Confronting Fascism in Egypt

Confronting Fascism in Egypt

Dictatorship versus Democracy in the 1930s

Israel Gershoni and James Jankowski

Stanford University Press

Stanford, California

Stanford University Press
Stanford, California

Printed in the United States of America on acid-free, archival-quality paper

Library of Congress Cataloging-in-Publication Data

Gershoni, I.
    Confronting fascism in Egypt : dictatorship versus democracy in the 1930s / Israel Gershoni and James Jankowski.
        p.   cm.
    Includes bibliographical references and index.
    ISBN 978-0-8047-6343-1 (cloth : alk. paper)—ISBN 978-0-8047-6344-8 (pbk. : alk. paper)
    1. Fascism—Egypt—History. 2. Democracy—Egypt—History.
3. Egypt—Politics and government—1919–1952.   I. Jankowski, James P., 1937–
II. Title.
    DT107.82.G425   2009
    962.05'2—dc22   2009022701

Typeset by Westchester Book Group in 11/13.5 Adobe Garamond regular

For Jonah, Owen, Moriah, Phoebe, Yehonatan, and Daniel

Contents

Acknowledgments

WE HAVE INCURRED DEBTS to many institutions, colleagues, and research assistants in the process of producing this work. It is impossible to list all those from whose advice and criticism we have benefited. Financial support for this study was provided by the National Humanities Center (NHC) at the Research Triangle Park in North Carolina and the Israel Science Foundation (ISF). We are grateful to these institutions for their generous assistance in providing support for over five years of research in Egypt, England, Italy, the United States, and Israel. We are especially indebted to these individuals from the NHC: Geoffrey Harpham, president and director; Kent Mullikin, deputy director; Lois Whittington, coordinator of the Fellowship Program; and Karen Carroll, coordinator of Editorial Services. The NHC provided a uniquely supportive environment and productive intellectual atmosphere that facilitated in the composition of the early drafts of part of this book. We also wish to express our appreciation to the staff members of *Dar al-Kutub al-Misriyya* (the Egyptian National Library) in Cairo and the Public Record Office in London for their assistance on several research trips to these institutions.

The Department of History of the University of Colorado at Boulder was unfailingly supportive of the research efforts of a retired colleague. We wish to express our gratitude especially to department chairs Thomas Zeiler, Peter Boag, and Susan Kent for facilitating the use of departmental and university facilities, and to Shelly Anderson and Kellie Mathews of the departmental staff for their invaluable aid in resolving technical problems.

Many colleagues and friends provided advice, stimulation, and criticism. Special thanks go to Nir Arielli, Orit Bashkin, Yoav Di-Capua, Haggai Erlich, Joel Gordon, Götz Nordbruch, Donald Reid, Shlomo Sand, Heather Sharkey, Ya'akov Shavit, Eve Troutt Powell, Esty Webman, Peter Wien, Eyal Zisser, and Meir Zamir. Insights provided us by Mustafa Kabha and Mahmud Ghanayim on complex Arabic texts, particularly cartoons, greatly enriched our understanding of the multiple layers of their meanings. We offer them our sincere appreciation for this help. We also thank Haya Naor and Susynne McElrone for translating parts of the manuscript in its initial stages.

Our sincere thanks goes to colleagues and friends in Egypt: the former chief justice of the High Court, Muhammad Sa'id al-'Ashmawy, Dr. Ahmad Shawqi Mahmud, and the late lawyer 'Ali al-Shalakany. They assisted us in the seminal stages of our research when this book was no more than an idea. All of them were generous enough to provide us with important materials; they helped us overcome obstacles and avoid embarrassing mistakes. They were patient in answering our questions and more than willing to help us understand the Egypt of the 1930s.

We are enormously indebted to our research assistants Avi Mor, Lisa Beinin Racz, and Arnon Degani. Avi Mor navigated us through complex Arabic texts and was responsible for collecting and organizing essential materials. Lisa Beinen Racz's editing skills proved indispensable in finalizing the manuscript and preparing it for publication. Arnon Degani's advice and production assistance in the last stages are highly appreciated.

We are most grateful to Kate Wahl, Joa Suorez, and the anonymous readers of Stanford University Press for their meticulous review of the manuscript and their constructive suggestions that improved the final quality of the work, and to the copy editor, Pat Cattani, and Barbara Goodhouse at Westchester Book Group for their excellent editorial assistance.

Finally, we would like to thank our families, who put up with numerous alterations and disruptions of their own lives and plans to facilitate our collaboration. Without the patient support and love of Mary Ann and Shani, John and Annie, Michal and Nimrod, this work never would have been completed. We offer our deepest gratitude to all these wonderful individuals. The book is dedicated to our grandchildren, Jonah, Owen, Moriah, Phoebe, Yehonatan, and Daniel, whom we hope may someday read it with profit.

Abbreviations of Egyptian Periodicals

AH	*al-Ahram*
BL	*al-Balagh*
FH	*al-Fath*
HL	*al-Hilal*
ITH	*al-Ithnayn wa al-Dunya*
JH	*al-Jihad*
JIM	*Jaridat al-Ikhwan al-Muslimin*
JMF	*Jaridat Misr al-Fatah*
MJ	*al-Majalla al-Jadida*
MLM	*Majallat al-Lata'if al-Musawwara*
MQ	*al-Muqattam*
MS	*al-Misri*
MSA	*Majallat al-Sarkha*
MSR	*al-Musawwar*
MTH	*Majallat al-Thughr*
ND	*al-Nadhir*
RS	*al-Risala*
RUY	*Ruz al-Yusuf*
TQ	*al-Thaqafa*

Confronting Fascism in Egypt

Part 1   Narratives and Contexts

Introduction
Narratives of Modern Egyptian History

THE 1930S HAVE OFTEN been described as a decade of crisis in Egypt. Politically, the constitutional parliamentary regime established in the 1920s was being undermined by the manipulation of autocratic elements supported by the Egyptian monarchy. Economically, the world Depression of the early 1930s had a severe impact on an Egypt dependent on the now-depressed price of agricultural exports. Sociopolitically, the Egyptian younger generation, raised with high hopes for the future of a newly independent Egypt but progressively disillusioned by the partisan bickering of their elders, was being attracted to more authoritarian and presumably efficient political models. Intellectually and culturally, the decade of the 1930s has been defined as one that witnessed a "crisis of orientation" in which Egyptian intellectuals retreated from the liberal values that they had previously espoused and turned to a neotraditional and reactionary romanticism rooted in the glorification of the Arabo-Islamic heritage. This decade of crisis is posited to have marked a sharp departure from the recent course of Egyptian evolution that had witnessed the introduction and dissemination of liberal and secular concepts and practices influenced by those of the modern West. Compared to what had come before, the 1930s are often presented as a regressive decade in Egyptian history.[1]

According to this master narrative of modern Egyptian history, the attitude of Egyptians toward political authoritarianism, most immediately toward the fascist model flourishing in much of Europe in the 1930s, became increasingly favorable. Egyptians are presented as having looked upon Fascist Italy and Nazi Germany as successful alternatives to a failing parliamentary regime. The appeal of Fascism and Nazism is posited to have derived from the apparent ability of Benito Mussolini and Adolf Hitler to transform their countries through economic rehabilitation, social mobilization, and the restoration of national self-confidence and pride. The greater emphasis on Islam in the 1930s is seen as having converged with this movement toward the acceptance of more authoritarian principles. Moreover, the continuing Egyptian nationalist struggle against British military occupation and political domination are believed to have reinforced a positive attitude toward Fascist Italy and Nazi Germany. With both states striving to overturn the post–World War I international order dominated by Great Britain and France, the two fascist powers are assumed to have been seen by Egyptians as the natural allies of an Egypt itself struggling against Western European imperialism. In the master narrative, the axiom "the enemy of my enemy is my friend" was applied to Egypt. The eventual result of this perceived parallelism of interest was the attempt by some Egyptians to collaborate with the Axis powers during World War II.[2]

Our study critically reconsiders this narrative. By undertaking a detailed examination of the relevant Egyptian primary sources, a corpus relatively neglected until now, it presents quite a different picture of Egyptian attitudes toward dictatorship and democracy in the years immediately preceding World War II. Through focusing on a hitherto-hidden discourse, located in absent spheres and populated by silent voices whom we will attempt to allow to be heard, we hope to demonstrate that liberal ideas about both politics and society continued to be expressed with considerable vigor by Egyptian intellectuals and publicists, and correspondingly that an infatuation with authoritarian or fascist concepts of political organization was the exception rather than the norm in Egyptian public discourse even in the period when fascism was at its ideological and political zenith in Europe and elsewhere in the world.

When and how did the view that the 1930s witnessed the decline of liberalism and a corresponding attraction to fascism in Egypt emerge? Two successive narratives—one political, the other intellectual—contributed to the emergence and consolidation of the interpretation. The first to take shape was a political narrative relating to the presumed pro-Axis inclinations and activities of Egyptians. Already before World War II, British officials in Egypt suspected leading Egyptian political figures, particularly the cluster of politicians around 'Ali Mahir (prime minister from August 1939 to June 1940) as well as Egypt's King Faruq and his Palace advisers, of harboring pro-Axis sympathies and possibly engaging in pro-Axis intrigue.[3] Fragmentary German documentation concerning secret Egyptian-German contacts during the war itself was first published, as a way of discrediting the Egyptian government and its involvement in the Palestine issue, in some of the polemical literature generated by the Arab-Zionist clash over Palestine in the late 1940s.[4] Suspicions of prewar and wartime Egyptian contacts with the Axis powers were highlighted and given an academic imprimatur in the authoritative survey entitled *The Middle East in the War* published by the Royal Institute of International Affairs in 1952.[5]

After the Egyptian Revolution of July 1952, external speculation concerning Egyptian pro-Axis activities during World War II was augmented and given substance by an Egyptian self-narrative relating to the war years. The military men who seized power in Egypt in 1952 were vehemently anti-imperialist. The early years of the revolutionary regime were dominated by the effort to end the British occupation of Egypt, a goal eventually achieved in 1956. To legitimize their stature as fervid Egyptian nationalists, the early self-narrative of the Revolution's leaders projected their anti-imperialist stance of the 1950s back into the 1940s. According to the collective remembrance they sought to disseminate to the Egyptian public in order to add historical depth to their anti-imperialist credentials, the anti-British activism of the Egyptian military went back to the difficult days of the war when the Egyptian army had been the locus of an underground movement directed against the British occupation, both considering (but not carrying out) an anti-British military uprising and engaging in (ultimately abortive) secret contacts with the Axis powers in the hope of weakening the dominant position of Great Britain in Egypt. The military's disillusionment with the existing order was consolidated by the humiliating incident of February 4, 1942, when the British forced King Faruq, under threat of ouster, to install a pro-British Wafdist government.[6]

The story of wartime Egyptian-Axis contacts found in the Egyptian self-narrative was incorporated into much of the Western literature written about Egypt in the 1950s and 1960s. It was in part confirmed and given often-lurid detail in the memoirs of German agents and British counter-intelligence officers who had been involved in wartime German espionage and British counter-espionage,[7] and was reiterated and augmented in the numerous Western journalistic and semi-scholarly accounts of the genesis of the Egyptian revolutionary regime that appeared in the 1950s and 1960s.[8] The final layer of the political narrative was provided by scholars working in the German archives, whose publications of the 1960s and 1970s documented German-Egyptian contacts based on archival materials.[9] By the 1970s, the narrative of Egyptian sympathy for the Axis powers during World War II had become accepted wisdom.[10]

In the 1960s, the political narrative developed in its basics in the 1940s and 1950s was overlaid by a more profound analysis of the unfolding of Egyptian ideological discourses offered by scholars working in the field of Middle Eastern intellectual history. The thesis of an Egyptian ideological rejection of liberal ideas and a corresponding turn of Egyptian discourse toward alternative principles of social and political life was initially articulated by Nadav Safran in his *Egypt in Search of Political Community*.[11] Safran's influential interpretation of the evolution of Egyptian intellectual life in the interwar era holds that, after a "progressive phase" of intellectual development through the 1920s in which the political and social values associated with nineteenth-century European liberalism were absorbed and advocated by Egypt's leading intellectuals, a "crisis of orientation" overtook many of these seminal thinkers by the 1930s. The most prominent manifestation of the crisis was the large-scale production of religiously oriented literature, particularly biographies of the Prophet Muhammad, the Rashidun Caliphs, and the early political and military heroes of Islam, by intellectuals whose previous writings had advocated a liberal orientation for Egypt and who had assumed that the adoption of European values and practices was the proper course of Egyptian development and modernization. By now embracing Islamic themes and emphasizing the glories of the Muslim past, these intellectuals were posited to have abandoned liberal-democratic and constitutional-parliamentary principles as the basis of their country's culture and having become advocates of more traditionalist and inherently anti-Western ideas as an alternative to a failed liberal order. Thus the 1930s marked the beginning of a more "reactionary phase" of Egyptian intellectual development.[12] For Safran, part and parcel of this reactionary phase was a rejection of parliamentary democracy and a turn toward more authoritarian concepts of government. As he summarized the latter process, "The great depression had given credence to the claims of Fascism, Nazism, and Communism that liberal democracy was a decaying system. The contrast between the misery, despair, and social discord that pervaded the Western democracies and the discipline, orderliness, and aggressive confidence that appeared to characterize the totalitarian regimes made a deep impression on Egyptians, who had seen in their own country a record of unmitigated failures of democracy."[13]

Published with the imprimatur of Harvard University Press at a time when serious scholarship of Arab intellectual history was in its infancy, Safran's interpretation that a transition from a "progressive" to a more "reactionary" phase in Egyptian intellectual life occurred during the 1930s has had wide currency. Although his construct of a "crisis of orientation" has been criticized as overly schematic, mistaking what was more a tactical shift in literary approach driven by considerations of popular appeal than a genuine fundamental change in outlook,[14] his parallel interpretation of Egyptian questioning of the effectiveness of parliamentary democracy and of a concomitant tilt toward authoritarian political principles has largely been accepted in subsequent scholarship. It was reiterated and reinforced by P. J. Vatikiotis's survey *The Modern History of Egypt*, two chapters of which deal respectively with the liberal "Attack upon Tradition" in the early twentieth century and "The Failure of Liberalism and the Reaction against Europe" in the 1930s and 1940s.[15] For Vatikiotis, "[t]he temporarily successful challenge Fascism and Nazism presented to the Western European democracies undermined constitutional government as a model for emulation by non-European societies. . . . The echo in Egypt was quite resounding. It was reflected in the rapid appearance of new social and political groups which, despite their different leadership, shared a belief in violence—the use of force for the attainment of political ends."[16] Thereafter, both Egyptian and Western scholars have generally accepted the broad outlines of the paradigm of a loss of faith in liberalism and a turn to authoritarian concepts on the part of Egyptian intellectuals and publicists in the 1930s. Afaf Lutfi al-Sayyid-Marsot's graphic description of the process is representative: "the crisis of democracies in the West had shaken the faith of many in the value of democracy. Admiration for Fascism grew when Mussolini made the trains run on time and forced the slackers to swallow castor oil. Some Egyptians believed that these methods might have more success in Egypt than those of the democratic institutions."[17]

Both the political and the intellectual narratives that postulate a decline of liberal values and a corresponding attraction to more authoritarian principles on the part of Egyptians are reconsidered in this book. The study focuses primarily on the later 1930s, years when Fascist Italy and Nazi Germany were at the height of their global influence and when Egyptian domestic conditions created a potentially favorable local context for the positive reception of fascist models. (Once World War II was under way, the imposition of strict wartime censorship in Egypt makes the evaluation of public opinion difficult, if not impossible.) Throughout, the work attempts to contextualize Egyptian opinion regarding liberalism versus fascism within the context of Egyptian domestic and international conditions, and within the context of heterogeneous and multivocal public sphere in which the public debate concerning fascism versus democracy occurred.

Three features of Egypt's political and intellectual development during the 1930s that are usually adduced as evidence for a decline of liberalism and a trend toward authoritarianism are addressed in this book. One is the emergence and growth of organized movements that did reject much of the liberal package of values that had been endorsed by an earlier generation of Egyptians and, in place of liberalism, expounded an alternative set of social and political principles. That movements such as the Muslim Brothers (1928–) and Young Egypt (1933–) shared and gave vehement expression to the mood of disillusionment with parliamentary representative government as practiced in Egypt during the interwar period is indisputable.[18] That an inclination toward more authoritarian concepts of rule can be found in the alternatives expounded by these movements is also the case.[19] Yet the characterization of these movements as "fascist" is inadequate. As Part III of this study demonstrates, spokesmen for the nonestablishment political movements of the 1930s articulated a variety of views on the merits and demerits of Fascism and Nazism, views that shifted significantly over time as the domestic and international agendas of both European movements unfolded and took on their full dimensions. Neither in regard to their domestic policies, where admiration for Fascist and Nazi efficiency and national mobilization was sometimes expressed but often accompanied by criticism of their perceived cultural totalitarianism and antireligious stance, nor in regard to their foreign policies, where Italian international ambitions in the Mediterranean and Africa were frequently viewed as a direct threat to Egypt and German expansionism was increasingly seen as threatening world peace and stability in general, were the views of the newer anti-establishment movements of the 1930s uncritical admirers of the ideas and policies of Italian Fascism and German Nazism. Over time, Young Egypt demonstrated a greater degree of admiration for fascist principles than did the more religiously oriented Muslim Brothers; but even in its case, admiration and emulation of some aspects of fascism was tempered by criticism and rejection of others.

The second feature of Egyptian politics cited to substantiate the claim of the growth of antiliberal tendencies by the 1930s relates to elite rather than to mass politics. It is the view that leading figures within the Egyptian political establishment, specifically the important politician 'Ali Mahir (chief of the Royal Cabinet in the later 1930s and prime minister in 1939–40) and his associates, as well as young King Faruq and his advisers within the Egyptian Palace, were by the late 1930s entertaining ideas of capitalizing on the mood of frustration with the operation of the existing parliamentary and party system to move in the direction of "fundamental reforms," specifically meaning the adjustment of the parliamentary monarchy in a direction that would diminish the power of both parliament and parties and in their stead centralize greater authority to the Egyptian monarchy.[20] This feature of Egyptian high politics is discussed in detail in Chapter 1. To anticipate its findings, it is our view that the putative authoritarian tendencies existing within the Egyptian Palace circle in the later 1930s bore little resemblance to the ruthlessly dictatorial and ideologically totalitarian systems of rule that characterized Fascism and Nazism, and that the tentative efforts to augment the authority of the Egyptian monarchy at the expense of parliament and parties that were attempted by the Egyptian Palace found little resonance as well as much opposition on the part of politically articulate Egyptians.

The third development adduced as evidence for an Egyptian turn away from liberalism in the 1930s is the perceived course of Egyptian intellectual life as first narrated by Nadav Safran and subsequently echoed by others. The literary corpus employed to demonstrate that the "crisis of orientation" experienced by Egyptian intellectuals in the 1930s produced a transition to a more "reactionary" and anti-Western outlook on the part of Egyptians is the literature devoted to Islamic themes produced in the

1930s by leading Egyptian intellectuals who in the 1920s had been advocates of liberal values. For Safran, this Islamically oriented literature of the post-1930 era was antirationalist, anti-Western, and as such antiliberal: "Its authors attempted a rational defense of those aspects of the Islamic heritage to which they were committed a priori on faith, while at the same time they attacked Western rationalism. . . . The only clear and universal aspects of that literature were a general emotional glorification of a vague Islam, and an aggressive attitude toward its antithesis, the West."[21]

In our view, the hypothesis that the turn to addressing Islamic themes by Egyptian intellectuals necessarily involved a rejection of liberalism is both methodologically flawed and misconstrued in its underlying premise. The automatic association between an "Islamic turn" in intellectual production and a corresponding retreat from liberal political ideas is reductionist. Simply put, it is looking for answers in the wrong place. It also reflects the traditional Orientalist assumption of a fundamental and irreducible incompatibility between liberalism and modernity on the one hand and Islam and tradition on the other. Under the impact of the Orientalist narrative, scholarship dealing with Arab intellectual history of the 1930s and beyond has focused on trying to understand the relationship between Westernism, secularism, and rationalism on the one hand, and Islam, tradition, religiosity, and spiritualism on the other. Scholarly endeavor has concentrated on measuring the movement of thought from the latter to the former. If intellectuals succeeded in assimilating and demonstrating European-inspired modernist and rationalist thinking, they were defined as enlightened and progressive; if they did not, they were termed traditionalists and reactionaries who had failed to meet the imperatives of the modern world. This scholarly paradigm channeled research toward the Islamiyyat corpus to the neglect of other, sometimes more pertinent, literary and cultural materials.

In our view, the Islamiyyat literature of the 1930s and after is neither the primary nor the best source for comprehending Egyptian attitudes on explicitly *political* questions relating to democracy and autocracy. These texts deal only marginally, and usually obliquely, with topics such as liberalism or fascism, democracy or dictatorship. Their function was different. Where the Islamiyyat literature played a crucial role in Egyptian history was in the cultural sphere, through rediscovering the Islamic-Arab heritage of Egypt and transforming it into a reservoir for the redefinition of a collective national identity that resonated with, and thereby linked, elite and non-elite sectors of society. It is only tangentially relevant to the central question that concerns us—the status of liberalism and the fascist alternative in Egyptian political, intellectual and cultural discourse.[22]

To learn about the liberal or antiliberal views expounded in Egyptian public discourse, it is necessary to examine those writings that deal directly with issues such as the respective merits of democracy or dictatorship, of representative versus authoritarian government, or of a pluralist social order that respects individual freedom of expression and civil rights and a totalitarian regime that subordinates the individual to the community. Outside the Islamiyyat literature, although often adjacent to it and written by the same authors, is a rich store of relevant texts produced by Egyptians. In brief, our research in this material—expressed in daily newspapers as well as in weekly and monthly journals of opinion, in books and pamphlets written in the period, and in visual expressions of opinion such as illustrations and caricatures—has found a more complex picture than the assumption that disappointment with the actual functioning of parliamentary democracy in Egypt led to enthusiasm for authoritarian or fascist alternatives would suggest. Rather than a prevailing inclination toward authoritarian concepts, we have found both multivocality and volatility in Egyptian attitudes about the relative merits of democracy versus autocracy. On the whole, the attitude of the majority of commentators—spokesmen of the older as well as the younger generation, of representatives both of the Egyptian political establishment and of the anti-establishment and subversive forces—were more pro- than anti-democratic, more supportive of what may generally be termed liberal values than of the illiberal ones embodied in Fascism and Nazism. Our study is an attempt to extricate and recover the ignored antifascist, pro-democratic discourse articulated by numerous producers of the print culture of the era.[23]

Our analysis of the Egyptian public discourse regarding dictatorship versus democracy is presented in Part II. It indicates that most of the shapers of Egyptian public opinion were by and large unreceptive to Fascism and Nazism, largely rejecting the ideas and practices that characterized European fascism. Even in the later 1930s, when fascist regimes were at the zenith of their popularity and power, the majority (although not all) Egyptian voices supported liberal democracy against the fascist challenge. The multiple difficulties Egypt was experiencing in the 1930s notwithstanding, most Egyptian commentators sought to reform and improve, rather than to replace or destroy, the existing Egyptian parliamentary system.

The dominant attitude toward contemporary fascism articulated in Egyptian public discourse can be summarized under three headings. The first was a general Egyptian rejection of fascism because of its totalitarian nature, its repressiveness, violence, and the use of rhetoric as well as force to achieve the regimentation of society and the subordination of the individual to the state. Fascism and Nazism were viewed as oppressive and brutal machines which had destroyed civil liberties, eliminated freedom of expression, and pulverized civil society. In both Italy and Germany, the individual had been subjugated to the service of an all-powerful state. To achieve this result, both fascist regimes had rejected and were in the process of destroying the cultural heritages of both nations. In contrast, constitutional democracy was defended as a system which, regardless of its defects, protected the rights of the individual and the best interests of the collective. Despite the problems liberal democracy was experiencing in the 1930s, the bulk of articulate Egyptians did not view fascist totalitarianism as an acceptable alternative.

The second feature of contemporary fascism that most Egyptian commentators found repugnant was Nazi racism. With a few exceptions, Egyptian observers rejected Nazi racial theory and practice. Included in this rejection was the condemnation of Nazi anti-Semitism and of the persecution of Jews in Germany as this accelerated and became more comprehensive over the 1930s. In regard to the implications of Nazi racism and anti-Semitism for the Middle East, Egyptians often found themselves with conflicting sentiments: while sympathizing with the dire fate of Jews in Germany and Europe, they nonetheless opposed the Zionist solution of the colonization of Arab Palestine as the answer to the Jewish problem.

The third and arguably the most important feature of contemporary fascism that concerned Egyptians were the international implications of Fascist and Nazi national aggrandizement and expansionism. Unlike the 1920s and the early 1930s, when there was an initial openness to the possible advantages of authoritarian rule in generating national regeneration internally, by the later 1930s Egyptian discussion of Fascism and Nazism focused on their foreign policies. Here a virtually uniform consensus emerged: Fascism and Nazism represented new and more pernicious forms of imperialism. The revisionist fascist states were seen as posing a definite threat both to world stability and to the existence of the "small nations" that stood in the path of Fascist or Nazi expansionism. The initial subject of Egyptian concern was Fascist Italy; in 1935–37, it was Italy's imperialist expansion into East Africa and military involvement in Spain that was the main focus of Egyptian concern. By 1938–39, their apprehension increasingly turned to Nazi Germany and the threat to world peace demonstrated by its use of political intimidation and military force to achieve the Nazi expansionist agenda in Central Europe. By the time of the outbreak of World War II in late 1939, the overwhelming consensus of Egyptian observers was that the two fascist states were an international menace, a manifest danger to world peace as well as to the independence of small states such as Egypt. In pre–World War II Egyptian public discourse, the axiom "the enemy of my enemy is my friend" did not apply.

To sum up, this book offers a new reading of the political and intellectual history of Egypt in the 1930s. It proposes a revision of our understanding of the responses of Egyptians to the issue of fascism and totalitarianism versus liberalism and democracy, a revision that parallels that now being undertaken by scholars in relation to the same issue elsewhere in the Arab world. While the study focuses on a specific historical period, its findings may also be relevant for today's debates about the relationship of Middle Easterners and Muslims to fascism. By examining Egyptian, mostly Muslim, views of fascism when classical fascism was at its peak, it questions the current assumption of an inherent Muslim predisposition toward authoritarianism, totalitarianism, or "Islamo-fascism."

1

The Historical Setting
Egyptian Politics in the Later 1930s

EGYPTIAN ATTITUDES TOWARD DEMOCRACY and dictatorship in the later 1930s must be situated in two contexts. One is the international arena—the increasingly fraught ideological rivalry and political confrontation between the liberal democracies and the Fascist and Nazi dictatorships, and how this rivalry and confrontation were read and refracted in Egypt. The other is the Egyptian internal scene—how domestic developments in Egypt made debate over the respective merits of fascist dictatorship versus liberal democracy a progressively more meaningful and vital subject for Egyptians. The external and internal contexts were intimately related; both played an essential role in conditioning Egyptian views of fascism and liberalism, dictatorship and democracy.

In their modern forms, both the liberal democratic and the fascist authoritarian models of political order were European in origin. For Egyptians in the 1930s, liberal democracy was exemplified primarily by Great Britain and France and more remotely by the United States. Authoritarian rule, on the other hand, reached its apotheosis in the two states of Italy and Germany where Fascism and Nazism had emerged and taken power, and in the Communist regime in the Soviet Union. When Egyptians reflected on the relative merits of democracy and dictatorship, the strengths or weaknesses of these foreign exemplars usually provided the raw material for their arguments pro or con.

The manifest failures of the Western democracies in the 1930s—mired in economic depression early in the decade, wracked by the partisanship seemingly inherent in pluralist political systems, and late in the decade apparently impotent in the face of Italian and German expansionism—had a powerful impact on Egyptian opinion. Correspondingly, the internal unity and vigor, the economic dynamism, and the ability to undertake bold international initiatives visible in the cases of Italy and Germany over the same period made an equally strong impression on Egyptians. The domestic difficulties of the Western democracies and the apparent achievements of the Fascist and Nazi regimes in the 1930s certainly played a role in Egyptian evaluations of both systems. But most salient for Egyptians over time were the international repercussions of the democratic-fascist rivalry, and most important, the possible implications of their international confrontation for Egypt itself. Indeed, the potential implications for Egypt of the international challenge of Fascist Italy and Nazi Germany to an international order previously dominated by Great Britain and France eventually came to bulk largest in the Egyptian debate over liberal democracy versus fascist authoritarianism.

The External Context: Fascist and Nazi Propaganda Activities in Egypt, 1935–1939

Egyptian attitudes toward Fascism and Nazism did not evolve in a vacuum. There is abundant evidence that first the Fascist regime in Italy, and subsequently its Nazi German counterpart, made strenuous efforts to influence Egyptian public opinion in the later 1930s. The available evidence also indicates, however, that it is questionable whether Fascist and Nazi propaganda endeavors in Egypt were worth the effort.

Through the mid-1930s, Fascist Italy took the lead in efforts to influence Egyptian public opinion in a favorable direction. Italian propaganda aimed at the Middle East, Egypt included, became more aggressive from the early 1930s onwards, as Italy prepared for the expansion of its empire in East Africa.[1] A benchmark in Italian propaganda activity in the Middle East was the inauguration of Arabic-language broadcasts by Radio Bari in May 1934. Accessible across most of North Africa and along the Red Sea, Radio Bari's blend of entertainment and news has been credited with attracting a growing audience of listeners, especially in public venues such as cafes.[2] An Arab Propaganda Bureau was created in Rome to establish contacts with Arab intellectuals and to disseminate Italian propaganda in the Middle East; the Ministry of Popular Culture sent an increasing flow of publications intended to burnish Italy's image to Italian legations and agencies in the region.[3]

Within Egypt, Italian propaganda activities from 1935 onward were carried out both by officials of the Italian Legation and by Ugo Dadone, the recently appointed director of the Italian news bureau Agence de l'Egypte et de l'Orient, a quasi-official entity operating under the supervision of the Italian Legation in Cairo.[4] Issuing daily press releases, and also presumed to be paying for pro-Italian news coverage in the Egyptian press, the agency was regarded by the British as "the major instrument of Italian propaganda activity in Egypt."[5] During the Ethiopian crisis of 1935, British assessments referred to "Italian efforts to corrupt the Egyptian press and politicians" in the hope of assuring a favorable or at least a neutral Egyptian stance in regard to the conflict between Italy and Ethiopia.[6] A January 1936 assessment of recent Italian propaganda efforts in Egypt cited several probable but unconfirmed methods used by Italian agents to influence Egyptian opinion, including providing subsidies to Egyptian newspapers, "prompting students to form groups on Fascist lines," and working through subsidies to students from Libya to influence opinion at al-Azhar.[7] A follow-up report of March 1936 cited both official and nonofficial sources that "all confirm the existence of bribery" of the Egyptian press carried out by Dadone and other Italian agents in Egypt.[8]

Italian propaganda efforts in Egypt at the time of the Ethiopian crisis and war appear to have had limited success. Certainly the tenor of on-the-spot British reports was that they had only a marginal effect upon Egyptian opinion. As the Ethiopian crisis developed in late 1935, the British view was that "public sympathy in Egypt is without doubt overwhelmingly and instinctively on the side of the Abyssinians."[9] A May 1936 assessment of the Egyptian attitude toward Italy engendered by the crisis and war in Ethiopia was that it had passed through several stages: initially one of alarm as the possibility of Italian aggressiveness threatening Egypt, subsequently one of relief as the arrival of British naval reinforcements reduced the prospect of an Italian menace to Egypt itself, and most recently a more pessimistic mood that Great Britain would be unable to defend Egypt successfully in case of Italian aggression.[10] The combination of fear over possible Italian aggression and concurrent apprehension over Great Britain's ability to defend Egypt was to be a recurrent feature of the Egyptian view of the international situation in the Mediterranean for the remainder of the 1930s.

After the extended international crisis over Ethiopia of late 1935 and early 1936, the period of the Wafdist ministry from May 1936 until the end of 1937 was a more placid one in international affairs as far as Egypt was concerned. Italian efforts to stimulate a favorable attitude in the Egyptian press apparently continued through the tenure of the Wafdist ministry.[11] Yet such Italian efforts to influence Egyptian opinion in 1936–37 again had limited success. The same British summaries of the Egyptian press of 1937 report vigorous press criticism of Mussolini's claim to be a protector of Islam and of recent Italian construction projects in Libya that were interpreted as being for military purposes,[12] and numerous Egyptian publications express apprehension over Italian military maneuvers in Libya that were seen as an implicit threat to Egypt.[13] That the Egyptian press was far from a pliable instrument in the hands of Italian propaganda is perhaps best indicated by the fact that in September 1937 both the Italian and German legations in Egypt lodged official protests with the Egyptian Ministry of Foreign Affairs concerning "allegedly absurd caricatures of the Duce and the Führer in certain Egyptian weekly reviews."[14]

A shift in the relative weight of Italian versus German propaganda activity in the Middle East occurred in 1938 and 1939. Efforts by Italian agents to stimulate anti-British sentiment in the region diminished substantially from early 1938 onward as a result of the Anglo-Italian Rome (Easter) Agreement of March 1938, which resolved the outstanding points of tension between Great Britain and Italy in the Mediterranean and in which Italy agreed to cease its anti-British propaganda in the Middle East.[15] According to a British evaluation of January 1939, "since the ratification of the Rome Agreement open Italian propaganda against Great Britain has largely ceased."[16] Italian charitable and propaganda activities in Egypt continued in 1938 and 1939, but reportedly became less overtly anti-British. The Italian Legation continued to subsidize Libyan, Eritrean, and Ethiopian students at al-Azhar, but apparently with limited political consequences.[17] Rather than seeking to erode the British position, as in the past, Italian efforts to influence the Egyptian press in 1938–39 appear to have been directed primarily toward deterring hostile criticism of Italy's international behavior such as Italian colonization efforts in Libya and its April 1939 invasion of Albania.[18]

These efforts at deterrence do not appear to have spilled over into generating a positive opinion of Fascist Italy on the part of Egyptians. By 1939, Italian officials were themselves estimating that Radio Bari was losing local audience for its Arabic-language programming.[19] British estimates of Egyptian opinion in the countryside in 1939 pointed in the same direction. A report on public opinion in Upper Egypt in early 1939 "failed to find any indication of Italian propaganda activity other than the educational and philanthropic work," and went on to say that "Italians are generally disliked" as a result of their brutal behavior in Libya.[20] A diplomat's report on sentiment in Lower Egypt in May 1939 came to similar conclusions: "I could find no marked evidence of Italian activity, and any propaganda they may be indulging in seems to have little effect. . . . The general feeling seems to be anti-Italian, especially since the invasion of Albania."[21] In her analysis of Italian propaganda efforts in the Middle East in the later 1930s, Manuela Williams concludes by emphasizing "the ephemeral nature of Italy's popularity in the Middle East," and provides the most likely reason for the fading of a positive view of Italy in the region: "[a]s Italy's colonial ambitions became increasingly manifest, mainstream nationalists began to distance themselves from Mussolini's policy in Africa and the Middle East."[22] A recent study by Nir Arielli comes to a similar conclusion: "[w]hile Fascism had a certain appeal in some young nationalist *Effendiyya* circles," overall Fascist Italy's brutal colonial policies in Libya, its imperialist war in Ethiopia, and its belligerent rhetoric and maneuvers in the Middle East all "alienated public opinion makers in the Middle East. Thus, when Italy joined the war the Italians had very few allies in the region."[23]

As Italian propaganda activity decreased, Germany in part filled the gap. Germany had given little attention to propaganda efforts in the Middle East prior to 1938. As late as March 1938, the British ambassador in Rome reported that "I have been unable to obtain proofs that there is any concerted move by Germany, either alone or in conjunction with Italy, to develop interests other than commercial in the Mediterranean."[24] A marker of Germany's relative disinterest in the Arab world for most of the 1930s was the absence of a full Arabic translation of Hitler's *Mein Kampf*. As Stefan Wild has shown, unauthorized partial Arabic translations of *Mein Kampf* were published in the Arab world before World War II.[25] Yet official German efforts to sponsor an authorized Arabic translation in the 1930s never came to fruition due to bureaucratic infighting over responsibility for the undertaking, dissatisfaction with the quality of the translations under consideration, and ultimately the cost of the project.[26]

Within Egypt, we have been able to identify only partial and generally critical translations of Hitler's personal statement of his aims. A 1934

Arabic work written by Ahmad Mahmud al-Sadati, *Adulf Hitlar, Zaʿim al-Ishtirakiyya al-Wataniyya maʿa Bayan al-Masʾala al-Yahudiyya* (Adolf Hitler, Leader of National Socialism, with an Explanation of the Jewish Question), contained a partial translation and analysis of excerpts from *Mein Kampf*.[27] The translation was unauthorized by the German government: the German Legation in Cairo was taken by surprise when Sadati visited and attempted to present a copy of the work to the Minister of Propaganda Joseph Goebbels.[28] Sadati's book appears not to have been widely circulated, and its public impact is unclear.[29] Another partial and problematic translation of the 1930s was ʿAli Muhammad Mahbub's *Kifahi fi Sabil al-Raykh al-Kabir* (My Struggle for the Sake of the Greater Reich, 1938). A translation of portions of *Mein Kampf*, it also contained critical commentary by the author that depicted Hitler as a menace to world peace. The German Foreign Office reacted angrily to the work, demanding that the Egyptian government prohibit its distribution within Egypt.[30]

Only in 1938–39, as tension with the Western democracies increased and as German officials became aware of the prospects of destabilizing the position of Great Britain and France in the Middle East, did Germany undertake systematic propaganda efforts in the region.[31] Once begun, German propaganda efforts in Egypt paralleled those undertaken earlier by Italy. The German News Agency [Deutsches Nachrichtenbüro] directed by Wilhelm Stellbogen took the place of the Italian Agence de l'Egypte et de l'Orient as the key organization attempting to stimulate pro-Axis coverage in the Egyptian press and in promoting Axis ties with Egyptian organizations. A British press summary of late 1938 claimed "circumstantial evidence" of German efforts to influence the press through advertising contracts and possibly bribery.[32] The same assessment that reported the diminution of Italian propaganda activity in Egypt by early 1939 immediately went on to note that "it has been replaced by German propaganda acting in the interests of both members of the Rome-Berlin Axis."[33] By 1939, the German Ministry of Propaganda was reported to be spending £3,000 a month on propaganda activities in Egypt.[34] Among such expenditures were financial subsidies to the Muslim Brothers provided through the Deutsches Nachrichtenbüro.[35] Like Italian propaganda in 1938–39, these German efforts to sway Egyptian opinion prior to the war appear to have been only marginally effective; a report on the Egyptian press of May 1939 concluded that "on the whole it may be said that the Egyptian press have not yet editorially reflected this [German] propaganda."[36] Overt German propaganda activities in Egypt effectively ended in September 1939, when the Egyptian authorities shut down official German agencies and interned German citizens resident in Egypt.

The position of successive Egyptian governments of the later 1930s—those of the Wafd and Mustafa al-Nahhas, in power from May 1936 until December 1937, and the coalition ministries headed by Muhammad Mahmud from the beginning of 1938 until August 1939—show little evidence of either ideological sympathy or practical collaboration with Fascist Italy and Nazi Germany. The Wafdist ministries of 1936–37 appear to have had no great sympathy for or substantive contact with either of the two fascist regimes. This does not mean that the Wafd was totally unaffected by European fascism. The party had since late 1935 organized and supported its own uniformed and increasingly militant youth movement, the Blue Shirts.[37] When on vacation in Europe in October 1936, Prime Minister Nahhas and Minister of Finance Makram 'Ubayd paid an unofficial visit to Berlin. In his posthumously edited and published diaries, Nahhas claims to have come away from a personal audience with Hitler with the distinct feeling that "this angry, agitated young man would inevitably drag the entire world into a world war."[38] In early 1937, Sir Miles Lampson's assessment was that neither Nahhas nor other Wafdist leaders were "as yet seriously affected by German influence."[39] For its part, Italy was reported, through its agents in Egypt, to be attempting to "undermine the Wafdist Government, whose interests were now so closely bound up with Great Britain."[40] After his dismissal from the premiership, a bitter Nahhas went as far to credit British acquiescence in his dismissal by King Faruq as being due to "his having become the avowed enemy of Italy" and thus an obstacle to the completion of Anglo-Italian negotiations for a relaxation of tension in the Mediterranean.[41]

According to the testimony of his posthumous diaries, Nahhas remained equally unsympathetic to Fascism and Nazism when out of office. The diaries record several initiatives of 1938–39 on the part of fascist or pro-fascist figures seeking Wafdist support for the Axis powers—a conversation with Italian Foreign Minister Galeazzo Ciano when Nahhas visited Rome in 1938, in which Ciano sought Wafdist support against British imperialism in the Middle East; a more indirect German approach, through an Egyptian student studying in Germany, for a Wafdist-Nazi "front against the English"; a conversation with the Mufti Amin al-Husayni of Palestine in which Husayni urged Nahhas to support Germany in case of war; and another Italian overture promising to install Nahhas as leader of an Egyptian "republic" in exchange for Wafdist collaboration. The diaries report Nahhas deflecting or rejecting all the approaches, and instead advocating Egyptian neutrality in any conflict among the European powers, all of whom were tainted by past records as imperialists.[42]

The public posture of the ministries of Muhammad Mahmud of 1938–39 also demonstrated no particular sympathy for Fascist Italy or Nazi Germany. Immediately upon taking office, Prime Minister Muhammad Mahmud assured the British ambassador that he was "fully alive" to the danger posed by potential Italian Fascist expansionism.[43] In May, Sir Miles Lampson reported that "as regards relations with foreign Powers, and more particularly Italy, the attitude of both the Palace and the Government of Mohammed Mahmoud Pasha has up to date been entirely satisfactory."[44] At the time of the Munich crisis, Prime Minister Mahmud made a public declaration to the effect that Egypt would fulfill her treaty obligations to Britain as specified in the Anglo-Egyptian Treaty of Alliance of 1936 in case of war;[45] for his part, the British ambassador reported that the stance of both the Egyptian government and the Palace during the crisis had been satisfactory.[46]

British assessments of how Egyptian views of Fascist Italy and Nazi Germany had evolved by the end of the 1930s suggest a differential impact of Axis propaganda upon different segments of Egyptian society. A detailed commentary by Sir Miles Lampson of early 1939 estimated that Axis propaganda had had its greatest appeal to the Egyptian aristocracy, but found less resonance among the educated middle class still largely under the sway of the Wafd:

Italo-German propaganda is extensive, but one of its favourite fields appears to be among what in Egypt corresponds to the aristocratic class, *i.e.*, the Court and those revolving around it, the Turks and Turco-Egyptians and the socially more eligible or more snobbish elements of Egyptian society. In this field the Italian and German propagandists find a more sympathetic hearing than in more bourgeois and popular circles, which, under the Wafd banner, still remain hostile to Italy at any rate.[47]

Lampson reiterated much the same view a month later, when he credited

the King of Egypt and the more "aristocratic" elements, using that term in its peculiarly Egyptian sense of those longer in possession of the spoils of power, must obviously dislike this democratic virus with which we have inoculated the Egyptian people. . . . [T]he authoritative (*i.e.*, totalitarian) regimes, with their contempt of democracies, must, in present circumstances, make a certain appeal to the Palace, which is ruling in opposition to the majority of the nation.[48]

After the outbreak of war in late 1939, Lampson repeatedly credited the Egyptian Palace and the Turco-Egyptian "aristocracy" as "tending to be anti-British and even-pro German."[49] Whatever the sentiments of the Egyptian Palace and aristocracy may have been through the 1930s, Lampson was unable to substantiate their presumed pro-Axis views being turned into pro-Axis activity. In November 1939, two months into the war, he reported that "[t]he anti-British intrigues of the Palace and its hangers-on still remain largely in the domain of talk and intention."[50]

The evidence of the Arabic primary sources concerning the response of the Egyptian public to Fascism and Nazism is the subject of the chapters that follow. To anticipate that analysis, here it is pertinent to note that the contemporary British view of the attitude of Egyptian public opinion toward Fascist Italy and Nazi Germany in the years preceding the outbreak of World War II was that Egyptian attitudes were not the passive object of manipulation by Axis propaganda but were determined primarily by Egyptian readings of the potential impact of that Italian and German foreign policy upon Egypt itself. As the British read the Egyptian scene, the Ethiopian crisis and war of 1935–36 planted an ominous seed of doubt in the minds of many Egyptians; that Great Britain was either unwilling or unable to protect Egypt from possible Italian expansionism in the future.[51] A report of May 1936 thus stated that "the natural conclusion [of Egyptians] is that, were Great Britain to do so, she would have stopped Italy, and the fact of her not having done so is simply an admission of inability and of weakness."[52] The British assessment thereafter was that apprehension concerning possible Italian military intentions toward Egypt, along with "doubt [in] the ability of the British to defend Egypt," continued to mark Egyptian public opinion even in the less turbulent years of the Wafdist ministry from mid-1936 until the end of 1937.[53]

International events of 1938–39 produced an intensification of Egyptian concern over the malevolent intentions and behavior of the European fascist states along with a deepening of apprehension over the likely implications of Fascist and Nazi aggressiveness for Egypt itself. At the time of Nazi Germany's incorporation of independent Austria (the Anschluss) in March 1938, a British report stated that "practically the whole [Egyptian] press expresses sympathy for Austria in her invasion by Germany."[54] The extended crisis over the Sudetenland in Czechoslovakia in the summer of 1938, culminating with Germany's annexation of the region as a result of the Munich Agreement of September, had a deeper impact on Egyptian public opinion. Egyptians viewed Neville Chamberlain's willingness to travel to Munich in order to appease Germany over Czechoslovakia as a sign of British national weakness with obvious implications for Egypt: "Great Britain is now regarded as having suffered humiliation greater than that caused by Abyssinia. Her ability and willingness to protect small States (including Egypt) against aggression are being seriously questioned."[55] The terms of the Munich Agreement were received in Egypt with ambivalence, reflecting continuing Egyptian concern over the implications of the policy of appeasement for small states such as Egypt:

Relief, when the news of the Munich Agreement was received, was no less sincere and universal in Egypt than elsewhere: but, after the first feeling of relief, reflection seemed to inspire the native press with some doubt as to whether the democracies had not been worsted by the autocracies and whether the former were no longer able to protect small States, such as Czecho-Slovakia, who had had to capitulate to force.[56]

Great Britain's appeasement of Nazi Germany at Munich was also interpreted as having regional implications for the Middle East and Egypt: a report of December 1938 concluded that many Egyptians "are now afraid that as a result of recent developments in Europe we [Great Britain] cannot adequately protect Egypt against Italian attack."[57]

Together, Nazi Germany's Austrian and Czech initiatives of 1938 were a crucial turning point in Egyptian attitudes toward contemporary international affairs. On one level, both Austria and Czechoslovakia were independent states like Egypt, both products of the post–World War I peace settlement; now one was wiped off the map and the other partially dismembered (and totally eliminated several months later) as a result of German expansionism. Preceded by Italy's imperialist conquests in East Africa, this international aggressiveness on the part of the fascist states, particularly their willingness to risk war in pursuit of their imperial ambitions, led many Egyptians to make the potentially negative implications of Fascist and Nazi international adventurism for their own country the overriding factor determining their attitude toward the European fascist powers.

In the British view, this outlook remained the dominant Egyptian perspective on Fascism and Nazism in the first several months of 1939, prior to the outbreak of war in September. Germany's absorption of the rump of Czechoslovakia in March and Italy's invasion of Albania in April reinforced Egyptian fears of fascist expansionism and heightened an Egyptian sense of dependence upon Great Britain for defense from possible aggression. "The successive shocks of the Czecho-Slovakian and Albanian tragedies, particularly the latter, have made it clear to Egyptians how precarious is their position without adequate support from their British ally. . . . The fear of Germany and Italy and disgust with the latter's action in Albania have generally made the population much more favourably disposed towards us and strengthened the realization of Egypt's need of England."[58] A review of May 1939 came to the conclusion that the "general consensus of opinion" in Egypt was that "Egypt's salvation lies in her association with the democracies."[59] As Sir Miles Lampson put it in July, "the fear and dislike of Italy and Germany have more or less forced the Egyptians into our arms."[60]

Yet not all trends set in motion by Fascist and Nazi international aggressiveness in 1938 and 1939 were favorable to the cause of the democracies. The imminent threat of war at the time of Munich inaugurated a yearlong debate over the extent of Egypt's obligations to Great Britain under the terms of the Anglo-Egyptian Treaty of 1936. According to information reaching the British Embassy, at the time of Munich in September 1938 unnamed members of the Muhammad Mahmud ministry had raised the possibility of Egypt remaining neutral in case of a general European war.[61] Although Prime Minister Mahmud hastened to assure the British that his government did not endorse the suggestion of Egyptian neutrality in case of war,[62] and while the British reading of Egyptian public sentiment during the crisis found "on the whole a resolve to stand by the [Anglo-Egyptian] alliance,"[63] the idea of possible Egyptian neutrality did not die. It was apparently a matter of private discussion in political circles after Munich, when jittery British reports claimed that the prospect of Egyptian neutrality continued to be a topic of discussion in Egypt, in part because of adroit stimulation by German and Italian diplomats resident in Egypt in their personal exchanges with prominent Egyptians.[64]

The idea of Egyptian neutrality became a matter of public discussion and debate in December 1938, when in a speech in Parliament former Prime Minister Isma'il Sidqi expressed the view that, while the Anglo-Egyptian Treaty of Alliance did "impose on Egypt the necessity of putting her resources at Great Britain's disposal" in case of war, nonetheless it "did not oblige Egypt to take part in a war in which Great Britain was engaged."[65] While Prime Minister Mahmud's parliamentary rejoinder was that his government intended to fulfill its treaty obligations to Great Britain "loyally and sincerely," Mahmud did not foreclose the possibility of negotiated revisions to the treaty that would reduce Egypt's treaty obligations in time of war.[66]

Sidqi's demarche set off a public controversy over the issue of possible Egyptian neutrality that lasted until the outbreak of war. As Sir Miles Lampson summarized the concern in early 1939, "Egyptians are anxiously groping for some way to get out of their being involved in the expected war."[67] Not all participants in the debate advocated Egypt avoiding involvement in the coming war: the politician who later was the strongest advocate of Egyptian entry into World War II, Ahmad Mahir of the Sa'dist Party, was vehement in rejecting Sidqi's suggestion and in insisting on the necessity of Egypt standing by the British in opposing Fascist and Nazi expansionism.[68] The Wafdist press, traditionally supportive of democracy and recently openly critical of the European fascist powers, initially maintained the necessity of Egypt fulfilling its treaty obligations.[69] This position was not consistently maintained; later in 1939 the British reported that the Wafdist press was advocating noncooperation with Great Britain in case of war on the grounds that "an Egypt deprived of its democratic rights has no inducement to fight for the democracies in the coming war."[70] Although the Egyptian Palace was not openly involved in the controversy, the always-apprehensive British Ambassador Sir Miles Lampson worried that

Italo-German agents are, through their tools in and around the Palace, definitely influencing King Farouk in the sense desired by the Rome-Berlin Axis, namely, in the direction of Egyptian neutrality in the event of war. . . . There is no doubt that German and Italian propaganda is at work to promote, among Egyptians, high and low, the feeling that Egypt should avoid being dragged into England's wars when they are on matters of no direct Egyptian interest.[71]

British suspicions of Palace reluctance to join the British in case of war have some independent verification: according to his diary, Italian Foreign Minister Galeazzo Ciano was informed in February 1939 that the Egyptian minister in Berlin, speaking in the name of King Faruq, had inquired if the Axis powers would provide support to Egypt in the case of an Egyptian declaration of neutrality.[72] A British evaluation of Egyptian sentiment on the eve of war perceived contradictory impulses regarding the tense international situation: while (as noted previously) estimating that "the fear and dislike of Italy and Germany have more or less forced the Egyptians into our arms," nonetheless it concluded that "there still persists considerable feeling in the country that Egypt ought to be allowed to keep out of a world conflict which does not directly concern her."[73]

This rolling debate over the possibility of Egyptian neutrality that took place in the year preceding the outbreak of World War II forms the indispensable background for Egypt's eventual decision not to declare war on Germany in September 1939. The outbreak of war placed the newly installed ministry led by Prime Minister 'Ali Mahir in a quandary. Although it promptly broke diplomatic relations with Germany and declared its intention to honor its obligations to Great Britain under the Anglo-Egyptian Treaty of 1936, Egypt formally remained a nonbelligerent in the conflict. This posture was in part due to the fact that Italy, the fascist country that in its Libyan colony bordered Egypt and thus presented a tangible military threat, remained a neutral through the early months of the war. Facing no immediate military threat, and composed of an assortment of less pro-British ministers than the one it had replaced, the Egyptian Cabinet refused to concur with repeated British requests for a formal declaration of war; its refusal was based on the grounds that a declaration of war would require parliamentary approval and that the Cabinet was uncertain of obtaining the same in light of the past year's growth of public sentiment to the effect that Egypt should spare itself from involvement in a struggle which did not directly concern her.[74] Although he angrily dismissed this justification for avoiding entry into the war as "a trifling pretext,"[75] Sir Miles Lampson was unable to suggest effective British action to bring Egypt in as a belligerent.[76] While fulfilling its technical military obligations of support to its ally under the Anglo-Egyptian Treaty of 1936,[77] Egypt had adopted the posture of de jure nonbelligerence, but de facto collaboration with the British war effort, that it maintained for almost all of the duration of World War II.

The Domestic Context: The Rivalry Between the Wafd and the Palace, 1936-1939

While Egyptian views of liberal democracy and fascist authoritarianism evolved in part in response to developments on the international scene, they were also shaped by conditions in Egypt itself. In particular, opinions regarding the new totalitarian regimes in Europe were at the same time an indirect commentary on domestic political events. The domestic Egyptian context is fully or more as important as the international one for understanding the course of the Egyptian discourse over liberalism versus fascism.

In 1922–23, Egypt had become a formally independent parliamentary monarchy, albeit one in which Great Britain retained a military presence, a number of advisers, and great political influence. The country's political evolution thereafter was complex. Egyptian politics during the era of the parliamentary monarchy have often been described as a triangular contest among three forces: the Wafd, the king, and the British. The Wafd was the nationalist movement that had led the post–World War I struggle for independence from Great Britain and thereafter was Egypt's most popular political organization. Its commitment to parliamentary ascendancy earned it the hostility of the Palace; its insistence on "complete independence" for Egypt through most of the interwar era made it the great opponent of the British occupation. The second force was the king (Fu'ad to 1936; his son Faruq thereafter) and the monarchy's political allies. Both Fu'ad and Faruq wished to rule rather than merely reign. They did so in part through the significant political powers granted the monarchy in the Constitution of 1923, in part through the agency of what are conventionally described as "minority" parties, elitist groupings of non-Wafdists or former Wafdists who were willing to ally with the monarch in order to gain ministerial office. The third actor was Great Britain, committed to preserving what it regarded as important imperial interests in Egypt. In normal times it exercised its influence through the medium of advice rendered to Egyptian officials; in times of crisis it used the threat of military force to work its will.

In reality, the triangle of king-Wafd-British represented only part of complex political universe of Egypt in the interwar era. Multiple other forces and voices, organized and disorganized, played a visible and important role in Egyptian public life. Among the most prominent was the venerable Muslim religious institution centered on the University of al-Azhar in Cairo. Committed to the maintenance of the hegemonic position of Islam in Egyptian society, and in practice often allied with the king upon whom the university was in part financially dependent, the faculty and students of al-Azhar were frequent participants in both the public debates and the political controversies of the 1920s and 1930s. A somewhat weaker countervailing force was represented by the faculty and students of the more secular Egyptian University, established in Giza in 1925 as a state-supported institution of higher education. By the 1930s the mix was complicated by the emergence of powerful and assertive extra-parliamentary sociopolitical movements such as the Muslim Brothers and Young Egypt. The most diffuse, but nonetheless vital, component of Egypt's public life was made up of the hundreds, if not thousands, of Egyptian intellectuals—some Muslim, some Christian, some Jewish; some conservative, some liberal, some radical; some affiliated with organized parties or movements, some independent of partisan ties—who expressed their views on current issues in the numerous newspapers and journals of opinion that flourished in Egypt in the interwar era. Egyptian public life in the 1920s and 1930s was a vibrant mix. The sheer number of different viewpoints and foci of expression found in interwar Egypt gave the system an inherently pluralist and democratic dynamic. Corruption, nepotism, and periodic authoritarian pressure notwithstanding, cultural diversity, freedom of thought and organization, and vigorous political debate and competition were the rule.

The central political feature of the later 1930s, the years upon which we focus, was the struggle for power between the Wafd and the Egyptian Palace. Concurrent with the Wafd's electoral victory of May 1936, the death of King Fu'ad (April 28, 1936) resulted in Egypt acquiring a new monarch in the person of Fu'ad's sixteen-year-old son Faruq. From the start of Faruq's reign, the Wafd and the Palace engaged in an increasingly bitter struggle for power. The rivalry of Wafd and Palace provided the primary domestic referent for the evolution of Egyptian attitudes toward democracy and dictatorship in the years from 1936 to 1939.

The initiative in the struggle came largely from the Palace. With his portly figure, poor Arabic, and contempt for things Egyptian, King Fu'ad (1922–1936) had never succeeded in becoming a genuinely popular figure in Egypt. His son and successor Faruq (1936–1952) at first possessed a much more appealing image. Young, attractive, untainted by the failures of the

past, and possessing a carefully cultivated aura of piety and devotion—
mujaddid (renovator) and *al-malik al-salih* (the pious king) were frequently
applied descriptors—Faruq inspired great popular adulation in the early
years of his reign. The young king's popularity led some Egyptians to view
the extension of the political role of the monarchy as preferable to the
maintenance of a parliamentary status quo that was being progressively
discredited by the partisan squabbles of the existing political parties.
Faruq was guided in the effort to expand royal power by ʿAli Mahir, a
skillful anti-Wafdist politician who briefly held the post of prime minister
in early 1936 and who served as Royal Chamberlain from October 1937 until
August 1939, and by the rector of al-Azhar, Shaykh Muhammad Mustafa al-Maraghi, who also served as the king's tutor in religious matters.
Mahir was the key figure constructing shifting coalitions of anti-Wafdist
forces—the minority parties and their affiliated newspapers; the students
of al-Azhar; newer extraparliamentary movements such as Young Egypt
and the Muslim Brothers—to harry the Wafd and to foster a political climate in which the monarchy would play a more prominent role; for his
part, Maraghi took the lead in a campaign to enhance the King's authority
by presenting him as a devout Muslim capable of playing a positive role
both domestically and in the wider Muslim world. Faruq's popularity
made him the focal point for the numerous parties and forces that by the
later 1930s were either competing with the Wafd or had lost faith in the
existing parliamentary system.

For its part, by the later 1930s the Wafd suffered from several im-
pediments in its contest with the Palace. The party had suffered schisms
virtually since its formation; many of the non-Wafdist political parties of
the interwar era were led by former Wafdists who had broken with the
party leadership at one time or another. The party's leader, Mustafa al-
Nahhas, successor to Saʿd Zaghlul since the latter's death in 1927, neither
possessed the personal charisma nor inspired the same degree of popular
adulation as had Zaghlul. Unprepossessing in appearance and blustering
in manner, Nahhas was a man of the people who inspired affection but
did not tower above his colleagues and rivals as had his predecessor Zaghlul. By the later 1930s, Nahhas's increasing reliance on his Coptic associate
Makram ʿUbayd, and rumors of rampant favoritism toward his in-laws in
the al-Wakil family, were eroding his public image. Out of both conviction
and self-interest, the Wafd was the great defender of constitutional government and parliamentary supremacy throughout the interwar period.

By the end of the era, however, the combination of internal schism, a tar-
nished leadership, multiple opponents in the political arena, and a popular rival in the king, seriously impaired its ability to defend the parliamentary order in which it believed and from which it benefited.

The struggle between Wafd and Palace commenced in May 1936,
almost immediately upon the accession of Faruq and the Wafd's return to
power as a result of parliamentary elections. In an effort to forestall any
Wafdist attempt to set the new king's majority at the age of twenty-one, a
step that would have delayed the king from playing an active political role
until 1940, a decree law issued by the caretaker ministry of 'Ali Mahir in
early May, just prior to its replacement by the new Wafdist ministry, set
his age of majority at eighteen by the Islamic calendar.[78] For its part, one
of the Wafdist ministry's first initiatives was to attempt to appoint a minister for the Palace to serve as liaison between ministry and monarchy. The
proposal was resisted as an unconstitutional infringement on the prerogatives of the throne by the three regents appointed to shepherd the young
king until he should attain his majority. Eventually, a parliamentary un-
dersecretary for Palace affairs was created as a substitute in an effort to
introduce ministerial supervision of Palace undertakings; the post existed
until July 1937, when Faruq reached eighteen and assumed his constitutional powers.[79] From the outset of Faruq's reign, the Egyptian Palace
made a conscious effort to keep the king in the public eye through con-
spicuous public prayer on Fridays as well as through well-publicized ceremonial receptions and visits, and tours of the countryside.[80]

By early 1937, the British anticipated that a Palace effort to oust the
Wafd from office would come in mid-1937, upon Faruq's assumption of
his constitutional powers.[81] The forecast was accurate. In the latter months
of 1937, upon Faruq's reaching the age of eighteen by the Islamic calendar,
the clash between Wafd and Palace came into the open. The formal investiture of Faruq as king of Egypt occurred on July 29, 1937, in a civil ceremony in Parliament in which the king took an oath to uphold the Constitution; the investiture was followed by lavish receptions and a military
review in Cairo and later public celebrations in Alexandria.[82] The Palace's
desire to parallel the civil ceremony of investiture in Parliament with a
religious follow-up, where Shaykh Maraghi would gird the king with the
sword of Muhammad 'Ali in a quasi-religious ceremony at the Citadel,
was firmly rejected by the Nahhas government as an unconstitutional in-
novation that would not accord with the king's status as the sovereign of a

parliamentary monarchy.[83] Popular enthusiasm for the king may have reached its peak during Faruq's investiture ceremonies of July 1937. A British report on the festivities concluded that the Palace policy of burnishing public Faruq's image had been a success: "On all these occasions manifestations of popular enthusiasm have marked His Majesty's appearance in public. There can be little doubt that the young King has caught the popular fancy. The policy inspired by the Palace entourage and by Ali Maher of showing the King to his subjects on every possible occasion, aided, no doubt, by the King's youthful and pleasant bearing, has borne fruit."[84]

Concomitant with the king's formal investiture, crisis struck the Wafd. A long-festering hostility between Wafdist grandees—the party's leader Mustafa al-Nahhas and his closest associate Makram 'Ubayd on the one hand, the influential party members Mahmud Fahmi al-Nuqrashi and Ahmad Mahir (brother of 'Ali Mahir) on the other—in late 1937 produced what may have been the most serious schism in the Wafd's history. The dispute between the two groups was in part personal, in part over policy. Nuqrashi and Ahmad Mahir resented Makram 'Ubayd's influence over Nahhas; their opposition to the granting of public contracts on the basis of what they maintained was favoritism also alienated them from Nahhas and 'Ubayd. When in August 1937 Nahhas submitted his new Cabinet to the king upon the latter's assumption of his constitutional powers, Nuqrashi had been dropped from the Cabinet. In September Nuqrashi was expelled from the Wafd, a decision which his ally Ahmad Mahir protested. Public invective between Nahhas and Nuqrashi through the fall of 1937, and more muted opposition within the Wafd to the leadership of Nahhas and Makram 'Ubayd by Ahmad Mahir, deepened the split. It reached its culmination in January 1938, when Ahmad Mahir was in turn expelled from the Wafd and the two ex-Wafdists established the new Sa'dist Party.[85]

The schism had serious repercussions for the Wafd as a popular movement. Throughout the fall of 1937, Nuqrashi publicly organized opposition to the Wafdist leadership that had expelled him from the party, opening an office to rally supporters and appealing to students on university campuses. The critical views of Nuqrashi and Ahmad Mahir of what they portrayed as a Nahhas-'Ubayd cabal are reported to have resonated particularly with younger and educated Egyptians. By October, Egyptian police reports reaching the British indicated that "Noqrashi's supporters are showing great activity in their propaganda among students apparently with considerable success, particularly in the Azhar. They claim that large numbers of students are now definitely anti-Government and in favour of Noqrashi."[86] Nahhas's position was not enhanced by his increasingly autocratic manner. The party meeting of September that resulted in Nuqrashi's expulsion also approved the text of a personal oath of alliance to Nahhas that would henceforth be required for party members.[87] A British report of late October, although undoubtedly reflecting the traditional British animus toward Nahhas and the Wafd, nonetheless portrayed a definite shift in public perception of the man and his movement by late 1937: "Nahas Pasha has not merely treated the old party leaders with contempt, but has either driven out or alienated all the constructive and intellectual elements in the Wafd itself. He has now also alienated a considerable section of the lay students, and the Azhar as a whole, and is appealing to the rougher elements represented by the Boulac workmen and the Blueshirts."[88]

Thus a divided and weakened Wafd faced the Palace assault that ensued upon Faruq's coming of age. Throughout the later months of 1937, the newly empowered monarch obstructed and provoked the Wafdist ministry over a number of personnel and policy issues.[89] The conflict between ministry and monarchy was also fought out in the public sphere. Makram 'Ubayd's being a Copt, with its implication of Coptic domination over the Wafd, was made an issue of public agitation by the Wafd's many opponents.[90] In turn, the Wafdist press accused the ministry's opponents of "fanning the latent antagonism of the Moslem and the Copt as one of the trump cards" in their tussle for power with the Wafd.[91] Demonstrations against the Wafdist government both by students at al-Azhar and at the Egyptian University occurred in the fall of 1937; those at the latter institution prompted the University's rector, Ahmad Lutfi al-Sayyid, to request the temporary suspension of classes. When the government rejected the request, he resigned.[92] Anti-Wafdist demonstrations were countered by others mounted in support of the ministry by the Wafdist paramilitary organization, the Blue Shirts, a movement which had grown over time and whose militants increasingly came to be used both as personal bodyguards for Nahhas as well as defenders of the government against its critics. When in October the king demanded the movement's dissolution, the behavior of the Blue Shirts became a central issue in the struggle between Palace and ministry. The anti-Wafdist press echoed the king's demand, repeatedly accusing the Blue Shirts of acts of aggression against the Wafd's critics and of having become "an instrument of terrorism" that was being utilized to support and maintain the "dictatorship" of the Wafd.[93]

The confrontation between Wafd and Palace eventually came to involve constitutional issues. By early October, the ministry was considering having Parliament pass legislation that would redefine and restrict the king's constitutional powers.[94] Faruq's unilateral appointment of the Wafd's bête noire ʿAli Mahir as Royal Chamberlain on October 20, 1937, without ministerial approval or even without informing the government prior to doing so, amounted to what the Egyptian historian ʿAbd al-ʿAzim Muhammad Ramadan characterized as a "declaration of war" on the part of the Palace against the Wafd.[95] The appointment prompted the Wafdist ministry immediately to demand that the king have no veto over government appointments and that royal appointments be subject to ministerial approval.[96] By late December, the Palace and the Wafdist ministry were engaged in unsuccessful negotiations concerning the composition of a committee that would delineate the respective powers of the ministry and the throne.[97] That a constitutional crisis was under way by late 1937 was also apparent to the Egyptian public. In the streets, one cry raised by pro-Wafdist demonstrators was "the Constitution over all"; yet another, more ominous in import, was "Nahhas or revolution."[98] This raising of the question of the definition of the constitutional powers of ministry versus monarchy was a foretaste of a debate that was to become increasingly salient in 1938–39, when the Wafd was out of office and the king and his allies dominated high politics.

On the personal level, relations between Prime Minister Nahhas and King Faruq became increasingly embittered. By October the meetings between the two parties were being described as "more than cold—they have been stormy and abusive on both sides."[99] According to a royal confidant, Faruq "hated Nahas and derived what he thought an innocent pleasure from baiting him."[100] For his part, by November Nahhas described the king's behavior toward him as "increasingly arrogant, insulting, and incorrigible";[101] in one meeting with the British ambassador, Nahhas termed the king's attitude toward him as "totally intolerable" as well as "entirely unconstitutional," and went on to "wonder whether further co-operation with His Majesty would ever be possible and whether in the country's interest King Farouk would have to go."[102]

In the end it was Nahhas, not Faruq, who went. On December 30, its public standing weakened by internal schism, by public confrontation

with a popular monarch, and by the unruly behavior of some of its supporters, the Wafdist ministry of Mustafa al-Nahhas was dismissed by royal
decree.[103] This royal dismissal of a ministry still enjoying an overwhelming
majority in Parliament amounted to what ʿAbd al-ʿAzim Muhammad
Ramadan has termed a "constitutional coup" by the Egyptian Palace.[104] It
marked the beginning of a period in which the Palace was the preeminent
force in Egyptian politics.

From December 30, 1937, until August 18, 1939, Egypt was governed by
coalition ministries of non-Wafdist parties headed by the Liberal leader
Muhammad Mahmud. Their right to rule was formally legitimized by
new parliamentary elections held in March 1938. Exceptionally corrupt even
by Egyptian standards—British reports on the methods used to secure a
pro-government vote include threatening local officials with dismissal if
they failed to insure a favorable result, the forcible exclusion of Wafdist
supporters from the polls, and the filling-out of blank ballots by election
officials—the election resulted in a Chamber of Deputies dominated by
opponents of the Wafd (77 Liberals, 84 Saʿdists, 12 Wafdists).[105]

The coalition ministries of Muhammad Mahmud were subject to
frequent interference in government affairs by a resurgent Egyptian Palace.[106] The dominant figure in Egyptian high politics in 1938 and 1939 was
the Royal Chamberlain ʿAli Mahir. As a British report of May 1938 described the political situation in Egypt, "[i]n view of the acquiescence of the
masses in the virtual disappearance of the Wafd from the Chamber, the Palace remains, for the moment, the arbiter of the political situation, and the
Palace to-day is synonymous with Ali Maher Pasha."[107] A mark of ʿAli Mahir's political ascendancy in the late 1930s is that he, not Prime Minister
Muhammad Mahmud, was unilaterally appointed by the king to lead the
Egyptian delegation to the St. James Conference concerning Palestine in
early 1939. Mahir's appointment was reportedly made despite the desire of
Prime Minister Mahmud to head the delegation, and without full Cabinet
discussion or approval.[108] Throughout the period, it was widely assumed
that Mahir aimed at becoming prime minister himself.[109] Eventually he did
so; in August 1939, his health deteriorating and his commitment to the premiership eroded by Cabinet squabbles and Palace interference, Muhammad
Mahmud resigned and was replaced by a ministry led by ʿAli Mahir.[110]

The Egyptian Palace was not a monolithic force in the later 1930s.
King Faruq—young, impulsive, and motivated in part by personal pique

over repeated lecturing from the overbearing British ambassador Sir Miles Lampson (whom he termed "Professor Lampson")—sometimes acted on his own initiative. His key political counselor, Royal Chamberlain ʿAli Mahir, was a politician of the old school. Skilled in political manipulation, with long-standing links with the assemblage of non-Wafdist parties (his brother Ahmad Mahir led the Saʿdist Party) as well as with the newer extraparliamentary movements that had become an important force in Egypt in the 1930s, the Royal Chamberlain was also beginning to build up a patronage network within the Egyptian military in order to ensure the loyalty of the latter to the monarchy.[111] Mahir's goal of crippling the Wafd in order to attain high office for himself as the preferred instrument of the monarchy nonetheless largely fit within the boundaries of the Egyptian political game as it had existed since 1923. Although holding no official post in the Palace, Shaykh Maraghi of al-Azhar continued publicly to advocate a greater role for Islam in Egypt domestically and was also the leading advocate of making Faruq caliph of the Muslim world, an aspiration that if realized would enormously increase the king's domestic prestige. A third and more radical trend within the Palace assemblage was represented by Muhammad Kamil al-Bindari. Briefly minister of health in Muhammad Mahmud's first ministry in early 1938, but excluded when the ministry was reconstituted after the elections of 1938 because of Muhammad Mahmud's suspicions that he was ʿAli Mahir's man, Bindari was immediately appointed assistant director of the Royal Cabinet. Where Mahir thought of advancing royal authority largely through manipulation and patronage, and Maraghi through capitalizing on Islam at the expense of the secular parties, Bindari thought in more generational and ideological terms. By his own admission an admirer of the ideas being expounded by Young Egypt by the late 1930s,[112] Bindari was the Palace voice arguing the need for sweeping change in Egyptian politics. In Bindari's vision of the future, the time had come for the discredited older generation of politicians to make way for Egypt's youth, including the king, to play a greater role in politics, which in turn demanded constitutional adjustments that would facilitate more effective government.[113] Bindari's ideas of governmental restructuring also envisaged a greater emphasis on the role of Islam in the state, an emphasis that corresponded with the ideas being advocated by Shaykh Maraghi as well as by Egypt's new extraparliamentary movements.[114] For most of 1938 and well into early 1939, ʿAli Mahir, "the man of old blood," and Muhammad Kamil al-Bindari, the champion of "new blood,"[115] vied for paramount influence over Egypt's impressionistic young king.[116]

British reports on the respective popularity and thus the political clout of the Palace and the Wafd in 1938 and 1939 indicate a shifting balance between the two main forces competing for hegemony in Egyptian politics. Throughout 1938, the young king still enjoyed great personal popularity. In large part, this was a default popularity stemming from the disillusionment of many Egyptians with the incessant partisanship of the country's established political parties. As a British assessment of August put it, "to-day, the indifference of the public to politicians and their *cliches* is so great that the King can do almost what he likes in the retention and dismissal of Cabinets."[117] Yet the king's popularity and hence his power had shallow roots. A November evaluation judged that "King Farouk, despite the enthusiasm excited by the romance of his youthful accession and his marriage, has not so far made any really deep appeal to the Egyptian people, with their innate dislike of the foreign reigning family and of Palace rule."[118] Royal interference in public affairs in time also produced a backlash, alienating part of the articulate Egyptian public from the king's effort to expand royal power. For the educated middle class, still the Wafd's core constituency, the assertion of greater royal authority by the Egyptian Palace in 1938–39 was read as an assault upon Egyptian democracy. Thus a British assessment of the mood in Upper Egypt in March 1939 concluded that "[t]here is no doubt that King Farouk's personal popularity has fallen very considerably," a decline in popularity that the report in part attributed to "the natural reaction of the growing educated middle class of Egyptians to His Majesty's autocratic tendencies. . . . There is, moreover, a real fear amongst the educated classes that he is aiming at a despotism of a selfish and intolerant type designed to glorify the house of Mohamed Ali rather than to serve the interests of the people of Egypt."[119] A similar report on the public mood in Lower Egypt in May 1939 found a prevalent apathy, rather than hostility, toward Faruq: "The King does not seem to arouse any popular enthusiasm these days, but there are no indications of his being unpopular, except in Sharkia province" (where the king's reckless driving had resulted in the death of a child).[120]

In contrast to the shallowness of royal popularity, that of the Wafd had deeper roots. The schism and turmoil of late 1937 definitely had an adverse effect on the party's standing but did not necessarily mean any increase in enthusiasm of its rivals. As a December 1937 report on political feeling in Lower Egypt put it, "there is little doubt that the Wafd as led by Nahas Pasha has lost a great deal of ground, but there is no strong indication, except in the provinces adjoining Cairo, that what the Wafd has lost any other party has gained."[121] By the summer of 1938, the squabbling of the parties in the government coalition and royal interference in government affairs produced a partial rebound for the Wafd.[122] By November, Sir Miles Lampson's estimate was that "the mass of the country has never ceased to be Wafdist. The faulty policy and bad administration of Nahas and Makram alienated from the Wafd a large section of its more educated supporters, but they did not find outside the Wafd any positive inspiration."[123] The ambassador's survey of the Egyptian scene at the beginning of 1939 concluded that "Egyptians have lost faith in political parties, including even the Wafd, but have found nothing to replace the Wafd, which still remains for them the symbol and bulwark of their emancipation. . . . Nearly all dislike Palace rule, but enthusiasm for the parliamentary system has disappeared."[124] By mid-1939, the Wafd was benefiting from this increasing apprehension concerning Palace ambitions: "[t]he position of the Wafd in the country has not appreciably weakened. The fears of a Palace dictatorship have, perhaps temporarily, strengthened the popular desire for more genuine constitutional government."[125]

Just how far the Egyptian Palace hoped to expand royal power at the expense of the Parliament and the parties in 1938–39 is an elusive subject. That it hoped to capitalize on the King's popularity in order to do so was certainly a common assumption at the time. As Isma'il Sidqi told a British official in February 1938, "a factor in Egyptian politics which must never be underrated now is that His Majesty both wishes and is determined to take an active part in politics."[126] In mid-1938, the Wafdist paper *al-Misri* reported that the Palace had proposed the creation of an arbitration committee to define the respective rights of the monarchy and the ministry under the Constitution.[127] Prime Minister Mahmud rejected the idea.[128] In August 1938, a public debate over the possibility of expanding royal authority at the expense of parliament is reported to have erupted when the weekly magazine *Akhir Sa'a* claimed that, in view of ministerial instability, a "high personality at the Palace had suggested that the best thing would be to suspend Parliament and let the King himself govern." When the Wafd's *al-Misri* demanded clarification concerning the unconstitutional suggestion, government officials rapidly issued declaimers asserting the king's dedication to the Constitution of 1923.[129]

The best-documented dimension of the Palace campaign to augment the power of the monarchy was the effort to enhance Faruq's authority through the use of religious symbols and claims. The Palace campaign to "create an Islamic aura round King Farouk" continued into 1938 and 1939.[130] In the external sphere, a conscious effort was made to present Faruq as a suitable figure to succeed to the position of caliph. (The Ottoman caliphate had been abolished by the new Turkish government in 1924, and subsequent efforts of the 1920s to claim the position by various Muslim rulers, including Faruq's father Fu'ad, had come to nothing.) Shaykh Maraghi of al-Azhar took the lead in this endeavor. In speeches and interviews in early 1938, Maraghi publicly promoted the idea of a reviving the caliphate in a modernized form.[131] Maraghi presented his ideas about a revived caliphate to various foreign Muslim leaders in 1938, and al-Azhar missions sent to other Muslim lands in the late 1930s may have also promoted the concept.[132]

The caliphal gambit clearly had domestic implications. Sir Miles Lampson saw two goals animating the shaykh's efforts: "[f]irstly to strengthen the position of King Farouq in Egypt by the assumption of the title of Caliph; and, secondly, to spread Egyptian influence thereby through Arab countries"; Lampson speculated that the first objective was "probably the one to which he [Maraghi] attaches most importance."[133] Various efforts to promote the concept of Faruq as caliph were directed at the Egyptian public in 1938: al-Azhar students at Friday prayer, presumably with the encouragement of Rector Maraghi, hailing Faruq as "Commander of the Faithful [amir al-mu'minin]," a term traditionally applied to the caliph;[134] Maraghi delivering a radio address on the king's birthday that called for reorienting Egypt's system of government in a more Islamic direction and that again raised the sectarian issue of alleged Coptic domination of the Wafd;[135] declarations by the leaders of Young Egypt hailing Faruq as "the most suitable" candidate for a revived caliphate and declaring that "[w]e call for Egypt to be the leader of Islam and for Faruq to be its caliph."[136]

The campaign to present Faruq as a claimant for the caliphate peaked from late 1938 to early 1939. At the opening session of the World Interparliamentary Congress of Arab and Muslim Countries for the Defense of Palestine, held in Cairo in October 1938, the audience (composed largely of members of Egyptian Muslim societies) again acclaimed Faruq as

"Commander of the Faithful."[137] One press report upon the conclusion of the congress stated that the subject of the caliphate had been discussed privately by the overwhelmingly Muslim delegates in attendance, with one suggested scenario being the convening of an international congress to designate King Faruq as caliph.[138] In January 1939, on the occasion of the ceremonial gathering at the Muhammad 'Ali Mosque of the Arab delegations on their way to London to attend the St. James Conference on Palestine, King Faruq took on the caliphal prerogative of publicly leading Friday prayer; afterwards, he was hailed by those in attendance with cries of "Long Live the Caliph."[139] An ominous feature of this event was the attendance of several hundred army officers at the mosque, the presence of whom raised fears of possible politicization of the Egyptian military as allies of the monarchy.[140] As had been the case with the interparliamentary congress in October, the January mosque incident was followed by press speculation concerning the possibility of convening a Muslim congress to select a new caliph.[141]

Agitation suggesting the possibility of Faruq as caliph in early 1939 was accompanied by the king himself publicly asserting the need for a reorientation of political authority within Egypt itself. On February 22, the beginning of the Islamic new year, Faruq delivered a holiday greeting on Egyptian radio. Broadcast while 'Ali Mahir was absent in London, and reportedly personally written by Faruq but under the guidance of Bindari, the address reflected the influence of Mahir's rival within the Palace camp.[142] Insisting that "confidence [thiqa]" and "faith [iman]" were essential for national success, Faruq expressed his personal conviction that "the youth of Egypt were proceeding with confidence toward glory, and will write an unforgettable page in the history of the nation. It is they who are achieving all of the dreams of this great nation, splendid, glorious Egypt. The realization of this dream rests on the youth alone."[143] The speech immediately set off public speculation that the Palace was about to pursue the constitutional reform of the parliamentary system in a manner that would enhance the role of the young king in government.[144]

The dual Palace initiatives of early 1939—the assertion of Faruq's claim to the caliphate and the king's own championing of youth, himself included, as the indispensable force of the future—marked the high point of the efforts of the Palace to enhance the role of the monarchy at the expense of the existing political parties and more broadly at the expense of the existing parliamentary order. What is crucial is that both initiatives met with a negative reaction by important constituencies. 'Ali Mahir, who had competed with Bindari for the ear of the king and whose ideas concerning the ways to expand royal authority did not extend as far as those of Bindari, was angered by the growth of Bindari's influence in the Palace during his absence in London. Upon his return from St. James Conference in March, a confidential Palace source in contact with the British reported an angry confrontation between Mahir and Faruq over the February speech in which Mahir "violently accused Bindari of having made mischief for him with the King."[145] Mahir subsequently threatened to resign as royal chamberlain. Perhaps aware that Mahir's connections and tactical skills were too vital to maintaining his own position on the domestic political scene, Faruq resolved the issue by removing Bindari from his post in the Palace and appointed him Egyptian minister to Brussels.[146]

Bindari's ouster from the Palace marked the end of the tentative effort of King Faruq to present himself as the champion of a movement of youth and of fundamental change in Egypt. Although Faruq still harbored thoughts of enhancing his domestic authority at the expense of the political parties, henceforth he did so in more conventional terms.[147] His victory over Bindari notwithstanding, the confrontation over the king's February speech also temporarily weakened Mahir's standing with Faruq, and led Mahir to seek both to repair his relations with Prime Minister Mahmud and to reestablish contacts with the Wafd.[148] Not dissimilar to the Wafd when in power in 1936–37, the Egyptian Palace at the height of its influence in 1938–39 was a political force with internal divisions that weakened its ability to permanently expand the scope of royal authority.

The Palace campaign to present King Faruq as a suitable candidate for a revived caliphate similarly fizzled by 1939. Domestically, it met with criticism and opposition from Egypt's many supporters of the existing primarily secular constitutional order. The thought of Faruq as caliph, with all that it implied in the way of an increased international role and thus augmented domestic prestige for the King, was anathema to the Wafd. In the press, the Wafdist *al-Jihad* editorially criticized the Azharite acclamation of Faruq as "Commander of the Faithful" and argued against "the revival of the caliphate question" in Egypt on the dual grounds of it being "a deliberate maneuver to distract the Egyptian people from the constitutional issue" and because it would be "viewed with misgiving in the other Arabic-speaking nations."[149] Nor was the idea of

Faruq as caliph gladly received by Egypt's non-Wafdist parties, particularly the Liberals and the Saʿdists in control of the government for most of 1938–39. Prime Minister Mahmud as well as other ministers in the government privately expressed their apprehension over a maneuver that would presumably weaken the entire parliamentary regime in Egypt.[150] Newspapers associated with both the Liberal and Saʿdist parties opposed the idea of the caliphate being brought to Egypt when the issue was raised at the World Interparliamentary Congress in October 1938 and again when the Arab delegations to the St. James Conference assembled in Egypt in January 1939, presenting the caliphate as an institution that would only saddle the country with unnecessary international obligations.[151] After the January 1939 mosque incident in which Faruq was hailed as caliph, attended by a number of army officers, Prime Minister Mahmud summoned senior officers and lectured them regarding the necessity to avoid involvement in domestic politics.[152] Their political rivalries notwithstanding, the leaders of Egypt's established political parties were too wedded to the maintenance of the ascendancy of a parliamentary system of which they were the prime beneficiaries to look with favor on the prospect of King Faruq ascending to international Muslim leadership.

It also appears that not all members of the King's entourage were wholehearted enthusiasts of the idea of Faruq as caliph. ʿAli Mahir in particular seems to have had reservations about the caliphal gambit. Although one hostile Wafdist source claimed that Mahir was "the chief sponsor of the idea,"[153] other evidence shows Shaykh Maraghi to have been its inspiration and prime advocate. Certainly Maraghi promoted the idea in public. One British report noted Mahir as being "rather apprehensive about Sheikh el Maraghi's Islamic campaign,"[154] and Mahir's close associate ʿAbd al-Rahman ʿAzzam later credited the caliphal initiative to Maraghi while asserting that "ʿAli Mahir and others went along but no one took it seriously."[155]

Faruq's caliphal aspirations also met with international opposition. From the initial rumors of Palace intentions to pursue the caliphate for Faruq, British reports commented on the likelihood of resistance from other Muslim countries, Turkey and Saʿudi Arabia in particular.[156] Immediately after Faruq was hailed as Caliph after Friday prayer in January 1939, the Turkish Foreign Ministry issued a demarche denouncing any attempt to revive the caliphate.[157] Among Arab states, both the Saʿudi and the Yemeni representatives present in Cairo at the January ceremony were reported to have been "considerably annoyed" by the incident, in which they felt that "their participation had been maneuvered."[158]

Together, this domestic and international opposition wrote *fini* to the Egyptian Palace's caliphal campaign. Within a few days of the mosque incident of January 1939, the Egyptian Embassy in London issued an official disclaimer to the effect that "there was no question whatever of His Majesty as Caliph of the Moslems."[159] Reports reaching the British after the incident claimed that 'Ali Mahir now felt that broaching the idea of Faruq as caliph had been "premature" in view of the hostility with which it had been received.[160] The notion of King Faruq as caliph effectively died in early 1939.

It is a mark of the limits of the current of opinion favoring more authoritative methods of government for Egypt that no substantial change in the constitutional distribution of authority between parliament and monarchy occurred prior to the outbreak of World War II. The tentative royal feeler in the direction of the same in mid-1938 (i.e., the Palace suggestion of a committee to redefine the powers of monarchy and ministry) was quickly rejected by the government and did not resurface prior to the war. As noted earlier, by early 1939 public apprehension over the king's presumed "autocratic tendencies" and of the prospect of a "Palace dictatorship" is reported to have produced a public reaction in favor of constitutional and parliamentary government.[161]

The resignation of the Muhammad Mahmud ministry in August 1939 and its replacement by one headed by the king's man 'Ali Mahir at first glance appeared to have increased the prospect of the institutionalization of an increased political role for the Egyptian monarchy. While undoubtedly self-serving, the closest thing to an explication of the extent of Faruq's autocratic aspirations at the close of the interwar era came in a conversation he had with a British official on August 20, two days after appointment of the Mahir ministry.

The King said that while he had little admiration for the European dictatorships, it was impossible to argue that the democracies were possessed of all the virtues. There was some good in both systems and, in times as grave as the present, it was surely advisable for Egypt to discard such aspects of democratic procedure as had proved useless or inapplicable and supplant them by something more calculated to "get a move on."

Yet Faruq immediately went on to indicate that the goals he envisaged for the new ministry largely fit within the bounds of the Egyptian political contest between the monarchy and the parties as it had existed since the inception of the parliamentary order: "Parliament (by which His Majesty undoubtedly meant the Senate, which is predominantly Wafdist) had become little more than a debating society with a distinct tendency towards obstruction, and many permanent officials did little more than draw their pay. Aly Maher Pasha was determined to 'give them a taste of his cocktail' by way of stimulating them all to more strenuous and effective effort." The king went on to assure his British interlocutor that neither he nor the new premier sought the elimination of the parliamentary order: "His Majesty asked me not to believe the rumours that were bound to be set on foot that a dictatorship was being set up."[162]

Whatever Faruq's opinion regarding the inadequacy of the existing parliamentary system, Parliament did remain a check on any movement in the direction of more authoritarian rule even during the 1939–40 ministry of 'Ali Mahir. As constituted in August 1939, Mahir's ministry was initially composed of eight independent and five Sa'dist ministers. The Sa'dist bloc in the Cabinet, former Wafdists who retained the traditional Wafdist commitment to "the sanctity of the Constitution,"[163] were not supporters of the idea of movement toward the institutionalization of royal autocracy. In October the prospect of major change receded further when Liberal members—less ardent defenders of parliamentary ascendancy, but nonetheless not advocates of significant constitutional change—joined the Cabinet. The Senate, where a sizable Wafdist contingent remained, served as a further barrier to any movement toward more authoritarian rule.[164] It is a mark of how limited the real prospects of increased autocracy in Egypt were at the close of the 1930s that, when an irritated King Faruq criticized parliamentary leaders for what he felt was a lukewarm parliamentary reception of the annual Speech from the Throne in November 1939, the speakers of the Senate and the Chamber of Deputies met with Prime Minister Mahir to protest the king's "unconstitutional" attitude; the latter promptly assured them that such imperious behavior by the king would not be repeated.[165] Finally and decisively, the prospect of constitutional change in Egypt was ultimately constrained by the British presence in Egypt, a presence that became larger and more assertive over Egyptian internal affairs with the outbreak of war in September 1939. It was the British who eventually, in June 1940 upon Italian entry into the war, ousted the king's man 'Ali Mahir as premier because of his presumed pro-Italian inclinations and contacts, and who thereafter ensured that Egypt was governed by compliant pro-British ministries for the duration of the war.

In conclusion, the interpretation that the later 1930s marked the decline of the Wafd and witnessed a corresponding growth in royal power is valid in general terms but in need of substantial qualification.[166] While the Egyptian Palace did succeed in more direct interference in the operation of the political system in 1938–39 than had been the case when the Wafd was in office in 1936–37, the manipulation of partisan rivalries by the Egyptian monarchy was hardly unprecedented; King Fu'ad had previously done so with considerable success during his reign, particularly in the early 1930s. The Palace's enhanced ability to shape the course of high politics in the late 1930s was based on a combination of temporary public enthusiasm for a young and untainted monarch and the prevailing exhaustion of the articulate public with the squabbling of the existing political parties.

Royal interference in Egyptian governmental affairs did not come anywhere close to the extent of control and domination of public life that was occurring in the authoritarian regimes across the Mediterranean. King Faruq possessed neither the personal drive and charisma, nor the institutional resources in the form of a loyal and ruthless mass movement, available to contemporary European dictators. Nor does he appear to have had anything approaching their totalitarian ideological agenda. Although testimony after the fact is always suspect, the Palace figure to whom ideological motivations have been attributed, Muhammad Kamil al-Bindari,[167] subsequently maintained that neither he nor Faruq were thinking in "fascist" terms when the king floated ideas of constitutional reform and the infusion of "new blood" into government in 1939.[168] Faruq's autocratic inclinations need to be located in realistic proportions; Egypt's young king was neither Mussolini nor Hitler. Moreover, the incremental growth of royal power in time produced a reaction against the prospect of the permanent entrenchment of a palace-dominated, more autocratic regime within Egypt's pluralist political universe. When faced with the prospect of the king augmenting his political authority, the commitment of articulate Egyptians to the ascendancy of parliamentary government was rekindled. All this put serious limits on the prospects for any definitive movement in the direction of authoritarian rule in Egypt.

The combination of accelerating political and ideological rivalry between the European dictatorships and the Western democracies on the one hand, and the aspirations of the Egyptian Palace to see the Egyptian governmental system evolve in a more authoritarian direction on the other, assured that the respective merits of democracy and dictatorship became a vital issue for Egyptians in the later 1930s. In those years, both the external context (the apparently unstoppable momentum of fascist regimes internationally) and the internal one (disillusionment with the existing political parties and the parallel effort of Egyptian Palace to augment its power) had a cumulative impact. Internationally, Fascist Italy and Nazi Germany seemed to be marching from political triumph to political triumph in 1938–39; the potential appeal of dictatorship as the way to achieve dramatic results was never stronger. Internally, the perceived shortcomings of the existing parliamentary system fed both the desire for and the prospect of fundamental reform centered around the then-popular figure of Egypt's monarch. Given the combined weight of the fascist surge in the international arena and the desire for a more efficient government at home, the question of what was the proper political system for Egypt became a matter of intense concern to politically articulate Egyptians.

The tension between theory and reality, between the noble values espoused in political rhetoric and the grubby realities of the political system as it operated in practice, framed Egyptian discussions of democracy versus authoritarianism in the later 1930s. Whereas the ostensible subject of Egyptian commentary may have been the virtues and vices of democracy and fascism as both manifested themselves abroad, the implicit referent was the possible relevance and utility of antiliberal authoritarianism for Egypt itself. If parliamentary democracy as it operated in Egypt was so flawed, why maintain the system? Were there better models to emulate? What could Egypt learn from the vigorous and seemingly effective dictatorial regimes that had recently emerged in Europe? Was the authoritarian alternative to representative parliamentary democracy better suited to Egyptian political realities? In short, was fascism worthy and capable of replacing parliamentary democracy in Egypt itself? The Egyptian answers to these questions are detailed in the pages that follow.

Part II Dictatorship versus Democracy in Egyptian Public Discourse

Prologue
Public Sphere and Public Discourse
in Interwar Egypt

THE EGYPTIAN DISCOURSE CONCERNING democracy and dictatorship developed within a public sphere that attained maturity and prominence particularly in the period between the two world wars. Exploiting the extensive print media of the period, mainly Egypt's flourishing press, a sophisticated civil society contributed to and in the process expanded and deepened the public sphere and the public discourse found within it.

Any discussion of public sphere and public discourse leans on the work of the German sociologist Jürgen Habermas and the inquiry into the nature of the public sphere it has stimulated in the social sciences and cultural studies. Since the publication of Habermas's pathbreaking study *The Structural Transformation of the Public Sphere* (original German edition, 1962; English translation, 1989) Habermas's theories have been revised and refined, even by Habermas himself. Our examination of the Egyptian public sphere critically appropriates insights suggested by Habermas and in the fertile academic discussions that ensued subsequent to the publication of his book. Habermas's theory of the public sphere is decidedly Eurocentric; hence we will cautiously and selectively attempt to adapt it to the distinctive experience of Egypt.

In *The Structural Transformation of the Public Sphere*, Habermas explored the historical development of the public sphere in European society. Habermas's public sphere was a historical category associated with the development of European bourgeois society. His emphasis was on the public sphere as a social and cultural arena separate from and independent of the state, one that occupied the expanding space between the state and its formal institutions on the one hand, and the private sphere of the individual and the family on the other. In his own words, "[t]he bourgeois public sphere may be conceived above all as the sphere of private people come together as a public; they soon claimed the public sphere regulated from above against the public authorities themselves, to engage them in a debate over the general rules governing relations in the basically privatized but publicly relevant sphere of commodity exchange and social labor."[1] The key characteristics of the public sphere—publicness, openness, accessibility, representativeness—were for Habermas an expression of the *moderna*; hence the public sphere is a distinctly modern entity.[2] In his historical analysis, Habermas went on to argue that over time, with the rise of mass society and mass politics, the commercialization of culture in the late nineteenth and particularly the twentieth centuries, and the shift from print media to the electronic and visual mass media, the public sphere changed profoundly (hence the "structural transformation" of his title), undergoing "decomposition" and ultimately "collapse."[3] For Habermas, the shift from what he termed "a culture-debating [*kulturräsonierend*] to a culture-consuming public" signified "the disintegration of the bourgeois public sphere."[4] His approach, inspired by the Frankfurt school of Adorno and Horkheimer, was historically pessimistic, if not bleak.

The work of Habermas has prompted an interdisciplinary academic discussion on the public sphere and public discourse. Particularly in the past two decades, critical analysis has revised and clarified both the boundaries and the characteristics of the public sphere.[5] Academic discussion of the public sphere has enlarged the concept from one historically specific to Europe to one of general applicability in modern societies. Moving beyond the European context that concerned Habermas, Nancy Fraser has redefined the public sphere as follows: "It designates a theater in modern societies in which political participation is enacted through the medium of talk. It is a space in which citizens deliberate about their common affairs, and hence an institutionalized arena of discursive interaction. This arena is conceptually distinct from the state; it is a site for the production and circulation of discourses that can in principle be critical of the state."[6]

Academic discussion has qualified or amended the concept of the public sphere in important respects. It has shown that Habermas's model of the decline and disintegration of the public sphere is overstated and that there is a continuing reality and vitality to the public sphere even in the "post-bourgeois" era. It has demonstrated that the public sphere was not exclusively bourgeois, but one open and accessible to other sectors of modern society. Where Habermas reduced the public sphere to a single, homogeneous entity, research has shown it to be a set of multiple, overlapping public spheres or a complex of different public spheres existing within a single society. Habermas's sharp distinction between state and society, between official ruling institutions and unofficial or nongovernmental entities, has been blurred. In historical reality, boundaries between the official and the unofficial are more porous and permeable. Where Habermas viewed this blurring as a process of disintegration, his critics argue that this blurring is essential to the nature of the public sphere, a feature that enables it to survive in its interactions with the state.

Habermas's interest was focused on the bourgeois public sphere as it had developed in Europe. Employing insights suggested by his critics, we suggest a framework whereby the concept of the public sphere can be applied to Egypt and other Middle Eastern societies.[7]

In its amended sense, Habermas's public sphere certainly existed in interwar Egypt. Readjusting Habermas's terminology of "the bourgeois public sphere," we can define the specific Egyptian public sphere as the *effendi* public sphere. The most prominent social cohort involved in the Egyptian public sphere—generating it, maintaining it, shaping and reshaping it—was Egypt's *effendiyya* population. By the interwar era, the *effendiyya* played the major role in producing and disseminating the public discourse of the day.

Originally a Greek term, the word *effendi* (Arabic *afandi*) was used in the Ottoman Empire to refer to state functionaries. In nineteenth-century Egypt, it came to be applied to the "new men," the cohort of professionally educated state servants generated by the modernizing regime of Muhammad ʿAli and his descendants. Over time, it came to be applied to the growing population of Egyptians who through their education and occupation were associated with, and who themselves identified with, the modern state, economy, and society developing in Egypt. Centered in urban areas, Western-educated in the liberal professions (doctors, lawyers), often but not necessarily state employed (bureaucrats, engineers, teachers), distinguished by their Western dress (*mutarbashun*, "tarbush-wearers," in contrast to more traditional *muʿammamun*, "turban-wearers"), the term *effendi* was both a social and a cultural construct that simultaneously indicated the "modern" training and profession as well as the "modern" lifestyle and life-orientation possessed by those to whom it was applied.[8]

In contrast to Habermas's model of a bourgeois public sphere that emerged apart from and in opposition to the state, in Egypt the public sphere dominated by the *effendiyya* did not emerge apart from the state. As it developed as social cohort over the nineteenth century, the *effendiyya* had its origins in education by and service to the state. Even as the social category broadened greatly over time, many of its members continued to hold or to aspire to official positions. Many of the leading *effendis* of the interwar era served in government or were members of the political parties competing for control for the state. Members of the *effendi* public sphere engaged in frequent interaction, collaboration as well as disputation, with state institutions and agencies.

By the interwar era, Egypt's *effendiyya* exhibited a strong collective self-image. Over time, the *effendiyya* had developed an increasingly assertive subjective self-consciousness that they, more than any other social group, truly represented the Egyptian national community. They and they alone expressed the common good; they and they alone spoke for the general public interest of the nation. The cartoon character Misri Effendi, so frequently employed in Egyptian illustrated publications of the 1930s as "the average Egyptian," the representative of and spokesman for the entire nation, was the stock image that captured—not without a degree of irony and self-criticism—the collective self-image of the *effendiyya*.[9]

Although the *effendiyya* played the major role in determining the content of Egypt's public sphere, it did not belong exclusively to them. By its very nature, the public sphere is inclusive. Other literate groups within Egyptian society contributed to the civic discourse developing within this sphere: the landed aristocracy, the indigenous commercial and financial bourgeoisie (sectors of the economy otherwise dominated by non-Egyptians), religiously educated *'ulama*, the more traditional urban middle class of artisans and merchants, and over time a limited number of spokesmen from more plebian social groups such as workers. To appropriate Nancy Fraser's terminology, one can say that there was "always a plurality of competing publics" and that interchange among them (conflict and confrontation as well as negotiation and compromise) characterized the Egyptian public sphere. Fraser is also correct in noting the existence of "counterpublics" within the public sphere, groups that produced and disseminated "counterdiscourses" that challenged the hegemonic discourse of the day and forced it to take into consideration the views of subaltern publics. In effect, the interplay among these diverse publics was marked by "interpublic relations" as well as "intrapublic relations."[10]

Gradually expanding in size, and progressively distancing itself from the state, Egypt's *effendi* public sphere reached maturity in the 1920s and 1930s. Largely self-contained and enjoying a well-defined civic identity, by then it was largely autonomous and propelled by an internal dynamic. As in Habermas's model, where "the public sphere's preeminent institution [was] the press,"[11] the *effendi* public sphere expressed itself through an entire industry of print media. The *effendiyya* made the press the major public means of communication in Egypt, both the market for practical information and the main theater for expressing public opinion. By the interwar years, the press was (to use Habermas's term) "a forum for rational-critical debate."[12] Existing under a liberal parliamentary regime where it was only occasionally subject to restrictive press laws, for most of the interwar era Egypt's press operated with substantial independence from state control or oversight. Its massive output, generated by literally hundreds of publications, demonstrated great intellectual diversity.

Alongside the press, various nonofficial institutions and organizations also contributed to Egypt's public sphere: civic associations, business groups, social clubs catering to the interests and needs of different segments of society (foreign communities, religious communities, women, youth, artists and writers), and political, cultural, and religious societies. The venues in which opinion was expressed were numerous: schools, coffee and tea houses, salons, theaters and cinemas, and social clubs of various stripes. In terms of religion, Muslims, Christians, and Jews all participated; in terms of gender, women by this time had begun to organize and play a public role; in terms of nationality, indigenous Egyptians as well as foreign residents contributed; in terms of generation, it gave voice to the views of both older and younger Egyptians. All of these agencies, groups, and social settings contributed to the vitality and strength of Egypt's public sphere by the 1920s and 1930s.

Increased accessibility and participation meant not "refeudalization," as Habermas asserted had occurred in Europe,[13] but the consolidation of the centrality of the *effendi* public sphere within Egyptian public life. The growth of mass society, mass culture, and the mass media by the 1930s, as manifested in the rapidly expanding cinema industry, the introduction of the new medium of radio, and the greater degree of mass political mobilization, did not undermine the liberal orientation of the *effendi* public sphere. The agents of the new mass culture and politics of the 1930s in Egypt were themselves primarily *effendiyya*; their prominence in these new means of expression strengthened *effendiyya* hegemony over an expanding public sphere and enabled the *effendiyya* to dictate norms and expectations to broader segments of society. The growth of new media and forms of political expression broadened and deepened the *effendi* public sphere, allowing more individuals and groups to participate in it.

It is arguable that the *effendi* public sphere reached its culmination in the second half of the 1930s. The autocratic ministries of Palace-oriented "strongman" Isma'il Sidqi in the early years of the decade, along with the replacement of the liberal Constitution of 1923 by the more authoritarian Constitution of 1930, had briefly brought greater restrictions on the Egyptian media. With Sidqi's fall in late 1933 and his replacement by less repressive ministries in 1934–35, and particularly with the restoration of the Constitution of 1923 and the conclusion of the Anglo-Egyptian Treaty of Alliance in 1936, both of which contributed to opening up the public sphere, a greater measure of media vitality and diversity returned to Egypt. This historical moment lasted until the outbreak of World War II in September 1939, when censorship was immediately introduced and (along with the wartime shortage of paper) severely constrained the volume and the range of divergent opinion expressed in the public sphere. In terms of both the variety and the independence of expression, the later 1930s were in many ways the golden age of unfettered public discourse in Egypt.

The "structural transformation" of the *effendi* public sphere seems to have occurred only after the military seizure of power in July 1952. With Egypt's transformation into a revolutionary republic in the 1950s and its adoption of a formally socialist social and economic orientation in the 1960s, many liberal structures and institutions (the press, political pluralism, an independent academy, a capitalist economy) were undermined or destroyed. In particular, the massive intervention of the state in the public sphere through the nationalization of the print and visual media put an end to the civil society and the liberal public sphere that had flourished between the two world wars. Clothing symbolized the transformation: the headgear of fez/tarbush, prime symbol of *effendi* status, after 1952 became the despised marker of the ancien regime and was rapidly replaced by the military or civilian cap.

Our study undertakes a systematic examination of one major dimension of the Egyptian public sphere at a particular historical moment. It attempts to reconstruct the public discourse concerning democracy and dictatorship that evolved in the later 1930s, when the public sphere regained its full vitality. It discusses the individual voices as well as the schools of thought that articulated the discourse. This discourse was not the only one that existed within the public sphere of the day. It took shape within a polysystem of overlapping discourses, including ones on the appropriate balance between tradition and modernity, the role of religion in modern Egypt, Egypt's relationship to the Arab and Muslim worlds, and the status and rights of women. Anwar al-Jundi aptly characterized this era of intellectual controversy as one of "cultural battles [ma'arik adabiyya]"—the contestation among different perspectives and orientations within both the "literary public sphere" and the "political public sphere," to use Habermas's terminology.[14]

Among these competing discourses, that relating to democracy and dictatorship had many dimensions. A heterogeneous network of issues and debates, it was characterized by multivocality. Many different agents contributed to producing and disseminating opinions regarding authoritarianism, militarism, and fascism on the one hand and parliamentary government, democracy, and cultural pluralism on the other. None of these rival concepts possessed universally accepted meaning and value within the *effendi* public sphere in the 1930s. Therefore, this study will pay special attention to how different individuals and groups interpreted these terms at different times and in different contexts. It will highlight the diverse and pluralistic nature of the public discourse in relation to democracy and dictatorship, and it will attempt to identify the prevailing positions and attitudes held by articulate Egyptians toward the burning issue of authoritarianism versus liberalism at a time when the clash between the two ideologies preoccupied people across the world.

2

The Fascist Threat as Seen in
the Egyptian Daily Press

EGYPTIAN DAILY NEWSPAPERS WERE the most influential medium of the interwar era. The daily newspaper was the dominant agent in print culture, the most widely read source of information with the highest circulation. The influence of the daily press in shaping public discourse was much greater than that of Egypt's many weekly or monthly journals of opinion. Daily newspapers presented Egyptian readers with a wider range of information on a wider range of subjects than did Egyptian periodicals. They were the primary source of news about Egypt and the world for educated Egyptians. In the interwar era in particular, Egypt's leading dailies were also Arab dailies that were distributed and read in other Arab countries. In addition to articulating the local Egyptian perspective on current events, they were an all-Arab medium influencing opinion across the entire Arab world.

The primary mission of the dailies was to react to current events in an immediate way. Although they occasionally printed more substantial essays probing a subject in depth, their focus was on providing a narrative account of current events. Appearing on a daily basis, their coverage of current affairs was fuller than that offered by publications that appeared less frequently. As with all narratives, their reports and commentaries were constructs that inevitably bore the mark of the ideological orientation and values of their producers. Tracing their coverage of and immediate reaction to international affairs gives an indication of how contemporary politics, specifically the political and ideological rivalry between the European democracies and their authoritarian challengers, was understood by Egyptians.

The coverage of international affairs found in four important Egyptian dailies—*al-Ahram*, *al-Muqattam*, *al-Misri*, and *al-Jihad*—from the Italo-Ethiopian crisis and war of 1935–36 until the outbreak of World War II in September 1939 will be examined in what follows. *Al-Ahram* was one of the oldest newspapers in the Middle East, having been published continuously since 1875. In the interwar era, it was arguably the most influential newspaper in Egypt and the Arab world. Privately owned and operated by the Taqla family, of Lebanese origin but long resident in Egypt, its publisher was Jabra'il Bishara Taqla; Antun al-Jamil served as editor. Not affiliated with any of Egypt's political parties, *al-Ahram* was a nonpartisan, modernist, and progressive forum that also tended to identify with Egyptian nationalist as well as with pan-Arab aspirations. Comprehensive in coverage, precise in reporting, serious in tone, it was "Egypt's greatest newspaper," as a British appreciation of late 1937 put it.[1] With an estimated circulation of 45,000–50,000 copies in 1937, a figure which by one estimate had risen to 150,000 by 1944, *al-Ahram*'s circulation far exceeded that of any other daily newspaper.[2]

The second establishment daily considered in the following section is *al-Muqattam*. Founded in 1889 by the Syrian journalists Ya'qub Sarruf and Faris Nimr, in political outlook *al-Muqattam* occupied a position at the fringe of the Egyptian daily press. Always relatively pro-British in orientation, in the interwar period also sometimes sympathetic to the positions of the Egyptian Palace, it expressed the views of and appealed particularly to the large and influential Syro-Lebanese émigré population resident in Egypt. By the interwar period it had acquired a reputation for substantial and serious, if somewhat dull, analysis of current affairs. In part because of its well-known pro-British orientation, its circulation, estimated at 8,000–10,000 in 1937 (a decline from perhaps 25,000 a decade earlier), lagged well behind that of *al-Ahram*.[3]

The other two newspapers were more recent and more partisan publications. *Al-Jihad*, established in 1931, was owned and edited by Muhammad Tawfiq Diyab. Early in 1938 it was purchased by the Wafd and amalgamated with another paper, *Kawkab al-Sharq*, thereafter appearing as an evening paper under the title *al-Wafd al-Misri*.[4] It resumed publication as *al-Jihad* after the bankruptcy of *al-Wafd al-Misri* in August 1938, but ceased publication for good at the end of September 1938.[5] *Al-Misri* was the youngest of the three, established in 1936. The initial founders and publishers of the paper were Mahmud Abu al-Fath, Muhammad al-Tabi'i, and Karim Thabit; the editor was Muhammad al-Shafi'i al-Banna. Pro-Wafdist from the start, in February 1938 the newspaper was purchased by the party to serve as the official organ of the Wafd (the first instance of the party actually owning and operating a newspaper).[6] With a circulation estimated at 20,000 in 1937 and 25,000 in 1944,[7] it was popular with the many Egyptians sympathetic to what was still Egypt's leading political organization. Since the Wafd was in political opposition to the Palace-supported coalition ministries in power, al-Misri can also be seen as representing the views of the Wafdist government in 1936–37 and as the leading voice of the Egyptian opposition in 1938–39.

Regardless of their differences in political orientation, in many respects the contents of these prominent dailies converged and may be viewed as representative of the views of the large center of articulate public opinion. Founded as commercial enterprises that needed to generate sufficient profit to continue to exist, they operated within the open market of supply and demand. Their circulation and viability was dependent upon the general congruence of their views with that of both their readers and their advertisers.[8] The need to sell papers, and not to alienate advertisers, pressured them toward a centrist viewpoint that was both understandable and acceptable to a broad range of consumer publics. As newspapers owned and operated by families of Syro-Lebanese background who, despite now being Egyptian citizens were nonetheless identified as immigrants ("those who have become Egyptian," mutamassirun), al-Ahram and al-Muqattam were in a particularly delicate position that led them to be politically cautious, ostensibly neutral, and "objective" on controversial issues. For their part, al-Jihad and al-Misri, while representing the Wafdist position on Egyptian internal politics, were also compelled to obey the rules of supply and demand. In line with the Wafd's own ideology that the party was not a partisan organization but the representative of the entire Egyptian nation in its search for national independence, they too sought to articulate positions representative of the broadest range of public opinion. The wide circulation of both al-Ahram and al-Misri, respectively the first and second most popular Egyptian daily newspapers in the later 1930s, leads us to conclude that both provide an accurate reflection of the position of the Egyptian public on international issues.

Through the prism of the daily press, the decisive event in which to view Egyptian attitudes toward Fascist Italy was the confrontation and war between Italy and Ethiopia in 1935–36. From the perspective of Egyptians, "the Ethiopian crisis (*al-azma al-habashiyya*)" was the most important international event of the mid-1930s. Throughout the summer, fall, and winter of 1935–36, the Egyptian press closely followed the confrontation between Italy and Ethiopia first in the diplomatic arena and eventually on the battlefield. The articulate Egyptian public reacted with shock and disgust to Italy's aggression against another independent African state as well as to the brutality with which Italy carried out its conquest of Ethiopia and its incorporation into a new Italian empire. Italy's invasion and occupation of Ethiopia permanently colored the Egyptian attitude toward the Fascist regime in Italy. The proximity of Egypt to the battlefield and the feeling that Egypt was now bordered on the west and the south by a powerful and aggressive European empire convinced many Egyptians that there was now a concrete Fascist threat to Egypt itself.

Al-Muqattam's coverage evolved considerably as the crisis between Italy and Ethiopia unfolded in the mid-1930s. In the early stages of the crisis, from the fall of 1934 until well into 1935, *al-Muqattam* expressed only cautious and restrained criticism of Italy's diplomatic maneuvering and military preparations for war. It repeatedly expressed the hope that the impending conflict between the two states could be resolved in a peaceful manner. Italy, the newspaper maintained, had an understandable desire for additional colonial expansion in order to balance its international position vis-à-vis the other European imperial powers. Nonetheless, it should not resolve its colonial ambitions at the expense of the sovereignty and independence of Ethiopia, a recognized member of the League of Nations.[9] The newspaper initially held that Italy had no interest in being dragged into war; Mussolini's threats of the same were only intended to bring pressure on the international community to recognize Italy's right to territorial expansion in east Africa.[10] The newspaper went on to suggest that Egypt could play the role of mediator between the parties, bringing each to the negotiation table to settle the crisis.[11]

In the summer of 1935, as the Italo-Ethiopian crisis deepened, *al-Muqattam*'s tone began to change. Although it continued to hold the view that a compromise and a peaceful resolution of the differences between Italy and Ethiopia could be reached, it became less tolerant toward Mussolini's bluster and threats. As international opposition to Italian demands mounted, the newspaper now dismissed Mussolini's demands for territorial expansion and held that Italy's imperialist ambitions were threatening world peace. Internationally "Italy is isolated," *al-Muqattam* maintained; the country's bellicose behavior had put it at odds with "the conscience of the entire world."[12]

When war between Italy and Ethiopia did break out, *al-Muqattam* placed the blame solidly on Italy and Mussolini. Although it occasionally expressed the belief that a negotiated solution to the Italo-Ethiopian dispute was still possible and might stop the hostilities,[13] elsewhere it accused Mussolini of waging a war primarily as a demonstration of Fascist power for the benefit of both the Italian public and world opinion.[14] It characterized the war as a prime example of "white imperialism [*isti'mar al-bid*]," presenting the conflict as being driven by an imperialist desire to conquer territory in order to obtain raw materials and other economic resources, as well as in this case to gain new land in order to ease demographic pressures within Italy itself.[15]

In contrast to its criticism of Fascist imperialism and Mussolini, *al-Muqattam* expressed unambiguous sympathy for the Ethiopian cause. Its solicitousness for the Ethiopians was in part an expression of solidarity with fellow Eastern Christians by this Christian-owned and operated publication.[16] The newspaper welcomed the imposition of partial sanctions on Italy by the League of Nations and praised the Egyptian government for supporting sanctions by restricting the movement of oil through the Suez Canal.[17] The unrestrained nature of Italian military operations, particularly "the aerial bombardment of defenseless towns and villages" and "the dropping of poisonous gas bombs which sow death and horror," was condemned as barbaric.[18] In as far as the conflict related to Egypt and its national interests, the newspaper cautioned that the war might carry direct repercussions for Egypt and warned Italy not to attempt any move that would cause harm to the Ethiopian sources of the Nile; Egypt needed to be concerned by the Italian takeover of the Blue Nile, and needed to act to secure and protect this essential Egyptian interest.[19]

Italy completed its conquest by the spring of 1936, and its subsequent annexation of Ethiopia to the Italian empire was criticized by *al-Muqattam*. The newspaper endorsed the Egyptian government's initial refusal to recognize the annexation as legitimate.[20] Nonetheless, as over the course of 1936 the world community gradually reconciled itself to Italy's conquest and annexation of Ethiopia, *al-Muqattam* similarly adjusted to the fact of Italian imperial expansion in East Africa. Expressing the hope that Italy had now satisfied its territorial and imperialist aspirations, the newspaper argued that it was necessary for Egypt to adopt a realistic approach and reconcile itself to a new situation.[21] In the summer of 1936, the newspaper congratulated the new Wafdist government for lifting economic sanctions on Italy,[22] and thereafter, in the context of the signing of the Anglo-Egyptian Treaty of Alliance, called on the Egyptian government to come to terms with the "real situation" and to work to ease tension and to improve relations between Egypt and Italy.[23] This attitude of accepting the Italian fait accompli in the international arena was paralleled by the publication in late 1936 carrying a sympathetic series of articles by its international editor Thabit Thabit about the domestic reforms and measures of modernization carried out by the Fascist regime.[24] Yet realism did not imply exoneration for Italian aggression in Ethiopia. Well into 1937, *al-Muqattam* continued to depict Italian expansion into Ethiopia as unjustified and racist, rejecting the Italian argument that its expansion was justified by the backward state of the country and praising the measures of modernization that had been inaugurated by the deposed Emperor Haile Selassie.[25]

Its gradual acceptance of the fact of successful Fascist aggression in East Africa notwithstanding, *al-Muqattam*'s apprehension concerning the potential negative implications of Italian international ambitions for Egypt itself did not disappear. One immediate concern was the fear that Italy had imperialist aspirations for taking over the Suez Canal.[26] More broadly, the newspaper warned that Mussolini's ambitions had not been sated by the conquest of Ethiopia, and that his Fascist regime viewed the entire Mediterranean and Middle East as a zone of Italian influence and expansion.[27] The Ethiopian crisis and war of 1935–36 permanently colored *al-Muqattam*'s attitude toward Fascist Italy and the possible repercussions of Fascist ambitions for Egypt.

Al-Ahram's coverage of the Ethiopian conflict paralleled that of *al-Muqattam*. The best-funded and staffed daily newspaper in interwar Egypt, *al-Ahram* had regular correspondents reporting from many foreign capitals, including Addis Ababa; thus it was able to provide its readers with detailed information as the confrontation in East Africa unfolded. It the months prior to the outbreak of war, reports in *al-Ahram* stressed the sympathy of Egypt and Egyptians for the people of Ethiopia. It repeatedly emphasized the Ethiopian desire for peace and cautioned against a war that would bring the destruction of an independent Ethiopia and adversely affect Egyptian vital interests by producing an Italian takeover of part of the sources of the Nile.[28]

Once war had begun, *al-Ahram* denounced Italy as the aggressor and criticized the League of Nations for its impotence in preventing Italian aggression against a member state.[29] Again warning that Fascist Italy, once victorious in Ethiopia, could use its territories in East Africa as a springboard for further expansion in the direction of the Nile Valley, the newspaper called on all national groups within Egypt to mobilize to defend "the national interest" against any Italian threat.[30] Yet, if war in East Africa posed danger, it also presented opportunity; *al-Ahram* argued that Egypt should attempt to take advantage of the tense international situation to persuade Great Britain to conclude a treaty of alliance with an independent Egypt, thereby establishing an effective defensive front against possible fascist aggression.[31]

Al-Ahram was particularly disturbed by the nature of the war Italy was waging in Ethiopia. The newspaper repeatedly condemned Italian brutality in bombing civilian centers, thereby destroying churches, hospitals, and other civilian facilities, and for the immeasurable human suffering that Italian military operations were callously inflicting on the civilian population of Ethiopia.[32] At one point terming the Italian campaign in Ethiopia a war aimed at "enslaving the people" of Ethiopia,[33] *al-Ahram* maintained that Italy's violation of the rules of war deserved condemnation by the world community. Italy's disregard of international compacts and its unrestrained and barbarous military operations made the conflict in East Africa an international problem. *Al-Ahram* called on the civilized world to join together to oppose Fascist imperialism. If Fascist aggression was not deterred, it would be "small nations" that paid the greatest price.[34]

Once the Italian conquest of Ethiopia was complete, *al-Ahram* termed the destruction of the Ethiopian state, "a vast empire" with an ancient and glorious historical tradition, as a "disaster [*nakba*]."[35] While its greatest condemnation of this result was naturally directed at Italy, the newspaper also criticized the hesitancy and impotence of the international community, headed by Great Britain and France, for their abandonment of Ethiopia. The lamentable outcome of the Ethiopian crisis was proof that in international relations might makes right. The international system established after the Great War had effectively come to an end; the League of Nations no longer had any meaning. The tragic outcome of the Ethiopian war was a lesson for small nations—that they could no longer place their faith in the League of Nations and its ability to maintain international order.[36]

The Ethiopian crisis over, *al-Ahram* continued to pay close attention to Italy and its presumptive international ambitions. Commentaries
and editorials through later 1936 and most of 1937 expressed ambivalent
views regarding Italy and its relationship with Egypt. The signing of the
Anglo-Egyptian Treaty of Alliance in August 1936, with its provisions for
mutual defense arrangements, seems to have reduced Egyptian fears of
Italian intentions. In the new "age of independence" *al-Ahram* played
down sympathy for occupied Ethiopia and sought ways to improve
Egyptian-Italian relations. Articles in the newspaper now expressed the
need for Egypt to come to terms with new facts in the Horn of Africa, to
accept de facto the annexation of Ethiopia to Italy, and to reopen diplomatic and cultural channels between Egypt and Italy.[37] The "gentleman's
agreement" of early 1937 between Great Britain and Italy, as well as the
somewhat calmer international situation in 1937, reinforced this position.[38] At the same time, commentaries on the international situation in
late 1936 and through 1937 gave continued expression to the fear that
Fascist Italy had imperialist designs for expansion into the Mediterranean and Middle East.[39] As one commentary put it, Mussolini's aspiration was to make the Mediterranean "an Italian sea like the Roman sea."[40]
Fascist Italy would continue to undermine world order in the pursuit of
imperial grandeur. Italy's involvement in the Spanish Civil War in support of the Nationalists proved its real intentions; Fascist Italy was preparing for war, not for peace.[41]

An editorial of April 1937, entitled "Italy and the Arabs: A New Orientation in Fascist Policy," typifies *al-Ahram*'s apprehensions regarding
Italy by 1937. The editorial examined recent Fascist propaganda efforts to
depict Mussolini and Italy as "friends of the Arabs and the Muslims." Its
view was that readers should not be misled by such mendacious propaganda. Mussolini's rhetoric was replete with hypocrisy. Italy's behavior
under the Fascist regime had not shown good will toward Arabs and Muslims, neither in its imperialist behavior in Libya nor in its declared imperialist intentions regarding the Mediterranean and Middle East. Nonetheless, *al-Ahram* held out to the possibility of a change in attitude toward
Italy. Mussolini bore the burden of proof. Everything depended on him.
If Italy proved that its actions matched its propaganda asserting "friendship for the Arabs," then the Arabs, including Egypt, would gladly agree
to rapprochement and cooperation with Fascist Italy.[42]

Whereas Italy's international intentions and actions became major subjects of concern in Egypt's premier newspapers in the mid-1930s, those of Nazi Germany—more remote from the Mediterranean world and as yet less overtly aggressive—received less attention and commentary. For its part, *al-Muqattam* did publish a number of editorials and commentaries critical of Germany's drive for military rearmament occurring under the Nazi regime, of the periodic warmongering found in Hitler's speeches and declarations, and of the danger of future expansionism under the Nazis.[43] The apprehensive tone of a May 1935 editorial summarizing German foreign policy is typical: "the German state is conducting vast military preparations in an effort to achieve, by means of force, its aspirations in Europe and to regain all that it lost as a result of the last war. . . . This is why German policy today greatly concerns the entire world."[44]

But *al-Muqattam's* warnings about the course of German militarism and foreign policy under the Nazis in the mid-1930s were paralleled by more positive reports on the perceived social and economic reforms that the Nazi regime was implementing and that were leading to a process of German national regeneration.[45] The Nazi concentration on transforming German society internally was sometimes presented as evidence that proved that Hitler was focused on domestic affairs and thus that Nazi Germany posed no threat to Germany's neighbors or world stability.[46] An enthusiastic series of articles on "Germany Today," written by Thabit Thabit after visiting Germany in 1936, exemplified this sympathetic perspective. The series presented a positive image of the Nazi regime and its leader, showing its achievements in the areas of economic revival, social reform, and cultural regeneration. The series maintained that Hitler and his policies had gained the support of the population of Germany.[47] According to Thabit, the success of the 1936 Olympic Games in Berlin were proof that Hitler and Nazism had brought a new spirit of confidence and pride to the people of Germany.[48]

The one area where *al-Muqattam* was utterly condemnatory of Nazi policy was in regard to the racism and anti-Semitism manifested by the new German regime. For *al-Muqattam*, Nazi theories about race and the effort to apply them in practice constituted a basic flaw in the Nazi project and placed an ugly stain upon Nazi Germany. As early as 1934–35, *al-Muqattam* was criticizing the new Nazi regime for its policies toward religious communities that legitimized the marginalization and persecution of Jews, stating that the Nazi premise that the inferior Jewish race was corrupting the

superior German race was both intellectually baseless and politically intolerable since it was directed against law-abiding citizens of Germany.[49] Contrary to Nazi doctrine, the newspaper maintained that German Jews had
made enormous contributions both to German culture and human civilization, in the process enhancing the name of Germany in the world. Hence it
was vital to oppose the racist ideology and anti-Semitic policies of the Nazi
regime.[50] *Al-Muqattam*'s criticism of Nazi racism in typified by an August
1937 article entitled "Germany Is Ousting Those with Hooked Noses." In
Nazi Germany, "the possessors of hooked noses [*ashab al-unuf al-maʿkufa*]"
were automatically suspected of being Jewish and thereby dismissed from
their occupations and expelled from the national community. A racist policy like that of the Nazis, that regarded physiognomy as the criterion of pure
Germanness, was irrational and uncivilized.[51]

Reported racist Nazi laws relating to the prohibition of Aryan-Semitic
intermarriage were a particular target of *al-Muqattam*'s wrath. Even prior
to its adoption, the newspaper denounced the proposed "new law for the
defense of German blood and honor," officially adopted by the Nazi Party
at its Nuremberg Conference in September 1935, that aimed at purifying
the German race by prohibiting marriage and extramarital relations between Germans and Jews.[52] Particularly offensive in the newspaper's eyes
was a reported Nazi regulation of 1936 prohibiting marriage between Germans and people of Middle Eastern origin, a provision that *al-Muqattam*
saw as an attempt to "remove all Semitic peoples [from Germany] and to
cut all ties and bonds between them and the German people."[53] A denial
of the reported ban on Aryan-Semitic intermarriage by the German Legation in Cairo notwithstanding,[54] the paper continued to protest any decision to the effect that, "because Egyptians, Iranians, and Iraqis are not
Aryan, marriage between Egyptians and Germans will not be recognized." It went on to deny the Nazi premise of inherent Semitic inferiority
to Aryans as unscientific, and turned the tables by proudly asserting Semitic precedence in the development of human civilization:

Who are these Aryans who boast of Aryan origin? After all, the Arab and Persian
peoples—Egyptians, Iraqis, Syrians, Palestinians, Iranians—who are assumed not
be Aryan are the ones who brought civilization as we know it to the world. These
peoples lighted the human path to life, and from them the three monotheistic religions emerged, religions that the so-called Aryans accept and believe. So what is the
advantage of these Aryan nations over them?[55]

Al-Ahram's reporting on German internal developments under the Nazis in the mid-1930s resembled that found in *al-Muqattam*. It too occasionally presented a positive picture of the processes of national change, reform, and rehabilitation being carried out by the Nazi regime, presenting Nazism as an authentic German movement oriented to achieving the national aspirations of the German people. The domestic measures of social welfare and economic relief introduced under the Nazis in the mid-1930s were sometimes portrayed as welcome developments that were improving the lives of the German population.[56] As was the case with *al-Muqattam*, the 1936 Olympic Games evoked admiration for the competence and achievements of the "new Germany."[57]

Yet the dominant concern of *al-Ahram* in relation to Nazi Germany was the country's foreign policy. In this area, coverage was more negative. The dominant trend of commentary on Germany's international ambitions and behavior was the depiction of Hitler and Nazism as a force challenging and undermining world stability and thus threatening world peace. Nazi Germany's withdrawal from the League of Nations, its remilitarization of the Rhineland, and its support for Franco and the Nationalists in Spain all demonstrated nothing but contempt for the international system; its rush simultaneously to rearm and to expand its military forces was seen as indicating that Nazi Germany was a militarist state preparing for military conflict in order to reverse its defeat in the Great War.[58] Its aggressive intentions were underscored by its claims for the return of German colonies in Africa and Asia, as well as by its assertion of the right to unify all Germans in a greater Germany.[59] The newspaper was a consistent supporter of the liberal democratic camp, expressing resolute support of the world order established after the Great War. The daily repeatedly took exception to the external strategy of the Nazi dictatorship, which in its eyes was intent upon territorial expansion, the conquest of German living space in Europe, and ultimately world hegemony.[60]

By August 1937, *al-Ahram* was presenting Germany's alignment with Fascist Italy and its support for the Nationalist forces in Spain as amounting to the formation of an antidemocratic alliance, a coalition of aggressive revisionist forces that constituted a direct threat to international stability and peace: "thus we see that the advocates of force [*ansar al-quwwa*] are striving to wage war in order to realize their goals and obsessions and in order to establish a new world order inspired by their principles and their leaders' teachings, while the supporters of peace [*ansar al-silm*] aspire to maintain justice and to strengthen the foundations of peace and harmony among humanity."[61] "Machiavellianism rules the world," Salah al-Din al-Sharif lamented in September 1937 in describing the manipulative and cynical international behavior of Nazi Germany. As Sharif surveyed the international scene in late 1937, he concluded that "Machiavellianism has succeeded in arousing extreme nationalism and stimulating the latent elements of reprehensible racial fanaticism [*al-taʿassub al-jinsi al-dhamim*]. It has transformed human culture into a chauvinist culture which knows no bounds except the nation and its borders." The greatest danger posed by the new Machiavellianism was not to the great powers, but to small and weak states. The militaristic and imperialistic rhetoric of Mussolini and Hitler was preparing the ground for an assault upon the "little peoples of the world."[62] Overall, *al-Ahram* presented Hitler's provocative foreign policy aimed at undermining the postwar international system as the most significant negative feature of the Nazi regime.

Al-Ahram initially took a more ambivalent position than *al-Muqattam* regarding the racism and anti-Semitism of the new Nazi regime. One report on the anti-Jewish Nuremberg Laws introduced in Germany in 1935 and on their attempt to exclude Jews from the German economy and German cultural life criticized the regime for its removal of Jewish professionals from public institutions such as the courts, universities, and medical facilities. Yet, while acknowledging that law-abiding Jewish citizens of Germany were being unjustly victimized by the "oppression, pressure, and injustice imposed on innocent people" by Nazi racial policies, the report nonetheless characterized such racist legislation as "a natural addition to the great Nazi revolution in Germany."[63] A later report on the Nuremberg Laws neutrally defined their purpose as the realization of one of the most important goals of the Nazi Party, namely, "the defense of the purity of the German race and German blood," and viewed them as providing a clear redefinition of the position of Jews within German society.[64] More offensive in the eyes of *al-Ahram* was the Nazi assertion of Aryan racial supremacy. Thus a 1937 commentary on Nazi relations with the Vatican rejected "the German ideology [*al-fikra al-jarmaniyya*]" being promoted by the Nazi regime, according to which Aryan racism and supremacy would in effect replace Christianity as the effective belief system of Germans. The effect of the Nazi assertion of Aryan supremacy was unquestionably negative, "brutally dividing human races by claiming that the German people are the only superior, chosen people."[65]

Whereas a firm picture of Fascist Italy and its international intentions took shape during 1935–36 as a result of the Ethiopian crisis and war, 1938–39 were the crucial years for the crystallization of Egyptian opinion regarding German Nazism. Three major events of 1938 initiated by the Nazi regime—externally, the German annexation of Austria in the spring and the summer's extended crisis over the fate of Czechoslovakia that resulted in the Munich Agreement; internally, Nazi persecution of Jews culminating in the barbarism of *Reichskristallnacht* in Germany in November—combined to produce an image of the Nazi regime as inherently brutal, relentlessly expansionist, and a manifest threat to world stability and peace. This image was progressively reinforced and strengthened in 1939 by further German expansion into Czechoslovakia and eventually by its instigation of a world war as a result of its territorial demands against Poland.

Al-Ahram's apprehension about the international intentions of the Nazi regime is apparent in the newspaper's reaction to the German incorporation of Austria into the Third Reich in March 1938. In February the newspaper carried several reports on Nazi agitation regarding Austria and Germany's growing influence on its neighbor through pro-Nazi forces.[66] The German takeover of Austria and Hitler's entry and triumphant progress through the country in mid-March were front-page news.[67] *Al-Ahram*'s editorial analysis of the Anschluss situated the Austrian annexation in relation to Germany's historical aspirations in Europe. Hitler's Germany had now adopted "a policy of strength" to revive the German nation and to rescue it from the humiliation it had suffered since its defeat in World War I. The newspaper summarized Hitler's master plan for Germany abroad as being "first, to rip up the Treaty of Versailles; second, to regain the Saar area; third, to annex Austria to Germany; fourth, to reclaim the German region of Czechoslovakia, which is nearly three million Germans; fifth, to regain the German colonies which the victors divided up after the war." The first two goals had already been realized; the third was in process; the newspaper speculated that, given the momentum of his past successes, the other goals were also within Hitler's reach. *Al-Ahram* now saw the international aggressiveness of the European dictatorships as a grave danger to world stability and peace, one that moreover directly affected Egypt. The Suez Canal was "Germany's road to some of its colonies, just as it is Italy's road to Ethiopia and Somalia." The looming crisis in European politics thus had definite implications for Egypt. Specifically, it required improved military arrangements for naval defense against possible aggression. More generally, national unity in the face of increased international tension was an imperative: "we must join forces and unify all components of national strength in the country in order to allow Egypt to demonstrate its international independence and determine its geographic position within defined borders."[68]

In the later 1930s, al-Ahram's commentator Muhammad Zaki 'Abd al-Qadir was a consistent voice warning of the global threat of fascism and calling for Egyptians to align themselves with the democratic camp. The impending crisis over Austria led 'Abd al-Qadir to reflect on the differences between democracy and dictatorship. It was clear that the hesitancy and restraint of the Western democracies were playing into the hands of "the dictator" Hitler, increasing his appetite for further expansion. This current weakness of democracy vis-à-vis dictatorship was presented as derivative of its openness and pluralism, its tolerance of interparty factionalism, the clash of personal and partisan interests, and its tendency to lapse into "sterile speeches and chatter." In contrast, "the advantage of dictatorship is that, like an arrow, it flies to its goal," with the target determined and the arrow controlled by the dictator. Should dictatorship triumph over democracy, 'Abd al-Qadir foresaw "tragedy for the entire world." If the democracies could not find a way to stop the rise of the dictators, power, violence, and intimidation would prevail in international affairs: "if the world comes under the influence of Hitler, Mussolini, Franco, and their ilk, it will suffer a ghastly regression into the Dark Ages when the military knighthood was the law and war was the symbol of glory." In the face of this threat, the democracies needed to find new ways to resist Hitler and to stop his march of conquest. 'Abd al-Qadir called on the democratic camp, Egypt included, to demonstrate its faith, courage, and determination in the defense of democratic values "in order to save our great cultural inheritance bequeathed to us by previous generations."[69]

By mid-1938, al-Misri had no illusions about Nazi Germany's domestic tyranny and its expansionist intentions abroad. Essays in the Wafd's main organ were critical both of Nazi domestic and international policies. A June review of contemporary European history "from Sarajevo

1914 to Vienna 1938" emphasized the role of pro-Nazi elements within Austria itself in facilitating "Germany's conquest and annexation of Austria to the greater Reich."[70] A July article sketching "How Hitler Proceeded Step by Step" credited Heinrich Himmler with a central role in advancing Hitler's career in the 1920s and in the violent consolidation of Nazi authority within Germany. The paper detailed the Nazi reliance on intimidation, violence, and bloodshed that had paved the way to Hitler becoming the all-powerful Führer of the Third Reich.[71] Another report expounded on the Nazi "dream of a greater Germany in Central Europe" that envisaged the incorporation of all German-speaking regions. According to the Nazi expansionist vision, the German-speaking populations of central Europe were part of the German race whose historical destiny was to be incorporated into "one greater German state." *Al-Misri* went on to report the view of experts who foresaw that "German cravings" would not be satisfied with Central European expansion, but extended to the Balkans and from there to "the spread of Germany's cultural and economic influence in the Middle East." Nazism was potentially a long-term threat to the independence of Arab states, Egypt included.[72]

Nazi racial policies were viewed by *al-Misri* as another negative and ominous feature of the dictatorial regime currently in power in Germany. During the summer of 1938, the deteriorating condition of Jews in Germany drew repeated coverage. The paper reported on the accelerating persecution of Germany's Jews, emphasizing the plight of Germany's highly educated and professional Jewish middle class who had lost occupations and property: "for all of these, it has become impossible to live and work in Nazi Germany."[73] In commenting on the Evian Conference of July 1938 that sought and failed to find a solution for the growing problem of Jewish refugees, the article sympathized with the fate of "the hundreds of thousands of European Jews" who had become a major international problem.[74]

The counterpoint to *al-Misri*'s criticism of the dictatorial Nazi regime in Europe was its parallel defense of democracy in Egypt. As a Wafdist organ, the newspaper was a staunch defender of parliamentary ascendancy at home. Throughout 1938 and 1939, numerous articles attacked the legitimacy of the incumbent coalition ministries of Liberals and Sa'dists headed by Muhammad Mahmud that had governed Egypt since the ouster of the Wafd at the end of 1937, and presented the Wafd as the guardian of democracy in Egypt. It accused both the Palace and the

present government, ruling with the support of the Palace, of undermining democracy in Egypt through its manipulative use of the King's constitutional prerogatives, in combination with electoral fraud and parliamentary maneuvering by the non-Wafdist parties, to subvert democracy by
marginalizing the Wafd, the one party that was the true representative of
the popular will in Egypt. In *al-Misri*'s opinion the Muhammad Mahmud
government, based as it was on a fabricated parliamentary majority, did
not represent the Egyptian people; "only the Wafd represents the Egyptian people." A slogan attributed to Sa'd Zaghlul, "right over power, and
the nation over the government [*al-haqq fawqa al-quwwa, wa al-umma
fawqa al-hukuma*]," was the iconic slogan employed by the newspaper in
its defense of democracy at home.[75] For *al-Misri*, the defense of democracy in Egypt was an indivisible part of the struggle to defend democracy
across the world.

Germany's second major international initiative of 1938, its aggressive and ultimately successful campaign for the incorporation of the
German-speaking regions of Czechoslovakia into the Third Reich, dominated international coverage in the Egyptian daily press in the summer
and fall of 1938. For its part, *al-Misri* was solidly hostile to Germany's territorial ambitions and demands concerning Czech territory. As early as
the spring of 1938, *al-Misri* commented sympathetically on Czech complaints of German aggression and the threat to Czech sovereignty found
in Nazi agitation over the Sudetenland.[76] It expressed support for the Prague
government, taking the view that Czech acquiescence to German demands
would lead to further German initiatives in regard to German minorities
elsewhere in Eastern Europe that would undermine the post–World War I
territorial settlement.[77] It similarly reported German acts of subversion
aimed at "undermining the democratic republic of Czechoslovakia," and
held that German claims of Czech mistreatment of its German-speaking
citizens were unjustified.[78]

While supporting Czech resistance to German demands, *al-Misri*
was ambivalent concerning the support the Czechs were receiving from
the Western democracies. In June the newspaper praised British Prime
Minister Neville Chamberlain's policy of negotiation as "realistic" and "positive" in view of the effective collapse of the multilateral security arrangements based on the now-discredited League of Nations. While the paper
viewed Chamberlain's policy in a generally favorable light, it also hoped
that Great Britain understood the potential military challenge that Hitler

was placing before it and the democratic world.[79] A month later, however, the paper took the view that Chamberlain's policy of negotiation had begun to exhaust itself and was becoming counterproductive. The paper's nationalist solidarity with the Czechs, "a stubborn and proud nation whose independence is engraved in their souls," now led it to express concern that, unless Great Britain took a firm stand against Germany, Czechoslovakia might be compelled to surrender to German demands and thus to lose its independence. Quoting British government opposition members, *al-Misri* now declared that the policy of peace at all costs was "an incorrect policy" that demanded fundamental revision if the fate of Czechoslovakia was not to be that of Austria, now "just an historical name."[80]

In August and September 1938, the Czech crisis was front-page news for *al-Jihad*. "The Czechoslovakian crisis is a danger to European peace," proclaimed one headline.[81] At the end of August, *al-Jihad* evaluated the Sudetenland issue as only one component of Hitler's expansionist designs in Europe. In the paper's opinion, Hitler and the Nazi regime in Germany may indeed have wanted war in late 1938. For its part, Germany's large and well-armed military was looking for battlefields on which to demonstrate its capability and might. Hitler "needs new military victories" to placate his generals and to impress the German nation with his leadership. "There is no doubt that the conquest of Czechoslovakia, if carried out quickly, will grant legitimization to the new German army which in large part is Hitler's intent. In addition, the Nazis are convinced that a military victory in the heart of Europe will arouse patriotic fervor at home and present Germany as a power than cannot be reckoned with or fought." *Al-Jihad* thus saw the issue of the Sudetenland as only a "pretext" for Hitler, one stage in the execution of his ambitious plan for European conquest.[82] The newspaper criticized the seemingly endless demands Hitler and Germany were making on Czechoslovakia and supported the desperate efforts of Czech President Edvard Beneš to satisfy the demands of the Sudeten Germans in order to preserve Czechoslovakia's territorial integrity.[83]

Commentary in *al-Ahram* at the time of the Czech crisis expressed a clear preference for the democratic as opposed to the dictatorial camp. An editorial of early September, on "The Crisis of Democracy and Our Duty in Preventing Its Perils," offered a vigorous defense of parliamentary government in the face of the autocratic challenge and a summons for the strengthening of bonds among the supporters of parliamentary government throughout the world.[84] In his reflections on the tension between Germany and Czechoslovakia over the Sudetenland, Muhammad Zaki ʿAbd al-Qadir perceived the root of the problem lying in the exclusivist, racially based nationalism now so prevalent in the world. In the crisis at hand, Hitler was demanding the inclusion of the Sudeten Germans in their "greater homeland" while the Czech leadership resisted "in the name of the nationalism which links them [the Sudeten Germans] to one land and which attaches them to one mother." More generally, ʿAbd al-Qadir lamented that "today nationalism is on every tongue." In particular, ʿAbd al-Qadir saw the pernicious doctrine of race as bringing the world to the verge of war. "Hitler makes race the basis of unity. For him, the nation can be composed of only one race." Hence he was expelling the Jews from Germany while simultaneously insisting on the gathering of Germans "from every place and every region" into Germany. ʿAbd al-Qadir disputed the link between race and nation, pointing the existence of multi-ethnic countries such as Belgium, Switzerland, and particularly the United States as disproving any necessary linkage between race and nationhood. Given the complex worldwide distribution of races, an insistence on the racial basis of the nation was bound to lead to international conflict. Racial nationalism was an anachronism in the modern age, when the world was one economic unit and nations needed to look beyond their boundaries and the narrow horizons imposed by race.[85]

In the wake of the Munich Agreement, *al-Ahram* found a number of lessons to be drawn from the recent crisis over the Sudetenland. Most related to the obvious collapse of the post–World War I settlement reached at Versailles and other postwar treaties and the inadequacy of current diplomatic procedures and mechanisms, such as the League of Nations, for resolving major international disputes. Institutionally, what was needed was a new international order, including an international court capable of resolving disputes peacefully. More profound and essential was a new international spirit of approaching international disputes, one that would eschew the "Machiavellian politics" that had prevailed at Munich.[86]

ʿAbdalla Husayn's reflections on the Munich crisis focused on what lessons the crisis held for small states such as Egypt. Husayn placed much of the blame for the lamentable results achieved at Munich on the Western democracies of France, Great Britain, and on their Soviet ally for their internationalizing of what in reality was an issue between

"Czechoslovakia and some of its citizens." Internationalization had been an error, legitimizing German involvement and resulting in Czechoslovakia alone paying the price for the preservation of world peace. For Husayn, one lesson of the Munich crisis was that a small state like Egypt could not place its faith in the great powers because "the great powers attend to their interests only by sacrificing the interests of small states." More generally, Husayn concluded that Egypt should rigorously avoid involvement in any conflict where its own interests were not directly at stake and where it did not know the ultimate price it might have to pay.[87]

An *al-Ahram* editorial of early November again reflected on the causes and results of the international crisis over the Sudetenland that had been resolved at Munich. The Munich Conference had created "a new world" in which "the autocratic, dictatorial powers" Germany and Italy, joined in a unified bloc, had emerged triumphant over their democratic rivals. The editorial had strong criticism of the behavior of the French and British governments at Munich. France had failed to grasp that the matter at hand was not merely the fate of the Sudetenland, but rather the question of "the integrity and security of the French homeland." For its part, England was simply not prepared, militarily or mentally, for war. While the editorial was sympathetic to Chamberlain's commitment to the maintenance of peace, nonetheless the position taken by Great Britain at Munich was described as "appeasement, retreat, and surrender" to Hitler. The policy of appeasement followed by the Western democracies at Munich, and their sacrifice of the territorial integrity of Czechoslovakia "on the altar of peace," was viewed by *al-Ahram* as a mistake that legitimized a dangerous trend in international politics in which political success was determined by intimidation of the weak by the strong. The editorial expressed doubt that the Munich Agreement was "a victory for those who support peace," as Chamberlain had presented it to the world. The victor at Munich was "the Nazi autocracy"; the democracies, on the other hand, had "suffered defeat."[88]

The editorial went on to relate the Munich crisis to Egypt and the Middle East. The clash over Czechoslovakia was part of a long-term struggle between autocracy and democracy. It predicted that, when France and Great Britain finally realized the severity of the Nazi threat to world order, they would not hesitate to go to war. In the looming confrontation between dictatorship and democracy, it was incumbent on Egypt and the

Arab world to support the Western democracies to which they were now linked by treaty: "the Arab peoples must know that the strength of their allies is preferable to the power of the autocratic camp [*al-fariq al-autuqrati*]." Yet, while *al-Ahram* clearly favored the democracies over the dictatorships, that support was not unconditional. In the post-Munich world, "in which the dictatorial countries are destroying the old world and creating a new one," the Arab Middle East could become a front should war erupt. It was necessary for the democratic powers to strengthen their relations with the Arabs. This meant granting them "true freedom and true independence" in order to gain their wholehearted support in the struggle of the democracies against totalitarianism.[89]

By late 1938, *al-Ahram* was decidedly pessimistic about the course of international affairs. The recent solidification of relations among Germany, Italy, and Japan in an Axis bloc, all of whose members relied upon "a policy of strength and violence in the world," was evaluated as threatening "the fate of humanity." While Nazi Germany's territorial ambitions threatened the peace of Europe "in the north," Fascist Italy was seen as a regime that had not yet satisfied its territorial aims "in the south" (i.e., the Mediterranean). In this struggle between the dictatorships and the democracies, the newspaper stood firmly with the latter. Reviewing the major developments of the past few years—Italy's invasion and occupation of Ethiopia; Japan's invasion and occupation of much of China; Germany's incorporation of Austria and the Sudetenland—*al-Ahram*'s position was that "the dictatorial countries have spread their rule over three continents, and the democratic countries have no choice but to use force to stop this domination."[90]

Recent developments in Germany itself only reinforced *al-Ahram*'s pessimism. The paper reported critically on the anti-Jewish brutality of *Reichskristallnacht*, seeing it as a new low point in Germany's persecution of "innocent Jewish German citizens" and sympathizing with "the awful tragedy" that had befallen German Jews. *Al-Ahram* feared that "expelling the Jews from Germany" had now become an official and systematic policy of the Nazi regime. The editorial went on to reiterate the newspaper's view that the new German-Italian Axis was an ominous event for Egypt. Both regimes were seen as almost identical in being domestic dictatorships with inherently aggressive foreign policies; the blend of dictatorship at home and a desire for expansion abroad made the two Axis powers a threatening combination.[91]

Muhammad Zaki 'Abd al-Qadir's assessment of Nazi Germany and its leader in the wake of the Anschluss, Munich, and *Reichskristallnacht* characterized the Führer as a dictator who was on the one hand obsessed with the extermination of Jewish presence not only in Germany but throughout Europe, and on the other ravenous to expand Germany's territorial sway first within Europe and ultimately in Africa and Asia. "The dictator's appetite knows no bounds," 'Abd al-Qadir wrote of Hitler. He went on to present Mussolini as "a dictator of the same sort" who, like Hitler, relied on "the rule of power and the use of arms" to attain his goals. Both dictators were a threat to world peace.[92]

Reviewing the events of the previous year at the start of 1939, *al-Ahram* evaluated the Munich Agreement as "the introduction of a dangerous feature" that had set new and ominous rules for the future conduct of international relations. Munich's precedents of "surrender to force as the way of avoiding war and evading commitments established through agreements and contracts between nations" were "the worst principles, worthy of the greatest denunciation." That "everything is allowed and everything is legal" in international relations were the conclusions that Fascist Italy and Nazi Germany were correctly drawing from what had transpired at Munich. Great Britain and France needed to replace the position of appeasement pursued at Munich with a stance of firmness against the Fascist and Nazi danger. Britain's and France's policy of appeasement placed its allies in peril as well. As long as the democratic camp continued to retreat and to "act according to the wishes of its enemies," then "it can expect to enter a dangerous and weak phase in which the freedoms of the countries allied to it will also die." The Munich Agreement had not insured peace; rather, "the ghost of Munich [*shabah munikh*]" was "the ghost of war [*shabah al-harb*]" knocking on the world's door.[93]

Apprehension about the international scene and the prospect of a military clash between the European democracies and dictatorships intensified in 1939. Two international developments of early 1939—the Nationalist victory over the Republicans in Spain that became obvious with the former's conquest of Barcelona in January, and Germany's unilateral incorporation of what remained of Czechoslovakia in March—reinforced *al-Ahram*'s and *al-Misri*'s warnings concerning the fascist threat to liberal democracy and world stability. For its part, *al-Misri* warned that the triumph of Franco and the Spanish Nationalists, by early 1939 emerging victorious in

Spain, was a defeat for democracy. "The other dictators," first among them Hitler and Mussolini, had through their aid contributed to Franco's assault on democracy in Spain. The paper criticized "the indifference of the democracies" over the Spanish Civil War, and noted that Nationalist victory was being perceived as proof that the authoritarian camp was "going from success to success" while "the Western democracies, particularly England and France, are mired in the mud." On the conceptual level, the Nationalist triumph in Spain was "another victory for fascist ideology . . . and therefore has great meaning from the psychological and propagandistic standpoint," one with negative implications for Egypt, the other Arab countries, and "other middle and small countries" who also faced the menace of fascist aggression and expansionism.[94]

Germany's next act of aggressive expansionism, when it absorbed the rump of Czechoslovakia in March 1939, was not a surprise to *al-Ahram*. Sensitivity to the danger a greater Germany posed for the world informed the paper's commentary on the event: As a result of the incorporation of Czechoslovakia, a greater Germany was now emerging "before our eyes." With ninety-five million people, Germany was now the largest power in Europe. "Germany is increasing its population and by doing so it is increasing its power, strengthening its influence, and widening the horizons of its ambitions." Given its augmented power, it would certainly put forward demands for colonies outside Europe as well. Within the continent, *al-Ahram* had no doubt that Germany's neighbors, specifically Belgium and Holland to the northwest and Hungary and Romania to the southeast, had cause for alarm for the integrity of their borders. The Nazi regime would not be satisfied until it brought them within the scope of Greater Germany as well.[95]

Beyond condemning the German incorporation of the remainder of Czechoslovakia as proof that "Hitler's appetite knows no bounds," *al-Misri's* commentary on the international situation by April 1939 went on to present what it believed to be the antidote to the current Nazi challenge to the international order. "The real, effective, response" that the democracies needed to pursue was military preparedness and rearmament. Endorsing the statement of a British leader that "it is essential that Britain be strong enough to prevent war and defeat aggression," *al-Misri* opined that the expansion of the British armed forces was the essential step necessary to forge "a powerful front against domination by force."[96] The paper had closely monitored the military buildup that was under way in both the democracies and the dictatorships in 1939, and had repeatedly argued that greater military preparedness by the former was the surest way to deter further aggression and to prevent war. Simultaneously, it accompanied its advocacy of military preparedness on the part of the democracies with repeated demands that Great Britain accelerate the strengthening of the Egyptian military by providing it with more up-to-date weaponry so that Egypt could stand as an ally of the democratic camp in their resistance to fascist expansionism.[97]

As had been the case in 1938, *al-Misri* continued to parallel its support of democracy abroad with demands for restoration of a properly functioning democratic government in Egypt. It continued to present Prime Minister Muhammad Mahmud as a dictator who was subverting Egyptian democracy in order to maintain a government that was unrepresentative of the will of the people in power. In contrast to Mahmud, Mustafa al-Nahhas of the Wafd was put forth as a guardian of democracy, a leader who had respected the Constitution and who now was the central oppositional figure to "the dictator Mahmud," whose mode of operation it compared to Mussolini, Hitler, and Stalin. The Mahmud ministry's steps to "curtail freedom of speech and freedom of the press" were termed a "tragedy for journalism and freedom of expression" and as such a policy which threatened to destroy one of the foundations of the democracy in Egypt.[98]

In its editorial commentary on the Italian invasion of Albania in April 1939, *al-Ahram* found it "very hard to believe" the Italian claim to the effect that "Italian interests are in danger in Albania" provided sufficient justification for outright invasion and conquest of the country, and went on to interpret the real reason for the invasion as being that, after Hitler's latest advance into Czechoslovakia, "the Italian regime believed that it was necessary to attain a substantial success to fortify its international prestige in the eyes of the Italian people, who had come to believe that Germany alone was benefiting from the policy of the Axis." Whatever the motivation, *al-Ahram* saw the Italian initiative as yet another development that "endangers world peace."[99] Muhammad Zaki 'Abd al-Qadir's assessment of the invasion expounded further on its probable causation. In analyzing "the psyche of the dictator," 'Abd al-Qadir maintained that the motivation for the invasion was as much internal as external, a measure intended to strengthen Mussolini's position at home by reasserting "control over the moral spirit of his people." The invasion was meant to "preoccupy the [Italian] people with false glory and the be-loved illusion of empire." Mussolini was trapped in an unfavorable com-petition with his fellow-dictator Hitler. The contrast between "what Mus-solini has obtained and what Hitler has obtained" was not to Mussolini's advantage. Although he had come to power well before Hitler, in interna-tional triumphs he now lagged well behind. Hence he was determined to seize the initiative. Since he could not compete with Great Britain or France for hegemony in the Mediterranean or take control of the Suez Canal, and since "there is no escape from action, action anywhere," Mus-solini had chosen "the smallest and least powerful" country, Albania, to demonstrate Fascist military might. For 'Abd al-Qadir, this Italian lash-ing out at the weak was an object lesson for Egypt as well.[100]

In April 1939, Mussolini's Mediterranean ambitions were just as alarming to al-Ahram as those of Hitler in Central Europe. Hitler's part-ner in "the dictatorial Axis," a commentary on a recent speech of Musso-lini observed, "supports Hitler's policy of using force to achieve political goals and desires." Moreover, geographic propinquity made Fascist Italy's expansionist intentions a more direct threat to Egypt itself: "Italy's de-mands are centered in the Mediterranean basin, and Mussolini demands this space in its entirety for himself." The danger posed by Italian imperial-ism to Egypt and the other Arab nations of North Africa, in al-Ahram's estimation, was a real one. The paper singled out the Italian threat to the Suez Canal, a strategic locale for consolidating Italian control of the Medi-terranean, as particularly menacing to Egypt. In view of the danger of Italian expansionism being directed against Egypt, al-Ahram called for Egypt to "reinforce its defensive armament . . . so that the adventurous state [Italy] understands that it is facing a substantial power."[101]

Al-Ahram saw numerous reasons for pessimism about the interna-tional situation by the summer of 1939. It could not envisage a peaceful solution to the Japanese-Soviet dispute over Manchuria, the cause of which it viewed as Japan's deepening penetration into China and conse-quent Russian fears concerning Soviet strategic interests.[102] The situation in Franco's Spain was no better: in effect, Spain had become part of "the dictatorial Axis" and represented another setback for the cause of democ-racy in Europe.[103] The fitful negotiations between the Western democra-cies and the Soviet Union, aimed at creating an effective deterrent to Nazi expansionism in particular, were going nowhere and held little prospect of creating an effective deterrent to the challenge of Hitler.[104] Closer to home, what *al-Ahram* termed "the Italian desire for hegemony in the Mediterranean" was a menace to Egypt itself. Italy was attempting to capitalize on its central location in the Mediterranean basin to realize political and strategic domination of the Middle Sea. Its modern navy had been created and augmented to achieve physical control over the Mediterranean and the Middle East should war occur. "The situation in the Middle East is growing more acute by the day," the paper warned. It called on Great Britain and France to demonstrate their military presence and commitment in the Mediterranean, a vitally important region for the Western democracies, in order to forestall the threat of Italian ascendancy.[105]

It was particularly German demands upon Poland, specifically the request for the incorporation of Danzig into Germany, that came to preoccupy the Egyptian daily press as 1939 progressed.[106] By July, *al-Ahram* was predicting that "the Danzig problem [*mushkilat danzij*]" could be the spark for a broader war: Danzig was "the source of the danger that threatens Europe with a bloody war."[107] The paper's commentary on the German-Polish crisis was sympathetic to the Polish position as well as to British and French support of Poland, declaring that "the entire world knows that only Germany is interested in aggression" and emphasizing that "Poland has put its trust in the help it will be given by the Western democracies."[108] Reporting on the growth of German influence and agitation through the formation of a pro-Nazi paramilitary "bigger than the Austrian Nazi or Sudeten Nazi volunteer armies" drawn from the city's German-speaking population, the paper surmised that Germany's goal was to subvert Polish control of Danzig from within much as it had previously done in Austria and Czechoslovakia.[109] Although the paper hoped for a negotiated solution, it was skeptical about the prospects of a peaceful resolution to the Danzig problem. Despite the professed desire of the two main parties to negotiate a solution, "until now no action has been taken [regarding negotiations] because the basis for negotiation does not exist." Moreover, it suspected that Hitler was being deliberately obtuse regarding Danzig and that he in reality he had "hidden intentions" to solve the Danzig problem by force.[110]

"The Danzig problem" was also the central international concern of mid-1939 for *al-Misri*. The paper carried regular reports on the accelerating international war of nerves over the status of Danzig. From the spring of 1939 onward, the paper's contributors understood that Germany's demand for the incorporation of the city into the Third Reich, Polish insistence that Danzig was an integral part of Poland, and British and French support for Poland posed the prospect of a general European war. The paper reasoned that, after the dismemberment of Czechoslovakia by Germany and the recent Italian invasion and occupation of Albania, the Western democracies had to stand firm lest Poland and other countries of Central and Eastern Europe fall under Fascist or Nazi domination. *Al-Misri*'s view was that "Britain will not let Germany take control of other parts of Europe"; France too "will help Poland in a war situation."[111] "The fate of Poland will not be like that of Czechoslovakia," the paper predicted.[112] It forecast that, given German intransigence regarding the German character of Danzig and Poland's declared intentions to defend its possession of the city, "there is no avoiding war."[113] While the paper's reporting of developments in the unfolding confrontation over Danzig was largely factual, editorial commentary expressed sympathy with "the courage and patience of Poland in the crisis"[114] and voiced Egyptian solidarity with Poland as a "small nation" being pressured by Germany, "which is much stronger than it militarily."[115] The paper was skeptical of regarding Hitler's claim that "he wants Danzig, but he doesn't want war,"[116] and reasoned that, while a peaceful resolution of the issue would require Hitler to abandon his claim to Danzig, this would be extremely difficult for the leader of "a dictatorial regime" like Nazi Germany.[117]

Al-Misri accompanied its reporting on the prospect of war resulting from the confrontation over Danzig with a call for the intensification of rearmament on the part of the Western democracies. As a headline of June asserted, Great Britain "must rearm in order to compel the rest of the world to respect it."[118] This was an imperative in view of the intensive military preparations that were under way in both Nazi Germany and Fascist Italy, the solidification of the military alliance that now linked to two dictatorships, and "the militaristic spirit" that permeated German behavior.[119]

By August 1939, both *al-Ahram* and *al-Misri* were convinced that war was inevitable. As an *al-Ahram* editorial titled "August 1914 and August 1939" put it, "the phantoms of war are frightening everyone." A general war would bring immeasurable destruction and tragedy to the world; it was necessary to take every possible step to prevent it. Voicing little confidence in the ability of the worlds' leaders to stop the speeding train of war, the editorial appealed to the consciousness of enlightened people everywhere to rally world public opinion against war, holding out the hope that mobilization from below could somehow avert the train wreck against which world leaders seemed helpless.[120] Nonetheless, with "twelve million armed soldiers alert and ready for war," a subsequent editorial expressed the view that the hope of maintaining peace was remote.[121] *Al-Ahram* held Hitler and the Nazi activists in Danzig responsible for the deteriorating situation. Few avenues for maintaining the peace were left: British-French-Russian negotiations for an anti-Nazi front were not advancing, and American efforts to call for a resolution in the form of sending letters to various European leaders had had no effect upon the tense situation.[122]

Al-Misri took a similar view of the deteriorating international situation by August 1939. The paper repeatedly lamented that, in view of unshakable German intransigence over Danzig and German-directed agitation against the Polish government within the city, the various international efforts to broker a peaceful resolution to the crisis had been futile.[123] One editorial attempted to turn Hitler's rationale concerning the German claim to Danzig against him. As it had done earlier with the Czech Sudetenland, the German government was attempting to justify its claim to Danzig on the grounds that the city was part of Germany's living space. *Al-Misri* now argued that the same logic "naturally must apply to Poland as well; that is, the present [Polish] government's insistence on Danzig [remaining Polish] is justified and warranted according to the principle of Polish living space." The paper speculated that the real issue in question was not Danzig but "the integrity of Poland" as established by international agreement after World War I. As had been the case with Czechoslovakia, in order for Germany to realize its *lebensraum*, "Poland needs to disappear from the world." This was Hitler's real aim. The editorial's conclusion was gloomy; war appeared to be the only way that the issue could be resolved.[124] If war did come, as the paper now assumed it would, *al-Misri* emphasized that it would involve more than just Germany and Poland; German use of military force against Poland would lead the Western democracies to intervene on the side of Poland, leading to a general European conflagration.[125]

The surprise announcement of the conclusion of a nonaggression pact between Nazi Germany and the Soviet Union in late August came as a bombshell to Egyptians; "the strangest and most startling event that has occurred in this era," as *al-Ahram* put it. The implications of the deal were deadly for Poland and for the cause of peace: while Great Britain and

France were geographically too remote to effectively assist Poland in case of German attack, Hitler had with one stroke succeeded in neutralizing Russia and its large army. The pact paved the road for a German assault upon Poland.[126] *Al-Misri* also saw the conclusion of a nonaggression pact between Germany and the Soviet Union as a "surprising and astonishing event," but predicted that "the agreement will not change the assistance that England and France give to Poland."[127] Only a few days before the German invasion of Poland began, *al-Ahram* concluded that Hitler's strong nerves had won the war of political maneuver against his more weak-willed democratic adversaries: it was "a new kind of war that Hitler had devised, just as he invented the Nazi regime."[128]

By the eve of World War II, both the independent *al-Ahram* and the Wafdist *al-Misri* had come to firm conclusions regarding the nature of the contemporary European Fascist and Nazi regimes. For its part, *al-Ahram* stressed three main contrasts between the two rival systems of political organization. The first contrast—the most important one for observers in a newly independent and fiercely nationalist country like Egypt—was the external aggressiveness and desire for expansion being manifested by Fascist Italy and Nazi Germany, and more proximately the possibility of fascist imperialism menacing Egypt. The second was the internal totalitarianism of the two fascist regimes, their violation of liberal and humane values by domestic suppression of freedom of speech, political pluralism, and legitimate dissent. The third—centered on Nazism in particular—was the nationalist chauvinism and racism that underlay both barbarism at home and disregard for the rights of others abroad.

An *al-Ahram* editorial of May 1939 expounded on the three basic characteristics of the leading contemporary European fascist movements. The first was imperialism, an imperialism that was more avaricious and dangerous than the imperialism of the sated imperial powers Great Britain and France. The editorial compared what it termed the "dictatorial nationalism" of contemporary Germany and Italy with the "democratic nationalism" of the Western democracies of Great Britain and France. Democratic nationalism was defined as moderate, open, and humane. It was a nationalism grounded in the universal values of freedom, equality, and tolerance that saw itself as part of a pluralistic international order of a family of equal nations in which no component was inherently superior to another. Quite different were those nationalisms that had emerged out of an "inferiority complex [*'uqdat al-naqs*]." This form of nationalism was prominent in newer nation-states that had been formed at the end of the nineteenth century and that suffered from feelings of inferiority as a consequence not having acquired colonial possessions. Italy and Germany were the archetype of such "dictatorial nationalisms." In contrast to Great Britain's and France's nationalisms that satisfied their imperial ambitions by acquiring large colonial empires and therefore could afford to be passive and moderate in their international behavior, Germany's and Italy's aspirations to revive the German and Italian empires were suffused with a feeling of national inferiority. Germany's defeat in World War I and the deep crisis into which Italy had fallen after the war had only intensified feelings of inferiority, producing in both a wounded national self-image of a victim who must revenge himself by any means possible. These feelings were the root of the powerful psychological need that drove both Hitler and Mussolini to relentless expansionism, to "conquer living spaces" and thereby expand the territorial boundaries of Germany and Italy. It also explained the extreme character of German and Italian nationalism, the insatiable hunger of each for material fulfillment through expansion. By their very nature, the contemporary dictatorial nationalisms were imperialist to the core, movements motivated by an obsession with "imperialist expansion [*al-tawassu' al-isti'mari*]." Such imperialist nationalism "does not believe in the rights of others," instead practicing a "policy of intimidation" of weaker nations in order to satisfy the urge for expansion.[129]

The second main characteristic of "dictatorial nationalisms" related to their domestic policies. This was their insistence on complete control of civil society and their sanctification of the nation and its leadership at the expanse of the rights of individuals. The editorial expounded on how the totalitarian Nazi and Fascist regimes had succeeded in "turning the individual into an atom devoid of his own will." The editorial analyzed the "internal terror [*al-irhab al-dakhili*]" that the Nazi regime was inflicting upon Germans through the violence and terror being carried out by its security forces. In order to satisfy the "will of the nation," the "will of the individual" was erased. It also noted the integral relationship between internal repression and external aggression, emphasizing that the purpose of the former was to facilitate the latter. The feeling of inferiority that marked fascist foreign policy had also burrowed inward, squashing the individual and enlisting their entire being in the service of the state. Under the Nazi and Fascist systems in effect in Germany and Italy, "the nation relinquishes its economic and societal freedoms and accepts the fact that it must fight with its entire being to achieve the [national] goal." Thus Hitler's demagogic speeches strove to harness the German nation in the service of the mission of national greatness, while Mussolini for his part had declared that "tens of millions of Italians are ready to arm themselves and to fight for their empire." In al-Ahram's opinion, both leaders were falsely leading their nations to believe in "the power of the state and its unquestioned greatness, its outstanding capabilities, and its superiority to other nation states" in order to assuage feelings of national inferiority.[130]

The third characteristic of "dictatorial nationalism" was racism. This type of nationalism was obsessed with "the merits of race [fada'il al-jins]" that "glorifies race and places itself as a race above all others." This characteristic applied primarily to Nazi Germany.[131] Believing that the German race was superior to all others, the Nazi regime was thirsty to realize not only geographical expansion but also racial lebensraum, based on the idea of a German race that was destined to rule over other nations.[132]

While in part overlapping with al-Ahram's critical view of Fascist and Nazi imperialism, totalitarianism, and racism, al-Misri's status as a partisan Wafdist organ led it to a somewhat different emphasis in its summation of the key issues involved in the confrontation of democracy and dictatorship. An editorial of July 1939 concentrated on defining the position Egypt and the other Arab nations who were "fighting for their national freedom" from British and French domination should take "in the struggle between democracy and dictatorship in wartime." Although al-Misri viewed Great Britain's and France's position in the Middle East as an imperialist one, and although it asserted the legitimacy of the Egyptian and Arab struggle for independence, the newspaper nonetheless viewed the Arab nations as part of the democratic camp opposed to fascist totalitarianism and expansionism. Fascist Italy and Nazi Germany were unacceptable allies for Egypt and the Arab world in their fight for freedom. Al-Misri fully shared al-Ahram's negative view of Fascist and Nazi aggressiveness and imperialism. The editorial acknowledged that Great Britain and France were far from blameless in international affairs; first among their flaws was their imperialism. Nonetheless, it was not from countries such as Italy or Germany that one could learn the meaning of respect for international agreements or the right of small nations. For its part, Italy had brutally conquered Ethiopia, "a member of the League of Nations," and later had facilitated Hitler's absorption of Austria and backed Germany in its destruction of Czechoslovakia, another member of the League of Nations "whose independence no one had the right to challenge." Italy had also invaded Albania "without justification." Ideologically the German Nazis were even worse than the Italian Fascists in their attitude toward the Arabs, in particular, Semitic nations "whom he [Hitler] places on the lowest level of the human races."[133]

The editorial went on to warn all Arabs against believing current Fascist and Nazi propaganda about assisting them in gaining their independence. Given the Fascist and Nazi track record of expansionism, their imperialism was likely to be far worse than that of democratic Great Britain and France: "If the Eastern Arab nations don't want the democratic countries to rule over them . . . it cannot be that they would agree to the dictatorial countries enslaving them."[134] For al-Misri as for al-Ahram, the axiom that "the enemy of my enemy is my friend" did not apply. This stance of hostility to fascist imperialism, clearly articulated in the Egyptian daily press before the outbreak of World War II, did not change once the war was under way.

Al-Misri's status as a Wafdist organ led it to place even greater emphasis on the need for Egypt to affiliate with the democracies than did al-Ahram. As the hegemonic political movement of the interwar era, the party that had emerged triumphant in Egypt's few relatively free parliamentary elections, the Wafd was a staunch defender of the Egyptian Constitution of 1923 and the system of parliamentary government it had instituted for Egypt. A clear political interest underlay the Wafd's defense of constitutional government and parliamentary ascendancy: the full implementation of a parliamentary regime insured the movement's political dominance.

This existential Wafdist commitment to democracy found expression in al-Misri. In an editorial published shortly after the outbreak of war, the newspaper presented the maintenance of democracy as the central issue in the war and the decisive factor in determining Egypt's position in regard to the conflict. "Democracy is the highest ideal of the Allied forces, our allies [hulafa'una] fighting against the tyranny of Hitler," it proclaimed. This was a fact of transcendent importance for Egyptians, a people who both in ancient and modern times had fought for "a democratic government that would promise it its freedoms and rights." Egyptians were inherently democratic: "the Egyptians today join the Allied forces with their bodies and souls in order to protect democracy because they are by their very nature democrats." The victory of the democracies over Hitler was essential to the preservation of democracy in Egypt as well as elsewhere in the world. The editorial praised England and France for their commitment to upholding constitutional procedures and their "respect for parliamentary life" even under the difficult conditions of war, so Egyptians also needed to "respect the Egyptian Constitution . . . and parliamentary government" in wartime. "Only parliamentary governments have the right to say that they are defending democracy and fighting Nazism and Hitlerism [*al-naziyya wa al-hitlariyya*]."[135]

3

Mockery and Terror
Fascism and Nazism in Visual Imagery

BY THE INTERWAR ERA, Egyptian commentary on contemporary issues was being presented in images as well as words. Photographs and caricature were a relatively new, but nonetheless an increasingly influential, form for the expression of political opinion. Egypt's mainline periodicals occasionally printed visual images relating to current affairs, including ones commenting on the respective merits of democratic versus authoritarian government. However, in Egypt's daily newspapers and weekly or monthly journals of opinion, visual imagery was the shadow of the written word, a supplemental means of commentary intended to dramatize views primarily expounded in textual form.

Whereas visual material was marginal in the mainline press, it was integral to the genre of periodicals that employed visual images as their primary means of expression. The illustrated journal was a unique press genre intended from the outset to serve as a medium of communication via the use of photographs, illustrations, and caricatures. Generally appearing as a weekly publication, illustrated periodicals began to appear in the cultural consumer market in the late nineteenth century. With the expansion of Egypt's politically aware consumer public under the parliamentary monarchy, it was a genre that developed rapidly and flourished between the two world wars. By the 1930s, against the background of political and economic crisis as well as rapid social and cultural change, the illustrated periodical reached new heights of popularity and circulation. From a marginal genre, it became a major medium both shaping and representing Egypt's political culture. Like Egypt's mainline newspapers, illustrated journals were an all-Arab rather than exclusively Egyptian medium that were distributed and sold elsewhere in the Arab Middle East.[1]

Visual images were a significant component of modern print culture in Egypt, one with a social impact transcending that of the written word. Visual imagery was arguably accessible to a more extensive audience than that whose views were shaped and molded primarily by written texts. Capable of being "read" by both the literate and illiterate public, photographs and caricature occupied a niche on the seam between print culture and oral culture. Photographs, illustrations, and cartoons were a mode of communication that gave condensed expression to the prevailing viewpoint of the day; without a discussion of the views presented though visual images, our understanding of the public discourse of the era would be incomplete.

Caricature was a particularly effective form of communicating political opinion. Stock figures representing distinct Egyptian social strata—"Misri Effendi [the Egyptian Effendi]" for the literate, Westernized middle class, "Ibn al-Balad [Son of the Country]" for the more traditional, less Westernized majority of the population—were used to present graphic commentary on current affairs. Most of the textual captions that clarified or expanded on the meaning of a caricature were written in the colloquial dialect (al-ʿammiyya) rather than modern standard Arabic. Through the use of popular characters and their pointed and often-trenchant observations, topical messages on contemporary problems were transmitted to a wider segment of the Egyptian public than that reliant upon the mastery of literacy. Although illiterate consumers had to rely upon reading agents, literate authorities who would read the captions on caricatures and initially decode the object's full meaning, nonetheless through the assistance of such authorities illiterate consumers of print culture were given access to the political discourse of the day. Illustrations and caricature brought nonliterate audiences into the political field.

The photographs and caricatures found in three weekly illustrated periodicals—al-Musawwar, Ruz al-Yusuf, and al-Ithnayn wa al-Dunya—will be considered in this chapter. Both al-Musawwar, which the Zaydan family's Dar al-Hilal publishing empire began to publish in 1924, and Ruz al-Yusuf, founded by the actress Ruz (Fatima) al-Yusuf in 1925, date from the mid-1920s. Both rapidly carved out an influential niche in the Egyptian publishing market, each having a reported circulation of 20,000 issues by the late 1920s.[2] Caricature, in particular the visual creations of the prominent cartoonist Rida, occupied a central place in *Ruz al-Yusuf*. *Al-Musawwar* relied upon photographic images first and foremost, caricature appearing only as a supplement to views expressed primarily in written text and photographs. The fortunes of the two weeklies diverged in the 1930s. Originally supportive of the Wafd, in 1935 *Ruz al-Yusuf* broke with the leadership of the movement and adopted a vehemently anti-Wafdist stance. Consequently it suffered a decline in advertising revenue and popularity, especially once the Wafd returned to office in 1936–37; a British report of 1937 estimated that *Ruz al-Yusuf*'s circulation had declined to as little as 3,500–4,000, a figure which reportedly rose to 7,000–8,000 by 1944.[3] More politically prudent, *al-Musawwar* succeeded in maintaining its popularity through the interwar era and into the war years. A British estimate gave a circulation of 24,000–26,000 for *al-Musawwar* in 1937; its circulation was estimated at 60,000 by 1944.[4]

The most popular of the three illustrated weeklies in the late 1930s was *al-Ithnayn wa al-Dunya*, founded by Dar al-Hilal in 1934. More than in its sister publication *al-Musawwar*, photographs and caricature were prominent in *al-Ithnayn wa al-Dunya*, often appearing on the front and back covers as well as in the body of an issue. The new weekly eventually became a huge commercial success. An estimate for 1944 calculated a weekly circulation in the range of 90,000 copies, one-quarter of which were distributed outside Egypt.[5] More than any other publication, *al-Ithnayn wa al-Dunya* embodied the visual conventions of Egyptian political caricature. The caricaturist Santis [Santez] was the most visual prominent artist of the Dar al-Hilal publishing house; his work was prominently featured in *al-Ithnayn wa al-Dunya*.

In what follows, we will focus particularly on visual images as an expression of Egyptian opinion regarding Fascism and Nazism. Visual representations of Fascism and Nazism appeared frequently in all three weeklies by the later 1930s. Individual images juxtaposed authoritarian versus liberal values, contrasted unitary and authoritarian political culture with pluralistic and democratic political culture, and compared the nature and potential of Italian and German imperialism with British and French imperialism. With specific reference to caricatures, there was considerable affinity among the multiple images dealing with these subjects in the three weeklies. Both from the standpoint of form, the shaping of the images found in cartoons, and from the standpoint of theme, the content and meaning implied by the image, a common caricature discourse can be identified. The similarities of form and theme outweigh the differences. The fact that the same caricaturist (Santis) was responsible for many of the caricatures published in *al-Musawwar* and *al-Ithnayn wa al-Dunya* added to the uniformity found in Dar al-Hilal's two illustrated weeklies. Its editorial distinctiveness notwithstanding, the caricatures found in *Ruz al-Yusuf* were also similar to those appearing in its more popular rivals.

Our concern is content more than form. By the later 1930s, the visual imagery appearing in all three weekly publications were firmly and consistently anti-Fascist and anti-Nazi. They frequently belittled both the leaders and the policies of both dictatorial regimes, denouncing their internal totalitarianism as well as their external imperialism. At the same time, their caricatures expressed an implicit affinity with and preference for democracy and for the preservation of liberal, pluralistic political culture in the world as well as in Egypt and the Middle East. As with the portrayal of authoritarianism and liberalism in written texts, a characteristic deserving of mention was the mobility of imagery between the external and the internal scene, between dealing with events in Europe and those occurring in Egypt. The portrayal of Fascism and Nazism was intimately connected with attitudes about the evolution of Egyptian domestic politics, as well as about the possible implications of the fascist surge for Egypt's national interests. Where the explicit subject of a visual image was external, in many cases its implicit reference was what was going on in Egypt.

To what degree may these visual images be assumed to have represented broader Egyptian views on the subject of dictatorship versus democracy? Our premise in what follows is that the relationship between production and reception is dialogic. As with written text, the images of reality presented in visual form were put forth with a presumed audience in mind and according to the feedback received from consumers. While there is no one-to-one correlation between the commercial success of any publication and its contents being a faithful representation of the prevailing view on a given issue, nonetheless we believe that the popularity of Egypt's illustrated weeklies does allow us to conclude that their visual imagery reflected widely held attitudes among the Egyptian public who continued to buy the weeklies and who may be assumed to some degree to have shared the attitudes about democracy versus fascism articulated in each.

The human figure is a natural object for political caricature. In Egypt as well as elsewhere, the figures and individual characteristics of the two fascist dictators, Benito Mussolini and Adolf Hitler, provided an ample reservoir of physical attributes to emphasize, to exaggerate, and to belittle. Egyptian caricaturists employed conventional portraits of the Duce and the Führer, iconic images that reappeared again and again. Mussolini was often presented in paramilitary garb, wearing the black shirt, tight white trousers, high black boots, and distinctive cap of the Fascist *squadristi*; sometimes he appeared in Italian military uniform. Usually portrayed as a portly figure with a menacing facial expression, the Duce's bulk was purposely exaggerated to create an impression of a physical bully. The conventional depiction of Hitler was also in paramilitary or military uniform, his Nazi Party affiliation designated by a swastika on the sleeve of his uniform. His head was usually uncovered, allowing the caricaturist to emphasize the distinctive fashion in which the German leader combed his hair. The conventional portrayal of Hitler's face was unflattering, prominently featuring a malevolent sneer and deep-set, glowering eyes. In contrast to Mussolini, Hitler was presented a trim figure. His slight stature notwithstanding, Hitler was unquestionably viewed as the greater menace; a ludicrous but very dangerous little man.

Visual portrayals of the two fascist leaders combined an overall message of menace and threat with one of ridicule and clownishness. On the one hand, Mussolini and Hitler were presented as monstrous tyrants, cruel and merciless dictators at home and militaristic warmongers thirsting for conquest and destruction abroad. Simultaneously, they were presented as grotesque, even preposterous, historical figures. In their images, a number of tropes blended; that of the vulgar and arrogant ruffian full of bombast, of the irrational megalomaniac obsessed with visions of greatness, of the capricious, reckless gambler who played with fire and risked destruction for the world. Together, this ridicule created an optimistic bottom line; despite the undoubted danger posed by both leaders and their regimes, in the end enlightened humanity would find a way to overcome these clowns and save mankind from their megalomania.

Most of the themes present in Egyptian press coverage of the Ethiopian crisis and war of 1935–36—the labeling of Fascist Italy as the aggressor for its imperialist expansion directed at Ethiopia; revulsion at the brutality with which the Italian conquest of Ethiopia was carried out; condemnation of Italy for its willingness to resort to war in its pursuit of national glory; fear that Fascist Italy harbored plans for further expansion in other parts of Africa, including Egypt—were present in visual form in caricatures published in Egypt's illustrated weeklies during 1935–37. In most of these, the figure of Mussolini—already being presented as a gross and rapacious brute—served as the personification of Fascist Italy and its dangerous policies of militarism and expansionism. Thus, as early as the mid-1930s, a critical and negative image of Italian Fascism and Mussolini had become commonplace in Egypt's illustrated weeklies.

Hostile visual images of both Fascism and Mussolini were the norm as early as 1935, as the crisis between Italy and Ethiopia accelerated and finally led to war. Thus a caricature in *al-Musawwar* of September 1935 condemned Fascist imperialist intentions by presenting the figure of Mussolini, dressed in Fascist paramilitary uniform (booted, wearing black shirt and tight white trousers) striding aggressively from the Mediterranean in the direction of the Red Sea and the Horn of Africa. Mussolini's image is unquestionably a malevolent one; eyes fixed intently upon his target and blazing with intensity, his hands are clenched as if ready to strike out. His right foot rests on the Mediterranean; his left foot, shown in the form of the Italian boot, tramples on Ethiopia, in the process crushing the dove of peace. The caption proclaims simply, "With his foot, Mussolini is crushing the dove of peace." The caricature carries a dual message: the first that nothing will stop Fascist Italy from invading Ethiopia, the second that a similar fate could await Egypt in the future.[6] (See Figure 3.1.)

A caricature in *al-Ithnayn wa al-Dunya* in November 1935 depicted a voracious Mussolini, now dressed in military uniform, in the process of eating a pizza shown in the form of Ethiopia. At his side, two figures apparently representing Emperor Haile Selassie and the Lion of Judah implore the Fascist leader not to continue with his attempt to consume his country. Determined to finish off the pizza/Ethiopia, Mussolini ignores the pleadings of the Ethiopian representatives. The message is clear: Mussolini will continue with his aggression until its aim, the conquest of Ethiopia, is completed.[7]

Ruz al-Yusuf participated in the chorus of visual condemnation of Fascist warmongering in 1935. A caricature of the same month depicted Mussolini, again in military uniform and festooned from head to toe with the tools of war (cannon, tanks, aircraft, a warship), on his way to attend

Figure 3.1 "With His Foot, Mussolini Is Crushing the Dove of Peace." *Al-Musawwar*, Sept. 6, 1935, front page.

a ceremony in commemoration of Armistice Day. While one caption at the bottom proclaims "a universal commemorative service was held on the occasion of Armistice Day; Italy also, my brother, participated in it," another mocks Fascist militarism by announcing that "Signor Mussolini is marching to the prayer service equipped with symbols of peace." For Mussolini and Fascist Italy, the "symbols of peace [*sharat al-salam*]" were an arsenal of lethal weaponry being directed against a weaker and more primitive adversary.[8]

Other caricatures of the mid-1930s expressed the view that the deterioration of international relations generated by the Italo-Ethiopian crisis was also a threat to Egypt. In early 1936, a caricature in *al-Ithnayn wa al-Dunya* portrayed Great Britain, in the figure of John Bull, beating a hammer upon an anvil bearing the face of Mussolini. However, every blow stuck upon the anvil/Mussolini is presented as also being a blow to Egypt, a map of which lies unrolled upon the top of the anvil. Stuck between the hammer of Great Britain and the anvil of Italy, Egypt was bound to pay the price for the growing hostility between the two great powers generated by the Ethiopian crisis.[9] When Italy's conquest of Ethiopia had been completed, the weekly again used culinary imagery to criticize Italian actions. As he devours Ethiopia, now presented in the form of a huge sandwich, the Duce is shown holding a wine glass with the name "Lake Tana." The caption presents Mussolini talking to himself: "Here I am devouring Ethiopia; will I also be allowed to drink the lake?" Having successfully devoured Ethiopia, Fascist Italy's imperial aspirations are represented as including a threat to a source of the Nile vital for Egypt's existence.[10]

Even with the Ethiopian crisis resolved, hostile presentations of Italian Fascism and Mussolini continued to appear in Egypt's illustrated press. At the beginning of 1937, a caricature in *al-Musawwar* estimating the prospects for the year to come offered a gloomy prognosis by depicting the dove of peace as an aircraft dropping bombs upon an unnamed civilian population (possibly Ethiopia, possibly Spain). Its caption held out little hope for the new year: "in 1937, the dove of peace has become a bomber sowing destruction and death."[11] *Al-Musawwar* also belittled Italian efforts to present itself as a friend of the Arab and Muslim worlds. Against the background of the completion of the construction of a better coastal road from Tripoli in Libya to the Egyptian border and a visit by Mussolini to celebrate the completion, the weekly offered a critical commentary regarding recent Italian propaganda efforts. Both mounted on horseback,

Mussolini is shown meeting a Bedouin chief. While Mussolini holds a flag inscribed with the words "There is no God but God and Muhammad is His Prophet" and states "Oh Arab, I am the protector of Islam," the Arab responds with the shocked reply "Heaven forbid . . . the only protector of Islam is God Himself!!" and points for Mussolini to leave the area.[12] By 1937, images of Fascist Italy as a menace equally to Egypt, to the Middle Eastern region, and to world peace were the common currency of Egyptian political caricature.

In 1938–39, Hitler and Nazi Germany came to be perceived and depicted as the greater threat to international stability in Egypt's illustrated weeklies. Now it was Hitler's expansionist maneuvers aimed at creating a greater Germany in Central Europe, more than Mussolini's imperial ambitions in the Mediterranean basin and Africa, that became the main subject of concern and caricature. The caricature mirrored reality: just as Hitler progressively seized center stage in the international arena from a marginalized Mussolini, so the real danger to the world came to be seen as Hitler and Nazi expansionism while Mussolini and his Fascist regime increasingly came to be presented as little more than frustrated camp followers of the Nazi war machine.

Al-Ithnayn wa al-Dunya opened 1938 with a gloomy prognosis as to what the new year had in store. A front-page cartoon featured an image of Mussolini, teeth bared and eyes glaring, threatening John Bull (Great Britain) and the figure of a young woman representing Egypt. Egypt's anxious inquiry of John Bull—"When will I find rest and well-being?"— expressed a definite Egyptian sense of apprehension concerning the year to come. John Bull's sober response was hardly reassuring: "When the ghosts of war disappear from our horizon!"[13]

Other caricatures of early 1938 reflected the relationship between European fascist movements and domestic Egyptian developments. Street brawling between the paramilitary Green Shirts of Young Egypt and more recently established Blue Shirts of the Wafd had presented a problem of public order in 1936 and 1937, one that indeed was a factor in the ouster of the Wafdist ministry of Mustafa al-Nahhas by the end of the year. A January cartoon in the anti-Wafdist *Ruz al-Yusuf,* showing Mussolini and Hitler facing a disgruntled Nahhas and removing their shirts in protest against the possible dissolution of Egyptian paramilitary groups, drew a link between fascist paramilitarism abroad and quasi-fascist paramilitarism, such as that of the Wafdist Blue Shirts, at home.[14] When in March the anti-Wafdist coalition ministry led by Muhammad Mahmud dissolved all Egyptian paramilitary youth groups, *al-Ithnayn wa al-Dunya* carried a cartoon showing the prime minister ordering the banning of "colorful" paramilitary uniforms and a defiant Mussolini attempting to evade the ban by responding with the sarcastic query "Is the black shirt colorful?"[15] In both caricatures, the fascist inspiration of Egypt's paramilitary groups was assumed and their unruly and antidemocratic behavior condemned.

The extended and escalating tension in Europe over Czechoslovakia in the summer of 1938 drew repeated commentary in Egypt's illustrated weeklies. *Al-Ithnayn wa al-Dunya* published several caricatures concerning the Czech crisis. One early in September, showing images of the stock comic figure Juha and his donkey wearing gas masks, expressed the fear that the confrontation over the fate of the Sudetenland could lead to a war that would menace Egypt.[16] Later in the month, on the eve of the Munich Conference, another depicted Neville Chamberlain as a fireman attempting to put out a blaze that threatened to engulf the entire world. The weekly's pessimistic prognostication was that "the fire cannot be extinguished."[17] Immediately after Munich, a caricature depicting a plucked dove being served on a plate at the dinner table and bearing the caption "The League of Nations no longer has any use for the dove of peace now that the states have plucked all of its feathers. Will she be broiled and eaten in the end?" was hardly sympathetic to the policy of appeasement adopted by the Western democracies at Munich.[18] Another image in the same issue of *al-Ithnayn wa al-Dunya* portrayed a pack of dogs, one of whom wears a gas mask. When informed that "the powers have agreed that there will be no war" and thus that he could remove his mask, he responds with a cynical "I am prepared for the unexpected."[19] A week later, another caricature portrayed an elegantly dressed woman, representing humanity, placing an olive branch on a table in front of the four co-signatories of the Munich Agreement (Hitler, Mussolini, Chamberlain, and Daladier), the two dictators in military dress and the other two in civilian garb. Her commentary mocked the recently concluded Munich Agreement by asking "now that you have saved me from war, can't you bring me a lovely dress?"[20]

Ruz al-Yusuf was more explicit in its criticism of what had occurred at Munich. Already in August, a caricature reprinted from the European press bore the caption "The International Lottery, or a War of Imperialism" in Arabic. It showed Mussolini and Hitler spinning a lottery wheel bearing the words "war/*Krieg*/*guerre*." For his part Mussolini declared his hope of winning "the shores of the Mediterranean, Tunis, and Spain"; Hitler's imperial aspirations were cited as "Czechoslovakia, the German colonies, and Danzig." The Arabic editorial commentary accompanying the image stated that together the foreign policies of the two dictators represented "a dangerous gamble that may cause some very great losses."[21] A cartoon a month later, when the crisis over the Sudetenland had intensified and war appeared possible, showed the faces of Mussolini and Hitler, their images flanked by heavy artillery, overlooking the Nile Valley while a mass of Egyptians look apprehensively in their direction. The river itself is overflowing its banks, as was often the case in late summer. As the caricature's caption put it, the country faced two threats in September 1938: "Egypt today faces two dangers—the danger of war and the danger of flood."[22]

On October 2, immediately after the Munich Conference, the front-page caricature in *Ruz al-Yusuf* that portrayed Czechoslovakia being sacrificed "on the altar of peace" left no doubt of the publication's disgust over the deal reached at Munich. Three figures dressed in clerical garb stand behind the altar: "Father John Paul" [a Czech primate?] weeping over the sacrifice of Czechoslovakia; Mussolini smiling benignly; and Hitler, armed with a sword, prepared to slaughter the lamb on the altar.[23] Another caricature in the same issue depicted Hitler, as usual dressed in military uniform and beaming with glee, lighting a bomb bearing the image of a swastika while around the Führer a throng of people of various nationalities and including Misri Effendi, together meant to represent humanity as a whole, look on in fear. The utterly reckless nature of the Nazi dictator's behavior in the Czech crisis is made clear in the caption: "Could Samson have brought the temple down on his enemies and I cannot? . . . Is he better than I?!"[24] (See Figure 3.2.)

Yet another caricature immediately after Munich, showing the artillery of several of the world's presumably antifascist countries—Russia (a bear), Great Britain (John Bull), France (Marianne), Czechoslovakia (a helmeted soldier), and Egypt (Misri Effendi)—pointing at the figures of Hitler and Mussolini, also surrounded by artillery, is noteworthy both for its inclusion of Egypt in the camp of the democracies and for its suggestion that a policy of firmness, rather than one of appeasement, was what

على وعلي أعدائى

الهر هتلر — أتمعنى شمشون هدم الهيكل على نفسه وعلى اعدائه . . . يعنى هوه . أحسن منى ! ! . . . .

Figure 3.2 "Upon Me and Upon My Enemies." Herr Hitler: "Could Samson have brought the temple down on his enemies and I cannot? . . . Is he better than I?!" *Ruz al-Yusuf*, Oct. 2, 1938, p. 10.

was needed to confront the fascist threat to world stability and peace.[25] A week later, as the German absorption of the Sudetenland was being effectuated, *Ruz al-Yusuf* presented Hitler as a satanic figure. A front-page caricature showed the German leader, dressed in black, juggling a globe representing the world as if it were a child's toy. The background of the caricature is a somber one, a dark night with only a few stars providing light. The caption is unambiguous about *Ruz al-Yusuf*'s fear of Nazi aggressiveness: "There is no limit to Hitler's ambitions; the world is like a ball in a game in the hands of a devil [*'ifrit*]."[26]

The danger Italian Fascist imperialism represented to Egypt in particular continued to be a frequent subject of visual commentary in Egypt's illustrated weeklies. Caricatures in *Ruz al-Yusuf* in late 1938 mocked Mussolini's presumed hopes for the expansion of Italian influence in Africa. One in December was a commentary on recent rumors that the Italian government was attempting to sign a nonaggression pact with Egypt. Showing an uncertain Prime Minister Muhammad Mahmud being tugged in opposing directions by John Bull and Mussolini, it had the prime minister asking Misri Effendi his opinion; the latter warned him to carefully examine what is involved before opting between the two rival Mediterranean powers.[27] The heading of another caricature in early December presented Mussolini, "the Italian raven," as the antithesis of the dove of peace. The body of the caricature, showing Misri Effendi in conversation with Mussolini, mocked the Duce's claim to be a friend of the Arabs and Islam. "Foreign telegrams claim that Signore Mussolini has decided that the Arabic language should be taught in Italy, and that he has ordered that Italian teachers be appointed to Fu'ad I University [Egyptian University]," the caption announced. Not persuaded by Mussolini's charm offensive, Misri Effendi tartly replies, "Do me a favor—keep away from me, stop stalking me like a cunning raven. You already got too much when we recognized the annexation of Ethiopia. I feel like hiding from the shame."[28]

At the close of 1938, the expansionist ambitions of the two fascist dictators and the threat they posed to Egypt were the subject of cartoons in both *Ruz al-Yusuf* and *al-Ithnayn wa al-Dunya*. A caricature in the former portrayed Mussolini and Hitler striding along the coast of the Mediterranean, approaching the Suez Canal from the west, while an angry Misri Effendi waves a club in the direction of the two dictators and defiantly declares, "I am the owner of the Canal and its protector. Anyone who dares take one more step will force me to beat him and break his skull.

I have no other weapon!!"; it simultaneously expressed Egypt's apprehension concerning the fate of the Suez Canal, resolve to defend it, and current military weakness in the face of possible aggression.[29] It was the Italian threat to the territorial integrity of the Arab countries of North Africa that drew the attention of *al-Ithnayn wa al-Dunya*. A caricature at year's end depicted a voracious Mussolini gazing covetously at the Suez Canal and Tunisia, together represented as edibles on a platter, while whining about the international opposition to his expansionist agenda in contrast to that of Hitler: "Every dish that Hitler cooks people eat. Why isn't my dish cooked and eaten?"[30]

Italy's imperial pretensions in the Mediterranean were a persistent concern in all three illustrated weeklies at the start of 1939. *Al-Ithnayn wa al-Dunya* used a photograph of a still image from a recent film about Egyptian history to warn Egyptians both of the imperial aspirations of Italy and of the need to be beware of Italian blandishments. The photograph showed an imperious Mark Antony appealing to a reluctant Cleopatra; the accompanying caption labeled the two figures as "Mussolini" and "Egypt." To Mark Antony's/Mussolini's appeal—"say yes—agree to my courting, and we will renew the [golden] age of Antony and Cleopatra"—Cleopatra/Egypt turns away from Antony and dismissively replies "By God! Forget it! After all, it is 1939."[31] A caricature in *Ruz al-Yusuf* continued the weekly's warnings of an Italian threat to Egyptian control of the Suez Canal. Showing Mussolini negotiating the issue of Italian access through the canal with British prime minister Neville Chamberlain, it used the figure of Misri Effendi to express the fear that the two powers will arrive at a canal agreement behind the back of Egypt, "the owner of the Canal." For his part, Chamberlain is presented as receptive to the Egyptian sovereignty over the canal. "The owner of the Canal is here," Chamberlain notes to Mussolini; "we have to hear what he has to say on the subject."[32] *Al-Musawwar* expressed its fear of an Italian threat to the Suez Canal in the words of its editor, Fikri Abaza, who in an open letter to Mussolini warned the latter that "Egypt only is the first and the last to have a say in regard to the Suez Canal." The fact that Italy's new African empire partially surrounded Egypt both on the west, along the Libyan border, and now to the south, in its new Ethiopian conquest that abutted the Sudan, was an issue of deep concern for a committed Egyptian nationalist like Abaza.[33]

Renewed international aggressiveness by the two fascist powers in the spring of 1939—Germany's takeover of the rump of Czechoslovakia in March, Italy's invasion and annexation of Albania in April—generated further visual presentations of Fascist Italy and Nazi Germany as a threat both to world peace and to Egypt. For its part, *Ruz al-Yusuf* saw the German absorption of Czechoslovakia as portending further Nazi expansionism and conquest. In one caricature entitled "Caught in the Claws of the Demon," Hitler, portrayed as a monstrous figure with long arms, claws, and a mouth with fangs, bends over a quaking Czechoslovakia, represented as an innocent girl. To the girl's frightened query, "Am I the first sacrifice or the last?" Hitler replies, "On the contrary, my dear, you are merely the 'aperitif' of the sacrifices!"[34] (See Figure 3.3.)

A particularly graphic caricature in the weekly a few weeks later showed Mussolini and Hitler, the "new Axis [*mihwar jadid*]," saluting Azrael (*'izra'il*), the angel of death. The demonic figure of Azrael, dressed in a white robe from which only his skull protrudes and brandishing a sickle, dominates the frame; the tiny figures of Mussolini and Hitler stand and salute in agreement to Azrael's query "What do you think about a covenant between the three of us that we will call the 'Rome-Berlin-Azrael' Axis?"[35] (See Figure 3.4.)

By 1939, Egyptian caricaturists did not view Fascist Italy and Nazi Germany as comparable powers and equivalent threats to peace. Unquestionably, Hitler was seen as the greater force and menace to world stability. The point was made in a caricature in *Ruz al-Yusuf* that brought together the figures of Mussolini and Franco, recently victorious in Spain. By showing the Spanish and Italian dictators racing with one another to be the first to congratulate Hitler for his recent takeover of Czechoslovakia, the caricature acknowledged the German dictator's primacy in the fascist cosmos.[36] Another caricature in *Ruz al-Yusuf,* depicting a giant Hitler standing alongside a smaller Mussolini, whom he calls "my son," as the two dictators gaze at such potential targets of aggression as Paris, London, Poland, Romania, and Holland, clearly subordinated Mussolini to Hitler in the Axis while also making no bones about the perceived aggressive intentions of the two European dictators.[37] *Al-Ithnayn wa al-Dunya* made much the same point about the Axis pecking order in a caricature showing Hitler and Mussolini at the dinner table on which the map of Europe is cut into edible portions. While Hitler's left hand plunges a fork into Czechoslovakia as his right hand sprinkles swastikas over his Czech meal,

بين براثن الغول ..

التشيك .ـ يا ترى انا « اول » الضحايا .. والا آخرها ١٢ .

المر هتلر ـ بالعكس ياعزيزتى .. انتى « ابريتيف » الضحايا ا .. ١

Figure 3.3 "Caught in the Claws of the Demon." Czechoslovakia: "Am I the first sacrifice or the last?!" Herr Hitler: "On the contrary, my dear, you are merely the 'aperitif' of the sacrifices!" *Ruz al-Yusuf*, Mar. 17, 1939, p. 9.

محور جـــديد ؟!..

عزرائيل — إيه رأيكم في عقد معاهدة بيننا احنا الثلاثة . . . ونسميها محور « برلين — روما — عزرائيل » . . . ؟

Figure 3.4 "New Axis?!" Azrael: "What do you think about a covenant between the three of us that we will call the 'Rome-Berlin-Azrael' Axis?" *Ruz al-Yusuf*, Apr. 2, 1939, p. 7.

a frustrated Mussolini is shown grumbling "How strange: I have been a dictator far longer than you, and all I do is watch you greedily gobble up everything and yet you are never satisfied!"[38] (See Figure 3.5.)

It was not long before Mussolini assuaged his appetite by invading Albania. This Fascist attempt to emulate Nazi expansionism drew scorn from Egypt's illustrated weeklies. A savage caricature in *al-Ithnayn wa al-Dunya* portrayed Mussolini as a muscular, half-naked bully of enormous size holding and trying to calm the frightened female figure of Albania by telling her "Come, my darling, I am longing to hug you." Albania's reply leaves no doubt that Mussolini's cordiality was not reciprocated: "Please, unhand me, stop squeezing me, I am dying!!"[39] (See Figure 3.6.) A later caricature depicted Albania as a child prostrate at the feet of Mussolini in a boxing ring as the Duce, dressed in typical Fascist uniform, bombastically declares "Victory!" over his infant opponent.[40]

Italy's aggressiveness in Albania notwithstanding, *Ruz al-Yusuf* saw Hitler, rather than Mussolini, as the dynamo impelling the world toward war in mid-1939. One of its caricatures belittled Italy's recent attempt to emulate German expansionism through its Albanian adventure. Depicting a frightened Mussolini sitting on the back of Hitler, here portrayed as "the Nazi lion," its caption explains that "the rider of the lion, who is trying to instill fear into people, is in fact more afraid than they are!" Misri Effendi stands in the corner of the caricature, enjoying the spectacle and expressing pity for the hapless Mussolini.[41] Nonetheless, the weekly also continued to emphasize that the immediate threat to the security of Egypt in 1939 came from Italy rather than Germany. A caricature of April with a domestic as well at external referent depicted Prime Minister Muhammad Mahmud, shown as "Marshal Muhammad Mahmud Pasha," appointed the Italian military governor of Egypt subsequent to Italy's occupation of the country, listening to an imperious Mussolini as the latter rebukes his Egyptian deputy for laziness and orders him to devote himself seriously to the administration of Italian-occupied Egypt.[42]

That the world was inexorably moving toward armed conflict was a recurrent theme in *al-Ithnayn wa al-Dunya* by the spring of 1939. A photo montage of April showed a fascist black boot trampling humanity as represented by an assemblage of faces of different backgrounds. "The tyrannical force marches on," the caption warned, "over the heads of humanity."[43] A photograph of May displayed a scowling and malevolent Hitler driving a tank, its four cannon pointed straight at the viewer. The caption

Figure 3.5 Mussolini: "How strange: I have been a dictator far longer than you, and all I do is watch you greedily gobble up everything and yet you are never satisfied!" *Al-Ithnayn wa al-Dunya*, Apr. 3, 1939, p. 3.

Figure 3.6 "Her Guardian . . ." Mussolini: "Come, my darling, I am longing to hug you." Albania: "Please, unhand me, stop squeezing me, I am dying!!" *Al-Ithnayn wa al-Dunya*, Apr. 17, 1939, front page.

beneath the cannon belittled Hitler's occasional verbal assurances of his pacific intentions: "Speech of the week; behind the loud-speakers [cannon]." [44] In this perilous situation, the weekly lamented the feeble state of Egypt's national defenses and argued that greater Egyptian military preparedness was a national imperative. Thus a photograph on the front page of one issue portrayed four Egyptian soldiers peering apprehensively from behind a pile of sandbags. "By God, until now we trained for a war of words," the caption reads, "now we need to prepare for a war of artillery and airplanes."[45] Another a month later, entitled "The Specter of War," again stated the Egyptian view that the immediate threat to world peace now came from the German rather than the Italian dictator. In it, Hitler and Mussolini are presented holding up a wooden figure dressed as a gigantic Teutonic knight, armored and helmeted for battle. Whereas Hitler's statement—"as long as the specter [of war] continues to stand we can do whatever we want without anyone being able to stop us"—indicated his reckless use of the threat of war to attain his goals, Mussolini's reply— "Right, but please be careful it doesn't become a serious matter!"— attributed greater caution to his Axis partner.[46]

Both caricatures and editorial commentary on the international situation in Dar al-Hilal's *al-Musawwar* and *al-Ithnayn wa al-Dunya* in July and August 1939, the months immediately preceding the outbreak of war, repeatedly expressed the prevailing Egyptian view that it was Hitler and the Nazi regime in Germany that was leading the world toward military conflict. Thus a photo montage of early July entitled "The Heroism of the Axis: Playing with Bombs" in *al-Musawwar* depicted a uniformed Hitler standing on the globe and juggling several bombs while in the background Mussolini, riding a horse, submissively salutes his fellow dictator. The addresses on the bombs—Danzig and the Balkans in Eastern Europe, the Suez Canal and Tunisia in the Mediterranean, and Germany's former colonial possessions—attribute a worldwide appetite for aggression and expansion to the Nazi dictator and his Italian junior partner.[47] In late July, a caricature reprinted from a French publication in *al-Musawwar* portrayed Hitler pressing a button labeled "Danzig" on a box. As he does so, the box abruptly opens and out emerges the figure of a woman pointing a bayonet at the Führer, forcing him to recoil. The caption—"The genie in the box: if Hitler dares to press on the button of Danzig, he'll be surprised by this frightening sight"—carries the reassuring message that the democratic world was now prepared to resist German aggression.[48]

The accompanying commentary on the same page similarly accused Hitler of expansionist intentions regarding Danzig and expressed the conviction that, "in view of Poland's determination to defend [its] justified rights," Great Britain and France would stand by Poland and force Hitler to retreat from his demands.[49]

Al-Ithnayn wa al-Dunya also presented Danzig as "the focal point of danger in Europe" by mid-1939. Like *al-Musawwar*, its editorial commentary placed responsibility for the Danzig crisis on Nazi Germany and justified Polish resistance to German demands.[50] A caricature captioned "The Ghost of Napoleon in the Twentieth Century, or Why England and France are Defending the Interests of Poland" that showed Hitler, dressed in Napoleonic garb but with a swastika on his sleeve, gazing at a map of Napoleon's earlier conquests, explicitly equated the military aspirations of the twentieth-century Führer of Germany with those of the nineteenth-century Emperor of France while implying that, like his predecessor, Hitler's imperial aspirations were doomed to failure.[51] Another caricature of July, "the Dove of Peace in Satan's Palm," depicted the dove of peace trembling in the hands of a fiercely grimacing soldier.[52] The annexation of Alexandretta, part of the Syrian Mandate, by Turkey in the summer of 1939 served as foil for a visual commentary on the tension between Hitler and Mussolini as the former seemed to be going from triumph to triumph while the latter lagged behind. A caricature of July depicted the shadowy figure of Turkey running, carrying the district of Alexandretta after having stolen it from Syria; above this image, the heads of Hitler and Mussolini are shown discussing Turkey's Alexandretta takeover. Hitler's observation on the Turkish initiative—"Don't they know that the rights of annexation are reserved [for me]?"—simultaneously criticized Turkey's annexation of an arguably Arab region and reiterated a long-standing conviction of Nazi Germany's expansionist intentions.[53]

The German-Soviet Treaty of Non-Aggression of August 1939 was greeted with dismay in Egypt's illustrated weeklies. Stalin's image in Egyptian caricature thereafter was equally as negative as that of Hitler. Once the arrangement had indeed led to the German and Soviet partition of Poland, *al-Musawwar* depicted "Communism" through an image of a beady-eyed, unshaven, slovenly dressed Stalin holding an enormous knife dripping with blood in his teeth.[54] For its part, *al-Ithnayn wa al-Dunya* predicted that the Soviet-German alliance would be short-lived. One of its caricatures after the war had begun showed Stalin placing a hangman's noose around Hitler's neck. To Hitler's inquiry—"What kind of rope are you placing around my neck?"— Stalin's response—"This is the rope of alliance and friendship; how can we be friends without it?"—envisaged further treachery by a dictator fully as deceitful as his German partner in aggression.[55]

The beginning of World War II in September 1939 only intensified the hostile portrayal of German Nazism in Egyptian illustrated weeklies. Both textual commentary and caricatures at the start of the conflict placed the blame for war solidly upon Hitler and Germany, situated Egypt as part of the alliance resisting Nazi aggression, and optimistically predicted the victory of the democratic camp over Germany's aggression in Poland. That Egypt's place in the war was in the democratic camp was the message of the front-page caricature in an early September issue of *Ruz al-Yusuf.* It depicted a two-gunned Hitler firing his pistols while trampling with his boots on a suffering humanity. At the edge of the caricature, his democratic opponents—John Bull, Marianne, and Misri Effendi—attempt to resist Hitler with clubs. The caption—"History repeats itself: The end of Hitler by the hand of democracy"—assumed that Egypt's natural place was with the Allies and that the Western democracies would eventually emerge victorious.[56]

Al-Ithnayn wa al-Dunya's initial prognosis was similarly one of successful Allied resistance to German aggression. One caricature of early September depicted Poland, Germany, and Great Britain as three sharks in a row, each successively larger. As the German predator shark attempts to swallow a smaller Poland, the even larger shark representing Great Britain in turn is prepared to devour Germany before it can consume Poland. To Germany's arrogant statement to Poland—"I plan to swallow you, what do you think of that?"—Poland confidently replies, "Leave me alone and look behind you."[57] Even when the German blitzkrieg in Poland was on the verge of military victory, a caricature of mid-September optimistically predicted German failure in Poland by depicting the face of Hitler attempting to swallow Poland but unable to get the country, cut in the form of a slice of bread, in his mouth because of its size. The caption expresses the (by-then-unrealistic) view that Nazi Germany's appetite had exceeded her capabilities: "He is unable to swallow her."[58]

4

Egyptian Intellectuals and Fascism, I
Fascism at Home: Denouncing
Totalitarianism and Racism

THIS CHAPTER AND THE NEXT FOCUS on the attitudes toward democracy and dictatorship expressed in several mainstream Egyptian journals of intellectual opinion. A consideration of the views expressed by the numerous intellectuals who contributed to four prominent Arabic-language cultural journals of the late 1930s—the monthlies *al-Hilal* and *al-Majalla al-Jadida*, the weeklies *al-Risala* and *al-Thaqafa*—offer the fullest understanding of the positions taken by Egypt's intellectual elite regarding the confrontation between liberal and authoritarian principles of political organization.

The discourse of intellectuals was pivotal in the field of Egyptian print culture. Their centrality to the public discourse of the era was fortified by the relatively broad freedom of opinion and expression existing in interwar Egypt. This favorable climate allowed them to develop a largely sovereign discourse. The embodiment of the ethos of the "liberal age," Egyptian intellectuals possessed symbolic capital that enhanced their stature within and influence upon society. Their reflections upon the issues of the day were often impressively well informed, demonstrating a deep understanding of the dynamics of their own society as well as an intimate knowledge of European society, politics, and culture. In most cases, they brought to the public arena a humanist, pluralist, and liberal worldview. Many considered their local discourse an integral part of the universal discourse of modernity. For all these reasons, the views articulated by Egyptian intellectuals in their journals of opinion constitute the most reflective, sophisticated, and probing corpus of opinion developed within the Egyptian public sphere.

Al-Hilal ["The Crescent"] was arguably the most prestigious and influential Egyptian intellectual journal of the era. Founded in Cairo in 1892 by the Lebanese émigré Jurji Zaydan and after his demise edited by his sons Emile and Shukri Zaydan, *al-Hilal* had been a major Arabic-language journal of opinion for decades. With a regular circulation of perhaps 20,000–30,000 copies of each issue by the interwar years, it was an all-Arab forum as well as an Egyptian monthly.[1] Egyptian and other Arab intellectuals contributed to its pages; it was sold throughout the Arab world. Although under Christian ownership and operation, many Muslim intellectuals contributed to its monthly discussion of contemporary issues. Unlike the other journals considered in the following discussion, its frequent use of photographs and illustrations gave it a visual as well as textual impact.

From an ideological standpoint, *al-Hilal* expressed the liberal and Westernizing outlook that had come to characterize much of the Egyptian elite by the early twentieth century. In addition to attempting to keep its readers abreast of current affairs as well as of social, cultural, artistic, and scientific developments across the world, the periodical gave considerable attention to Egypt's Arabic-Islamic heritage. Its implicit purpose was to promote a synthesis between modern ideas and practices on the one hand and the indigenous Arab cultural legacy on the other. A publication owned and edited by Christians in a primarily Muslim environment, its editors followed a cautious and prudent strategy of publishing mainstream and generally moderate opinions on controversial issues, thus appealing to the broadest intellectual common denominator in order to reach the widest readership possible. Nonetheless, in a journal that was a product of the Westernized elite culture of early twentieth-century Egypt, the views articulated in *al-Hilal* were usually supportive of liberal values and social modernism.[2]

The weeklies *al-Risala* ["The Message"] and *al-Thaqafa* ["Culture"] were more recent entrants on the Egyptian cultural scene. In scope and outreach, they resembled *al-Hilal*. Like the latter, they were wide-ranging in content, incorporating articles on current affairs, social trends, and cultural currents. *Al-Risala* in particular was also similar to *al-Hilal* in its Arab emphasis, publishing the writings of non-Egyptian Arab intellectuals as well as of Egyptians and seeking an audience throughout the Arab world. Yet, whereas *al-Hilal* had been in operation for decades, the two weeklies were distinct products of the 1930s that reflected the social and cultural changes of the decade. In general terms, whereas *al-Hilal* gave voice to and spoke for the established intellectuals of the older Egyptian and Arab generation, *al-Risala* and *al-Thaqafa* often expressed the sentiments and attempted to meet the cultural expectations of the younger educated generation of the new *effendiyya* who were becoming a prominent social and cultural force by the 1930s. The contributions appearing in both weeklies were on the whole less Westernizing and more traditionalist than those that predominated in *al-Hilal*, advocating the revitalization of the Arab-Islamic heritage as a viable alternative to wholesale Egyptian and Arab imitation of the West.

Al-Risala was established in 1933 under the ownership and editorship of Ahmad Hasan al-Zayyat. Under Zayyat's direction, the journal expounded an Arab-Islamic cultural stance that fit the worldview of the new generation of educated Egyptians and Arabs. It promoted both Egyptian nationalism and an Arab cultural identity. While not adverse to the incorporation of elements of Western culture into modern Egyptian and Arab culture, on the whole its contributions gave greater attention to the reform and revival of the indigenous heritage as the fundamental basis for contemporary Arab thought and practice.[3] Appealing to a rapidly expanding audience of educated readers with a similar cultural orientation, the journal became an impressive commercial success. By the later 1930s, the circulation of regular issues was about 20,000 copies; up to 40,000 copies of special issues addressing specific topics sometimes appeared.[4]

Al-Thaqafa began publication in January 1939. It was the official publication of the Committee for Composition, Translation, and Publication of the Ministry of Education. Its editor, who set the tone for the journal, was the historian and literary critic Ahmad Amin. In content, *al-Thaqafa* saw itself as a journal devoted to the promotion of "Eastern" culture in general. It regarded "the East," a loose term sometimes denoting the Arab world but at other times signifying a broader unit including the civilizations of the Indian subcontinent and East Asia, as a unique cultural entity that needed to be harmonized with modern Western culture. *Al-Thaqafa* was also somewhat more open to European influences than was the case with *al-Risala*. As Amin put it, the aim of the journal was to present readers with "the finest creations of the Eastern and the Western intellect in science, literature, art, politics, and society."[5] Within a year of its appearance, the journal was reporting a circulation of 20,000 copies per issue.[6]

Salama Musa and his journal *al-Majalla al-Jadida* occupied a unique niche in Egyptian intellectual discourse during the 1930s. Editor of *al-Hilal* for much of the 1920s, Musa founded *al-Majalla al-Jadida* ["The New Magazine"] in 1929. The journal had a fraught publishing history in the early 1930s, being suspended for much of the tenure of the ministries headed by Egypt's autocratic strongman Isma'il Sidqi. It appeared without substantial interruption and reached the height of its influence in the mid- and late 1930s. Musa turned editorial responsibilities over to others in 1942; the journal ceased to be published in 1944.[7] Estimates for the circulation of *al-Majalla al-Jadida* are not available.

Coptic by birth, a Fabian socialist in conviction, Salama Musa was a leading advocate of the non-Marxist variant of socialism that appealed to segments of the Egyptian elite in the interwar era. Reflecting his personal orientation, *al-Majalla al-Jadida* stood at the cutting edge of Egyptian secularism in the 1930s. Its avant-garde message was, as its title implies, relentlessly antitraditionalist and radically modernist. The pages of *al-Majalla al-Jadida* advocated parliamentary democracy in opposition to monarchical autocracy, called for social and economic reform to bridge the chasms of wealth and privilege that characterized Egyptian society, promoted the wholehearted acceptance of technology and science as the levers of progress, and preached the need for Egyptians to abandon outmoded social and cultural practices and in their place to adopt values and customs appropriate to the modern age. Along with this modernist message went an espousal of a secular and territorially based Egyptian nationalism and a commitment to insuring the success of the new Egyptian nation-state that had been created in the wake of the Revolution of 1919.

The modernist views of Musa and the group of intellectuals who coalesced around his journal in the 1930s appealed particularly to two constituencies. One was the select cohort of older Egyptian liberals, like Musa the product of a heavily Europeanized socialization earlier in the century, who shared the Westernizing outlook expressed in *al-Majalla al-Jadida*. The other was the growing educated and professional class of younger Egyptians who were disillusioned with the shabby performance of the established political parties of the older generation mired in unproductive partisan competition, but who were not inclined to the alternative more radical but also more nativist agenda being espoused by newer extraparliamentary movements such as the Muslim Brothers or Young Egypt, and as a consequence found the journal's secular reformism attractive.[8]

Al-Majalla al-Jadida's aggressively secularist orientation appealed to Egyptians whether of Muslim, Christian, or Jewish background who found many of the specifics of their inherited religious traditions out of tune with the values they had absorbed from the heavily Westernized intellectual milieu of the interwar era. Concomitantly, the journal's outlook was of little appeal to the bulk of more traditionally inclined Egyptians. As a result, the distinctive discourse presented in *al-Majjala al-Jadida* was a phenomenon that appealed to a narrower range of opinion than *al-Hilal*, *al-Risala*, and *al-Thaqafa*.

Al-Hilal, *al-Risala*, *al-Thaqafa*, and *al-Majalla al-Jadida* contributed to the unfolding Egyptian discourse on democracy versus dictatorship in two ways. The first was through publishing substantial articles of analysis that attempted a systematic examination of various facets of liberal democracy and authoritarian government as both systems had developed historically in the West and as they operated in the contemporary era. Essays offering a comprehensive assessment of such topics as the parliamentary system as it existed in the Western democracies, of the opposing Fascist and Nazi systems currently found in Italy and Germany, of the historical roots and prerequisites of each, of the general characteristics and merits of one-party rule versus multiparty pluralism, of the opposing principles of individual freedom versus totalitarian rule, and of related issues such as nationalism and racism, appeared frequently in all four publications. A common feature of such analytical commentaries on developments in Europe was the conceptual and practical relevance of these foreign political concepts and currents for contemporary Egypt and beyond that for the Arab world as a whole.

The other way in which views on democracy and autocracy were expressed was in news reports and commentaries on contemporary events in Europe and the world. Like other Egyptian publications of the period, these journals of opinion followed current events closely, reporting on the major developments and crises of the week or month. Thus the growing tension between the democratic and fascist camps of the later 1930s—the international crises of 1935–36 over Ethiopia and those over Austria, Czechoslovakia, and Poland in 1938–39, and the gradual descent of Europe into war by late 1939—were all major subjects of concern and commentary. As with the more systematic analytical articles found in the journals, such reports and discussions of current events frequently reflected on their implications for Egypt and the Arab world.

Our discussion will consider both the more reflective analyses found in these journals of intellectual opinion and their commentaries on the world crisis as it unfolded over the later 1930s. This chapter addresses how Egyptian intellectuals viewed the historical origins and the domestic characteristics of Italian Fascism and German Nazism, specifically their interpretations of the philosophical as well as the conjunctural roots of contemporary fascism, their evaluation of the merits and flaws found in democratic versus totalitarian forms of government, and their conclusions regarding the intellectual falsity and moral evil of Nazi racism. The following chapter examines how Egyptian intellectuals interpreted the international actions of the fascist states, the danger to world stability as well as to Egypt posed by Italian and German imperialism and aggression, and discusses the measures that needed to be taken to counter the spread of fascist totalitarianism, racism, and expansionism.

Intellectual discourse on these issues was typified by a large measure of continuity. The anti-fascist perspective that had developed in the early and mid-1930s, largely in reaction to rise of Nazism in Germany, dominated intellectual discourse into the late 1930s. If anything, the intellectual rejection of both Italian Fascism and German Nazism became more prevalent over time. Whereas earlier in the decade occasional admiration had been expressed for the perceived domestic "achievements" of the authoritarian regimes in both countries, their apparent success at extricating their societies from economic and social crisis and in restoring national vitality, prestige, and power, by the late 1930s Egyptian intellectuals showed far less sympathy for the internal as well as the external policies of the fascist states. As time went on, an awareness of the dark side of both regimes domestically, their reliance on repression and terror, and especially of the threat to world stability and peace apparent in their agendas of external expansion, became the dominant themes in the analyses of Fascism and Nazism written by Egyptian intellectuals.

Explaining the Roots and Rise of Fascism

The intellectual as well as the conjunctural roots of fascism were a major subject of concern for intellectuals writing for Egypt's premier cultural journal *al-Hilal*. What were the philosophical and ideological sources of fascist ideology? What were the historical conjunctures that accounted for the successful rise to power of fascist movements in Italy and Germany?

Above all, did the current fascist surge portend the demise of liberal democracy as an effective system of governance for a modern society such as Egypt was in the process of becoming?

By and large, Egyptian intellectuals accepted that contemporary fascism, both as ideology and praxis, was not merely an outgrowth or reproduction of traditional autocratic rule but was a consequence of the rapid process of modernization that European society had undergone over the course of the nineteenth and into the early twentieth century. Writing as intellectuals, they paid particular attention to ways in which European philosophers had reacted to modernity and tried to impose new patterns of meaning on it. The focus of much of their concern was the relationship between leader and mass. Rightly assuming that the essential fascist concept of an absolute leader was a modern phenomenon, one intimately related to the emergence of contemporary mass society, they went on to dissect how the massive changes in social structure wrought by industrialization, urbanization, literacy, and the growth of the mass media paved the way for fascist success. Although the ostensible subject of their discussion was fascism in European countries, the implicit referent of much of their analysis was an Egypt and an Arab world that was undergoing similar processes and therefore might be expected to follow a similar trajectory of political development. Thus, when they wrote about fascism in Germany or Italy, they were often thinking about what the future held for Egypt and the Middle East.

Two articles by ʿAli Adham in 1938 offered a wide-ranging analysis of the contributions of several seminal European thinkers to the complex mix of ideas that underpinned the emergence of contemporary fascist ideology. Adham located the philosophical origins of Italian Fascism, the archetype of the species, first and foremost in the writings of Thomas Carlyle and Friedrich Nietzsche. According to Adham, Carlyle's view of the role of the hero in history and Nietzsche's cult of the will to power and the superman laid the ideological infrastructure for Fascism and Nazism. Adham was well aware that neither philosopher had anticipated historical figures such as Mussolini or Hitler as the incarnation of their historical hero or superman; what had happened was that Fascism and Nazism had appropriated their ideas and made them the foundation for the centrality of the leader in modern totalitarianism.

Carlyle was the starting point for understanding modern fascism. Adham declared that "the basis upon which Carlyle predicated his philosophy is precisely the same on which the philosophy of the fascists is based." It was Carlyle's theory of heroes and heroism that provided the intellectual rationale for totalitarian dictatorship. According to Adham, Carlyle assumed that the majority of humanity was incapable of understanding the intricacies of governance. "Most people are unable to rule themselves independently"; they need leaders to think for them, to direct and to lead them. For Carlyle, "worship of the leader and heroism is a basic instinct and need of the human spirit." Although Adham noted that the kind of heroism and leadership envisaged by Carlyle was quite different from that currently being demonstrated by Hitler and Mussolini, nonetheless Carlyle indirectly provided a conceptual basis for absolute rule on the part of a hero-leader who could bend the masses to his will; "that is precisely the basis for fascism."[9]

The contribution of Nietzsche's ideas of the cult of power and the will to power to the emergence of contemporary fascism was even more substantive. One of Nietzsche's major contributions was to provide legitimacy for the undermining of liberal democracy by fascism. Nietzsche had viewed democracy as "stifling the passions of the people and robbing them of their vitality," seducing them with appealing but fallacious ideas about "freedom, equality, and brotherhood" that destroyed spontaneity of feeling by restraining man's natural instincts and drives. What Nietzsche called for was the liberation of human spontaneity and the fostering of the human will to power, both of which would be achieved by the superman. Nietzsche's concept of "the superman [al-insan al-a'la]" laid the intellectual as well as the emotional foundation for the rise of fascist dictatorship. Whereas Nietzsche had conceived of the superman as an ideal that would be realized only in the distant future, in actuality "the impact of Nietzsche's philosophy was quite different than Nietzsche's intent." Nietzsche's contribution to contemporary fascism was direct: "every dictator regards himself as Nietzsche's superman."[10]

In another essay, Adham credited other European thinkers with constructs that also contributed to modern fascism. Georg Wilhelm Friedrich Hegel, for whom the state was the end-all and be-all ("according to him the state is the shadow of God on earth"), had developed the concept of the state as the supreme force in history and consequently could be viewed as the prophet of the totalitarian state. Johann Gottlieb Fichte's idealization of the German nation laid the philosophical basis for the worship of the nation and the passion for national grandeur so prominent in fascism. Adham regarded Georges Sorel as a particularly important influence upon Mussolini and Italian Fascism. Sorel's view of the masses as merely a herd thirsting for a strong leader and his insight into the importance of the "mythical factor ['amil al-ustura]" in mobilizing the masses were crucial contributions to fascism. Sorel instilled in fascism the belief that it was myth, rather than reason or science, that was the engine capable of motivating action and changing society. Sorel also provided legitimization for "the heroism of violence" and for "violent revolution" as the way to change the political and social order.[11]

Another extremely influential intellectual source for fascism for Adham was the intuitive philosophy of Henri Bergson. In his challenge to science and rationalism, Bergson had appealed to intuition and instinct as the primary forces behind human thought and action. Intuitive drives and the subconscious, the dynamic movement of the "élan vital," were the engines propelling human progress. As Adham saw it, this philosophy privileging intuition and the irrational posed a serious challenge to democracy: democracy was based on "gradual progress and consistent, systematic effort, while Bergson's philosophy is predicated on a sudden leap and split-second development [al-wathba al-mubaghata wa al-tatawwur al-mufaji']." Moreover, like others of his time, Bergson had assumed that modern mass society was comprised of an "ignorant and irrational mob" that had to be directed by leadership blessed with instinct, emotional power, and the ability to manipulate myth. Given these elements, Adham found Bergson's theory of the intellect and intuition to be anti-liberal and anti-democratic. He also perceived a direct link between Bergson on the one hand and Mussolini and Italian Fascism on the other. He found an additional intellectual connection in the fact that Bergson, like Sorel, had been a critic of Marxism. Both had objected to what they perceived as the impersonal dialectical materialism of Marxism, and in its place held that the "excellent leader" was the dynamic agent in the march of history, a force capable of igniting a "revolution in one dramatic leap," thereby destroying an antiquated order and creating a new one in its place.[12]

Lastly, Adham identified Vilfredo Pareto, "Sorel's friend and Mussolini's teacher," as having made a vital contribution to the ideology of Italian Fascism. Pareto's concept of "self-selected elites [al-safawat al-mukhtara]" was the opposite of democracy in positing that it was a leader's self-perception and deep conviction that only he knows the will of people and in which direction to lead it, and hence that he alone was entitled to the right to rule.

Effective leadership was not to be determined by democratic elections but by self-designation and personal assertion. The masses would accept such leadership because of a leader's ability to persuade them, through the adroit use of propaganda, that it was rescuing them from crisis and guiding them to a state of security and prosperity. For Adham, the anti-democratic vision of Pareto, "the constant and eternal struggle between self-selected elites, is a theory upon which Mussolini's school of Fascism is modeled."[13]

When considering the rise of contemporary fascism, elitist Egyptian intellectuals sometimes revealed a fear of modern mass society and culture, a direction in which Egypt was inexorably moving. In an article in *al-Hilal* in the spring of 1938, 'Abd al-Rahman Sidqi located the success of European fascist movements in the creation of modern mass society and the innate characteristics of the masses that formed its largest social element. Because of the enormous number of people involved, the masses in modern societies were, by their very nature, a politically immature and submissive herd. "The masses are like infants," the title of Sidqi's essay proclaimed. Blindly following their baser instincts, the masses worship strength and are enthralled by shows of heroism. Emotional rather than rational in their approach to social affairs, they lack a critical sense and could easily be aroused by demagogues and propagandists "who know how to appeal to them in the language they understand." Dominated by "a spirit of concern and fear," in times of crisis they tended to submit and to follow. Thus both "the success of fascism in Italy" and "its facile acceptance in Germany" had been made possible by the infantile nature of the masses. Mussolini had appeared to Italians as a decisive leader who demonstrated fearlessness in imposing his will upon the nation; for his part, Hitler, in his *Mein Kampf,* had displayed an acute awareness of the herdlike nature of the German masses, and thereafter had skillfully employed simple language and platitudes to win their submission to his leadership. Sidqi warned that, given the fertile soil afforded by modern mass society, there was the constant danger of the growth of totalitarian dictatorship.[14]

Ibrahim al-Misri similarly believed that the modern masses "pay no heed to culture or rational thought." What appealed to the masses was the mass culture of amusement and entertainment, a culture of "imaginings and foolishness that confuse the mind and are of no benefit." Contemptuous of the higher culture of their societies, the masses ignored the writings of the educated elite. The intellectual production of higher culture in mass society remained the province of an isolated group of intellectuals; it did

not reach the masses or influence them. This deplorable situation characterized not only European societies, but contemporary Egypt as well. Again,
modern mass society was seen as offering fertile soil for the irrational, for
the demagogue, and thus for fascism.[15]

In their discussions of the rise of fascism in Europe, Egyptian intellectuals did not ignore the temporal context in which the fascist surge was
occurring. Most immediately, Fascism was seen as a product of the enormous shock of World War I and its aftermath. For Muhammad Husayn
Haykal, contemporary dictatorship was a phenomenon specific to the
"weak nations" that had emerged defeated and broken from the catastrophe of the Great War. Citing Italy, Germany, and the Soviet Union as his
examples, Haykal saw Fascism, Nazism, and Communism as temporarily
fulfilling a positive function, providing a way of overcoming the structural and psychological disruption produced by the war. For such states,
dictatorial regimes were providing the competence and dynamism necessary to carry out economic and social rehabilitation as well as to restore
national self-respect and pride. In contrast, the "strong nations" such as
Great Britain and France that had emerged victorious from the war had
been able to maintain strong and healthy democratic governments with
strong and functioning political systems capable of insuring stability.
While his sympathy clearly lay with such "strong nations" and their functioning parliamentary systems that he believed Egypt should emulate,
Haykal nonetheless saw dictatorship as temporarily suitable for "weak nations" that had developed along a more troubled historical trajectory.[16]

For Niqula al-Haddad, the rise of Fascism in Italy and Nazism in
Germany was not accidental or arbitrary. In both countries, dictatorship
was popular since it was viewed as the only way to rescue each from a
profound state of crisis. However, like Haykal, Haddad viewed contemporary dictatorship as temporary, a transitional state existing in unique
conditions and as such one that would eventually give way to modern
democracy. Nor was dictatorship the only possible antidote to structural
crisis. For Haddad, the democracy of the United States served as antithetical and preferable model to the dictatorship of Nazi Germany. In the
United States, despite severe economic crisis, the American nation was
recovering through democratic means. In this well-established democracy, there had proved to be "no need of even a shred of dictatorship" to
resolve acute crisis. The American model was the one that should be emulated by Egypt.[17]

In a 1938 essay, 'Abd al-Rahman Sidqi expounded on the subject of the temporal causes of dictatorship in a pessimistic tone. For Sidqi, the state of economic dislocation, cultural disorientation, and psychological shock that afflicted European countries in the wake of the Great War had created "an agonizing atmosphere of crisis." Parliamentary democracy, while an adequate form of governance in calmer times, had proved itself incapable of managing the postwar crisis. Too often, parliamentary parties and their representatives in elected parliamentary assemblies had proved helpless in extricating their societies from economic distress and social angst. Moreover, many parliamentary institutions were marred by corruption, bickering, and opportunistic dedication to the advancement of partisan interests at the expense of the general good. Faith in liberal democracy had been shaken as much of the educated public had reached the conclusion that "parliaments are noisy, raucous institutions that have no practical benefit."[18]

This "crisis of parliamentarianism" in turn had led to a wider crisis, "the crisis of democracy." In those countries where democratic institutions had failed to meet the novel demands placed upon them, "the journey to one or another form of dictatorship took place." In such conditions, "the suffering people dreamt of great men" who promised a way out of crisis. The inability of democratic governments to cope with unprecedented structural crisis had opened the door for dictatorship. Even people who had previously opposed forms of despotism or autocracy now forgot the defects of authoritarian rule and, due to "the shock of the long, horrible war," hastened to embrace dictatorship as the answer to their problems. Dictatorship also had its appeal to specific economic groups who became supporters of dictatorship because they believed that authoritarian rule would safeguard their economic interests, assure stability, and prevent the rise of socialism or communism. What they got, however, was a form of dictatorship far more thoroughgoing than the autocracies of the past. Decentralized liberal democracy had given way to the absolute rule of a single dictator who concentrated all power and authority in his own hands "without any restrictions or limits." Desire for a redeemer had only paved the way for the terrible tyranny of an individual.[19]

Egyptian intellectuals also identified fear of communism as a crucial factor contributing to the rise of fascism. As an *al-Hilal* editorial of March 1939 put it with respect to Italian Fascism, "it is impossible to understand Fascism if we do not understand that this political, economic, and cultural school was merely a violent reaction to a pre-existing violent situation, or that it is a radical extremist force that arose to fight against a similar radical extremist force." The editorial saw "the Fascist revolution" of 1922 in Italy as a direct reaction to "the Communist revolution" of 1917 in Russia. Fascism rode on the wave of the "great fear" of Communism. The editorial analyzed Italy's postwar economic and social crisis, the hunger, unemployment, and despair that had prevailed throughout the country, as creating conditions apparently favorable to a Communist takeover. This situation in turn produced a reaction in the form of a desire for a strong leader who could insure that "Communism would not gain control" in Italy. Enter Mussolini and the Fascists, who adroitly exploited the fear of Communism as their springboard to power. Promising to serve as a barrier against Communism, Mussolini created an atmosphere of national emergency in which the liberal establishment and much of the country's political elite, even while disapproving of their violent methods, acquiesced in the Fascist rise to power. The result was Mussolini's "conquest of Rome" with the assistance of other nationalist forces and the cheers of the masses.[20]

In general terms, Egyptian intellectuals regarded Nazism as an outgrowth of many of the same historical processes as had occurred in Italy. The crisis of German society after World War I, the weaknesses of the Weimar government, hyperinflation and economic collapse, ideological disorientation alongside the rise of mass culture as well as mass politics, and the consequent yearning for a redeeming leader, were all processes parallel to those that had occurred in Italy and that had paved the way for the ascendancy of Italian Fascism. But analysts also identified unique social, cultural, and political features of the German context and the German historical tradition that in their view made it easier for a ruthless dictatorial regime like that of the Nazis to gain control of the country by the 1930s. Germany, they argued, had a distinctive authoritarian tradition of its own that prepared the way for the rise of Nazism. Moreover, Germany had an ideological tradition of racist anti-Semitism that helped explain the rise of the Nazi movement and gave the German variant of fascism a distinctive and virulent cast.[21]

In an essay published shortly after the start of the war, 'Ali Adham complemented his earlier analyses of the roots of Italian Fascism by elaborating on what he saw as basic features of German political culture that he felt contributed to the success of Nazism. One such tendency was the

German predisposition to "glorify and sanctify power," a trait which he regarded as an indelible component of the German national character. To that he added the German tendency to regard "the state as the supreme end." Each in his own way, Fichte, Hegel, and the "Iron Chancellor" Otto von Bismarck had provided the philosophical and practical rationale for the cult of the nation-state. The German Empire created by Bismarck in 1871 had been born in war, and from its inception had a militaristic orientation. Militarism was an organic component of the modern German state. This new state also fostered the ultranationalist, pan-German ideal of a greater Germany as well as the worldwide dominance of German culture. According to Adham, German leaders believed that "this culture will not achieve hegemony in the world merely by means of persuasion and propaganda. German victories in war have proven that force is the only means for achieving these aims." Since the late nineteenth century, this militant ideal had become anchored in the German national mentality, conditioning the nation for the acceptance and ascendancy of Nazism.[22]

Another fundamental German national trait, one intimately connected to the German fixation on power, was German insistence on order and discipline. As Adham saw it, Germans believed that "there can be no power without order or discipline; hence orderliness is in essence German!" This in turn led to the German bondage to the concepts of duty and obedience. Among Germans, "duty" had taken the place of "right" as a determinant of behavior. A parallel feature of German national character for Adham was the tendency to "despise emotion." Germans suppressed their natural feelings, particularly feelings of compassion, replacing emotion with a stern devotion to duty. It was this predisposition that led Germans to accept "totalitarian government [al-hukuma al-shamila]," and fed the militant mentality that led them to tolerate the use of "absolute force without any restrictions, the force of conquest and control, devoid of any emotion," thereby producing the aspiration to "organize the world" along German lines.[23]

Adham was convinced that the concept of "culture [al-thaqafa]," meaning "the effort to educate a person to be in harmony with humanity by educating and refining his feelings and uplifting his thoughts," had been totally destroyed in Nazi Germany. A leader in the development of global culture in the past, a nation that had given the world "heroes of philosophy and culture, pillars of thought and science, geniuses in art and music," Germany had now fallen into a state of cultural barbarism. Germany today was a nation whose concept of culture "has divested man of his humanity and denies him his respect and freedom, turning him into the submissive slave of what German philosophy calls the 'state.'" The goal of "this culture that is dependent on the state" was that "man should be an educated barbarian." For Adham, modern Germany was "the savage nation [al-umma al-jamiha] with uncontrolled, barbaric passions and evil intentions, a nation that knows only force and more force." Writing just after the war had begun, Adham predicted that Germany's drive for world domination was doomed to failure. Just as the ancient Assyrian state fell due to its "brutality and terror," so Nazi Germany will surely fall.[24]

Assessing Fascist Totalitarianism versus Liberal Democracy

Numerous contributors to *al-Hilal*, *al-Majalla al-Jadida*, *al-Risala*, and *al-Thaqafa* in the later 1930s addressed the respective merits of liberal democracy versus fascist authoritarianism. Overwhelmingly, their judgments came down on the side of democracy. While sometimes acknowledging the material achievements of Fascism in Italy and Nazism in Germany, their overall conclusion was that the economic and social successes of the two fascist regimes were far outweighed by the political despotism and cultural tyranny that characterized both systems.

A partial exception to this generalization was the position expressed by Salama Musa and his modernist journal *al-Majalla al-Jadida*. Musa's personal views of Fascism and Nazism stemmed from the fact that Musa was a socialist whose overriding concern was to promote socialist principles as the essential basis of Egypt's economic and social reconstruction. The process of modernization was clear to him: mechanization of agriculture, industrialization of the urban economy, rationalization of the economic and social systems on a scientific basis, a technological revolution in all spheres of life, and as an aid to the preceding the intensification of Egyptian contact with and the free flow of knowledge from the more advanced societies of Western Europe. In Musa's vision, an advanced and modernized Egypt would be directed by the new professional middle class of scientists, engineers, technicians, and managers. For Musa, the state was the central, sometimes the sole, agent of change, reform, and progress. He did not believe that a transformation on this scale could be realized without the massive involvement of the state in planning, investment, and coordination. It was the task of the state to build a modern economy operated by the professional class and to create a welfare society that would provide and operate a social security network that would care for the needs of all segments of the population.[25]

In order to establish the state as an effective agent of change and modernization, Musa for much of the 1930s was prepared to forego, to a certain extent, liberal values, civil liberties, and the right of free expression. In the context of the economic and social crisis of the 1930s from which Egypt, like many other countries of the world, was suffering, the classic liberalism of the eighteenth and nineteenth centuries seemed to him anachronistic. Musa was convinced that a modern society and economy could not be created in Egypt without the state assuming many powers and without its massive intervention in directing social and economic development. The regime of the future, he stated, would be a "socialist regime" led by a "government of specialists" which through the power of the state would reshape Egyptian life on a modern basis.[26]

Looking abroad, Musa initially found an attractive model for his étatist socialism, one suitable for the world crisis of the 1930s, in German National Socialism. Musa was particularly captivated by the apparent synthesis of nationalism and socialism in German "National Socialism [al-ishtirakiyya al-wataniyya]," the Nazi regime's ability to blend nationalism and socialism into one dynamic process creating both a national and a social revolution in Germany. The Nazi state was demonstrating in practice the constructive involvement of the state in the economy, the society, and culture. Nazi Germany was showing how it was possible, rapidly and effectively, to impose a socialist system in all spheres of life.[27]

Musa was enthused by what he saw happening in Germany in the mid-1930s. On the psychological level, the restoration of the nation's pride and self-respect, the mobilization of the population of Germany for the implementation of large national projects of revival, and the assignment of a key role to youth in the creation of a new Germany, were all impressive achievements.[28] Through accelerated industrialization, the elimination of unemployment, the increase in economic productivity, and the construction of a modern transport infrastructure, Hitler was leading the way to "absolute independence" in the economic sphere.[29] At the top of the list of successes of National Socialism was the rapid assimilation of science and technology by German industry, its manufacture of improved products ranging from modern appliances for home use to highly sophisticated weaponry. Rapid industrialization and the creation of an efficient bureaucracy under the Nazi regime meant jobs for the new class of professional specialists who in Musa's view were the natural leaders of a modern society. Thanks to this new elite of professionals, Germany was making rapid strides toward becoming a progressive socialist society. At the same time, Nazi industry was producing cheap goods and products for the masses and generating an overall rise in the standard of living for all Germans.[30] Musa also expressed admiration for the Nazi educational agenda that combined the expansion of elementary and secondary education with the spread of nationalist values among the masses. This new education was creating a generation of dedicated German youth prepared to enlist in the cause of national revival and to make sacrifices for the sake of the nation. Musa was envious of what he perceived as the enthusiasm of German youth, their readiness to obey their charismatic leader and to make every effort for the promotion of national aims.[31] As an example of the successful mobilization of youth, Musa praised the promotion of sport by the Nazis. Awareness of the importance of physical activity had increased greatly in Germany under the Nazis, with an improvement of both the physical and moral fitness of Germans due to the mass addiction to sport. Like other Egyptian commentators of the mid-1930s, Salama Musa and *al-Majalla al-Jadida* viewed the hosting of the 1936 Olympic Games in Berlin as proof of the existence of a new Germany, a muscular and optimistic Germany, that was taking shape as a result of the revolution inaugurated by National Socialism.[32]

In the mid-1930s, Salama Musa was not totally oblivious to the fact that the achievements of the Nazis had been attained at the price of dictatorship and repression on the part of the regime. His response to Nazi tyranny was not always coherent. Sometimes it contained internal contradictions. On the one hand, he argued that a social revolution on the scale of that undertaken by the Nazis could not be carried out without a strong centralized state directing the process.[33] On the other hand, he maintained that the invasiveness of the Nazi regime in the daily lives of the people of Germany was legitimate only in the crucial formative stage of social revolution; once a socialist society had been established and institutionalized, a more advanced stage should develop in which the state would relinquish its control over society and decentralize into a more pluralistic system regulated by a democratic parliamentary regime. From this perspective, Musa was able to praise the "democratic socialist" model such as Franklin D. Roosevelt's New Deal in the United States as a model for the socialist reorganization of society that was also worth emulation in Egypt.[34]

In general, Musa was far less enthusiastic about the desirability of copying the dictatorial features of the Nazi state in Egypt. He still regarded himself as belonging to the liberal democratic camp and a supporter of the constitutional parliamentary order in Egypt.[35] While often praising what he saw as the economic and social accomplishments of German National Socialism, he was also aware that a considerable part of the industrial and technological dynamism realized under the Nazis was being directed to military rearmament and the building of modern weapons of war. Even the civilian technological achievements of the regime were two-edged: "That same cheap car [the Volkswagen], manufactured to serve the German worker and farmer in peacetime, will serve the German state in wartime."[36]

Musa's views of fascism became less favorable over time. In two articles in *al-Majalla al-Jadida* of early 1938, he reconsidered the question of democratic versus authoritarian government in the changing context of the later 1930s. A March 1938 essay entitled "Germany after Five Years" presented an ambivalent assessment of the achievements and shortcomings of the National Socialist regime in Germany after a half-decade in power.[37] The essay was also a personal account-taking in which Musa, previously an enthusiast of Nazism, reevaluated the phenomenon in more sober terms.

Musa's views concerning the domestic economic and social policies of the Nazi regime remained largely positive in early 1938. In the economic sphere, he credited the Nazis with creating jobs for millions of previously unemployed Germans, with increasing the gross national product and raising the German standard of living, with promoting further industrialization of the economy, and with setting Germany on the path to economic independence. In the social sphere, Musa praised the improvement of the social and material position of German workers in what he termed the "Nazi welfare state." Beyond creating new jobs, the Nazis had guaranteed a fair salary to workers, had initiated new housing projects, and had installed social welfare programs to provide for the basic needs of weaker members of German society. Nazi concern for social well-being went beyond satisfying the material needs of the population: social welfare programs in Nazi Germany included state sponsorship of entertainment and holiday programs for the masses. In material terms, there was no doubt that the National Socialist regime had improved the lives of millions of Germans.[38]

Its material achievements, however, were only one side of the Nazi coin. The improvement of economic and social conditions in Germany under the Nazis had to be weighed against the regime's political authoritarianism. Here Musa's view was that the Nazis had destroyed the open civil society that had existed in Germany up to 1933. As state control of the economy and the society grew, "so are liberties diminished and increasingly limited." Freedom of the press was a thing of the past; teachers could no longer freely express their opinions in the classroom; public criticism of the regime was impossible in Nazi Germany. On balance, Musa's liberal inclinations led him to conclude that the political tyranny brought by Nazism outweighed its material successes: "if you treasure individual liberties and believe in the value of freedom—freedom of thought in literature, ethics, philosophy, and religion—then there is no doubt that you will hate this regime which supports economic efficiency over freedom, or in other words sacrifices the latter for the sake of realizing the former."[39]

In an essay of the following month on "The Problems of Egyptian Youth," Musa assessed the relevance of democratic versus authoritarian principles for Egypt itself. The essay was staunchly pro-democratic. For Egypt, a country currently debating its national identity and in the process of assimilating to and internalizing modernity, Musa was convinced that liberal democracy was the preferable form of government. His reasoning was functionalist, a reflection of his personal commitment to the modernization of Egyptian society. With its allowance for the participation of a wide variety of groups in national discourse, representative and parliamentary government was the way to include more and more of the population in national life and thereby to encourage the adoption of modern views and practices by broad sectors of society. Musa regarded liberalism as a synthesis of freedom and progress, a system of values that permitted political liberty at the same time as it fostered social reform. In his highly idealized overview, nineteenth-century European liberalism was presented as having insured civil liberties at the same time that it worked for economic improvement and social betterment. Liberals had "spread for the first time programs for social reform, and it is they that made education universal and available to all." Liberalism had worked in the name of the weak: for improving the subsistence of workers and the elderly, for unemployment protection and sick pay, for the enhancement of the power of labor through the establishment of labor unions, for health insurance for laborers. Liberal movements had also preached religious tolerance, the acceptance and advancement of science, and the development of new technologies. Much that was good in modernity stemmed from liberalism. Thus, instead of resorting to any anachronistic form of authoritarian government that would substantively be "no different from the tyranny of the Mamluks or the absolutism of Eastern rulers," what was needed was "spreading democratic education and imparting the principles of liberalism in Egypt."[40]

Rather than presenting authoritarian models as the necessary agent of social change and progress, as he had occasionally done in the past, Salama Musa now argued that a liberal order was the best path to modernity for Egypt. Only a liberal system of government could establish a modern welfare state that would improve the lives of all citizens without at the same time sacrificing political freedom. Egypt, he concluded, needed a democratic political system that would simultaneously work for the advancement of the weak, encourage initiative by the middle class, and limit the ability of the ruling class to constrain the freedom of others. Such an enlightened liberal regime would relieve social pressures and forestall social unrest or class war in Egypt. Only by improving the lives of Egyptians would Egyptian youth be prevented from turning to forms of political radicalism that would destroy individual freedom.[41]

By late 1938, Salama Musa was accepting a new conceptual framework, that of the totalitarian state, for understanding fascism as a political system. Now his heightened sensitivity to the repressive and tyrannical dimensions of Nazi rule led him to abandon, once and for all, his previous view of German National Socialism as a regime working toward the creation of a progressive socialist system. From this point onwards, the concept of totalitarianism served Salama Musa and *al-Majalla al-Jadida* as the key to decoding the essence of Nazism.

In an essay of December 1938, Musa contrasted the two fundamentally different types of government that had developed in the twentieth century: "the totalitarian state" and "the democratic state."[42] "The democratic state [*al-dawla al-dimuqratiyya*]" was a liberal political regime based on a lively civil society. What distinguished the democratic state was that it was limited in its scope and power, operating within the constraints imposed by a constitution and choosing its political leadership by means of free elections conducted in pluralist, multiparty competition. Great Britain, France, and the United States were contemporary representatives of the democratic state. In opposition to this form of government stood "the totalitarian state [al-dawla al-jamiʿa]" in which there was only one party and one leader, in which all pluralism was repressed by agencies of the state, and in which civil society was made subservient to party, leader, and state. Fascist Italy, Nazi Germany, and the Soviet Union were the leading contemporary examples of the totalitarian state.[43]

Musa identified the distinguishing feature of the totalitarian versus the democratic state as the degree of control each exercised over society. The totalitarian state was one in which an all-powerful centralizing regime concentrated in its own hands, in an unrestrained fashion, all political, economic, social, and cultural authority. Totalitarian regimes "centralize and endeavor to rule over everything and to pervade all matters. Governmental functions and roles are concentrated exclusively in the hands of the state. The individual is swallowed up by state mechanisms." Education, the print media, commercial and industrial enterprises, the multiple associations found in civil society: all were controlled by an omnipresent state whose agents "oversee every movement and action." In contrast to the totalitarian state, the democratic state "does not dominate [all aspects of life] and concentrate authority in the government. In a democratic country, the governing authority is found in the hands of the individual. The powers of the state are limited to the power and authority given to it by individuals." In the democratic state, citizens enjoyed "full and private lives" that were not controlled or interfered with by the state and its agents.[44]

Other contributors to *al-Majalla al-Jadida* shared Salama Musa's negative view of European fascism by the close of the 1930s. In an essay entitled "Democracy and Dictatorship,"[45] Rushdi Saʿid came down firmly in favor of the former. While acknowledging that democratic states had their limitations and flaws, Saʿid nonetheless felt that dictatorial regimes were far worse. After reviewing the historical development of democracy from ancient Greece to the modern era, Saʿid concluded that a democratic government that respected and insured the existence of a pluralist political culture was the natural political order for a complex modern societies with a diverse and sophisticated public opinion. Dictatorship, on the other hand, was a transitory phenomenon characteristic of societies in crisis. To those who argued that the current spread of authoritarian regimes indicated that democracy was failing, Saʿid responded that the human desire for freedom and liberty insured that "democracy will never fail."[46]

Cultural life in Nazi Germany served Saʿid as the prime example of the evils of dictatorship. Characterizing the Nazi regime as engaged in no less than "the destruction of German culture," Saʿid termed Hitler and the German minister of propaganda, Joseph Goebbels, as "the wardens of the prison of culture" whose policies had placed German literature, journalism, theater, music, and film in "an intellectual jail." The Nazis had turned culture into propaganda enlisted in the service of the state. This intellectual domination of the population was paralleled by the regime's physical domination of Germans. Whereas Goebbels was "the agent of intellectual terror," Hermann Göring was "the agent of physical terror" supervising the regime's use of imprisonment, deportation, and violence to intimidate Germans. Above these agencies of control and domination stood the cult of the Führer: "the nation's obedience and servitude to the Führer, the leader, is total, and the sanctity of his thoughts and ideas an absolute imperative for the nation."[47]

Commentaries on the respective merits of fascism versus democracy in *al-Hilal* and *al-Risala* in the later 1930s were more consistently negative about all forms of fascism. Different intellectuals focused their criticism of different aspects of Fascism and Nazism. The political methods demonstrated by Nazism in particular drew vehement criticism from ʿAli Adham. Employing the term "Machiavellianism [*al-makyafiliyya*]" to characterize Nazi methodology, Adham may have ascribed more ideas and themes to Niccolo Machiavelli and his political treatise *The Prince* than they in actuality possessed; but there is no question that he meant the term as one of utter condemnation. By "Machiavellianism," Adham meant a new style of politics based on manipulation, a cynical disregard for the truth, and extreme opportunism, a politics in which naked power reigned supreme. All methods were legitimate in Machiavellianism, including the use of force, for the sake of achieving the chauvinistic Nazi aims that were totally dismissive of liberal and universal values. According to Adham, the original Machiavellianism of *The Prince*, transmitted and refined through Hegel's cult of the state, Nietzsche's Superman, and Bismarck's realpolitik, had reached its monstrous twentieth-century apogee in Nazism and Hitler. Nazi Machiavellianism was the politics of "the worship and glorification of the state," of "the triumph of absolute dictatorial rule," that if unchallenged threatened to "shatter civilization and turn it into a heap of debris."

Writing in 1936, Adham called on the forces of democracy to defend human culture against this destructive Machiavellianism. The survival of civilization itself demanded the restoration of humanitarian values, the consolidation of democracy, the fostering of mutual understanding among peoples, and the total rejection of "coarse, violent Machiavellianism."[48]

Fascist control over cultural life and its accompanying persecution of intellectuals was a particular item of concern to intellectuals writing for both journals. In an essay in *al-Hilal* in 1937, Ibrahim al-Misri lamented the obliteration of personal freedom and the suppression of expression under dictatorial regimes. In the contemporary fascist states, every critical voice or oppositional movement had been silenced by the brutal steamroller of tyranny. Intellectuals lost their raison d'être in dictatorships; in Italy and Germany intellectuals, the bearers of free thought and scientific truth, had either been viciously persecuted and expelled, or assimilated by the sinister mechanism of the state and forced to serve it against their will. The intellectual elite in such countries had become, like the population as a whole, a herd living in a "huge military camp" at the disposal of Duce or Führer.[49]

An editorial in *al-Hilal* in late 1938 was devoted to what it termed "the tragedies of freedom in the modern age." The editorial lamented the persecution and expulsion of liberal intellectuals occurring in Nazi Germany, Fascist Italy, and Franco's Spain, how in all three countries liberal spokesmen had been "compelled to escape to freedom in exile." Nazi Germany was depicted as the most ruthless oppressor of intellectuals, a land where there was no longer any space for independent intellectual life. Such persecution was occurring regardless of religious affiliation: the "deported" and the "escapees" included non-Jewish as well as Jewish scientists, writers, artists, musicians. Albert Einstein, Emile Ludwig, Thomas and Heinrich Mann, and hundreds of other intellectual luminaries had been forced to flee "from the regime that despises the voice of opposition and persecutes freedom of thought," not only "in the political sphere but also in all the spheres of cultural creation, in literature, history, art, and philosophy." While pointing out the distressed circumstances as well as the alienation for their homeland that such exiles were suffering, the editorial praised their heroism for choosing to preserve the spark of intellectual creativity in exile.[50]

Al-Risala was equally condemnatory of the cultural policies of the Nazi regime. As a cultural forum dependent upon freedom of expression,

it was natural for the journal to take a stand against what one of its contributors, Muhammad ʿAbdalla ʿInan, as early as 1935 was characterizing
as the "totalitarian tyranny [*al-tughyan al-shamil*]" inherent in fascism.[51]
Thus an editorial of the same year denounced what it termed "the persecution of the German press in the shadow of the Hitlerian terror."[52] An
earlier essay by ʿInan similarly had lamented that Nazism "has killed the
German press." Free discourse in Germany's splendid press had posed a
threat to the consolidation of Nazi power; accordingly, the regime had
concentrated the dissemination of information in its own hands. By suppressing the free press through closing some outlets, co-opting or nation-
alizing others, and exiling dissident journalists, Hitler asserted absolute
control of the public sphere, eliminated every critical voice, and imposed
the truth of the regime as the only truth. In ʿInan's view, the extermination of the free press and its replacement by a compliant "Nazi press" was
a tragedy. Through it, Hitler was demonstrating a level of coercion and
violence "stronger and more frightening than that of the Fascist or Bolshevik dictatorships."[53]

Denunciations of Nazi cultural policies continued to appear in *al-
Risala* throughout the 1930s. As an editorial of mid-1939 put it, "Nazism
by its very nature is contradictory to freedom of expression and freedom
of opinion; it is based on the rule of force." Although the mendacious
propaganda of the Nazis proclaimed that the regime had succeeded in
"removing sin and liberating the human conscience," in reality "this dictatorship debases the value of man." By effacing the autonomy of the individual and sacrificing the individual on the altar of the state, Nazi policies
were destroying the human conscience.[54]

Commentators writing in *al-Risala* were particularly attuned to the
pernicious power of propaganda in the modern world. The journal repeatedly expressed criticism of the state monopoly over the production and
dissemination of culture under fascist regimes. The prime example was
the role and power of Joseph Goebbels within the Nazi regime. The very
terms used for the man and his office, "minister of propaganda [*wazir al-
diʿaya*]" and "Ministry of Propaganda [*wizarat al-diʿaya*]" carried negative
connotations. Goebbels had turned German culture into a military culture, turning artists into soldiers obliged to think, act, and create in ac-
cordance with directives issues by the Ministry of Propaganda. All creative work in Germany was now meant to serve the state and the Nazi
dictatorship. Artists had lost their independence and freedom to create

autonomous artistic creations; their sole purpose was to satisfy the cultural needs of the state and its propaganda apparatus.[55]

Subsequent commentaries on the issue of intellectual freedom in *al-Risala* emphasized that, in a world in which "ninety percent of our knowledge comes from the written word," from what we absorb "with our eyes," the totalitarian state's takeover of all means of producing and distributing printed information was both unprecedented and dangerous. The introduction of radio and the dissemination of information "through the ears" only exacerbated the domination of culture by the state, since the new medium was even more susceptible to state control.[56] Democratic regimes decentralized the distribution of information by placing the same in many hands. In contrast, dictatorships had "with force and barbarism [*bi quwwa wa wahshiyya*]" harnessed all print and broadcast means of communication and employed them to "spread propaganda among the masses."[57] Goebbels's Ministry of Propaganda, through its control over "no less than three hundred newspapers" throughout all of Germany and the countries it had recently annexed, and through "an army of journalists" spread across the entire world, now "solely and totally controls all the means of propaganda and communication." The German government now exercised strict censorship over every word printed or broadcast in Germany. In addition to the media, the Nazi dictatorship controls all levels of education in the Third Reich, shaping educational values and supervising how they are imparted to the younger generation of Germans. The regime's absolute control over all sources of information and knowledge subjugated mass society to the demagogic propaganda of the fascist state.[58]

The revulsion of Egyptian intellectuals against fascist cultural totalitarianism was eloquently captured in a Taha Husayn essay of early 1937. In it, Husayn postulated the existence of a cultural distinction between "the Fascist culture [*al-adab al-fashi*]" and "the Communist culture [*al-adab al-shuyu'i*]" of contemporary dictatorships such as Italy, Germany, and the Soviet Union, and "the democratic culture [*al-adab al-dimuqrati*]" of the Western parliamentary democracies. Under the repressive totalitarian regimes characterized by fascist culture, writers and artists were forced to create for the sake of national aims "outside of themselves" that were determined and defined by the totalitarian state. The creative personality of the artist or writer withdrew inward when faced with "the power of the sole leader, the superman," who through suppression and terror imposed his own artistic doctrine and demands. Under such regimes, the creative spirit had only two options: either exile from his homeland, or subjugation of his creative intellect in the service of the official propaganda and demagogy of the state. Husayn lashed out at contemporary dictatorships for their persecution and subjugation of intellectuals and the resultant annihilation of free creative expression. In Nazi Germany and Fascist Italy, he stated, "people think and create the way that Hitler and Mussolini direct them to think and create." Totalitarian regimes erased the individuality of intellectuals. "They live like a society of insects. They must behave like ants in an anthill or like bees in a hive."[59]

Husayn's thesis was clear: only under democracy was there the possibility of giving full creative expression to the human spirit. Only in democracies, where the freedom of the individual was a supreme value and where the individual was able to express their personalities with no dictation from the outside, could culture, literature, and art develop and flourish. Democracy was the only system that created a balance between individual and society, between the needs of the individual and the needs of the collective. It was only in a "democratic environment [al-bi'a al-dimuqratiyya]" that the human spirit could achieve authentic philosophical, scientific, or artistic creativity.[60]

The differential position of women under democratic and totalitarian regimes was an additional point of contrast in favor of democracy. In his December 1938 comparison of the totalitarian to the democratic state, Salama Musa used the position of women as an example of the gulf between the two types of states. The totalitarian state's rejection of individual liberty was demonstrated in its treatment of women. The Nazi government in Germany was a male chauvinist regime that suppressed and marginalized women by limiting their entry into the bureaucracy and the state apparatus. Musa again contrasted this to the United States: "the woman in the United States is a completely free person; she can become a university professor, a priest in the church, or an elected representative in the parliament."[61]

A 1939 commentary in al-Risala similarly criticized the status of "Women in the Shadow of Dictatorship."[62] Like Musa in al-Majalla al-Jadida, al-Risala presented the position of women under fascist regimes as a faithful representation of the masculine nature of fascism. Since Fascism and Nazism are "based on physical force, then the status of women is always secondary, under the influence of the man who goes to or returns from war and the killing fields." Women in Fascist Italy had but one function, "to be a tool to produce the man and to serve him in time of war." The journal cited Mussolini to the effect that "if I permitted women to enter the arena of elections the world would laugh at me," and claimed that in the legal sphere Fascist legislation discriminated against women. The situation of women under the Nazis was equally humiliating. "The Nazi regime treats women's rights harshly and abuses them. The German woman is like her Italian sister in her position, subject to the rule of tyranny." Draconian regulations discriminated against women and perpetuated male supremacy. In Nazi Germany, "first and foremost the place of women was in the home." The journal cited a variety of disadvantages imposed on women under the Nazi regime, including their marginalization in government service and holding public office. Educational opportunities for women were also being reduced in Germany, with restrictive quotas for women's enrollment in universities. When women did enter the public sphere, it was predominately in menial service positions. As *al-Risala* saw it, the status of women under fascism was reverting to one comparable to what had obtained in the Middle Ages.[63]

One of the fullest evaluations of the respective merits of authoritarianism versus democracy came from the pen of ʿAbd al-Razzaq al-Sanhuri. Sanhuri was one of Egypt's most distinguished jurists. French-trained, briefly dean of the Egyptian University School of Law, a judge on the Mixed Courts, and one of the founders of the Saʿdist Party, in early 1938, Sanhuri contributed two essays to *al-Hilal* considering how best to give "expression to the opinion of the nation."[64] The question he addressed is directly relevant to our analysis since one of the claims of fascist movements and regimes was that democracy had failed to give due expression to the will of the nation, and that for its part authoritarian rule could do so. Sanhuri was indeed relating to a major question of the day which, beyond being at issue in Europe, also touched directly upon Egypt's form of government. Sanhuri was implicitly offering a liberal rebuttal to those Egyptian voices that in the late 1930s were criticizing Egypt's parliamentary system as hopelessly cumbersome, that were denouncing the existing political parties as mired in self-serving factionalism, and that were maintaining that the will and the interests of the Egyptian people could best be met through the authoritarian leadership of a virtuous ruler such as young King Faruq.

Like other Egyptian intellectuals, Sanhuri was well aware of the current worldwide crisis of democracy in which extremist movements such as fascism and communism were "replacing democratic regimes with dictatorial regimes." Sanhuri rejected as unfounded the presumption of those who maintained that authoritarian rule was better suited than democratic government for representing "the opinion of the nation." Fascism's use of ostensibly democratic procedures and institutions such as constitutions, parliaments, and elections was mendacious, he asserted, a smokescreen masking a new tyranny of the most rigid and totalist variety. "Fascist dictatorship is based on the rule of a strong individual controlling all affairs," Sanhuri emphasized. Fascism brooked no pluralism, dissent, or opposition; "whether it be honest and capable or corrupt and dishonest, is not capable of existing other than by suppressing the voice of the opposition and demolishing it." What distinguished democracy was that "it is reconciled to the existence of oppositional entities that are entitled to criticism." In turn, it was this pluralism in democracies, the existence of multiple political parties and their competition in elections, that insured that the opinion of the nation would be expressed and become a determining influence in affairs of state. Fascism's claim to represent the popular will was fallacious. In fascist dictatorships, the ruler determined the wishes of the nation without asking the people what their wishes were. In actuality, "fascist dictatorship has nullified the opinion of the nation." What fascist systems did represent was the view of the ruler who arbitrarily claimed, without justification, that he knew the will of the nation and represented it. For Sanhuri, "the democratic system is still the best, most appropriate system that the human race has even known."[65]

One Egyptian commentator found an historical precedent for Nazi totalitarianism in ancient Sparta. In an essay in *al-Hilal* of January 1939, Ibrahim al-Misri held that "the principle of the absolute rule of the state and the disintegration of the individual in it" was "a Spartan principle" that the Nazis had only revived. Misri analyzed at length what he saw as the Nazi parallels with the Spartans that had made Germany a similar "military authoritarian society."[66] Misri's critical analysis of the structure of the Nazi regime was comprehensive. It was ultimately based on force, all oppositional voices silenced through state harassment, imprisonment, or death. National or religious minorities had no living space in Nazi Germany; their fate was "expulsion and exile." Germany was ruled by a totalitarian system in which "the state supervises and controls everything, big and small, in economic, social, intellectual, and cultural life, as well as everything in the life of the individual." The totalitarian power of the state was based on its police and military forces, and was reinforced by state efforts to instill a militaristic spirit in society and culture. All sons and daughters of the German nation were regarded as soldiers subjected to the discipline of the state and to the service of its objectives. Women were devalued and suppressed by the dictatorial Nazi state just as they had been in the dictatorship of Sparta. The cult of masculinity and the worship of masculine heroism marginalized women in Nazi Germany; their role and destiny were merely "to give birth in order to provide the maximum number of healthy men" for the state. Just as in Sparta, where "the nation became a military barracks, the people as a whole became an army," so "in the new dictatorial countries, all efforts and forces are mobilized to turn the nation into a military barracks and the zealous, intoxicated people, who are addicted to the charms of demagogy, into an army." Overall, the Nazi totalitarian state was an updating of ancient Sparta.[67]

This catalog of evils notwithstanding, Misri ended his essay on a positive note. The story of Sparta had come to a bitter ending, one of failure and defeat. "What has remained of that Sparta," Misri rhetorically asked his readers; "what benefit did the world receive from the culture of Sparta?" His answer was a curt one: "Nothing!" In contrast to its rival Athens, which represented the values of enlightenment and democracy, Sparta represented "neither science nor art," but only "an experiment in the rule of warriors based on force and force alone." Athens left posterity the ideals of hostility to war and led man to aspire to "the triumph of justice and to offer help and succor to the weak." Contrast the Spartan legacy: "all we learned from it was a distorted, negative sort of heroism, contrary to logic and reason, a heroism that idolizes human pain and death, a heroism that fills with pride and flourishes when it spreads the horrors of hunger, suffering, and death!" Just as Sparta failed and disappeared without leaving positive traces, so the Nazi totalitarianism would fail and pass into oblivion.[68]

Egyptian intellectuals were sensitive to the differences between Italian Fascism and German Nazism. A 1939 *al-Risala* essay by Muhammad Lutfi Jumʿa offered an analysis of the differences between Fascism and Nazism. In Jumʿa's opinion, Nazism "is not an imitation of Fascism nor is it a type of fascism." Although the Nazi regime in Germany, like that of the Fascists in Italy, had emerged in alliance with the industrial and financial bourgeoisie, and was putting an enormous effort into internal social reform as a counter to the threat of communism, they differed greatly in their ultimate objectives. Nazism in Germany was unlike Fascism in Italy. In the latter, a state that had emerged a victor in World War I but faced a postwar internal crisis, the dominant issues propelling Fascism were domestic. In contrast, Nazism in Germany was externally oriented. The primary Nazi agenda was one of "defending the homeland against foreign external enemies and redeeming it from the restrictions of the Versailles agreement." The overriding goal of Nazi foreign policy was the realization of German international hegemony in Europe. The main aim of "Hitlerian Nazism [al-naziyya al-hitlariyya," a reoccurring term in Egyptian discourse] was "a greater Germany and the glorification of the Third Reich."[69]

Their differences of external orientation notwithstanding, Jumʿa perceived great similarities in their internal orientation. Here his critique paralleled that of other intellectuals in its emphasis on the assault on individualism under Fascism and Nazism. Jumʿa saw both regimes as being devoted to the creation and maintenance of tyrannical dictatorships that were unprecedented in their power and oppressiveness. Both regimes have "swallowed up the rights of the individual and made the state the supreme goal, even if this means discriminating against the individual and sacrificing him on its altar." In the Nazi dictatorship in particular, the will of both individuals and groups were "subordinated the will of the leader, and their personalities merged with the personality of the leader who embodies the common will." While Nazism was not a carbon copy of Fascism, nonetheless both movements had created a totalitarian police state of an entirely new type devoted to crushing the individual and subordinating him to the regime.[70]

Assessments of Italian Fascism and the Fascist state were as negative as those of German Nazism. When al-Hilal's March 1939 editorial reviewing the rise of Fascism in Italy moved on to discuss the Fascist Party in power, it presented the Fascist regime as a totalitarian one that had destroyed Italian democracy:

The Fascist movement is in essence a movement that calls for the destruction of the parliamentary order and the democratic principles which gained ascendancy over the European mentality in the nineteenth century. It is a movement for the total concentration of all authority and power in the hands of the state, for the elimination of the freedom of the individual and for assimilating him into the state, and for placing all powers of implementation in the hands of the leader of the state. That is what has actually happened in Italy.[71]

A subsequent *al-Hilal* editorial of May 1939, dealing with the operation of the Fascist Grand Council, presented a close critique of the relationship between party and state under Fascism.[72] The editorial highlighted the differences between the position of the Fascist Party in Italy and that of political parties in democratic regimes. In today's Italy, the Fascist Party was "a unique institution . . . similar in fact to a church comprised of masses of believers who are totally, blindly submissive to its head, namely to Mussolini." The Fascist Party resembled a religious organization in that its principles were similar to religious articles of faith that took precedence over and above the wishes of the individual. The Fascist regime required "total obedience to the Duce, obedience that precludes any argument or dissent," from its subjects. The Party "creates for all citizens one religious dogma and one faith, shared by all."[73]

This detailed presentation of the character of the Fascist regime had a clear didactic goal: to prove that Fascism had created a new form of dictatorship possessing an extraordinary power of oppression of the individual. The chief sin of this totalitarian state was "the annihilation of the individual" to a degree unprecedented in past history. *Al-Hilal*'s litany of the evil characteristics of the Italian regime—"the blind obedience, the oppressive rule, the personality cult of the leader, the absolute denial of freedom of thought, and the sacrifice of all of the individual's rights and wishes in order to bolster the greatness of the collective and to enhance its influence, authority, and control"—focused particularly on the individual's loss of autonomy under Fascism. In Fascist Italy, the individual no longer had any substance:

the individual sacrifices his freedom, namely, his right to think as he wishes; he gives up his ability to express his thoughts and to criticize the government. His right to manage his own affairs . . . He sacrifices everything for the sake of the interests of the state that transcend any other interest. The individual is meant to have complete religious faith in the state and to believe that the leader at its head is infallible, free of any defect or error, just as the Catholic believes in the Church and the Pope who both care for him and govern him.[74]

When compared to totalitarian Fascism, *al-Hilal* had no doubt that democracy as it existed in "the two democratic states, France and England," was a preferable form of government. The advantage of democracy rested both in the fact that it restricted the power of the state by decentralizing authority among various autonomous agencies, and in the fact

that it gave priority to the individual over the state. Democratic governments respected the rights of the individual, honored ideological and political pluralism, allowed freedom of thought and expression, and maintained a heterogeneous political arena in which various parties representing
diverse sectors and perspectives could operate. Observing how the French
and British democracies reacted to danger and crisis, *al-Hilal* concluded
that they had learned to cope with stress through a prudent process of
self-examination and self-reform by their representative parliamentary
institutions. This insured that democratic states undertook reformist measures only after obtaining broad public consent and support. When a
democratic system had to enhance the powers of the state apparatus in
order to address a danger or crisis, it did so only on a temporary basis, with
a clear commitment that emergency measures "would disappear when the
danger passed and that the country would return to its previous form of
government." Democratic systems, if properly conducted, offered overwhelming proof that economic, political, or cultural crises, no matter how
severe, did not require dictatorship for satisfactory resolution. National
crisis was thus no reason to "invite an omnipotent redeemer" who would
assume all political authority. *Al-Hilal* was convinced that democratic
systems possessed effective means for coping with danger and crisis, and
moreover with doing so while simultaneously safeguarding stability and
insuring the rights of the individual would not be negated by the state.[75]

A periodic feature in *al-Hilal* was the journal's symposia, in which
the editors posed a question to several prominent Egyptians and published their views on the issue. It was a mark of the degree to which ideas
of authoritarianism versus democracy were under debate in Egypt at the
close of the 1930s that the journal's symposium of February 1939, the time
when Palace initiatives aimed at enhancing the authority of the Egyptian
monarchy were under intense public discussion, dealt with the question
"Will Dictatorship Succeed Among Us?"[76] The precise question posed to
the interviewees—"Would enlightened dictatorship [*al-diktaturiyya al-
'adila*] be better for the Arab nations and constitute a guarantee of their
happiness, or is genuine democracy [*al-dimuqratiyya al-sahiha*] more beneficial and more enduring?"—is significant in its implication that some
forms of authoritarian rule might be preferable to democracy. The views
of three leading figures on the Egyptian cultural scene—Ahmad Lutfi al-
Sayyid, rector of the Egyptian University; 'Abbas Mahmud al-'Aqqad, poet,
critic, and currently a Sa'dist Deputy in Parliament; and 'Abd al-Hamid

Sa'id, veteran Islamic activist, president of the Young Men's Muslim Association, and a member of Parliament for the Nationalist Party—were solicited. Their varying responses indicate that, while antipathy to totalitarian dictatorship on the Fascist or Nazi model was the rule, some voices were open to the possibility of presumably progressive forms of authoritarianism for the Arab East.

When Lutfi al-Sayyid, the doyen of Egyptian liberalism in the early decades of the twentieth century, addressed the possibility of an "enlightened dictator" emerging in the Arab world, he saw no possibility that any progressive form of authoritarianism "would succeed or be of benefit in Egypt or in the nations of the Arab East." In his view, "an enlightened dictator" could only emerge in a stable, mature, and well-established society, rather than in the developing countries of the Arab world that were still suffering from backwardness, internal social divisions, and political instability. In more general terms, Lutfi expressed the view that "democracy, despite all of its flaws, is better than and preferable to dictatorship." Limited in scope and respectful of individual rights, democracy was "the least harmful of all forms of government." Lutfi foresaw a democratic future for Egypt and the Arab world, calling on Egyptians and Arabs elsewhere to correct the present flaws in their parliamentary systems "so that they can enjoy genuine democracy," which in his view was the only path to modernity as well as economic and cultural well-being.[77]

'Abbas Mahmud al-'Aqqad was totally dismissive of the possible utility of any authoritarian form of government for Egypt or the Arab world. The distinction between "enlightened" and other forms of dictatorship was not a meaningful one for 'Aqqad. Dictatorship was dictatorship, wherever and whenever it existed. Citing postwar Germany and Russia as clear examples of the destructive power of despotic governments, 'Aqqad maintained that dictatorial regimes had brought only destruction and ruin to the peoples they ruled. Dictatorship was a temporary and unnatural political system for human societies in general and for modern ones in particular. Democracy was the form of government best suited for the modern age and for facing the challenges of modernity. Dictatorship represented backwardness and the past, and as such constituted a challenge to human progress. It was an aberration even in the West: "dictatorship will not succeed and endure in Western countries and in my view will be decisively defeated in the near future." Turning to Egypt and the Arab world, 'Aqqad asserted that, if the Arab world wished to progress and to enter the modern age, it had no choice but to opt for democracy over dictatorship. This was indeed the trajectory he saw currently under way: "every step in our development attempts and hopes to bring us closer to democracy, and distances us from dictatorship." 'Aqqad summed up his pro-democratic stance with the declaration that "dictatorship would not work in our Eastern [Arab] countries unless there was a need for it; but until today we see the reality that the fulfillment of the needs of these countries can by ensured only by democratic governments existing in them."[78]

More conservative than either Lutfi al-Sayyid or 'Aqqad and a vehement opponent of Western imperialism, 'Abd al-Hamid Sa'id situated his contribution to the symposium in the context of both the Arab and Muslim struggle for emancipation from colonialism and their efforts to realize progress and modernity. This twofold agenda required "competent individuals and institutions to conduct these efforts and to achieve fruitful results as quickly as possible and with the fewest procedures." Sa'id was willing to entertain the possibility that a "benevolent authoritarian ruler" would best facilitate "the revival of the East." His response did not go into specifics on how enlightened authoritarian rule would be implemented in Egypt or the Arab world. What mattered for him were results rather than form: "I am not preaching for dictatorship, but am calling for revival by means of any type of political regime that will succeed in bringing it about."[79]

A month later, the poet 'Abd al-Rahman Shukri supplemented the symposium with an essay bearing the same title. Shukri argued the viability of democracy was conditional on particular circumstances and experiences and that, in special circumstances in the life of a nation, dictatorship was indeed an appropriate form of government. Unlike 'Aqqad, Shukri did not regard dictatorship as an aberration from modernity. While rejecting the Fascist and Nazi forms of totalitarian dictatorship, Shukri did not dismiss all possible forms of authoritarian rule. In his view, a moderate, temperate authoritarianism, what he termed a "people's dictatorship [*diktaturiyya sha'biyya*]" based on popular consent and accepted by the people, could be of benefit to the nation. In certain unique circumstances, an authoritarian ruler could advance a nation's progress and modernization. Shukri cited Egypt's own Muhammad 'Ali, the man who "created modern Egypt," as an example of beneficial authoritarian rule. As a contemporary example, he mentioned Turkey under Ataturk, "although it would not be correct to draw from it the general conclusion that every nation would benefit from a dictatorial regime such as Turkey has." But in most historical circumstances, where there was no political, economic, or social need for authoritarian leadership, then democracy was preferable. Addressing the current state of Egypt and the Arab world from this perspective, Shukri saw no "historical necessity" for dictatorship at the present time.[80]

The qualified acceptance of the possibility of a beneficial form of authoritarian rule emerging in the Arab world was a minority position among Egyptian intellectuals by 1939. Although residual admiration for the perceived internal achievements of fascist regimes continued to be voiced by some, opposition to the untrammeled despotism that characterized fascism was the dominant note in Egyptian commentaries. Thus Ahmad Hasan al-Zayyat of *al-Risala* in May 1939, even after expressing a measure of admiration for Hitler's success in achieving many of the goals of the Nazi movement, rejected Hitler and Nazism as a potential model for Egypt. Zayyat offered a largely positive overview of what he saw as Hitler's achievements. Domestically, Hitler had brought stability to Germany, enabling the country to overcome the economic privation and psychological humiliation of the postwar era, and had done so "in the course of only six and a half years." On the foreign scene, Hitler had overturned the terms of the postwar Versailles settlement and brought Germany further international advances, including the annexation of first Austria and then Czechoslovakia, and all this "without a revolution and without a war."[81] But, when Zayyat turned to consider the question of whether a thoroughgoing dictator such as Hitler was a possible model for Egypt, his answer was in the negative. "The leader we earnestly desire," Zayyat suggested, must "possess the ability to lead but not to control, to be ready to consult and not to rule arbitrarily, to be open to struggle and sacrifice but not to enslavement and egotism." More religiously oriented than many other Egyptian intellectuals, Zayyat also emphasized that in his view Islam served as a barrier to the adoption of fascism. "The man we want as a leader for us, and for every friendly nation in the East, cannot be a tyrant because he is a believer . . . , a Muslim, and the law of Islam is one of liberty for man and consultation [*shura*] in matters of governance." Certainly as personified by Hitler, the fascist model was unsuitable for Muslim lands.[82]

The antitotalitarian perspective that had come to characterize the outlook of Egyptian intellectuals was exemplified in two pieces published in *al-Hilal* in June 1939. In an essay analyzing the main "social schools" currently vying with each other for world ascendancy, ʿAbbas Mahmud al-ʿAqqad reiterated his unqualified endorsement of democracy over dictatorship and predicted that, in the long run, dictatorship was not a viable alternative to democracy whether in the Middle East or elsewhere. Posing the question for his readers of which of the two polar systems would survive the seemingly inevitable clash between them, ʿAqqad saw no future for dictatorship which "by its very nature is a temporary phenomenon." Individual dictators did not live forever and, since a dictator does not easily give way to another dictator, there was "no continuity" in dictatorship. More importantly, no nation would agree for long to an absolute dictatorship in which the individual was ignored. Nations could not be held captive by the rousing demagogy of the dictator forever; people would not indefinitely "sacrifice and suffer hardships for the sake of a goal that the dictatorship wishes to achieve and for which it channels all hopes and aspirations." Regardless of its success or failure, dictatorship did not have a long shelf life.[83]

ʿAqqad believed that only democracy would survive the coming world conflict. Unlike dictatorship, democracy offered "continuity, stability, and permanence." The flaws of democracy were "human flaws," problems in the management of democratic institutions and hence correctible, rather than the "inherent flaws" that characterized dictatorship. Democracy was always open to reform and revival. Unlike infallible dictatorship, which by its very nature could not admit to error, democracy knew how to admit and to rectify its shortcomings. It was the only system that could cope successfully with tensions between classes, with economic and social crisis, and which offered solutions from which all members of the nation would benefit. ʿAqqad concluded by stating that "our clear preference is that in the future democracy will exist among all peoples on the globe." "Human reason," he summed up, "can imagine the survival of democracy after dictatorship and communism, but it is incapable of imagining the survival of dictatorship or communism after democracy." For ʿAbbas Mahmud al-ʿAqqad, the triumph of democracy was assured as long as human reason prevailed.[84]

Niqula al-Haddad similarly saw fascist dictatorships as regimes that had totally destroyed freedom of expression and individual liberty and had violently repressed civil society. Speaking specifically of today's Germany, under its "Nazi military regime," the individual was regarded as akin to "a soldier in wartime . . . who stands ready to totally obey the Führer." In Nazi Germany, the individual had been deprived of all civil rights: "he has absolutely no freedom of work, or freedom of expression or thought. He is a tool in the factory of the Third Reich, namely an instrument in the idolatrous worship of the Hitlerian government, who acts and works, against his own will, in everything the controlling government imposes upon him." In the police state that was the Third Reich, the individual had been enslaved, all his movements and actions under surveillance. The Nazi regime "maintains terrible pressure on personal freedom . . . pressure that has reached a level unprecedented anywhere else or at any other time."[85]

For Haddad as for ʿAqqad, dictatorship was no substitute for democracy. Whereas dictatorial regimes "have turned the life of the nation into the means and governance into the goal, namely that the nation exists in order to serve the government," in contrast "the democratic system makes the government into a means for the sake of the nation and its life, and made the well-being of the nation its goal, namely that the government exists to serve the nation." Democracy was the only form of government that protected the rights of the individual, possessing mechanisms that limited governmental control over the individual and hence insured his freedom and autonomy. Writing in mid-1939, Haddad predicted that "the dictatorial regime will not last for long." He likened dictatorship to "a sudden, passing fever," a temporary illness of which society would eventually cure itself, then returning to democracy and to liberal political culture.[86]

Critiquing Nazi Racism

Their common totalitarian nature notwithstanding, European fascist movements, as well as the regimes several of them eventually established, differed in significant respects. The most prominent fascist state of the era, that of the Nazis in Germany, was distinguished in particular by the ideological racism and practical anti-Semitism that stood at its core. More than any other fascist movement of the twentieth century, Nazism had turned the theory of race from an abstract academic construct into an operative agenda that it attempted to implement in the here and now. By arming nationalism with the weapon of racism, Nazism greatly accentuated German ethnocentrism, intolerance of others, and aggressiveness both internal and external. The racist ideas and anti-Semitic policies that permeated the German version of contemporary fascism could not be ignored by Egyptian intellectuals when they assessed Nazism.

In its evaluations of Nazi racism, Salama Musa's *al-Majalla al-Jadida* again expressed a more sympathetic position than that of other journals of intellectual opinion. Almost uniquely among leading Egyptian liberal intellectuals, for much of the 1930s Musa accepted and endorsed the basic elements of Nazi racism and anti-Semitism. The concepts of racial superiority and inferiority, of the necessity of racial purity and consequently of separation on the basis of race, as well as the assumption that racial engineering through eugenics was a positive element in achieving social reform, were repeatedly endorsed by Musa in the pages of *al-Majalla al-Jadida*. Musa's acceptance of racist thought was grounded in his belief in the power of the new science of eugenics. As Vernon Egger has demonstrated, from an early date Musa was fascinated by eugenics. Based on the premise that genetic and biological factors were determinative in human development, he was an advocate of engineering the biological improvement of human beings through selective breeding and careful racial separation. By planning and implementing the matching and crossbreeding of individuals from superior racial stock, while simultaneously minimizing or avoiding the mixture of inferior with superior racial stock, he believed it possible to produce healthier, fitter, and more highly developed human beings. Given the sophisticated scientific and technological nature of modernity, he indeed believed such genetic engineering was necessary in order to produce human beings capable of dealing with modern science and technology.[87]

With respect to Egypt itself, Musa encouraged intermarriage between local Egyptians and Egyptians resident in Europe for the purpose of improving the overall level of Egyptian intelligence, and discouraged intermarriage between Egyptians and peoples of darker skin whom he regarded as inferior racial stock that would dilute the superior racial characteristics of Egyptians.[88] Looking abroad, Musa praised the Nazi regime for implementing racist laws such as the sterilization of criminals, social deviants, and individuals with natal defects. He also viewed Nazi measures aimed at preventing intermarriage between Aryan Germans and people of inferior races, such as the Jews, as legitimate. Hitler's goal of purifying the German race in order to strengthen it was a worthy aim that advanced the National Socialist agenda of carrying out a social revolution in Germany.[89] Referring to other eugenic projects in Sweden, Switzerland, and the United

States, Musa noted that the Nazis were not the first to attempt to apply the science of eugenics to society; but at present they were the great example of "positive eugenics [al-yujaniyya al-ijabiyya]." By mobilizing the resources of the state and through careful planning and supervision, the Nazis were institutionalizing eugenics in Germany and demonstrating its positive results.[90]

Along with selective breeding, Musa believed that the separation of different races was essential to racial improvement. Musa assumed different races to be distinct biological entities with different intellectual as well as physiological traits that could be isolated and identified. The separation of these distinct entities was vital to correctly implement the science of eugenics. Only after a given race had been purged and cleansed of the pollution of its racial stock by alien races could it fully realize its potential and capabilities. The mixing of different races, such as "the black with the white and the yellow with the brown," leads at best to "the adverse mixture [al-khalt al-sayyi']" of races in which the qualities of the more superior race would be polluted by the inferior; on the other hand, racial purity was the way to maintain the inherent superiority of the more highly developed race. Given this perspective, Musa regarded the racial policies of the Nazi regime as a model for others, Egypt included.[91]

Musa's acceptance of Nazi racism in the mid-1930s extended to the regime's anti-Semitism. In his view Nazi hostility toward Jews was justified. The Jews were a foreign element in Germany that needed to be excluded and ousted; it was essential to purge Germany of its alien Jewish population in order to maintain and refine the superior qualities of the Aryan German race. The anti-Semitic measures introduced by the Nazis were therefore largely acceptable to Musa as part of their project of racial purification and improvement.[92] To justify his endorsement of Nazi anti-Semitism, Musa sometimes echoed the prevailing anti-Semitic stereotype regarding purported Jewish domination of the German economy, at one point asserting that "Jews control the stock exchange, the legal system, the bar association, the press, and the theater."[93] On both the theoretical and practical levels, al-Majalla al-Jadida offered little criticism of Nazi racism and anti-Semitism prior to 1938.

The explanation for Salama Musa's initial tolerance of Nazi anti-Semitism lies partly in his Coptic background and in the concept of the Pharaonic national identity of Egyptians that was of particular appeal to Egypt's Copts. A component of the Pharaonicist premise that Egyptians were a historic nation whose ethnic origins and national character derived from ancient Pharaonic Egypt was the belief in the non-Semitic racial composition of the Egyptian people. Since they postulated that Egyptian national origins lay in a non-Semitic Pharaonic race, Nazi anti-Semitism was personally irrelevant to adherents of Egyptian Pharaonicism. Nazi anti-Jewishness was equally not a major concern, since Egyptians were "a Pharaonic people" who were distinct from "the people of Moses."[94]

Salama Musa's and *al-Majalla al-Jadida's* view of Nazi racism and anti-Semitism evolved considerably over time. By 1938–39, the evils of Nazi racism were receiving more attention in *al-Majalla al-Jadida*. Musa's review of "Germany After Five Years" of March 1938 contained a negative critique of both Nazi religious policies and Nazi anti-Semitism. In terms of the former, Musa now protested against "the spiritual and institutional destruction" of Catholicism, Protestantism, and Judaism that was resulting from the Nazi effort to subordinate religious institutions in Germany to the Nazi state. Musa rejected Nazi pretensions to be creating a new religion that revolved around the worship of nature, race, and national history. He denounced "the German national religion" that, in its elevation of "biology and environment" to the level of basic principles, was a "total heresy" standing in complete contradiction to the universalism of monotheism. Whereas he had previously viewed the Nazi use of neopagan symbolism as a positive exercise in national self-representation, Musa now criticized Nazi reliance on the myths of the pre-Christian German past. In his view, by its very nature religion was not national; the Nazi sanctification of Aryan blood and the Aryan race was fundamentally irreligious. On the practical level, Musa now went on to decry the anti-Jewish policies followed by the Nazi regime once in power. The pernicious premise of Aryan racial superiority had led the Nazi regime to intensify the persecution of Jews to a degree far exceeding that traditionally present in Christian societies. Based as it was on what were believed to be unalterable biological differences between Aryan Germans and Jews, Nazi discrimination against and persecution of Jews was a "racial fanaticism [*ta'assub 'unsuri*]" far more invidious than traditional "religious fanaticism [*ta'assub dini*]." In this regard, Musa was convinced that the German national religion being propounded by the Nazis was an instrument intended to serve their more fundamental racist doctrines and to mobilize religion in the service of racism.[95]

This new criticism of Nazi theory of race notwithstanding, remnants of racist-influenced thought could still be found in Musa's writings in the late 1930s. Another lead editorial in *al-Majalla al-Jadida* a few months later saw the journal's editor reiterate a qualified acceptance of some of the premises of anti-Semitism.[96] In a classic example of blaming the victim, Musa's historical overview of anti-Semitism placed a considerable measure of blame for the durability of the phenomenon on Jews themselves. In discussing the case of Jewish flight from ancient Egypt, Musa demonstrated the resentment of an Egyptian nationalist and Pharaonicist over the negative depiction of the ancient Egyptians in the Biblical account of the Exodus; even Nazi anti-Semitic propaganda "was not equal to the descriptions [of the Pharaonic persecution of Jews] in the Biblical story." Musa maintained that subsequent Jewish historical memory had made instrumental use of the Exodus. Because the Jews had maintained themselves as a religious community through their historical memory of collective isolation and persecution, they were in part responsible for the persistence of anti-Semitism into the modern era. Since they themselves had emphasized their distinctiveness as a people, Jews had no right to complain if the Nazis continued to regard them as such. Long before the formulation of the racist ideology found in Nazism, "the Jews made Jewish blood a basis for belonging to their religious group." What the Nazis had adopted was simply "the classic Jewish principle" of biologically based distinctiveness; "a firm stand regarding the superior Jewish race, to which non-Jews cannot belong." The reciprocity of Jewish racism with Nazi racism led Musa to conclude that the correct solution to the Jewish question was the separation of Jews and Germans. Both had an equal right to adhere to their principles of ethnic purity. Racial separation was presented by Musa as a progressive policy. In the age of distinctive nationalisms, the mixing of races resulted in "anarchy"; a people that could not distinguish its own ethnic and racial characteristics "may appear from the outside to be civilized, but on the inside it is barbarian [*hamajiyya*]." The separation of Germans from Jews, and thus "the assurance of the ability of each to preserve its blood," was a progressive solution that would ensure the future of each ethnic group.[97]

Musa's account of contemporary anti-Semitism in Nazi Germany went on to accuse the Jews of intentional exaggeration of their treatment at the hands of the Nazi regime. The purpose of this rhetorical exaggeration was clear; it was designed to present Jews as victims and to "convince the enlightened world of the need for them to have a homeland as a refuge for Jewish refugees who were victims of persecution." Musa denounced "worldwide Jewish propaganda" for invoking the Jewish situation in Germany in order to advance its agenda of colonization in Palestine. The ultimate victims of Nazi anti-Semitism were the Palestinians.[98]

While sympathizing with their cause, Musa's relentless modernism also led him to criticize the Palestinian Arabs. In the same essay, Musa emphasized the technological backwardness of the Palestinian Arabs to the economic dynamism and progress apparent within the Zionist community in Palestine. Musa presented the relative failure of the Palestinians vis-à-vis Zionism not as a result of Zionist colonization, but as a consequence of their traditionalist social structure and of the divisive rivalries among the Palestinian elite. He posited that the Palestinians could wage and win their just struggle against Zionist colonization only if they faced the challenges of modernity and undertook significant economic, social, and cultural reform. In a characteristically paternalistic tone, Musa called on the Palestinians to learn from external models such as Bank Misr in Egypt and even from their Zionist rivals in Palestine. Musa's overall attitude to the Jewish question was thus an ambivalent one: while partially justifying the racially based persecution of Jews in Germany and expressing sympathy for the Palestinian Arabs, he also demonstrated admiration for the modernism so visible in Zionism, which itself was a reaction to anti-Semitism.[99]

Salama Musa's partial acceptance of racist reasoning did not extend to an endorsement of the specific Nazi concept of the superiority of the Aryan race. In September 1938, in responding to a reader's query as to "what is the source of the term Aryan, and who are the Aryans?" *al-Majalla al-Jadida* explained the term as a purely linguistic one referring to the family of Indo-European languages rather than as a term defining a distinct biological group. The response went on to state that "German propagandists have altered the meaning of the term 'Aryan' to designate a race." This was the unscientific politicization of philology; "the meaning of the term today is more socio-political than scientific." By implication, the concept of Aryan racial supremacy had no scientific basis; it was a myth of Nazi ideology.[100]

As the persecution of Jews in Europe accelerated through 1938, *al-Majalla al-Jadida* came to take a more critical view of the racism being manifested by the fascist states. A November 1938 editorial on Italy's new policies of institutional anti-Semitism, adopted under German inspiration and influence, made the point that, although the policy was in effect directed against the country's Jewish population, it theoretically applied to all "inferior races." Highlighting the clause that specified a ban on intermarriage between Italians and "men of women of the Hamitic and Semitic races or others among the non-Aryan races," the editorial made clear to readers that Fascist Italy now considered Egyptians and Arabs to be members of an inferior race.[101] An editorial in the same issue of the journal criticized the simplicity of Hitler's biologically-based view of race. The slogan "one blood for one nation" indicated that Nazi Germany would not rest until it had united all Germans, "people of one blood," in a "state of one blood." This Nazi insistence on racial unity had dreadful implications; in effect, it legitimized the future conquest of much of Europe in pursuit of incorporating all Germans into the Third Reich. Nazi racism was not only anti-Semitic; it also carried with it a desire for imperialist expansion.[102]

Other contributors to *al-Majalla al Jadida* were more hostile than Salama Musa to both the theory and the practice of anti-Semitism. Michel 'Abd al-Lahad's February 1939 essay on "the Wandering Jew" provided readers of the journal with an unambiguously critical overview of anti-Semitism in its various forms.[103] Its historical account made a sharp distinction between the persecution of Jews prior to the modern era and their increasingly precarious position in the twentieth century. Whereas discrimination against Jews in medieval Europe had been religiously motivated, and that of the early modern era primarily economic in character, contemporary Nazi and more recent Fascist anti-Semitism was ideologically motivated. It was also comprehensive in intent, amounting to a total war against Jews with the goal of purifying Europe of their presence. 'Abd al-Lahad's analysis of anti-Semitic movements in nineteenth- and twentieth-century Europe emphasized that modern nationalism had given traditional hatred of Jews a more vicious twist, resulting in the systematic and brutal anti-Semitism current in Germany and Italy. The Jewish response to this modern anti-Semitism—Zionism and its effort to find a permanent national home for "the lost and wandering Jew"—was for 'Abd al-Lahad a legitimate reaction to this new and more virulent anti-Semitism.[104] Unlike Salama Musa, 'Abd al-Lahad dismissed the intellectual validity of the anti-Semitic propaganda being disseminated by the Nazis. The anti-Semitic literature that told Germans that Jews were "defiling your honor, belittling your faith, destroying your churches, corrupting your culture, and polluting the purity of your noble race" was, while effective in the German context, nonetheless "completely groundless." In his view, the worthless propaganda of the Nazis that took advantage of "the primitive mentality of the masses" was intellectually not only "a crime against Jews," but also "a crime against the truth of science and against humanity and civilization."[105]

Liberal intellectuals writing for *al-Risala* and *al-Hilal* were more consistently critical of Nazi racism and anti-Semitism. They mobilized both the norms of the monotheistic religions and the liberal values of the Enlightenment to counter what they saw as the paganism and barbarism that characterized Nazi racist theory and anti-Semitic practice. The evil of Nazi racism was reinforced and augmented by its being associated with a totalitarian regime possessing absolute power over its society. The connection between dictatorship and racism endowed the Nazi regime with a monstrous singularity.

Essays in *al-Risala* in the second half of the 1930s frequently addressed the topic of Nazi racism. Their general consensus was that "racism [*al-ʿursuriyya* or *al-jinsiyya*]" was the most singular feature of Nazi ideology and policy. As with Nazi totalitarianism, Muhammad ʿAbdalla ʿInan took the lead in *al-Risala*'s denunciations of Nazi racism. For ʿInan, totalitarianism and racism were the two defining characteristics of the Nazi regime. "German National Socialism (Nazism or Hitlerism) developed the newest form of contemporary dictatorship in the sense that it systematically implemented violence and the suppression of general civil rights and liberties. However, its most important and unique trait and principle is its racist ideology, or the ideology of origins and blood." Focusing specifically on Nazi racism, ʿInan saw racism and behavior as amounting to a reversion to "barbaric paganism [*wathaniyya barbariyya*]." Reviewing Nazi racist theory in order to refute it, ʿInan evaluated the Nazi attempt to provide a scientific and factual basic for their racist beliefs. The effort to premise a hierarchy of races, with "the German race as the most supreme and noble of all races," was totally unfounded. It would be bearable if such theories, lacking in any scientific basis, had remained on the theoretical level; but in Germany they were being systematically applied in daily life. The most obvious effect of Nazi theories of race was the persecution of Jews. The Nazi aim was to purify Germany of alien Semites. ʿInan's analysis went further, noting that Nazi anti-Semitism was capable of being directed against all "Semitic easterners," including Arabs. In Nazi racial theory, all such non-Aryans were "inferior races [*ajnas munhatta*]" destined for subordination and exploitation for the benefit of the superior Aryan race.

Nazi racial theory simply denied any Semitic contribution to the construction of human civilization throughout history.[106]

Both the ideological anti-Semitism of the Nazis and the anti-Jewish policies it inspired were denounced in the pages of *al-Risala*. A 1935 article that reported on the Nazi claim that Jewish medical scientists had developed microbiological techniques intended to pollute "pure German blood" denounced Nazi laws aimed at protecting Germans from such biological contamination as "fallacious, extremist laws that not only reveal racist fanaticism but also blacken the good name of science and scientific factual truth."[107] The journal reinforced its dismissive position regarding racist theory with the authority of outside experts. Reporting on the findings of a survey of academic specialists conducted in France concerning human development and the question "is it possible to verify the existence of pure, distinct, isolated races as a biological scientific fact," it summarized their evaluation of racist theory as unequivocally negative. According to the report, the scientific consensus was that no pure race existed in reality. Moreover, it reported that, since in the view of those surveyed "all human races are equal," racial mixture and crossbreeding could actually improve and enhance genetic quality. Not only was the Nazi theory of race lacking in any scientific basis, in some cases, the opposite could be true: racial mixture improved the genetic quality of humans.[108] "The idea of a racist division between the Aryan and the Semite is groundless," *al-Risala* concluded in 1938, "lacking in any scientific basis and without any foundation in human reality." Given the complex historical development of ethnic groups, races and peoples had over time "mingled and mixed with one another" to the point where it was impossible to identify any pure race or to prove its superiority over others, The Nazi effort to locate and map the original homeland and current territorial boundaries of the Aryans was also fundamentally erroneous; it was just as impossible to realistically identify any territory with any particular race. "This is a nonsensical idea that takes root only in the mind of a deceitful imperialist or a fanatical racist [*musta'mir makir aw muta'assib haqid*] filled with hatred."[109]

Interpreting the local implications of Nazi racist theory for its readers, the journal emphasized that it granted ultimate and perpetual superiority to the "German, Aryan, Nordic race" over all other human races. Nazi branding of the Semitic race in particular as inferior was a collective slander against all Semitic peoples, including Arabs and Egyptians. This Nazi theory of race was currently being disseminated and instilled in the population of Germany by means of the regime's propaganda apparatus, thereby becoming a popular perspective embraced by most Germans. In the process, Germany had become both "the cradle of racist fanaticism [*mahd al-ta'assub al-jinsi*]" and "the cradle of anti-Semitism [*mahd al-khusuma al-samiyya*]."[110] Although Nazi racist theory was a myth, an irrational manifestation of chauvinistic nationalism rather than of science, the fact that "it is the soul of the Nazi regime" was seen by the journal as evidence of the danger Nazi racism represented for all "Eastern Semitic peoples."[111]

The practical policies that followed from the flawed theory of racism drew similar criticism. An essay of January 1938 condemned the Nazi effort to purge Germany of Jews, "to persecute them to the point of destruction, to confiscate and expropriate their property, to exile them and to spit them out."[112] For his part, Ahmad Hasan al-Zayyat termed the Nazi policies that "expel Jews from their homes and rob them of their property" to be "a denial of humanity and a defiance of civilization."[113] The negative institutional effects of Nazi anti-Semitic policies were also noted. In an editorial of November 1936, the journal condemned the Nazi regime's attempt to purge the German legal system of legal texts written by Jews. Noting that Jewish jurists had made a vital contribution to the formulation of modern German civil law, the journal lamented that "the disappearance of Jewish textual influences from German legal literature" would disrupt the integrity of the law and facilitate its further subordination to the whims of the Nazi dictatorship. *Al-Risala* mocked the attempt to "purge Judaism" from German legal literature as a counterproductive effort to "create a new era in writing German law, in which the Aryan intelligence would on its own express its purity and genius in composing legal texts." In reality, without the Jewish contribution the German legal system would be a sorry state.[114]

Essayists writing for *al-Risala* eventually came to explain Nazi racism as the inevitable product of German history and national character. For Germans it was race, more than language, history, culture, or territory, that defined national identity; the modern German nation was "a product of the German-Aryan race."[115] As it developed in the late-nineteenth and early-twentieth centuries, the modern German nation had inscribed in its DNA the aspiration to "fulfill dreams of a strong greater Germany" based on "the purity of the German race."[116] In addition to positing the existence and the right to unity of a pure German race, Nazism also had as a fundamental premise the inherent superiority of the Aryan race. "The superiority of the German-Aryan race and its preeminence over other human races in all political, social and intellectual spheres" was a deeply ingrained principle in German collective identity.[117]

But modern racism was not solely a German invention. On the intellectual level, al-Risala credited Ernest Renan and his invidious distinctions between the qualities of Aryans and Semites with a major role in inspiring modern anti-Semitism. Hitler had appropriated Renan's concept of "the division of human beings into Aryans and Semites" and his premise that the Semite was the antithesis of the Aryan. Where the Aryans were a pure human race, inherently creative and superior by nature, Semites were a deformed hybrid, degenerate and inferior. In order to preserve Aryan purity and superiority, it was necessary to eliminate the Semitic germ from Aryan society. The journal emphasized that it was Hitler's tirades in Mein Kampf that turned anti-Semitism into a political doctrine and a program for action. Mein Kampf had made Renan's racism into a political agenda that held that "only the select German people have the right to leadership and command because it is a supremely creative people, while the Jews and the Semitic people have never created anything."[118]

By the end of the 1930s, al-Risala's editor Ahmad Hasan al-Zayyat was unequivocal in his rejection of Nazi racism. Against the background of the crisis that led to Munich in September 1938, Zayyat posited an inseparable connection between racism and the unrestrained despotism that characterized Nazism. The Nazi theory of race stripped human beings of "religion, civilization, and philosophy," he asserted, causing them to lose their sense of belonging to humanity. Abandoning God, under the influence of racism, people turned to "the language of force, so that they squabble with the logic of wolves, falling upon one another with the fanaticism of paganism [bi 'asabiyyat al-jahiliyya]." With moral restraints removed, racism intensified the Nazi thrust toward totalitarianism, providing it with validity and vitality. The Nazi premise that they ruled a racially unique and racially unified people facilitated their dictatorial thrust and the subjection of the community to "the tyrant of the chosen race." With the Czech crisis clearly in mind, Zayyat went on to assert that Hitler was externalizing the aggressive and tyrannical approach of Nazism, imposing it on the general discourse of international relations.[119]

Historical discussions of what was termed "the German school of racism [madhhab al-'unsuriyya al-almani]" in al-Hilal dealt with the intellectual sources of Nazi racism, analyzing the contributions of fore-runners such as Gobineau, Wagner, and Chamberlain who had laid the theoretical foundations for the racist doctrines that permeated Hitler's *Mein Kampf*.[120] To this racist substratum, the combined philosophical and political legacy of Nietzsche and Bismarck had added "the cult of force that became a permanent element in German philosophy and German thought."[121] It was Bismarck in particular, "who united Germany by blood and iron," who provided the model of the all-powerful and aggressive state that Hitler was emulating.[122]

In the later 1930s, ʿAbd al-Rahman Sidqi was a consistent critic of Nazi racism. In a 1937 commentary on the subject of racism in *al-Hilal*, Sidqi totally rejected the Nazi claim of the racial superiority of the Aryan race and its alleged seminal role in the development of human civilization. In defiance of Nazi pretensions, Sidqi held that civilization emerged and developed through the shared endeavor and contribution of all racial groups. It was impossible to isolate the role of a specific race in the evolution of civilization; it needed to be understood as a multiracial and multicultural product, the fruit of constant human interaction and mutual stimulation. For Sidqi, modern democracy and progress also demanded interracial cooperation and the participation of all races in an effort to further develop and improve civilization.[123]

A mid-1939 essay expanded on Sidqi's negative view of Nazi racism. In his view, racism was a fundamental component of the Nazi regime in Germany; "Nazi Germany bases her revival on racism," the title of his essay asserted. As Sidqi described it, the Nazi theory of race was founded on the premise of the biologically derived reality of race as well as of the existence of essential differences between different races. It posited that the unique physiological and psychological characteristics of each human race could be scientifically determined and assessed. Race was the basis of the unique culture of each national collective. National identity, thought, culture, and political system all derived from the particularities of race. Concomitantly, any talk about "the unity of the human race" was totally unfounded, indeed was a "foolish hypothesis." Races were separate and distinct, and could not meld.[124]

To this racist essentialism, Nazism added the premise of a hierarchy of races in which some were superior and others inferior. Specifically, Nazi racism assumed the superiority of "northern white" races and the inferiority of "southern yellow and black" ones. Within the northern racial cluster, the Aryan race was the best, embodying the strongest and highest racial qualities. Finally, Nazi racism assumed the existence of the possibility of racial contamination, that there was "the danger that the superior race will be mixed with the blood of the inferior race," resulting in the "degeneration and decline" of the superior by the inferior. This meant that the superior northern Aryan race should not mix with the inferior southern Semitic race that had originated in the Middle East. Racial separation was necessary, and in the case of pollution, purification was essential in Nazi racist ideology. Sidqi had no doubt that Nazi racist ideology was a "myth [*ustura*]." But, thanks to the Nazis, it was a myth with enormous influence at the present time. The Nazi regime in Germany had harnessed the power of the state to a cult of the myth of the Aryan race. In Hitler's Germany, "this pure blood is the most important thing and nothing else is more important"; indeed, "the act of purifying German blood is the platform of the Nazi government, its first and last mission."[125]

Ibrahim al-Misri described the nature of "the Nazi racist state" slightly differently. In his view, modern Nazi racism was in sharp contradiction to the antiracist humanism of liberal democracy. Reviewing the development of what he termed the "humanistic school" from the classical Greco-Roman era through the Renaissance to the modern period, Misri analyzed the challenge that contemporary racism posed to the humanist tradition. He left no doubt that Nazi racism was thoroughly antithetical to liberal humanism. In unquestionably hostile terms, Misri stated that the supreme goal of Nazism and Hitler was "to establish an enormous, frightening, chauvinistic state, pure in blood and made up of one race, whose political rule will spread throughout a vast empire that resembles a huge military barracks containing despised inferior peoples whom the empire will treat with clemency provided that they give up their personal freedom to the ruling elite." For Misri, Nazi racism was an instrument in the service and exultation of the state, an ancillary to the Nazi "spirit of militarism, namely a mentality characterized by devotion to order and discipline, the sanctification of obedience, and a cult of force and military glory."[126]

An *al-Hilal* essay by 'Ali Adham analyzed the historical development of racist ideology.[127] After surveying various phases in the development of nineteenth-century racist thought, Adham placed "the contemporary German theory supported by the Nazis, the theory of the superiority of the Aryan race," at the apex of the theoretical and practical evolution of modern racism. The Nazis had perfected the theory of race and were now implementing it as a practical policy carried out by the apparatus of the German state. For the Nazis, the Germans were the most authentic representative of the Aryan race and its racial superiority to other races; "this people is the supreme exemplar of high culture in the civilized world and the most sublime product that human civilization has created from ancient times to the present." Given this inherent superiority of the Aryans, the aim of the Nazi state was "to preserve the Aryan people as a pure people free of any flaws or stains of racial mixture."[128]

Adham's purpose in dissecting modern racism, culminating with the Nazis, was to expose the theoretical poverty of racist ideology as well as to stress the danger it represented to humanity. He dismissed the reality of racist thinking, totally rejecting the possibility of the existence of biologically pure or distinct races. By citing the antiracist theories as expounded by leading scientists to the effect that "peoples and races are equal and none has any superiority over another," Adham attempted to discredit the Nazi pretension of Aryan superiority. The human race was one unit, a single biological entity in spite of diverse cultural features and traditions that had their origin in different physical environments and historical experiences.[129]

Was racism an integral component of modern nationalism? For Adham, nationalism and racism were unrelated concepts. Historical circumstances, not race, were the basis of nationalism; "a nation is a political unit based on similar components that grow and develop in a shared environment, created by the force of economic factors and linguistic and religious connections, or by a collective cohesiveness in the face of invasion or as a defense against an act of military or economic aggression." Additional components of nationalism included "a specific geographical location and shared historical memories." A nation was not biologically derived, but "comprises a diversity of peoples and races." In terms of their value, nationalism was a positive and essential feature of the modern age while racism was a negative and destructive feature. In his eyes, nationalism was by its very nature opposed to racism. Nationalism was an authentic phenomenon associated with modernity, by which the peoples of the world demarcated themselves into territorial units in order to survive and prosper. Moreover, nationalism assumed the existence of a "family of nations," an egalitarian composite in which each distinct nation drew on its particular historical and cultural reservoir in order to make a unique contribution to human civilization in general. In marked contrast, racism assumed "the superiority of one nation and the inferiority of the rest." By positing a hierarchy of races, racism denied and threatened the unity of humanity. Again asserting that racist theory was absolutely groundless and lacking any empirical basis, Adham went on to condemn racism as simultaneously fallacious and pernicious; "it is the myth of myths [*ustura min al-asatir*], a legend and superstition that functions as a veil behind which political aims hide, as well as a type of propaganda aimed at inciting and inflaming national emotions and arousing a patriotic spirit." He called on his readers to adhere to rational analysis and empirical research based on objective evidence, and not to believe in "mythical fallacies." His call was for "strengthening the humane trend" among the peoples of the world as a weapon with which to fight against "the myth of racism."[130]

The intellectuals who decried Nazi racism were well aware of the fact that, while theoretically condemning all non-Aryans to an inferior status in the hierarchy of races, it was the Jewish people who were the proximate target of Nazi racist ideology. They clearly understood that Nazi anti-Semitism, although ostensibly aimed against all "Semites," was primarily directed against Jews. As 'Abd al-Rahman Sidqi put it in June 1939, "Germany is founding its revival on racism and on the uncompromising purge of the Semitic races [*al-'anasir al-samiyya*] from it, in particular Judaism [*al-Yahudiyya*]."[131] Numerous reports in *al-Hilal* in 1938–39 dealt with the increasingly severe persecution Jews were experiencing in Nazi Germany. In the wake of the savage anti-Jewish attacks of *Reichskristallnacht* in November 1938, the journal's regular in-house commentator on current affairs, Sami al-Jaridini, attempted without success to find any "element of justification" for this latest wave of anti-Semitic brutality by the Nazis. "Even if we allow ourselves to leave aside logic or reason for a moment, and to assume that the Jews of Germany . . . are the enemies of the National-Socialist regime," Jaridini mused, "even if we assume all that, we still cannot understand or digest the implementation of these abusive, arbitrary actions." He went on to denounce Nazi confiscation of Jewish property as well as the incarceration of German Jews in concentration camps or their expulsion from their "birthplaces" in Germany.[132] News commentaries in *al-Hilal* reported on the continuing persecution of German Jews by the Nazi regime, highlighting particularly the pressure being placed on Jewish intellectuals such as Albert Einstein because of the

Nazi determination to "distance the Jewish race from Germany."[133] In mid-1939, the journal estimated that the German government had earned "an enormous financial profit" of approximately five hundred million marks from the draconian levies imposed upon German Jews as the price of their being allowed to flee their homeland.[134]

Were the Jews indeed a "race," as Nazi doctrine insisted? One analysis in *al-Hilal* disputed this fundamental premise of Nazi ideology.[135] Just as the Nazi theory of race was groundless in its general postulates, so its specific claim that "the Jews are a defined race" was equally fallacious. *Al-Hilal* denied the existence of particular Jewish physiological traits such as a distinctive nose ("the nose attributed only to the Jews is in fact shared by them and many races and peoples of mankind"). This commentator went further, also arguing that the Jews of the world neither had a common ethnic origin nor shared in one historical experience based on ancient Israel/Palestine. Most Jews of today, three-quarters according to *al-Hilal*, originated from "the land of the Khazars;" only one-quarter originated "in the region of the Mediterranean," including "the original Jews of Palestine." A map accompanying the article attempted to provide cartographic proof of the claim that most of the Jews of Europe in particular were of Khazar descent.[136]

This theoretical argument had implications for contemporary affairs in the Middle Eastern context of the 1930s. It led *al-Hilal*, at the same time as demonstrating sympathy for the European Jewish plight in the face of rampant anti-Semitism, to oppose the Zionist claim to a Jewish national home in Palestine. Jews were not a race; in addition, their claim to nationhood was shaky. According to *al-Hilal*, Jews lacked the minimum number of "shared unique traits and common elements" that could be found in other historic nations. The most that could be said was that the Jews, beyond sharing a common religious tradition, were a cultural community with a common language ("most of them speak the Hebrew language") and "cultural unity." The Zionist claim that the Jews "are like all the nations," and therefore that they needed to be united in a revived national home in Palestine in order to realize their national sovereignty, had no basis.[137] Articles in *al-Hilal* in 1939 continued to dispute the Jewish claim to a national home in Palestine, asserting "the irrefutable truth that Palestine has been a purely Arab homeland for thousands of years" and noting that "a large part of the Jews were opposed to this Zionist idea, and believe that it is best for the Jews to remain as they are—dispersed among the nations of the globe." A Jewish national home in Palestine was unacceptable on national grounds, and also did not represent the desire of most of the Jews in the world.[138]

Al-Risala and al-Thaqafa, both newer journals of the 1930s whose contents expressed and appealed to the more Islamic-Arabist mood of the decade, were even more vehement in their opposition to the Zionist project for the settlement of Jews in Palestine. Like most Egyptians, they argued that the solution of the problem of the Jews of Germany, produced by the intolerable racism and anti-Semitism of the Nazis, could not be resolved at the expense of the national rights of the Arab people of Palestine. As an editorial in al-Risala put it in late 1938, "nothing stands between us and the Jews except the matter of Palestine" and "there is no antagonism between the Muslims and the Jews except Palestine." Were it not for "the fact that the Zionists and Zionism want to turn Palestine into their national home at the expense of the Arabs," which has led to the current violent clash between the Jews and the Arabs in Palestine, it would have been possible for the journal to identify totally with the plight of the Jews and to embrace them as victims of Nazi anti-Semitism who fully deserved support. Al-Risala maintained that the historical relations between Muslims and Jews in the lands of Islam, in particular in Spain, the Ottoman Empire, Egypt, and Syria, had been harmonious and tolerant "for hundreds of years." Jews and Arabs were "cousins, identified with the Semitism [al-samiyya] that is being persecuted in the lands of dictatorship, [suffering from] an anti-Semitism based on the fanaticism of race and color that violates both humanism and religion." Zionism was the problem, not the solution: "after all, Egyptian Jews, Iraqi Jews, and others who do not believe in Zionism and do not support this English pawn, live with the Muslims everywhere in absolute harmony and complete brotherhood."[139]

Upon its appearance in 1939, al-Thaqafa adopted a similar stance regarding Zionism. Against the backdrop of the London (St. James) Conference of early 1939, an editorial under the title "the modern Shylock" criticized Zionism. As al-Thaqafa saw the current situation, "the position of the Zionist leaders in Palestine is identical to the position of the Venetian merchant Shylock in Shakespeare's play." The editorial contrasted the position of the Jews in Europe, perennial victims of Christian anti-Semitism, and tolerance shown by Arab-Islamic society toward Jews. In their efforts to colonize an Arab-Muslim land, Zionists were demonstrating crass ingratitude toward those Arab and Muslim lands which, unlike the anti-Semitic states of Europe, "had taken in the Jews exiled from the places of their birth, opened their doors to them, and gave them shelter and security in place of fear, respect and pride in place of humiliation and debasement, justice in place of injustice." In all stages of its long history, Islamic civilization and successive Muslim empires had provided Jews with the opportunity "to participate in all spheres of cultural, political, and economic life." For its part, Egypt had fully integrated Jews, "taking them out of a situation of injustice and persecution and raising them to a lofty position of esteem and justice." This positive Muslim attitude toward Jews, demonstrating "feelings of brotherhood, solidarity and love," stood in sharp contrast to "the sinister, exploitative demands of the Zionists" who intended to steal the lands of the Palestinians, metaphorically biting the very hand that had fed them.[140]

Al-Thaqafa reiterated its anti-Zionist position upon the publication of the British White Paper on Palestine in May 1939. Although viewing the White Paper as a start in the right direction, the journal urged the British to go further than the White Paper and to adopt a position closer to that of the Palestinian Arabs that was "shared by all the Islamic Arab nations." It endorsed the Palestinian Arab demands for the end of the British Mandate over Palestine, the annulment of the Balfour Declaration pledging British support for a Jewish national home, and "the establishment of an independent Arab state [in Palestine] with sovereignty, linked to Great Britain through a treaty of friendship" similar to those concluded with Iraq and Egypt, as the minimal demands for a just solution to the problem of Palestine. Once again, the Zionist enterprise was rejected as a solution for the distress of the Jews of Nazi Germany.[141]

'Abd al-Rahman Shukri's essay on "The Problem of the Jews of the World," published in *al-Risala* in mid-1939, is emblematic of the crosscutting sentiments of sympathy with Jewish distress and opposition to the Zionist movement generated among Egyptian intellectuals by the related phenomena of the current persecution of Jews in Europe and the Zionist attempt to establish a Jewish refuge from anti-Semitism in Arab Palestine. Shukri was unequivocal in his rejection of the Zionist effort to create a Jewish national home in Palestine. In his view, the Zionist fixation on Palestine was an atavistic impulse that was "contradictory to Jewish economic interests." As Shukri saw it, "the populist religious trend [*al-naza al-sha'abiyya al-diniyya*]" of Jewish attachment to Palestine challenged "the global trend [*al-naza al-'alamiyya*]" in which Jews today were inevitably enmeshed. Zionism contradicted Jewish economic globalism, the dominant trend of cosmopolitan involvement of Jews in the modern world economy. Shukri used the phrase "the global Jew [al-yahudi al-'alami]" to characterize the modern, secular Jewish elite whose economic interests would be imperiled by the realization of the Zionist project in Palestine. The idea of concentrating the Jews of the world in the small area of mandatory Palestine, populated mainly by Arabs and with a backward economy, was both impractical and counterproductive; it would only have a harmful effect on the Jews "whose numbers in the modern world have grown greatly and whose global economic interests have increased immensely." Zionism was contrary to the cosmopolitanism that was the dominant course of development pursued by Jews in the modern era.[142]

His rejection of Palestine as a solution to the Jewish problem notwithstanding, Shukri was not unsympathetic to the Jewish call for self-determination and nationhood. Acknowledging the gravity of "the problem of the Jews in the world" caused by rampant anti-Semitism and persecution, Shukri endorsed the creation of a Jewish homeland and refuge in an unspecified area other than Palestine. "The Jews should be persuaded into accepting a more fertile land than Palestine, a more extensive area, and one in which there is a sparser population." He optimistically suggested that "it would be possible to satisfy the popular sentiment [attaching Jews to Palestine] by calling this new homeland the 'New Palestine' or even 'Zion.'" In that land, "the Jews could establish cities with ancient Jewish names," and perhaps go as far as to transfer "sacred" artifacts from the old promised land to the new in order to erect a new Temple. "This solution," he concluded, "would combine the need to satisfy [popular] sentiment with economic advantage."[143]

5

Egyptian Intellectuals and Fascism, II
Fascism in the World: European Imperialism in a New Style

OVER TIME, it was the aggressive and potentially destructive character of Italian and German foreign policy that came to predominate in Egyptian critiques of fascism. From 1935 through 1937, the main subject of concern for intellectuals writing for *al-Hilal*, *al-Risala*, and *al-Majalla al-Jadida* was the expansionist intentions and actions of Fascist Italy as manifested particularly in its invasion and conquest of Ethiopia; in 1938–39, it was German aggressiveness and its threat to world stability and peace that took center stage in the same publications as well as in the new weekly *al-Thaqafa*.

Warning Against the Threat of Fascist and Nazi Imperialism

Salama Musa and his journal *al-Majalla al-Jadida* were vigorous opponents of Italian Fascist imperialism in the mid-1930s. Italy's conquest of Ethiopia and its continuing threat to establish Italian hegemony in the Mediterranean basin drew repeated criticism in the journal. Sensitivity concerning prior and potential European colonial conquest in the Middle East played an important role in the journal criticizing "imperial Fascism [*al-fashiyya al-imbarialiyya*]" and resolutely rejecting possible Fascist "imperialist expansion [*al-tawassuʿ al-imbaraturi*]" directed against "the small, weak nations" of the Mediterranean, the Middle East, and East Africa.[1]

In 1935–36, it was the Italo-Ethiopian crisis and war that provided *al-Majalla al-Jadida* with evidence of Italy's imperialist intentions. "The question of Ethiopia [*al-masʾala al-habashiyya*]" was a major subject of discussion in the journal. Editorials and articles condemned Italian threats directed against Ethiopia and expressed solidarity with the Ethiopian people and the country's right to an independent and sovereign existence. Fascist Italy's clear intention to aggress against and to conquer Ethiopia in order to expand the Italian Empire in East Africa was illegitimate. Criticism of Italian behavior often centered on the person of Mussolini, who was presented as a captive of his megalomaniac personality; he was a man in a state of "self-enchantment [*istihwaʾ dhati*]" who had persuaded himself that he was Julius Caesar or Napoleon.[2]

The actual outbreak of war, and the savage course it took, intensified the journal's condemnation of Fascist Italy. In particular, Italy's use of poison gas and its repeated attacks upon civilian sites shocked Salama Musa. In a December 1935 editorial entitled "The Gases and the War," Musa analyzed the effects of modern technology when applied to warfare. Now qualifying his previous admiration for modern technology, he presented the energies of the Fascist revolution as being channeled into the pernicious development of new and more devastating techniques of killing. "The war is a terrible catastrophe," he stated, since most of its casualties were innocent civilians. It was a barbaric war, blind and impersonal in its effects, that with its modern technology possessed a previously unparalleled destructive power.[3] In early 1936, as the Italian conquest rolled on, another editorial defined the war as "Italy's savageness [*tawahhush Italiya*]." "Never, in any other war in the past, have such barbaric acts been perpetrated," the editorial protested.[4] The journal's condemnation of Italian behavior in Ethiopia continued well after the end of the war. Thus an editorial of May 1937 entitled "Mussolini and the Ethiopian Mothers" rejected Italian propaganda attempting to justify the war with the claim that it was the Ethiopians who had provoked the confrontation. The article condemned the hypocrisy of the attempt of Mussolini and his generals to rewrite the history of the conflict. Italy was now trying to place the blame for this destruction upon its victims while "tens of thousands of Ethiopian mothers remain licking their wounds and mourning for their children who were murdered by Italian gas and bombs."[5]

The Ethiopian conflict concluded, *al-Majalla al-Jadida*'s attention shifted to other and closer potential sites for Italian aggression and expansionism. In April 1937 an editorial analyzed the possibility that Fascist imperialism, fueled by exaggerated self-confidence after its success in

Ethiopia, would now direct its militarist and imperialist energy to other regions of the Mediterranean basin. Mussolini's declarations to the effect that "the Mediterranean is a Roman Italian sea" needed to be taken seriously, the journal predicted. Mussolini was indeed preparing to fulfill the Italian fantasy of imperial greatness, "the madness of the Fascists," by means of war. The possibility of a military attack upon Egypt or Tunisia was concrete, the editorial warned. In its Libyan colony, Italy was presently making methodical preparations for war by creating an extensive transportation infrastructure, erecting fueling facilities for mechanized war, and constructing bases and fortifications—all as preparation for war directed against Egypt. If Egyptians in addition considered the fact that Italian engineers were at this moment diverting the waters of Lake Tana to provide for the expansion of agriculture in Italy's new Ethiopian colony, thus threatening the diversion of one of the main sources of the Nile, "then we will be able to grasp the magnitude of the danger we are facing."[6] By 1937, al-Majalla al-Jadida's viewed the expansionist policies of Fascist Italy as a direct threat to Egypt itself.

Another Egyptian Cassandra who repeatedly warned that Fascist expansionism was a threat to the world as well as for Egypt was the dissident Wafdist intellectual 'Abbas Mahmad al-'Aqqad. In his editorials on the Italo-Ethiopian crisis in al-Hilal, 'Aqqad had nothing good to say about Mussolini. Italy's imperialist and criminal war against Ethiopia had exposed the Fascist dictator as conquest-driven warmonger, in the process eclipsing what credit he had gained through the Fascist domestic rehabilitation of Italy. "Mussolini and freedom," 'Aqqad wrote, "are basic enemies of one another." Mussolini was a dangerous dictator, and the model he presented was clearly not one Egypt should consider emulating: "I do not want such a ruler for Egypt."[7]

'Aqqad continued to warn against Fascist Italy and its leader's aspirations for a revived Roman Empire in the Mediterranean through the mid-1930s. The Duce's provocative declarations to the effect that "the Mediterranean is our sea (Mare Nostrum)" indicated Fascist Italy to be preparing for further expansion that could now threaten Egypt itself.[8] 'Aqqad used the stepped-up emphasis on military rearmament in Italy, and to Italy's recent military deployments, as evidence of Mussolini's intention to undertake further military expansion directed against the countries of the Mediterranean basin.[9] By 1937, Nazi Germany had been added to 'Aqqad's list of dangerous states. He now warned that Germany had become one large "military camp" intent upon preparation for war. The Nazi regime was treating "all Germans like soldiers in closed barracks," obliging them to dress in uniforms, to participate in intensive sports activity, and to regulate their behavior according to the directives issued under the "absolute rule" of the Nazi leadership.[10]

Faced with the danger posed to world peace by Fascism and Nazism, and disillusioned regarding the possibility of Great Britain taking more resolute steps to deter their aggressiveness, in 1937 'Aqqad pinned his hopes on the United States and President Roosevelt as a role model for effective democratic leadership. 'Aqqad praised Roosevelt's New Deal for extricating the United States from terrible economic crisis by democratic means. In contrast to Mussolini and Hitler, Roosevelt was clearly proving that a stricken nation could be rehabilitated and an effective recovery program instituted by means of creating a democratic welfare state. All this had been accomplished in America without dictatorship, without violence, and without channeling the nation's energies into plans for territorial expansion. Roosevelt's America represented the model for democracy in the future. In addition America, devoid of any "imperialist passions," could in his view potentially stem the wild dash toward war being led by Mussolini and Hitler. Roosevelt's democratic America was the world's hope for avoiding a destructive war.[11]

The most systematic critique of the danger to world peace and to Egypt posed by the aggressive and imperialist foreign policy of Fascist Italy in the mid-1930s appeared in *al-Risala*. More than the generally restrained *al-Hilal*, perhaps even more than the stridently secularist *al-Majalla al-Jadida*, *al-Risala* was an anticolonial forum. Beyond being an outlet for the expression of Egyptian opinion, from its inception in 1933, *al-Risala* manifested an Arab and Islamic orientation. In its pages, first Fascism and later Nazism were depicted not only as a threat to Egypt and its democracy, but also to the Arab Middle East, to the Islamic world, and beyond these to all "Eastern" countries.

Two writers—*al-Risala*'s founder and editor Ahmad Hasan al-Zayyat, and its main commentator on international affairs Muhammad 'Abdalla 'Inan—took the lead in the journal's denunciations of Italian Fascist foreign policy. As early as late 1934, 'Inan was interpreting tension and military skirmishes along the Somali-Ethiopian border as a "struggle between Western imperialism and Ethiopia" and a "plot by imperialism to attack and conquer her [Ethiopia]." Italy's provocative military behavior was part of a plan for Fascist imperialist expansion in East Africa, an ambitious project to realize the imperialist goal of an Italian empire in the Mediterranean, the Middle East, and Africa.[12] In a subsequent essay analyzing the geographical and historical links between Egypt and Ethiopia, ʿInan emphasized that Egypt's sympathies in the conflict should naturally lay with Ethiopia, an ancient nation seeking only to defend its freedom and independence against "the aggression of Western imperialism [ʿudwan al-istiʿmar al-gharbi]."[13]

By the summer of 1935, the imminent threat of war between Italy and Ethiopia led al-Risala's editor Ahmad Hasan al-Zayyat to employ his rich repertoire of condemnatory adjectives to level a strident attack upon "bloody, barbaric Fascism [al-fashistiyya al-damawiyya al-mutawahhisha]." The crisis in East Africa being engineered by Mussolini was artificial, a fictitious pretext for an unprovoked war of conquest aimed at "destroying an ancient, free, and independent country." Ethiopia had never shown any hostility toward Italy, and Italy had no legitimate reason for aggressing against her. The entire purpose of the impending war was imperial in nature; the desire to make Ethiopia an Italian colony settled with Italian immigrants. To achieve his imperialist goals, Mussolini was prepared to wage "organized murder by way of war." Never restrained in his use of words, Zayyat summed up the Italian imperialist project in East Africa as "unabashed looting [al-salb al-jahr]" and "blatant piracy [al-qarsana al-mujarrada]."[14]

Zayyat had little confidence in the willingness or the ability of the international community to restrain Italian aggression. In his view, a tacit alliance existed among Western countries with similar imperialist interests to protect. The indifference of the European powers to the fate of Ethiopia also reflected European racism, which was prepared to accept the brutal conquest of an African nation because its people were black.[15] In a subsequent editorial calling on Egyptian public opinion to rally behind Ethiopia and to denounce Italy's "criminal act of aggression," Zayyat voiced his deep disappointment in the hesitant behavior of the members of the League of Nations in the crisis. "There is no chance that we will see the League of Nations supporting, even once, an Eastern state or nation regarded as weak, even if law and justice are on its side," he proclaimed. As a consequence of European hypocrisy and opportunism, the League of Nations was impotent: Mussolini's road toward aggression against Ethiopia was clear.[16]

The actual outbreak of war in East Africa led Zayyat to vitriolic denunciations of Italian imperialism. What Italy was perpetrating in East Africa was a "crime [*ithm*]" fueled by European arrogance and chauvinism. In the racist eyes of Mussolini, "the Ethiopians are unquestionably a barbarian multitude because they do not eat spaghetti and do not drink Chianti. . . . They have not developed past the stage of being slaves for [other] nations." Mussolini's predatory imperialism was leading the world back to a new age of "barbarism [*jahiliyya*]," of might is right, of tribal chauvinism and the sanctification of war. In particular, Italy's use of poison gas as a weapon of mass destruction leveled against civilian populations proved the barbaric nature of the war. In the Italo-Ethiopian conflict, humanity was descending to a level of bestiality.[17]

Muhammad 'Abdalla 'Inan's numerous commentaries on the Italo-Ethiopian war in 1935–36 were less florid in tone but equally critical in substance. 'Inan analyzed the conflict against the background of what he termed "the collapse of world order." Surveying the recent history of international relations, 'Inan observed that the international arrangements put in place after the Great War, intended to promote international stability, were in dissolution by the mid-1930s. The militaristic drive now being manifested by Italian Fascism was undermining the international system that had been intended to promote peace between nations and to guarantee the security of the "small nations" that had emerged in the wake of the Great War. Italian Fascism was a destructive force that was shattering international agreements and treaties in pursuit of its ethnocentric imperialist agenda. The gutting of existing agreements in order to create a new world power system favorable to itself was the ultimate Fascist aim. From this standpoint, 'Inan saw Fascism as a reactionary and antimodern phenomenon, a force seeking to annul the values of freedom, tolerance, progress, and peace among nations.[18]

'Inan believed that Italy's savage attack upon Ethiopia was reflective of the inhumane nature of "barbaric Fascism [*al-fashistiyya al-hamajiyya*]." He denounced both the internal and external policies of the Fascist regime in Italy. Whereas internally it was based on "murder, imprisonment, banishment, confiscation, and other means of organized violence," externally it was now oriented toward "expansion, imperialism, and the exploitation of the natural resources found in abundance in the recesses of Ethiopia." 'Inan posited a direct connection between Fascist dictatorship at home and Fascist militarism abroad. The use of such barbaric force against

Ethiopia paralleled and reflected Fascist internal policies. Anyone who employed violence and the techniques of terror against legitimate opposition domestically would not shrink from the use of weapons of mass destruction, such as poison gas, against external opponents.[19]

'Inan's analyses repeatedly warned of the probable negative consequences of Fascist expansionism and the destruction of Ethiopian independence. In a global context, he saw the Ethiopian war was only the first phase of a global fascist strategy to establish the hegemonic place of Fascism within the international system. By means of "arbitrary Fascist dictation," Italy was establishing new international norms whereby might made right and anyone who threatened the use of force was successful. The major and immediate danger of Fascist militarism was to the "weak nations" of the Mediterranean, the Middle East, and Africa. Like other Egyptian observers, 'Inan worried that Fascism, victorious and heroic in Ethiopia in its own eyes, would continue its unrestrained foreign policy and be unstoppable in the international arena. Captive of the belief in the "absolute necessity of fulfilling the dream of establishing a new Roman Empire," Fascist Italy would not stop with the conquest of "the small weak nation" of Ethiopia; in addition, "she is eyeing other weak nations," including Egypt and the Arab states.[20]

'Inan occasionally presented an optimistic long-range scenario concerning the Fascist threat. While the emergence and success of Italian Fascism was a "tragedy [ma'sa]," in late 1935 he saw it as a temporary and reversible one. For 'Inan, "the destruction of Fascism is essential." 'Inan believed that a reactionary historical phenomenon like Fascism had no chance of persistence. The destructive impulses it was displaying and the terrible damage it was currently causing would in the final analysis operate against it, arousing the forces of peace and democracy to mobilize and to defeat it. In the end, Fascism would be unable to prevail against the forces of modernity and democracy. Despite its victory in Ethiopia and the prospect of a continued imperialist assault in other parts of the world, Fascist Italy was bound to encounter the determined opposition of a coalition of democratic states and small nations and hence be stopped. The blocking of its external momentum would in turn produce the collapse of the Fascist regime from within once Mussolini's imperialist megalomania had been exposed as hollow bombast. 'Inan predicted that eventually a "brave political coup" within Italy, supported by the democratic powers, would put an end to the tragedy of Fascism.[21]

Occasional expressions of optimism notwithstanding, 'Inan's commentaries later in 1936–37 were usually marked by a pessimistic tone concerning the danger Fascism represented for world peace. In late 1936, his analyses of international affairs emphasized the apparently unstoppable force represented by the fascist powers. The international community had been unable to prevent Italy's conquest and annexation of Ethiopia. The tacit acquiescence of the democratic states in the elimination of a member state of the League of Nations was fueling Mussolini's ambitions for territorial expansion. The recent creation of the Rome-Berlin Axis, bringing together the dictatorial regimes in Italy and Germany, further augmented fascist power. The new war in Spain, where "fascism has ignited a civil war" and in which Italy was supporting the antidemocratic forces of Franco in their drive to overthrow a democratic regime and to establish an authoritarian one, proved that fascism was on the offensive and working its will in the international sphere. Those most threatened by these ominous developments were "weak nations" who could no longer rely on the League of Nations or international law to serve as their protector against aggression.[22]

For 'Inan, Egypt was definitely one of the countries threatened by the international successes of Fascist Italy. In a commentary of late 1937 entitled "Egypt and Italy: The Lessons of the Past Are Guides to the Present," he examined the implications for Egypt of the intensified Fascist presence in the Mediterranean. In his view, Fascist Italy posed a definite menace to Egypt. 'Inan rejected Italian declarations denying any aggressive Italian designs upon Egypt. Egypt could not remain indifferent to the fact that the "grand imperial dream" of Italian Fascists was "a Roman Empire in which Egypt, like Libya, was only an ancient Roman province [*wilaya rumaniyya sabiqa*]." Egypt must not be seduced into believing Mussolini's protestations of goodwill. For Fascist Italy, "right and law are merely force." Italy currently "acts according to a naked Machiavellian policy that justifies all means for the sake of achieving the aim." Armed with the finest modern weaponry and the captive of an imperial dream, Italy will be unable to restrain itself when it comes to Egypt. The Fascist threat to Egypt was a real one, and "Egypt has every reason to be very much concerned." Its defensive alliance with Great Britain notwithstanding, 'Inan maintained that Egypt not be seduced into relying on external protection. As a small nation threatened from the outside, it needed to rely on itself, mobilize its resources, and strengthen its own armed forces in order to defend its sovereignty in an age when "the only determining factor is force."[23]

'Inan's pessimistic analyses of the international scene in the mid-1930s paid less attention to Nazi Germany as a threat to world peace. In a late 1936 overview of European politics, he did denounce Nazi Germany for providing, along with Fascist Italy, substantial aid to the antidemocratic Nationalists in the Spanish Civil War. From a broader perspective, Nazi Germany was a disruptive power, one that was resolved to achieve hegemony in Europe by force or the threat of force. For 'Inan, Nazi Germany was "a militaristic, aggressive power that annihilates all individual rights and liberties, denies universal rules, and challenges all international principles of justice. It has revived the ancient German world view in its most dangerous form, that might makes right [al-haqq huwa al-quwwa]." 'Inan emphasized the monumental shift in the world balance of power currently underway. With the emergence of threats to international stability coming from Fascist Italy and Nazi Germany, and with the entry of an expansionist Japan into the ranks of the revisionist camp, the Western democracies were no longer the hegemonic force in international affairs. The moves at rapprochement recently set in motion between the German-Italian Axis powers on the one hand and imperial Japan on the other were developments that potentially "threatens all the forces of democracy and peace" led by Great Britain and France. The aim of all three authoritarian states was to shatter existing international agreements and forge a new world order; in the process, this emerging tripartite alliance threatened to lead mankind into a new world war. The democratic camp needed to vigorously resist the unrestrained international behavior of the authoritarian states.[24]

In his frequent commentaries of 1936–1937 on the Spanish Civil War, 'Inan continued to present a gloomy portrait of a European continent now divided into two rival camps between which war was inevitable. The open affiliation of Nazi Germany with the camp of war on the battlefield in Spain had greatly escalated the fateful contest between dictatorship and democracy. The proxy struggle in Spain between the dictatorships and the democracies was in his view a zero-sum game in which one side would win decisively and the other lose completely. In language nearly as florid as that used earlier by his colleague Zayyat in regard to the Italo-Ethiopian war, 'Inan defined the struggle in Spain as a black-and-white conflict between "absolute justice" on the one hand and "absolute evil" on the other, an existential "war of life and death" between two irreconcilable ideologies.[25] Throughout, his message was that the world's democracies could not remain indifferent in the struggle in Spain. As 'Inan saw it, "the future of peace depends on democracy and is in its hands."[26] There was no room for the kind of acquiescence that the democracies had shown regarding Italy's aggression in Ethiopia. The democratic camp needed to mobilize all its resources to face the threat to democracy made so obvious by the Spanish Civil War. "If democracy is to win this decisive battle for the fate of civilization, it will be a victory for a [form of] civilization based on respect for law and liberty. However, should the principles of barbaric force [*mabadi' al-quwwa al-hamajiyya*] adhered to by Fascism and Nazism prevail, the enlightened civilized order will collapse and Europe will return to the systems of the Middle Ages."[27]

As the confrontation between the liberal democracies and the fascist dictatorships accelerated as a result of the expansionist actions of Germany in 1938–39, Egyptian intellectuals increasingly came to perceive that Nazi territorial aspirations and international aggressiveness were becoming the greatest danger facing the world. Their commentaries on the successive international crises of 1938–39—the German annexation of Austria in March 1938; the summer's confrontation over the Sudetenland in Czechoslovakia that culminating in the Munich crisis in September; the Nationalist defeat of the Republicans in Spain by early 1939; the German takeover of the rump of Czechoslovakia, soon followed by the Italian invasion of Albania, in the spring of 1939; and finally the crisis over the status of the city of Danzig in the summer of 1939 that led to the German assault on Poland and the beginning of World War II—demonstrate a solidifying consensus that Nazi Germany and Fascist Italy were an immediate threat to international stability and peace, a threat that Egypt needed to resist by aligning itself with the liberal democracies who, for all their diplomatic blunders, nonetheless represented the best hope for the future of the world as well as the only realistic option for Egypt and the Arab Middle East.

Al-Hilal's "Register of the Days [*Sijill al-Ayyam*]," written by Sami al-Jaridini, was a monthly commentary on current affairs. It provides a convenient barometer of the journal's position in regard to the international crises of the period. In March 1938, Germany's incorporation of Austria into the Third Reich led Jaridini to ominous conclusions regarding Nazi Germany's imperialist aims. Hitler's dream of establishing a German empire was on the way to being realized, he warned. The "German danger [*al-khatar al-almani*]" was now becoming immediate. Reminding his readers of Hitler's long struggle to overturn the Versailles peace arrangements, Jaridini warned that "the barbarism of the German race [*hamajiyyat al-'unsur al-almani*]" now threatened European and international stability. Hitler's *Mein Kampf,* the "holy book" of Nazi Germany, had placed "Germany over all"; Nazi foreign policy was now striving to actualize that vision. Germany's aim of achieving "the unity of the German race under the flag of one state" recognized no bounds or restraints. Jaridini regarded Hitler as dedicated to fulfilling the historical ambitions of German imperialism, a goal that reflected the long-standing aspirations of the German nation and hence enjoyed the backing and support of the German people.[28]

By mid-1938, Jaridini's view of the international situation was a pessimistic one. The polarization between the European democracies and dictatorships was deepening, and beyond that confrontation between "freedom" and "tyranny," an additional struggle was being waged between "the Nazi dictatorship" and "the Bolshevik dictatorship." Jaridini, a supporter of liberal democracy who believed in "liberty and freedom of thought and expression in both political and non-political affairs," saw little or no difference between the totalitarian regimes in power in Germany, Italy, and Russia. Although Hitler was waging "a war of words" against Bolshevism, in reality "Bolshevism is another form of extreme socialism that sacrifices the individual on the altar of the state." For their part, "Fascism and Nazism are also based on the same principle—deification of the state and the loss of the personality of the individual in the state." The conflict between fascism and communism stemmed not from ideology but from a clash of interests and the striving for power of ruthless rulers. Already in mid-1938, Jaridini foresaw that the crosscutting tensions across the continent would lead to armed conflict in the near future.[29]

Other commentaries in *al-Hilal* of mid-1938 reacted in a similar manner to what one defined as "the raging struggle between the two camps: democracy and dictatorship." An August editorial analyzed the current diplomatic maneuvers among the European powers. It criticized "the dictatorial axis, the Rome-Berlin Axis," for their international provocations and reacted favorably to the growing awareness in the democratic camp, especially Great Britain, of the danger these aggressive actions posed. The editorial cited numerous potential crises on the international agenda in the summer of 1938—Hitler's claims versus Czechoslovakia and the Sudeten-land; an intensified Italian military presence in the Mediterranean and the Red Sea that posed a threat to Egypt and the Middle East; the civil war in Spain, which was also an arena of competition between the two camps—and warned that the struggle between the democracies and the dictator-ships was growing more intense. Great Britain and France were on the cusp of a momentous decision: could the danger to the international sys-tem be averted "through diplomatic maneuvers, or will the well-known methods of fascism—provocation, manipulation, adventurism, and sur-prise attack—in the final analysis compel them against their will to enter into a great war" in the defense of liberalism and democracy?[30]

The extended crisis of the fate of the Sudetenland that culminated in the Munich Agreement awarding the disputed territory to Germany drew intense attention in Egypt. An overview of the international situation on the eve of the Munich Agreement by *al-Risala*'s editor Ahmad Hasan al-Zayyat attempted to situate the Czech crisis in the historical development of the ideological clash between democracy and dictatorship. The democ-racies, emerging triumphant from the First World War, had created what they hoped would be an "order of peace" in the world. That international system was now being undermined by "the absolute tyranny [*al-tughyan al-mutliq*]" of Fascist Italy and Nazi Germany. Democracy was on the de-fensive in face of this challenge, forced to defend both its own existence and the continuation of an enlightened world order.[31]

Zayyat was an equal-opportunity critic in September 1938. On the one hand, he saw little hope that the democracies would be able to appease the Nazi appetite for expansion into Czechoslovakia, evaluating Western diplomatic efforts as likely to have the effect of "a tiny watering can in the face of a huge fire." In his view, the weakness and impotence of Great Brit-ain and France in the crisis were largely responsible for its degeneration into a situation that was likely to lead to war. On the other hand, Zayyat also condemned Nazi Germany for unjustified aggression in the pursuit of territorial expansion. Zayyat's harshest rhetoric was reserved for Hitler, who had opened his "hellish voice [*fahu al-jahannami*]" in order to devour one of Germany's neighbors. Nothing could now restrain Hitler's aggres-sive drives. Never at a loss for extravagant language, Zayyat compared con-temporary totalitarian dictatorship to "the re-infection of a bestial disease in enlightened and civilized man"; it was similar to "the disease of rabies." In the florid neoclassical language favored by Zayyat, the Munich crisis threatened to return man to a state of primitivism in which "the man of the twentieth century," who had achieved such marvelous scientific and cultural achievements, was now "forgetting everything and reverting back to the wilderness of dark and barren rocks to which his ancestors were expelled from the Garden of Eden, naked and stripped of all the glory of civilization, his spirit emptied of the nobility brought by religion, his feelings depleted of the glories and beauty of culture. He looks down upon his bleeding prey, his mouth drooling, his dagger dripping blood."[32]

The Munich Agreement of September 1938 and the subsequent annexation of the Sudetenland to Germany were perceived by *al-Hilal* as an escalation, rather than a resolution, of tension on the international scene. Munich only heightened the journal's antipathy toward the aggressive methods of the fascist states. For his part, Ibrahim al-Misri saw the Munich Agreement as a failure. The confrontation between democracy and dictatorship was a zero-sum game: "each time that history records a failure for democracy, it records a victory for dictatorship." Thus Munich had not worked to alleviate international tension but rather had served to heighten it because through it "the two dictators, Hitler and Mussolini," appeared as victors. The democracies' misguided restraint toward Hitler and his demands "went a long way towards appeasing dictatorship, compromising and giving in, and this was now forcing them to make a difficult choice between two options: absolute submission or all-out war." The dictatorships were bound to view democratic weakness of will at Munich as the opportunity for additional demands, for "a continued campaign of victories by dictatorship over democracy." The territorial hunger of the two dictatorships knew few limits. Munich was indeed a harbinger of future cataclysm: "the bitter truth is that the fate of Europe and the world in the wake of Chamberlain's policy has created a situation in which Europe has bound itself to the passions of the dictatorial front," a situation that would potentially lead to "a horrible war of the sort that history has never known!"[33]

The specter of the Munich Agreement haunted Egyptian intellectuals thereafter. An editorial in *al-Risala* in August 1939, the eve of the war, revisited Munich. It lamented the results achieved at Munich in the previous year and the collapse of "the resolve of Great Britain and France" in the face of Hitler's threats. The weekly attributed the powerlessness of the democracies at Munich in large part to their military inadequacy in comparison to Nazi military strength. Nazi Germany had engaged in an enormous national effort to enhance the size and power of its military. "Hitler understands the meaning and value of the army for the state, and has assigned it the role of shaping and enhancing the spirit of masculinity and force among Germans, educating them to be prepared to die at any moment if necessary." At Munich, Hitler had terrified Chamberlain with the threat of provoking a war for which the Western democracies were unprepared. *Al-Risala* invoked a pathetic image of the British leader "whom the world will never forgive for his strange behavior in the affair. . . . It will never forget the photograph taken of Chamberlain, the British prime minister, emerging from his car after returning from Munich and waving a document which read: 'We have brought peace to the world.'" The journal denounced the Western democracies for not having given sufficient attention to military preparedness. In contrast to Germany's massive military buildup, Great Britain and France were beset by "lethargy and weakness." The former was "content to remain with her small army"; the latter, "despite her large army, is paralyzed in the face of the overall anarchy" in Europe that had been produced by recent Nazi initiatives. The democracies were simply not sufficiently aware of the importance of strength and that, in order to defend the values of democracy against fascist totalitarianism, military preparedness was essential.[34]

While Nazi aggressiveness and expansionism was perceived as the major threat to world peace, Egyptian intellectuals were also aware of the more proximate danger to Egypt and the Middle East that continued to be posed by the imperial ambitions of Fascist Italy. In December 1938, in the face of recently intensified Italian efforts to "tighten the cultural links between Egypt and Italy, especially in the area of education," *al-Risala* cautioned its readers that "we should be careful and on guard." In Fascist Italy, culture, religion, and literature were all "in the service of politics." The imperialist designs of Italy in the Middle East were well known. Egyptians needed to be wary of cultural cooperation with Italy, "whose open policy is conquest of the East and the re-establishment of the Roman Empire after the submission and enslavement of the eastern peoples to it." Italy's offer to provide teachers of Italian for Egyptian schools was in *al-Risala*'s eyes "part of that same policy, one of a whole array of means that Italian propaganda is employing to prepare the way for the Fascist strategy [of expansion]."[35]

Al-Hilal's and *al-Risala*'s critical view of Fascist and Nazi foreign policy was paralleled in *al-Majalla al-Jadida* by late 1938. For Salama Musa, a crucial difference between "the totalitarian state" and "the democratic state" was their international behavior. Totalitarian despotism externalized itself through aggression abroad. Perceiving Nazi Germany through a new lens after the Munich crisis of 1938, Musa now held that "the aim of the totalitarian state is to maximize power on its way to war." In Nazi Germany, domestic reform had been undertaken in the service of imperialist expansion. Hitler was obsessed with "material and mental preparations" for a future war, preparations that went beyond the production of new weaponry and operational planning to include the enrollment of German youth in paramilitary youth organizations intended prepare them for war. Nazi Germany's slogan was "guns before butter." All this stood in sharp contrast to the priorities of the democratic state: "the democratic state always attempts to supply an abundance of butter, that is, to produce and distribute food to the masses ahead of every other goal." Thus, whereas Nazi Germany was investing massive sums in the production of new weaponry, post-Depression era America was investing millions to feed its poor. On the ideological level, Nazi Germany's obsession with militarism and preparation for conquest stood in equally sharp contrast to America's sponsorship of pacific international cooperation: "whereas Germany has produced Hitler, a propagandist for war, the United States produced Wilson, the originator of the concept of the League of Nations."[36]

In an essay weighing the respective merits of nationalism and internationalism, Niqula Yusuf complemented Musa's denunciation of contemporary Fascist and Nazi aggressiveness through contrasting what he saw as the internationalist patriotism of Giuseppe Mazzini, an Italian committed to working for both the national liberation of Italy and the welfare of mankind as a whole, with the solipsistic and anti-universalist nationalism of Mussolini. Yusuf's view of Hitler and Nazism was equally negative. Citing *Mein Kampf* to the effect that "true grandeur in this world can only be achieved by the powerful conqueror," Yusuf denounced such militant nationalism as chauvinist. The goal of a genuinely modern and enlightened society should be to create "an empire of humanity," not "a nationalist empire."[37]

The apprehension expressed by Egyptian intellectuals concerning the fascist tide apparently engulfing Europe intensified in 1939. Commencing publication in January 1939, the new weekly journal *al-Thaqafa* from its inception provided regular coverage of the global struggle being waged

between what it termed "the democratic camp [*al-mu'askar al-dimuqrati*]"
and "the dictatorial camp [*al-mu'askar al-diktaturi*]."[38] "This huge struggle
between giants" was, in the words of the journal's political editor, "the
most immense struggle that the world has ever known between two political and social systems"; it was "the axis of European politics, in fact,
the axis of global politics."[39] In its inaugural overview of the global scene,
al-Thaqafa presented the recent crisis that had resulted with the Munich
Agreement as only one phase in an intensifying international confrontation that had begun in the mid-1930s and that thus far had been marked
by "victory after victory for dictatorship and defeat after defeat for democracy." Germany's success in remilitarizing the Rhineland; Italy's invasion and conquest of Ethiopia; the German takeover of Austria; the Munich accord that had prepared the ground for the collapse of the Czech
Republic; Franco's imminent victory in the Spanish Civil War; the creation of the Axis between Germany and Italy and the policy of "threat,
defiance, and provocation" that they were pursuing: all these triumphs by
the fascist powers had reversed the balance of power between the two opposing camps in favor of "the dictatorial camp." Democracy was now on
the defensive, forced to defend both its existence and the continued progress of the world as a whole.[40]

Al-Thaqafa placed the main blame for the international crisis on
the dictatorial camp. Germany, Italy, and Japan all had "an aspiration to
achieve imperialistic aims" whether in Europe, the Mediterranean and
Middle East, or Asia; "that is the real reason for the alliance among them."
It was the aggressive and expansionist policies of Italy and Germany in
particular that the journal saw as "likely to ignite a new world war." But
al-Thaqafa was also critical of the craven behavior of the Western democracies. At Munich, Czechoslovakia had been offered to Germany as a
sacrifice for saving the peace. But the respite gained was illusionary. What
happened at Munich was that "dictatorship gained an immense victory
while democracy suffered an overwhelming, humiliating defeat." While
Munich was "perhaps the end of the tragic disaster of Czechoslovakia, it is
only the beginning of the huge, terrible, and most serious disaster of all,
the disaster of the European continent." The awful consequences of Munich were already becoming apparent: while the democracies clung to "a
policy of submission and compliance," Nazi Germany was perfecting its
strategy for achieving "control over the entire continent of Europe." The parliamentary democracies of the West appeared powerless to take a resolute,

decisive stance; the structural weakness of parliamentary government was being fully exploited by the dictatorships in which one man ruled and decided. It seemed that democracy "emerged from one defeat only to fall into another; every crisis ends in further capitulation and submission on its part."[41]

This gloomy portrait notwithstanding, *al-Thaqafa* had not lost all hope that democracy could eventually succeed in its confrontation with dictatorship. The journal rejected the defeatist, and in its view hasty, conclusion that the international crisis signified "the decline of democracy." It was convinced that the democratic powers, led by Great Britain, France, and the United States ("which today is the strongest power in the world"), could reverse course and successfully challenge the dictatorial camp. The democratic camp possessed both quantitative and qualitative strengths that the dictatorships lacked: it had greater economic and human resources to mobilize in support of democracy, and was capable of winning the arms race with the dictatorships and of ultimately gaining military superiority in case of a new world war. Although currently on the defensive, the democratic camp "has time on its side, and its vast resources are the surest guarantee of its superiority in the long-term, worldwide military contest."[42]

The early months of 1939 witnessed further setbacks for the democratic camp. For *al-Majalla al-Jadida*, the Spanish Nationalist conquest of Barcelona in January 1939, an event signifying impending Nationalist victory in the Spanish Civil War, was a disheartening development, indeed "a new chapter in the tragedy of European politics." The journal, which throughout the war had supported the Republican cause, presented Franco's victory as a negative shift in the European balance of power in favor of the antidemocratic forces now on the offensive against democracy. Referring to the previous year's Munich Agreement and its object of deterring fascist expansionism through diplomacy, its assessment was that "the talk about saving peace has become empty words. . . . The League of Nations is dead." The defeat of the democratic forces in Spain meant an undermining of democracy in the Mediterranean basin, an event that, by shifting the balance of power, also had the potential to affect Egypt adversely.[43]

Several articles in *al-Hilal* in the early months of 1939 were devoted to warning about the fascist threat to world stability and peace. Writing at the beginning of 1939, 'Abbas Mahmud al-'Aqqad accompanied his vehement criticism of the totalitarian character of fascist internal policies with the advocacy of Arab support for the efforts of the Western democracies to resist fascist international aggressiveness. ʿAqqad presented a utilitarian rationale for the view that the Arab nations needed to support Great Britain and France in the case of war. In his view, the Arab world needed to solidify its ties to the two democracies in an effort to use the fraught international situation to promote Arab national interests. The international crisis was an opportunity for furthering the goals of Arab freedom and independence, for increasing the weight of the Arab states in the international arena, and for strengthening the ties among the Arab countries as well as for fostering their increased cooperation with the developed world. He predicted that current international tensions would work to enhance "the good relations between the Arab nations and the two great powers, Great Britain and France," thereby bringing mutual benefits for both sides. Support for the Western democracies would serve the cause of Arab independence.[44]

Ibrahim al-Misri, in a February essay entitled "Germany Advances Towards the East," cautioned Egyptians that Germany's imperialist aspirations were pushing it in the direction of the Balkans and beyond that toward the Mediterranean and the Middle East. A map accompanying the essay delineated Nazi Germany's efforts at expansion. Germany was a state of eighty million people after its incorporation of Austria and the Sudetenland in 1938, and the Munich Agreement had provided an opening for its further economic expansion into Eastern Europe. After Munich, the rump of Czechoslovakia "from an economic standpoint was now at Germany's mercy." The Third Reich was continuing its pressure against Czechoslovakia, threatening its existence as an independent state. More broadly, Germany's expansionist aims had perturbed the international balance of power, placing the entire world in an accelerating cycle of tension. In Misri's view, this expansionist impulse would impel Nazi Germany to "expand towards southeastern Europe" from whence it could pose a real threat to the Arab Middle East.[45]

A month later, Sami al-Jaridini's review of Germany's aggressive foreign policy expressed a clear fear of Nazi intentions of world domination. Hitler now controlled the course of events in the European arena. His political and military strength was growing to the point where, should he wish to do so, he could "imitate Napoleon" and expand in various directions, the Middle East included. Germany's international aggressiveness was now directly challenging the international position of Great Britain. The latter faced a moment of decision: either the British Empire would display the courage to "defend all parts of the world" threatened by Hitler and Nazism and "learn how to overcome the enemy," or "it would no longer exist."[46]

Writing in the same issue of *al-Hilal*, Niqula al-Haddad was vitriolic in his denunciations of Mussolini and Hitler, terming them "merchants of death who are dragging the peoples towards war." "World peace is in danger," he warned in March 1939. In his opinion, Fascism and Nazism needed war in order to maintain themselves as dictatorial entities. Without the war in Ethiopia, Mussolini would not have survived in power; he needed a powerful military to reinforce his personal dictatorship. Similarly, "Hitler's dictatorship would not hold out for even one day were it not for his acts of adventurism and provocation in tearing the Treaty of Versailles to shreds and in reclaiming areas of Germany lost in the Great War." Expansion was an imperative for maintaining the momentum of Hitler's leadership; "his very dictatorship depends on constant incitement to war."[47]

The eventual conclusion of the civil war in Spain in March 1939 was viewed in Egypt as another international advance for the dictatorial camp. In a commentary in *al-Thaqafa* entitled "The Spanish Tragedy," Muhammad 'Awad Muhammad credited the support of Fascist Italy and Nazi Germany for Franco's forces as having ensured Nationalist victory over the Republicans. In Muhammad's opinion, Nationalist Spain was dependent on Italy in particular, and it was possible that Italy would prod Spain, at last no longer absorbed in civil war, to play a more active part in the international arena alongside Italy and Germany. What price would Italy demand of Franco after helping him win the war? Would Spain become an Italian satellite? Although expressing the hope that Spain, "known for its hatred of foreign influence," might resist Italian domination and conduct an independent foreign policy, Muhammad was not certain that this would indeed be the case. While calling on Spain to "keep a distance from the painful problems of Europe," Muhammad expressed the fear that the Spanish tragedy was more likely to increase the strength of the dictatorial camp.[48]

A month later, *al-Thaqafa* cast the danger of the enhancement of Italian influence in broader terms. The Italian view that "the Mediterranean is a Roman-Italian sea" and that the lands around its shores were Italy's "living space [*mintaqa hayawiyya*]" for national aggrandizement had grown stronger with Franco's victory in the Spanish Civil War. This victory for fascism, along with the Germany's takeover of Czechoslovakia in March, was proof positive of the impotence of the democratic powers and an incentive to Italy to realize her vision of Italian domination of the Mediterranean. The Duce's desire of hegemony in the Mediterranean was turning control of the Mediterranean into a crucial international issue and "a source of danger to world peace."[49]

The German absorption of the rump of Czechoslovakia in March 1939 reinforced the prevailing Egyptian perception of the continuing expansionist desires of Nazi Germany. *Al-Thaqafa* 's editorial commentary on the event pointed out that within one year two once-independent states in Central Europe, Austria and Czechoslovakia, had "fallen prey to the German passion for expansion." The journal's sympathies were clearly with Czechoslovakia. Hitler's willingness to use military force in the pursuit of living space for Germany had resulted in a "terrible disaster and tragedy for Czechoslovakia." Once again, the democratic powers had proved helpless in the face of Nazi aggression. The devouring of Czechoslovakia by Hitler was "a direct result" of the futile policy of appeasement that the Western democracies had been pursuing since the Munich Agreement. Reiterating its earlier position that "the Munich Conference was a real disaster for democracy and for Europe, and was the opening of a new and dangerous era of German military expansion," the journal predicted that Hitler would continue to pursue the territorial expansion of the Third Reich. The enhancement of Germany's "living space" was Hitler's ultimate objective. The liquidation of Czechoslovakia's status as an independent state should put an end to any international faith in Nazi Germany's moderation. "Nazi Germany understands only the language of force," the journal declared, "and she will be stopped only by decisive, crushing force." Accordingly, *al-Thaqafa* called for the democratic camp to "mobilize all of its strength and power" and to adopt a resolute policy of deterrence in the face of "Hitlerian Germany's military and economic campaign of imperial expansion."[50]

An April editorial in *al-Majalla al-Jadida* also viewed Germany's absorption of independent Czechoslovakia as but one more step down the road of imperial expansion. The journal reminded its readers that exactly a year earlier, in March 1938, Germany had unilaterally annexed Austria to Germany. Now that the Germans had entered Prague and taken effective control of Czechoslovakia, "no one can fathom which European capital Hitler will decide to conquer next year, or sooner." Its Austrian and Czech additions had together increased Germany's population from seventy to ninety-five million, meaning that "the new Germany is the largest and strongest power" in Western and Central Europe. "Only the blind," the journal's readers were told, "can believe that Germany will calm down and be satisfied with the conquest of Czechoslovakia and its erasure from the map." In all probability, "the German campaign of aggression" would next be directed toward smaller nations such as Romania with its rich oil reserves or even the agricultural cornucopia of the Ukraine.[51]

Italy's invasion and occupation of Albania in mid-April was additional proof of the expansionist dynamic inherent in the fascist dictatorships. For *al-Thaqafa*, Italy's resort to unabashed aggression in order to conquer "a tiny, brave nation" and to turn it into an Italian protectorate clearly exposed Fascist Italy's militaristic nature and imperialist ambitions. Albania's status as a small state, as well as its Muslim nature, heightened Egyptian identification with it. According to *al-Thaqafa*, the entire Muslim world should be shocked by Italy's "liquidation of Albania's independence in a violent and objectionable manner." Islamic nations, "in particular the Islamic nations of the Mediterranean," needed to regard this brutal action as "a new warning sign that once again exposes the truth about Fascist policy and the truth about its intentions and the methods it employs." The Albanian example revealed Mussolini's true intentions; he was a "predator [*muftaris*]" who preyed upon smaller nations in his desperate effort to compete with Hitler's territorial successes. The Italian adventure in Albania proved that Fascist Italy was "following the Nazi path of territorial expansion and occupation."[52]

Writing in *al-Thaqafa* in the wake of the invasion of Albania, Muhammad 'Awad Muhammad offered a comprehensive assessment of what policy Egypt should adopt in relation to the current international situation. As he saw it, Egypt could not ignore the grave crisis developing in international affairs. The examples of Ethiopia, Austria, Czechoslovakia, and Albania, the fact that "more than once, small states have been neglected and abandoned to their fate," needed to give Egyptians grounds for concern. The immediate danger for Egypt came from Fascist Italy and its desire to dominate the Mediterranean as well as to control the Suez Canal, an integral part of Egypt. When the time came, Italy would not hesitate to challenge Great Britain as the hegemonic power in Egypt. Muhammad analyzed the threat posed by Italy as manifested in Italy's military position in Libya and along Egypt's western border, the strength of the Italian military, and the Italian regime's obvious expansionist ambitions. Despite

Egypt's Treaty of Alliance with Great Britain and its clauses relating to the defense of Egypt, Muhammad was not convinced that Egypt was safe from aggression. Britain's current military dispositions in Egypt were meager; whether these were sufficient for the defense of Egypt was problematic. More broadly, "we are living in an age marked by the tearing up of treaties and the violation of alliances." In his view, it was imperative for Egypt to augment her military preparedness and to create an autonomous military force capable of defending the country in case of Italian aggression. "We cannot deny that we are living in some of the most difficult and cruelest of times, times in which small states can no longer enjoy security and tranquility." Egypt had no choice but to assume responsibility for her own fate, to "assume the burden of defending herself and her soil."[53]

Al-Risala was equally apprehensive regarding Fascist and Nazi imperialism in the spring of 1939. In April, the journal repeated its earlier warning to the effect that the danger of the imperial ambitions of Mussolini actually menacing Egypt had been increased by the recent tightening of the Rome-Berlin Axis. It was "weak states," including the Arab states, who were the most likely victims of the imperialist drives of the two fascist powers.[54] In a May editorial entitled "there is no friendship between Islam and imperialism," the journal evaluated Italy's latest act of aggression from an explicitly Muslim perspective, arguing that the invasion of Albania was proof positive of the concreteness of the threat Italian imperialism represented for Muslims. The editorial argued that the Muslim world should not be deceived by Fascist and Nazi claims that they were also "fighting against the two imperialists, England and France," and consequently were allies of Muslims in their struggle against imperialism. The new imperialism of the Fascists and the Nazis was worse than that of the old imperialist powers. Italian imperialism had shown its ugly face in the wars it had waged against "weak peoples," both Muslim and non-Muslim, in Libya, Ethiopia, and now Albania. Mussolini was "the new emperor, reviving the glory or ancient Rome, on whose head the crowns of Ethiopia and Albania have been placed." His next likely target was Tunis; he also had designs for controlling the Suez Canal. For its part Germany was "demanding colonies for itself while giving its imperialism a Nazi basis built on hatred and contempt for the colored races." Since Italian and German imperialism was a more racist and oppressive form of imperialism and not merely an imitation of the French or British versions, "The Islamic world has no alternative but to abhor their imperialism and to consider this imperialism an enemy . . . for Islam cannot have any cordial relations with imperialism."[55]

The international crisis that eventually did lead to a new world war was of course that between Germany and Poland over the fate of the city of Danzig. As early as May 1939, al-Thaqafa viewed the crisis developing over Danzig as another example of unjustified German expansionism. "Hitlerian Germany continues to act systematically, with all its force, to erase every trace of the Treaty of Versailles," the weekly's political editor observed. By claiming Danzig as a German city with a German-speaking majority in its population, Hitler was recycling his pattern of provocation by deliberately inciting the German population of the city to protests and violence that would in the end compel Germany to use military force to occupy Danzig. "The mask has fallen off the face of Germany . . . and its true intentions at conquest and expansion have been exposed" by its demands regarding Danzig. The editorial speculated that Hitler's demands on Poland would not stop with Danzig; after Danzig he would demand other parts of Poland, such as Polish Upper Silesia, eventually leading to "the dismantling and demolition" of the Polish state as a whole. If Hitler was successful in his demands, Poland could anticipate "the fate of Czechoslovakia." Danzig was a second Sudetenland, a pretext for the German takeover of Poland. "This is the true aim which Germany is striving to achieve." Al-Thaqafa was pessimistic regarding the prospect of deterring Germany and Hitler in the Danzig crisis. Given the weakness which the democratic states were showing in regard to Danzig, the editorial speculated that Germany would once again succeed in its expansionist aims. "There is a high likelihood," it stated, that the crisis over Danzig would end in a "peaceful compromise" in which Great Britain and France, along with Poland, would meet most of Germany's demands.[56]

One possible deterrent to German aggrandizement at the expense of Poland was a strategic rapprochement between the Western democracies and the Soviet Union. Al-Thaqafa closely tracked the desultory negotiations between the Western powers and the Soviet Union in the spring-summer of 1939. Regarding the Communist state as a key player in contemporary international affairs, the journal applauded the attempt of Great Britain and France to reach out to the Soviet Union in order to "build a front of opposition to the aggression of the Hitlerian and Fascist dictatorships." A show of strength by the democracies, in concert with Russia, was the only way to restrain Mussolini and Hitler and to save the peace.[57] Al-

Thaqafa was optimistic about the possibility of Stalin's committing himself to alliance with the democratic powers both because of the historic enmity between fascism and communism, and because of Soviet fears that "the German policy of expansion eastwards" would eventually threaten Soviet territory.[58] The weekly had great hopes that a successful Western-Soviet rapprochement would result in a "defensive alliance [*mithaq difāʿi*]" that would serve as an effective counter to the Rome-Berlin Axis. *Al-Thaqafa* saw such an alliance as "a firm guarantee of peace" that could block German and Italian aggression. Such an alliance would provide solid security for "all the countries neighboring on the Soviet Union." No less important, the alliance would have a reassuring effect for all small states, offering refuge in its shadow "from the aggression of the two dictatorial powers."[59]

Ibrahim al-Misri's June 1939 overview "The Political Situation in Europe" in *al-Hilal* again traced the seeds of war to the previous year's Munich Agreement. Munich had been "a disaster [*nakba*] for the Western democracies and world peace." According to his interpretation, the Munich accord had been reached because the governments in power in Great Britain and France wished to block the possible expansion of the Soviet Union. They preferred to satisfy Hitler's demand regarding the German-speaking portion of Czechoslovakia in the hope that Nazi Germany would serve as a barrier to Communist expansion to the west. But "Chamberlain and Daladier had made a fateful error!" They had failed to understand Germany's own aggressive and expansionist intentions. Territorial concessions would not satisfy the Nazi desire to "establish a German empire." Poland, the Danube basin, and the Balkans would surely follow after Austria and Czechoslovakia. Chamberlain and Daladier had totally failed to understand Hitler's shrewdness. Since he had no present interest in clashing with the Western democracies backed by their considerable colonial resources, Hitler had adopted a circuitous strategy that Misri termed "the politics of threats and crises." The tragedy of democracy at Munich was that Hitler had found naïve statesmen who played into his hands and actually facilitated his policy of German expansion "by peaceful means."[60]

Fascist Italy's recent conquest of Albania and "Italian aspirations in the Balkans and Asia Minor" augmented and intensified the danger posed by Nazi expansionism. Misri stressed that Italy already ruled Ethiopia and Libya in Africa and thus was "a close neighbor of Egypt and the Sudan." Moreover, Misri warned that "Italian imperialists" also had a vision of "annexing Egypt to the Italian empire" in order to create territorial contiguity from Libya to the Red Sea, Ethiopia, and the Indian Ocean. Together, the imperialist intentions of Nazi Germany and Fascist Italy posed a serious threat to the world position of Great Britain and France. Fortunately, the latter were currently in "a process of opening their eyes and awakening" to the magnitude of the danger to themselves, to their empires, and to all of Europe. Even the United States was coming to realize that Hitler and Mussolini posed a threat to world stability and peace. Hitler's most recent threats against Poland over the Danzig issue and the perception that Poland could become "a second Czechoslovakia" were leading the Western democracies to the conclusion that Hitler could be stopped only by war. Thus Hitler's "bellicose strategy of threats and more threats," Misri concluded, was inevitably leading to a state of war.[61]

The confrontation over the fate of Danzig reached its peak in the summer of 1939. In July, al-Thaqafa offered a global perspective on what was at stake in the Danzig crisis. Its political editor did not see how "Great Britain and France can remain indifferent, marking time, when confronted with the mockery and contempt with which Germany is overturning peace and the balance of power in Europe." If the Western democracies did not show resolve this time, "the entire basis of the European order will collapse and Germany will become the unrivalled ruler of Europe, doing whatever it likes on the continent." By this time, the journal was imploring Great Britain and France not to flinch over Danzig. They needed to take a clear and resolute position in support of Poland, giving Hitler an unmistakable message that if Germany did not withdraw its demands regarding Danzig it would be responsible for the outbreak of war. Now arguing that "only force can overcome force," the journal expressed the hope that "the adoption of a firm, bellicose stance" by England and France could at the last moment "prevent the danger of war."[62]

In mid-August, commemorating the twenty-fifth anniversary of the start of the First World War and two weeks before the outbreak of the second, al-Thaqafa compared the factors that had produced war in 1914 with those obtaining in 1939. "Does history repeat itself," the journal asked? After noting both similarities and differences between the situation in 1914 and those of 1939, its cautious prognosis was that history did not necessarily have to repeat itself. But the outcome was still in doubt. Everything depended on Nazi Germany. "Can those playing with fire, mocking the peace of the world, threatening war in order to fulfill dreams of grandeur and reign of empire, think again about their actions? . . . Are they capable of acting in concert with others to preserve and defend peace and civilization?"[63]

Al-Thaqafa's commentaries on international affairs in mid-1939 had viewed a rapprochement of the Western powers with the Soviet Union as a potential deterrent to Nazi aggression and a subsequent world war. When in August Stalin instead concluded a nonaggression pact with Germany that facilitated and endorsed German military action against Poland, the reaction in Egypt was surprise and disappointment. *Al-Thaqafa*'s initial account of the Soviet-German détente was entitled "A Moscow Bomb." The Ribbentrop-Molotov agreement demolished the hopes that the weekly had previously placed in the creation of a possible antifascist front. Whereas the world had anticipated that Russia would join "a strong front to struggle against Germany and block its expansion," now Stalin had chosen the opposite course. The agreement fundamentally changed the balance of power in the international arena. For its part, the Soviet Union apparently insured against the German "expansion to the east" that was of great concern to Stalin. The pact had also effectively separated Germany from any possible anti-Communist front directed against the Soviet Union. The weekly pessimistically predicted that the long-term result of the German-Soviet nonaggression pact would be the enhancement of the Communist aim of world hegemony and the eventual emergence of the Soviet Union as the world's dominant power. What was more immediately critical about the agreement was that Germany had both insulated itself from Soviet counteraction in Poland and had neutralized Russia as a possible partner in an anti-Nazi alliance with the Western democracies. Hitler's path to an assault on Poland was now open. The weekly's analysis concluded with a question: "will Germany embark on that path to rapidly take over Danzig, and by doing so push the whole world into the terrible disaster [*al-karitha al-ʿuzma*] that must inevitably destroy all those taking part in it?"[64] *Al-Thaqafa* and the world did not have long to wait for the answer.

Faced with the prospect of an international cataclysm provoked by Fascist and Nazi imperialism, contributors to Egypt's intellectual journals intensified their support for liberal democracy. In the months immediately preceding World War II, essays in *al-Majalla al-Jadida* repeatedly expressed support for democracy. Democratic government in its various forms—Republican France and its democratic legacy dating from the French Revolution; Great Britain and its well-rooted tradition of parliamentary monarchy; the United

States with its fusion of political freedom and social reform—were repeatedly analyzed and praised in editorials and essays.[65] By 1939, much of the admiration the journal had previously expressed regarding the perceived economic and social achievements of the National Socialist regime in Germany was transferred to the democratic example of the United States. Editorials of May and July 1939 praised the New Deal as the most important program of social reform to appear in the world in recent years. The New Deal proved that it was possible to stimulate the economy, eliminate unemployment, and provide new jobs through democratic means, without sacrificing individual liberties or freedom of expression as had occurred in Germany. By showing the world that economic recovery and social progress could be achieved through democratic processes, the American case demonstrated the falsity of the assumption that only authoritarian rule was capable of resolving deep economic and social crises. The United States was proof that democracy was "the only form of government that can guarantee both economic growth and liberty."[66] Nor were worthy exemplars of progressive tolerance to be found only in the Western world; the East also had notable examples of the reconciliation of nationalism with internationalism. Several times in 1939, *al-Majalla al-Jadida* commented approvingly on the personality and ideas of Mahatma Gandhi, presenting him as a leader who combined a commitment to national liberation with an equal concern for nonviolence and the brotherhood of man.[67]

Similar to *al-Majalla al-Jadida*, *al-Risala*'s editor Ahmad Hasan al-Zayyat praised Roosevelt's New Deal on the grounds that "when you kill hunger you kill war." Whereas Fascist Italy and Nazi Germany had chosen to resolve the economic crises in their respective countries through programs of rearmament and preparation for war, Roosevelt had chosen to honor the humanistic tradition of the great religions by addressing economic crisis through programs of economic and social reform. Through adopting policies that simultaneously quelled hunger and bridged the social divide, the American New Deal had avoided any domestic impulse toward war.[68]

Al-Thaqafa's outlook on the international situation in mid-1939 combined a fervent hope that world peace could somehow be preserved with solid support for the democratic camp in the case of war. The journal maintained that Egypt was a nation that desired peace, indeed that it would be "the first to be pleased if peace and harmony prevail."[69] It repeatedly warned that any war carried the possibility of grave injury to Egyptian national interests. Egypt had nothing to gain from a new world war; it could only emerge damaged.[70] In regard to its own region of the world, al-Thaqafa argued that Egypt had a vital interest in maintaining tranquility in the Mediterranean arena and in finding a way to contain Italian imperialism short of military conflict. In reviewing recent diplomatic maneuvers among Mediterranean powers in July 1939, the journal supported signs of rapprochement between Turkey and France on the one hand and Egypt and Turkey on the other. Such steps were positive and essential for the creation of an effective line of defense against Italian imperialism in the Eastern Mediterranean and the Red Sea. By virtue of her geostrategic location and control of the Suez Canal, Egypt was a key component of such a front. The editorial went on to deride Fascist and Nazi propaganda efforts directed at the Middle East, stating that the people of the region "understand all too well that the expressions of identification with them in current circumstances are merely a mask hiding desires and drives." The Arab and Muslim nations "will not be deceived" by Axis propaganda; it "will not blind them to the true reality" of Fascist Italy and Nazi Germany as imperialist warmongers who posed a tangible threat to the nations of the Middle East.[71]

Al-Hilal's warnings of the looming threat of war were often accompanied by appeals for the democratic powers, first and foremost Great Britain, to adopt a policy of rearmament and solidarity in order to deter the threat of war.[72] Contributions to al-Thaqafa in early 1939 perceived a need for rearmament on several fronts; for the Western democracies to rearm as rapidly as possible, for Turkey to do the same in view of its strategic location in the Mediterranean, and most vitally for Egypt to strengthen its military capabilities to face a possible Italian Fascist attack.[73] Calls for democratic steadfastness and rearmament were accompanied by predictions to the effect that eventually the Western democracies would prevail over their authoritarian challengers. When evaluating the probability of war in mid-1939 and its likely repercussions for the Middle East, al-Hilal's Sami al-Jaridini expressed confidence that eventually Great Britain would act decisively to protect her interests and strategic position, thereby serving as a protective wall against Italian and German imperialism extending into the Mediterranean region.[74] For his part Niqula al-Haddad came to the conclusion that, if war did come, the military forces and resources at the disposal of the democracies had a clear advantage over that available to the dictatorships and would lead to democratic victory in the long run.

"The superiority of the democratic states over the dictatorial states is absolute," Haddad predicted.[75] *Al-Thaqafa* echoed this view. In speculating on "the prospects of war and peace" in May 1939, the journal argued that Germany and Italy had no chance of winning the war that their actions were provoking. *Al-Thaqafa* was convinced that "these dictatorial, tyrannical regimes that have been forcibly imposed on Italy and Germany are incapable of sustaining a war for a long time." The resources of "the bloc of democratic countries" far exceeded those of the two Axis powers. Another great strength of the Western democracies was "the position of America, that will undoubtedly stand behind the democratic states and provide them with its support." Germany in particular needed "not to forget the role of this factor in her defeat in the Great War."[76]

Al-Hilal had no doubt that Egypt's natural place was at the side of the democracies should war erupt.[77] Despite his opposition to British imperialism, in the current international crisis, Sami al-Jaridini placed his trust in "the glories of the English." Today Great Britain was the light of hope for the preservation of democracy, a nation whose parliamentary form of government was a model of liberal and enlightened rule. England was the most advanced and progressive society of the modern era. In defiance of Aryan Germany's racist claims to world hegemony, Jaridini asserted that "if any one race of all the races of mankind deserves to rule [the world] . . . it is the inhabitants of the British Isles." Other peoples would not agree to replace British world hegemony with the dominance of Germany, "the nation of fanatic Aryans who are using force against individual freedom, whose lives are devoted to the persecution of others, who show contempt for others out of overweening pride and a sense of superiority."[78]

By the eve of World War II, *al-Majalla al-Jadida* similarly asserted that Egypt was unquestionably part of "the family of democratic nations frightened for the fate of the legacy of equality and justice in which we take pride, due to the challenge of the dictatorial nations to this legacy."[79] When war did break out in September 1939, *al-Majalla al-Jadida*'s long march from its initial infatuation with European models of authoritarianism to its eventual unconditional support of liberal democracy was complete. The lead editorial in the first wartime issue of the journal left no doubt as to its sympathy for the antifascist cause: "all that remains for us is to hope that the war will lend in victory for the Allied forces, because this is a victory for humanity."[80] Niqula Yusuf's accompanying analysis of the long confrontation between dictatorship and democracy that had finally resulted in war in terms unmistakably sympathetic to the latter; it was the result of "the twenty-year struggle between the messengers of peace and the myrmidons [*zabaniyat*] of war."[81]

Confronting Fascism and Nazism

What was the antidote to the totalitarian, racist, and imperialist virus threatening Egypt and the world? Egyptian intellectuals considered how to counter the fascist menace on two levels. One was internal; the measures of internal strengthening and reform that needed to be undertaken within Egypt to inoculate and protect Egyptian society from the insidious virus of fascist ideas. The other was external; how to promote international cooperation and the brotherhood of man in place of the chauvinistic racism and aggressive imperialism inherent in fascism.

The education of the Egyptian masses in order to acquaint them with the values and virtues of democracy, thereby diluting the attractiveness of concepts of authoritarianism, was perhaps the most widely shared solution to the internal challenge of fascism voiced by Egyptian intellectuals. Writing in 1936, Niqula al-Haddad called for a special emphasis on "education in the values of democracy" as an essential means for the consolidation of democracy in Egypt. Education for democracy in his view meant the promotion of a moderate, tolerant form of patriotism that remained open to the world and that entered into dialogue with other peoples as equal members of the universal family of nations. Only such an education in liberal patriotism was capable a serving as a barrier against "the blind chauvinism [*al-taʿassub al-aʿma*]" that was the foundation of ethnocentric Fascist nationalism and Nazi racism.[82]

In an essay prompted by the increasing street brawling of Egyptian paramilitary youth organizations that was occurring by 1936, Ibrahim al-Misri forcefully counseled Egyptian youth against being seduced by the forms of youth organization and activism characteristic of fascist movements. It was wrong for youth to emulate the violent ethos or methods of Fascism or Nazism, he warned. Fascist movements that worshipped power and were based on "the principle of the cult of force for the sake of force itself" were making a negative use of the dynamism of youth. Their real aim, "the glorification of dictatorship [*tamjid al-diktaturiyya*]," meant the obliteration of the individual and his mobilization for aggressive imperialist ends and, in the case of Germany, for the demonstration of the power of the chosen race over others. Misri called on Egyptian and Arab youth to channel their energies into activities "appropriate to our temperament and our historical experience." The vitality of youth needed to be directed toward positive, creative goals such as the anticolonial struggle, economic development, cultural progress, and national solidarity. Egyptian and Arab youth should concentrate on the national cause that "rebels against any form of tyranny," whether that of imperialism from without or dictatorship from within.[83]

Contributors to *al-Risala*, a new journal of the 1930s that saw itself as speaking for and appealing to the new generation, emphasized that the models of youth mobilization and indoctrination characteristic of dictatorial governments should not be emulated by Egyptian youth. Asserting that "Egypt is very far from the idea of dictatorship," in 1937 *al-Risala*'s editor Ahmad Hasan al-Zayyat repeatedly called for Egyptian youth to base their activity on liberal and democratic values.[84] His admonition was echoed by Khalil Hindawi, who called on Egyptian and Arab youth to strive for their goals only through democratic means and procedures, thereby "protecting their souls from any form of political and spiritual enslavement" by forces that wished to make manipulative use of their energies.[85] From a different perspective, 'Abd al-Majid Nafi' called on youth to become aware of the substantial affinities between Islam and democracy. Criticizing all those who postulated an antithesis between the values of Islam and the principles of democracy, Nafi' advocated that youth ought to understand that the values of liberty, equality, and humanism, as well as opposition to tyranny, were common to both the democratic and the Islamic outlooks. In his view, a correct combination of Islamic and democratic principles offered youth an authentic framework within which to realize their aspirations. Egyptian and Arab youth needed to find indigenous ways—Egyptian, Islamic, Arab—to achieve their goals, but only through democratic means and within the framework of democracy.[86] These admonitions reflect a basic theme of *al-Risala*: the desire to educate youth in Egypt and the Arab world in order to curb their potential fascination with the ostensible success achieved through youth mobilization under dictatorial regimes.

In 1938, Salama Musa argued for the necessity of implanting democratic norms and values in the Egyptian younger generation in his *al-Majalla al-Jadida* essay "The Problems of Egyptian Youth." Lamenting that "our youth are ignorant of liberal principles, of the meaning of democracy and of the forms of democratic government," Musa worried that as a result younger Egyptians were increasingly susceptible to the fascist alternative to parliamentary democracy. "We must beware of political extremism," he warned; "it is incumbent on us to distance our youth from radical political models such as fascism or communism." His answer was a call for "spreading democratic education and imparting the principles of liberalism in Egypt." Musa called on Egyptian youth to adopt "liberal principles that are based on a spirit of benevolence, humanitarian justice, and mutual respect," and to accept that a democratic political order was capable of achieving the political and economic reform they so ardently desired.[87]

Both 'Abd al-Rahman Sidqi and Ibrahim al-Misri similarly saw education as the solution to the ignorance of the masses, and hence as the essential barrier to the spread of fascist tendencies in Egypt. Understanding that "the masses are the ammunition for every future revival that we desire," Sidqi called for the intellectual elite of Egypt to strive to educate the masses.[88] Intellectuals needed to demonstrate and realize their power through the education of the masses. They could not neglect "fulfilling this mission of theirs in relation to the masses of the people," in the process creating a unified and enlightened national culture shared by both elite and masses.[89] Similarly, Misri believed that the power of Egyptian intellectuals in relation to the masses needed to be realized and demonstrated through their taking the lead in educating the nation in the values of democracy.[90] Both authors held that such education for democracy would save Europe and Egypt from the threat of fascism and dictatorship.[91]

Faith in the power of education as a deterrent to the spread of fascism continued to be expressed throughout the late 1930s. In January 1939, al-Hilal republished the section from Taha Husayn's recent book The Future of Culture in Egypt [Mustaqbal al-Thaqafa fi Misr] in which Husayn, one of Egypt's most prominent educators and intellectuals, insisted that compulsory education was "the major basis for creating genuine democratic life" in Egypt. The nation could not be prepared for implementing democracy, nor could there be any expectation of the thoroughgoing democratization of Egyptian life, without education for democracy from an early age.[92] Al-Majalla al-Jadida also called for fostering the spread of democracy in Egypt through the strengthening of democratic values in Egyptian education. Democracy "must be implanted in our children at home and in our youth at school so that its principles and values can be assimilated into their souls until they feel that they are democrats by nature, not only because of their political system."[93]

Other commentators went beyond education in democracy to argue for a need to refine and improve the operation of Egypt's existing democratic institutions. Egyptian intellectuals certainly acknowledged that democracy as currently practiced both in Egypt and elsewhere had its flaws, particularly that of partisan divisiveness and factionalism. But they also argued that, by its very nature, which allowed for pluralism, dissent, and the addressing of shortcomings, democracy's flaws were subject to correction in a way that was not the case in authoritarian and dictatorial systems of rule. However imperfect, democracy nonetheless was capable of learning from its mistakes and thus was "constantly open to growth and progress," as 'Abbas Mahmud al-'Aqqad stated the case in June 1939.[94] Niqula al-Haddad shared 'Aqqad's view that the defects of democracy were not inherent but stemmed from the flawed implementation of its principles by imperfect human beings. Such defects were correctible, and once they had been corrected, democracy's advantage over dictatorship would be manifest.[95]

Critiques of democratic versus dictatorial government occasionally offered detailed suggestions as to how to improve the internal operation of Egypt's own democratic institutions. The bulk of 'Abd al-Razzaq al-Sanhuri's two essays dealing with how best to "express the opinion of the nation" offered a series of practical suggestions for improving parliamentary government in Egypt so that the Egyptian parliament would become a more effective institution, "a parliament which is indeed an echo of the view of the nation." "A free, honest, and independent press" was one essential prerequisite for democracy. It was no less important in his eyes to nourish the nation's political parties, which were "not only a means of expressing the view of the nation but also one of the most important factors establishing this collective view." For Sanhuri, political parties were the vehicle for representing the view of the nation: "in actuality it is impossible for any nation to establish a comprehensive, organized position on social, economic, and political matters unless the party system has a firm basis." He called on Egypt's political parties to formulate precise platforms and agendas relating to both internal and external affairs, and insisted on the need for open, transparent parliamentary debate of national issues. With regard to the electoral system, Sanhuri advocated "general, open, and direct elections every five years." In a largely illiterate country such as Egypt, "elections are the best school for the mature political education of the masses of the nation," an opportunity both to educate them about national issues and to insure that their opinions played a role in determining the view of the nation. Elections were an essential mechanism for educating the masses in the values of democracy as well as for drawing them into the political life of the country. Finally, "a major and most important element in a healthy democracy is the existence of a genuine, honest opposition." Elections needed to be protected "against the suppression of the minority by the majority." Such improvements in Egypt's parliamentary system would serve to make it more genuinely democratic and thereby prevent any possibility of the emergence of dictatorship in Egypt.[96]

As we have seen, Egyptian intellectuals were particularly incensed by the cultural totalitarianism they perceived as integral to fascist regimes. In the view of *al-Risala*, the satisfactory resolution of the question of cultural totalitarianism versus cultural freedom rested with democracy. Only democracy, "which relies on the good sense of the individual and on his autonomous intellectual capacity to understand and master events," could insure an open cultural system.[97] The journal's solution to the threat of such cultural barbarism was to insist on the independence of the means of communication and of the dissemination of information from the control of the totalitarian state and the restoration of the autonomy of the media within an open civil society. Only through independence "can the media provide us with a genuine, reliable picture of the conditions and the situations that the world is experiencing, and explain the true reasons for their existence in as objective a manner as possible." The free flow of information was a general public necessity, the basis for a functioning democratic society, just as a democratic society was a guarantee of free, multivocal media.[98]

'Abbas Mahmud al-'Aqqad was one of Egypt's staunchest advocates of cultural freedom. In an essay of November 1938, he criticized the control of the press and the lack of freedom of expression under fascist regimes, lamenting that "in fascist countries, a special law exists that enables the relevant minister to issue a government decree discharging a journalist, who may be banned from all the newspapers in the country without any possibility of appealing this decree." In contrast, "in democratic countries anyone who wants to can write, and anyone who wishes can publish a newspaper. Anyone can work in the press without needing any approval from the government or a license to publish a newspaper." 'Aqqad's analysis of the subject of press freedom was penned in the context of the Speech from the Throne of November 1938 that called for reform of the press laws in a fashion that would elevate journalistic standards. His verdict on the current state of the Egyptian press was that it stood somewhere between the poles of fascist control of the press and press freedom in democratic countries, between the fascist situation in which journalists were "officials in the government apparatus" and that in democracies, where journalists were responsible only to "press ethics and the moral criteria of the community of readers." His opinion was that "we are not fascists, that is true; but we also have not achieved the degree of democratic freedom accepted in the United States and England. In fact, we are somewhere between these two poles." 'Aqqad clearly hoped that Egypt could and would move closer to the democratic norm of press freedom, expressed the hope that the Egyptian government's declared intention to encourage "freedom of expression" was serious. What Egypt needed was to achieve a level of journalistic freedom of expression in which "the readers are the only authority that determines the nature of the culture and of journalism, without any reference to press laws or restrictive government regulations."[99]

Avant-garde playwright and bold secularist, Tawfiq al-Hakim was one of Egypt's leading intellectual luminaries of the 1930s. In an April 1939 article in *al-Thaqafa* entitled "Do Our Contemporary Writers Understand the True Nature of Their Mission?" Hakim criticized Egyptian and Arab intellectuals for their failure to mobilize in defense of universal values. "The mission of the writer" today, Hakim asserted, was to affirm and support "liberty," "justice," and "free and critical thought" as well as to create "aesthetic beauty." Public intellectuals needed to stand up to and when necessary to challenge the state, which often tended to pervert these values. Hakim's model in this respect was Emile Zola, whose support of Alfred Dreyfus had been a noble example of "the defense of human justice against the powerful opposition of the government and against the tyranny of the state." The liberal intellectual needed to understand the gravity of his mission at this perilous moment in history, when "the future of thought in Europe" was "endangered by barbaric warmongers" who threatened to destroy libraries, museums, and scientific institutions. Wherever books were burned and cultural treasures destroyed, the intellectual needed to speak up in defense of all he held dear. For Hakim writing in

1939, this imperative transcended national boundaries: in the present state of emergency, every intellectual needed to disregard his distinctive national identity "in order to enter the temple of eternal thought . . . for the sake of defending universal human values."[100]

When they turned their attention from the domestic scene to the international arena, the suggestions offered by Egyptian intellectuals as the antidote to the threat of fascist totalitarianism and imperialism sometimes became more visionary. As noted above, the most obvious counter to fascism internationally suggested by Egyptian intellectuals was steadfastness and improved military preparedness on the part of the democracies, Egypt included. But for some, this was perceived as insufficient to make the world permanently safe for democracy. In their most idealistic moments, a number of Egyptian intellectuals saw the ultimate deterrent to fascism as lying in the promotion of internationalism, international cooperation, and the universal brotherhood of man.

In a November 1938 essay in *al-Majalla al-Jadida*, Niqula Yusuf considered contemporary fascism in terms of its relationship to the competing ideals of nationalism and internationalism. Announcing himself to be both a "patriot" and a supporter of the concept of "world unity," Yusuf called for a balance between nationalism and internationalism, arguing that they were complementary rather than contradictory loyalties. Nationalisms that put their own nation on a pedestal above all others, ignoring the norms of the international system, were illegitimate in his view. Yusuf was well aware of the utopian character of this message in late 1938, when the world was facing numerous crises. Nonetheless, it was precisely because the current danger was so great that people needed to mobilize "the conscience of mankind" in order to cultivate a "global mentality" capable of resisting the brutal tribalism visible in contemporary nationalism, and hence prevent the world from falling into destructive conflict.[101]

A similar internationalist perspective was expressed by 'Ali Adham in *al-Hilal*. Writing at the close of 1938, Adham found the root causes of present international tension to lie not only in "the struggle between democracy and fascist dictatorial nationalism" but also in a parallel "struggle between nationalism and internationalism." Adham denounced the chauvinist form of nationalism characteristic of fascism that sanctified the idea of the unique nation while rejecting universalist values and promoting international conflict. Nationalism in the fascist states was marked by "imperialist extremism and aspirations for territorial expansion," and as such constituted a total antithesis to the pluralist form of nationalism that assumed all nations had an equal right to self-determination and sovereign, independent existence. Despite the current fascist challenge to this vision of a world of equal and tolerant nations, Adham was convinced that internationalist values would triumph in the end, and that justice, right, and freedom for all nations would prevail.[102]

Al-Majalla al-Jadida's Salama Musa also reflected on the relationship of nationalism to internationalism. In an essay entitled "A Human Culture or Multiple National Cultures?" of February 1939, Musa criticized contemporary nationalist movements such as Fascism or Nazism for promoting a new form of radical nationalism in isolation from and opposition to a global identification. He decried the efforts of the fascist regimes currently in power in Italy and Germany to exaggerate national distinctiveness by fostering a specifically Italian or German national economy, national history, or even national science. Such solipsistic nationalism denied the unity of humanity and bred hatred for others. Obsessed with the self and the ways in which it was distinct from and superior to the alien and inferior other, such extreme particularism was "a nationalism that enlists culture to serve the nationalist state without any commitment to humanity or humane values. The meaning of this was that the nationalist state takes the place of humanity. This is a great danger." In Musa's opinion, such nationalization of culture perverted its value; instead of culture being a way to the brotherhood of man, it became a means of fomenting hostility and aggression among nations.[103]

Musa went on to ask whether identification with a specific nationalism stood in contradiction to the notion of the solidarity of humanity. Like others, he concluded that nationalism and internationalism did not have to stand in opposition; both were expressions of legitimate human affiliations. On the one hand, he endorsed the preservation of distinctive national identities derived from specific natural surroundings and particular cultural heritages. Each nation had its own language, literature, and art; each was entitled to develop these to their fullest potential. On the other hand, Musa also maintained that, over and above different national cultures, a "human culture [*thaqafa bashariyya*]" also existed that was "the product of the sum total of the progress" of humanity as a whole. Whereas every nation had its own unique culture, all were also connected to the cultural system shared by all mankind. Musa asserted that national cultures could not develop their full potential in isolation. National cultures needed to strengthen their ties to the common culture of mankind, drawing from and contributing to the latter. Every nation had not only its own cultural essence, but was also part of a larger cultural universe with which it was in mutual dialogue. The individual was first and foremost a member of the human race rather than a member of a national community, "a man of the world [*rajulan 'alamiyyan*] who is in the service of humanity before belonging to and acting in the name of a particular nation," and, Musa cautioned, "the civilized, enlightened individual" should strive to insure that his nation was "in the service of humanity and acting in its name . . . since we all belong to this world."[104]

A faith in humanist values and the brotherhood of man continued to be expressed by intellectuals even as the specter of war came closer and closer. In May 1939, 'Abbas Mahmud al-'Aqqad went as far as to advocate the creation of a "worldwide government [*hukuma 'alamiyya*]" to supplement the forms of nationalist government that had proved so turbulent in the past. The brutal wars and massive bloodshed of the twentieth century, 'Aqqad believed, proved the limitations of the system of independent nation-states. He expressed the hope that a "worldwide government" embodied in "one world parliament" could extricate humanity from the cycle of confrontation that nationalism, particularly the fascist form of chauvinist nationalism, had imposed on it.[105]

Ibrahim al-Misri also endorsed a need for the assertion of universalist values in the face of the challenge of exclusivist nationalism. He did so in the context of chastising the defenders of universalism for their past shortcomings. In his view, a major part of the world's problem by mid-1939 was the lack of commitment on the part of the world's democracies to the vigorous defense of universalism in light of the current ideological and political assault being mounted by fascism. The past sins of the Western democracies had encouraged the emergence and rise of the fascist alternative: "it is the imperialism and exploitation of the democracies that gave birth to the violence of the dictatorships." In place of continuing to act as imperial powers, Misri called on the Western democracies to adhere to universalist values. This adherence was indeed the source of their strength and their ultimate hope in the face of the fascist challenge: "the source of the world's identification with the democracies is their support of the school of universalism [*madhhab al-bashariyya*], their deep ties to it and their defense of it, as their supreme ideal." Misri called on all peoples, under the leadership of

the democracies, to adhere to "the school of universalism" that represented the "general interest" of humanity, guaranteeing justice for all and
beyond that teaching "the principles of love, compassion, and human solidarity and brotherhood." Misri had no doubt that "the democracies have
the ability to convey this message of universalism again, and through it to
disarm the dictatorships and to save the world from their tyranny, destroying their regimes and their philosophy."[106]

Part III Egypt's New *Effendiyya* and Fascism

Prologue
The New *Effendiyya* of the 1930s

THE MAINSTREAM EGYPTIAN JOURNALISTS, commentators, and intellectuals that we have examined thus far were not the only parties active in the production of Egyptian print culture. While hegemonic in national discourse, they did not monopolize the field of public opinion. From the end of the 1920s and more prominently in the 1930s, a new and significantly different set of actors began to participate in public discourse: the "new *effendiyya* [*al-afandiyya al-jadida*]."[1]

The "new *effendiyya*" denotes those younger Egyptians born mostly in the early decades of the twentieth century, young men who had reached early adulthood and came to political consciousness and involvement in the wake of the Egyptian Revolution of 1919 and under the institutions of the new independent parliamentary monarchy. Chronology differentiated them from the older generation of Egyptians born in the less turbulent later decades of the nineteenth century. Not all Egyptians belonging to this chronological age cohort were *effendis*: the term properly refers to urban males, often with a professional or semi-professional education obtained in the secular and heavily Westernized educational institutions created by the new Egyptian state, possessed of modern skills and employed in modern occupations, and viewing themselves as an emerging middle class.

The new *effendiyya* were a product of a different context from earlier generations. The common historical experience that shaped their political and social opinions was first that of growing up during World War I, witnessing the postwar collapse of the Ottoman Empire, and sharing the powerful influence of the memory of the heroic nationalist Revolution of 1919 that produced formal but restricted Egyptian independence by 1922. Thereafter, their views were heavily influenced by the sense that over time the nationalist movement that had succeeded in attaining formal independence was internally corrupt and externally was incapable of completely liberating Egypt from British domination, as well as by the trauma of economic depression and political repression that afflicted Egypt in the early 1930s. These shared historical experiences marked the new *effendiyya* as a distinct historical generation.

Developments of the interwar era specific to their age group and educational cohort also influenced the outlook of the new *effendiyya*. By the 1930s, the growing supply of graduates of schools that trained professionals (doctors, lawyers, engineers, teachers, bureaucrats, and journalists) exceeded the ability of the Egyptian economy to absorb the product of an expanding school system. This "crisis of the educated [*azmat al-mutaʿallimin*]," exacerbated by the Depression of the early 1930s, produced great frustration among a younger generation educated in the modern world of values according to which a professional education should lead to a rapid ascent on the socio-economic ladder. Personal frustration combined with the perception of national failure (establishment corruption and impotence vis-à-vis the foreign occupier) was a potent brew that generated great dissatisfaction with and alienation from the existing political as well as social order among many of the new *effendiyya*.

The result was the emergence of a distinctive new *effendiyya* political discourse as well as new sociopolitical movements appealing to the new *effendiyya*. Common to both the discourse and the movements was lack of faith in the performance of the parliamentary system of government instituted by the Egyptian Constitution of 1923. From their perspective, the existing political system had failed to live up to its liberal values. As they observed the actual operation of the parliamentary monarchy, they saw an undemocratic and manipulative structure that internally served and preserved the interests of the upper classes of the older generation (particularly landowners) and obstructed badly needed social and economic reforms at the same time that externally it colluded with the British occupier and perverted the national struggle for complete Egyptian independence. The corrupt Egyptian establishment of existing political parties dominating parliament and government reflected neither the aspirations nor the interests of the new *effendiyya*.[2]

Their search for a more successful alternative to a failed sociopolitical order led many younger Egyptians to establish or to support new anti-
establishment, extraparliamentary organizations. The first stirrings of independent new *effendiyya* activism can be dated to the later 1920s, with
the formation of the explicitly religious "Society of the Muslim Brothers
[*Jam'iyyat al-Ikhwan al-Muslimin*]" in 1928.[3] Five years later, a more secular paramilitary movement appealing to youth, the "Young Egypt Society
[*Jam'iyyat Misr al-Fatah*]," also appeared on the Egyptian scene.[4] Many
younger *effendis* had their political baptism of fire in the large-scale and
prolonged student demonstrations of late 1935 that forced the restoration
of the Constitution of 1923 that had been replaced by a more autocratic
substitute in 1930. Their involvement in sustained and ultimately successful political protest simultaneously staggered the political establishment
and gave younger Egyptians a sense of their ability to act effectively on
behalf of the new urban mass society emerging in Egypt by the 1930s.[5]
New *effendiyya* political activism accelerated greatly in the later 1930s: this
period saw the rapid growth of the Muslim Brothers; the less extensive
growth but even greater political notoriety of the Young Egypt Society
(which became a formal political party in 1937); and the more short-lived
success of the Wafdist paramilitary alternative to the latter, the "Squadrons of the Blue Shirts [*Firaq al-Qumsan al-Zarqa'*]" that flourished,
thanks to the patronage of a Wafdist government, in 1936 and 1937.[6] In
the later 1930s, before greater controls on public activity and expression
were instituted by the Egyptian government for the duration of World
War II, the Muslim Brothers and Young Egypt in particular were enjoying a quantitative upsurge and coming to manifest significant weight in
the overlapping spheres of public discourse and national politics.

The views expressed by spokesmen for the two premier movements
of the new *effendiyya* as both flourished in the later 1930s form an important layer of Egyptian thought concerning liberalism and fascism, democracy and dictatorship. Aware of and concerned with the spread of fascism
abroad as well as of the domestic Egyptian struggle between the Palace
and the Wafd for hegemony over the Egyptian state, spokesmen for both
movements gave considerable attention to issues of political legitimacy,
authority, and efficiency. The first chapter of this section considers the political views of spokesmen of the Society of the Muslim Brothers on questions of democracy versus dictatorship; the second examines the positions
articulated by the leaders and publicists of the Young Egypt movement.

6

The Muslim Brothers Consider Fascism and Nazism

THE SCHOLARSHIP DEALING WITH the early history of the Muslim Brothers in Egypt is rich and diverse.[1] We see no need to elaborate further on its detailed findings. Nonetheless, existing research on the Brothers has not sufficiently clarified the organization's attitudes regarding fascism, democracy, and the ideological confrontation of the 1930s between liberal versus authoritarian principles of political order. In particular, it has not been sufficiently attentive to the multivocal and pluralist context of interwar Egypt in which the movement emerged and in which it had to operate, and the degree to which the views articulated by its spokesmen were constrained by a need to accommodate to that context. Contrary to ex post facto interpretations of the movement's ideology, the Muslim Brothers' complex view of Italian Fascism and German Nazism in the 1930s and its perspective on the alternative political systems found in the Western liberal democracies were not totally at odds with the consensus regarding democracy and dictatorship found in mainstream Egyptian public discourse as demonstrated in the preceding chapters.

Several authors, Western and Egyptian, have regarded the Muslim Brothers as either inspired by the example of European fascism, sympathetic to Fascist Italy and Nazi Germany in their confrontations with the Western democracies, or as itself partially "fascist" in ethos or organization.[2] For observers for whom fascism dominated the global landscape of the 1930s and 1940s, there was a natural tendency to assume that the impact of European fascist movements was an inescapable influence on contemporaries elsewhere. "Fascism" served as an immediately comprehensible label for locating and deciphering both the inner code and the outer behavior of political movements of the same era such as the Muslim Brothers.

Unquestionably, features of the movement's organization and ideology resembled contemporary fascism: the society's hierarchical and autocratic structure; its revulsion over the flaws of partisanship, always labeled and denounced with the deprecatory term "factionalism [*hizbiyya*]"; the cult of a venerated leader whose very title "guide [*murshid*]" echoed the total submission expected of a Sufi acolyte to his *shaykh*; the preaching of obedience, discipline, and dedication to the achievement of sanctified goals; the establishment of a youth branch with quasi-military features such as physical training and uniforms; and the adherence to a comprehensive doctrine providing guidance for all spheres of life. All these characteristics paralleled but did not necessarily derive from or imitate those found in contemporary Fascism and Nazism.[3] There are also essays written by members of the movement that voice admiration for aspects of Fascism and Nazism. In one essay Hasan al-Banna expressed admiration for the "militarism [*'askariyya* or *jundiyya*]" and "masculinity [*rujula*]" of the Nazis, both of which could serve as a model for the Muslim Brothers.[4] Banna also spoke favorably of the centralized nature of the Fascist and Nazi regimes, as well as of their ability to impose order, discipline, and obedience to a charismatic leader.[5]

Yet in our view, "fascist" is an inadequate descriptor for the Muslim Brothers, a misleading characterization that obscures rather than clarifies its complex character and fails to account for its phenomenal appeal. In particular, the designation fails to allow for the uniquely *Muslim* nature of the movement. The essence of the Muslim Brothers was a tireless striving for Islamic authenticity. Its quest for authenticity was first and foremost directly inward, against the stagnant traditionalism of the Muslim religious establishment of the *'ulama* and the irrational escapism of Sufism (even though the movement was influenced by the latter). The heart of the Brothers' "message [*da'wa*]" was the urgent need to revivify Islam. First and foremost, this meant infusing contemporary Muslim belief and practice with a dynamism and activism that could effectively meet the demands and pressures of modern life, thereby enabling Muslims to integrate into the modern world. Second, the movement's search for a distinctively Muslim modernity was directed outward, against the contemporary current of Europeanization and secularization that threatened to swamp Muslim culture. Although the society did adopt and incorporate particular European ideas and practices, it regarded itself first and foremost as a movement working to purge "imperialist" Western influences from Egypt as well as from the wider Muslim world.

Along with its commitment to the search for Islamic authenticity and a distinctively Muslim path to modernity, the Muslim Brothers was at root an anticolonial movement —"anticolonial" in the broadest sense of the term. The anticolonial struggle of the movement was directed not only at ousting the foreign occupier politically, but also and equally important, at eliminating any form of control by Western imperialism over the life of Muslims: European economic exploitation, the infiltration and domination of Western social practices, Western cultural hegemony, and Western constructs of community and nation. Of course, the movement's anticolonial struggle began in Egypt, but Egypt in its ideology was not an isolated entity unto itself but rather an inseparable part of a wider Muslim community. The anticolonial struggle extended from the Nile Valley to all parts of the Arab Middle East currently under European domination and beyond to the entire Muslim world.[6] This wider community was the basis for the enormous effort the movement devoted to the Palestine issue in particular. For the Muslim Brothers, the Palestinian Arab revolt against British rule and Jewish immigration of the later 1930s was a battle that concerned all Muslims and in which every Muslim nation needed to become involved. Palestine was the practical arena in which the movement first demonstrated the depth of its commitment to Muslim authenticity and solidarity. The movement expended a vast propaganda and practical effort in aid of the Palestinian Arabs during their uprising against imperialism and Zionism from 1936 to 1939. Movement publications dealt with the Palestine question on a daily basis; a considerable effort was given to issuing petitions, mounting demonstrations, undertaking fund-raising, and eventually dispatching volunteers to assist the Palestinian Arabs. More than any other Egyptian organization, the Muslim Brothers were the Egyptian spearhead supporting the Palestinian Arabs in their struggle against the Zionist movement and the British Mandate.[7]

The crucial point for our analysis is that, in the context of the 1930s, for the Muslim Brothers the imperialist "West" included both the liberal democracies of Great Britain and France, who together still dominated most of the Arab world, and the totalitarian regimes of Europe such as

Fascist Italy (ruling Libya) and Nazi Germany. A sharp distinction needs to be made between the occasional admiration expressed by movement spokesmen for the perceived organizational advantages of authoritarian exemplars, and their consistent opposition to the expansionist and imperialist tendencies they saw as inherent in Italian Fascism and German Nazism. Themselves adherents of a hierarchical organization critical of the pluralism and partisanship of their own parliamentary system, spokesmen for the Muslim Brothers were less concerned with the authoritarian attributes of Fascism or Nazism but were vehement in their opposition to the prospect of Fascism or Nazi imperialism in the Muslim world. Their opposition to Fascism and Nazism at first focused on the imperialist character and actions of both European movements, and later on the imminent threat to international order and world peace represented by the external initiatives undertaken by both.

Politically, only the slightest indication of a concrete link between the Muslim Brothers and either Fascist Italy or Nazi Germany in the 1930s is available. There is no evidence of clandestine support for the movement by Italian Fascist agencies or agents prior to World War II; given the vehement denunciations of Italian colonialism in Libya penned by the movement's spokesmen in the 1930s, a positive connection is unlikely. Such is not the case with Nazi Germany. The society's involvement in the Palestine conflict in support of the Palestinian Arab revolt briefly drew it into tangential contact with Germany. Documents seized by the British when Germans in Egypt were interned upon the outbreak of the war in late 1939 indicated that, through Palestinian Arab intermediaries in contact with the Germans, the Muslim Brothers had briefly received clandestine subsidies from the German News Agency in Cairo in order to facilitate its anti-British activism.[8] The outbreak of the war and the internment of all German nationals in Egypt apparently terminated the relationship. While British assessments of the wartime Egyptian scene are replete with apprehension concerning the presumed "defeatist" tendencies of extraparliamentary movements such as the Muslim Brothers or Young Egypt, nonetheless a British intelligence report on the Muslim Brothers in December 1942, by which time the tide of battle had changed, concluded that "there is however very little evidence of their contract with Axis agents since the outbreak of the war. . . . Though the Ikhwan have perhaps imitated the Nazi-Fascist organization, they have no particular sympathy for their ideology as far as is known."[9]

In ideological terms, the Muslim Brothers' stance toward Fascism and Nazism must be situated in the effort of the movement's ideologues to define and promote a form of collective identity in terms appropriate for and acceptable to Muslims. Movement ideologues did not totally reject modern nationalist concepts. What they did do was to attempt to reformulate nationalism in Islamic terms by stripping it of its European referents and symbols and instead endorsing forms of nationalism that they viewed as congruent with Islamic principles and values. In effect, they attempted to offer an Islamic alternative to existing European-derived forms of nationalism.

This adaptation was done most definitively in Hasan al-Banna's several "messages [*rasa'il*]" of the 1930s, the authoritative programmatic statements of the movement's ideology in its early years. In *Da'watuna* [*Our Message*, 1937], Banna systematically discussed acceptable and unacceptable forms of both "patriotism [*wataniyya*]" and "nationalism [*qawmiyya*]" for the edification of his followers. His position in regard to both was a nuanced one that accepted more moderate and benign forms of both concepts of identity while rejecting their more extreme and divisive variants. Thus Banna spoke favorably of several kinds of patriotism, including "the patriotism of sentiment [*wataniyyat al-hanin*]," love of one's homeland; "the patriotism of freedom and greatness [*wataniyyat al-hurriyya wa al-'izza*]," the desire to liberate one's country and insure its freedom and greatness; and "the patriotism of community [*wataniyyat al-mujtama'*]," the bond of social solidarity and the willingness to work for the common good.[10] On the other hand, the Brothers' general guide vehemently rejected "the patriotism of partisanship [*wataniyyat al-ahzab*]," "the dividing of the nation into factions" engaged in "mutual competition and vituperation"; such extreme partisanship was "counterfeit patriotism [*wataniyya za'ifa*]."[11] In another of his programmatic messages, Banna also rejected both "geographical patriotism [*al-wataniyya al-jughrafiyya*]" and "blood patriotism [*al-wataniyya al-damawiyya*]" as artificial limitations on the concept of community.[12] Beyond his categorizing of these acceptable and unacceptable forms of patriotism, Banna insisted on the overriding primacy of an Islamic loyalty for all Muslims: "the difference between us and them is that we define the boundaries of patriotism according to creed, while they define it according to territorial borders and geographical boundaries. For every region in which there is a Muslim who says 'There is no God but God and Muhammad is His Prophet' is a homeland [*watan*] for us, possessing its own inviolability and sanctity, and demanding love, sincerity, and striving for its welfare."[13]

Hasan al-Banna's view of "nationalism [*qawmiyya*]" was on the whole more negative. He did find some forms of nationalism acceptable for Muslims: "the nationalism of glory [*qawmiyyat al-majd*]," a desire to emulate one's ancestors and replicate their achievements; "the nationalism of the national community [*qawmiyyat al-umma*]," loyalty and devotion to one's people and nation; and "the nationalism of discipline [*qawmiyyat al-tanzim*]," the willingness to work diligently for the good of the nation.[14] But Banna was vehement in his denunciation of "the nationalism of paganism [*qawmiyyat al-jahiliyya*]," by which he meant the contemporary effort of modern nationalists in some Muslim countries (Egypt is not specifically mentioned in the passage but is certainly implied) to "revive the customs of the *jahiliyya*" [i.e., pre-Islamic pagan Arabia] that had been superseded by the monotheism of Islam. The effort to replace the bond of Islam by such racially based nationalism was reprehensible in the view of Banna. He made his categorical rejection of such anachronistic nationalisms in the contemporary Arab world explicit, proclaiming that the Muslim Brothers "do not call for Pharaonicism, Arabism, Phoenicianism, or Syrianism."[15] Most important, Banna also explicitly condemned "the nationalism of aggression [*qawmiyyat al-'udwan*]," referring specifically to "racial self-aggrandizement to a degree that produces disdain for other races, aggression against them, and their victimization for the sake of the glory of the nation and its existence, as advocated for example by Germany and Italy and indeed is claimed by every nation that announces it is over all; this too is a reprehensible idea."[16] Banna reiterated this rejection of the aggressive forms of nationalism that had emerged in contemporary Europe in his *Nahwa al-Nur*, where he firmly denounced the pernicious consequences of such slogans as "Germany Over All," "Italy Over All," and "Rule Britannia" and went on to state that "the principle of domination in Western nations did not define its goal without fallacious chauvinism [*al-'asabiyya al-khati'a*], and because of this it brought about internecine warfare and aggression against weak nations."[17] Banna insisted that a huge gap existed between Islam's advocacy of strength and the character of the militarism embedded in contemporary totalitarian movements: "Mussolini's Fascism, Hitler's Nazism, and Stalin's Communism are based on pure militarism [*'askariyya*]. But there is a vast difference between all of these and the militarism of Islam, for the Islam which has sanctified strength [*al-quwwa*] has also preferred peace [*al-salam*]."[18]

Hasan al-Banna's keynote address at the Fifth Congress of the Muslim Brothers, held in January 1939, provides an authoritative statement of the movement's stance on current global issues.[19] Delivered shortly after the Munich crisis of late 1938, the speech gave considerable attention to defining "the Brothers' position regarding the states of Europe." Banna first situated the movement's international stance in its attitude toward nationalism in general. Reiterating that the Islam of the Muslim Brothers "does not recognize geographical boundaries or differences of race and blood," he reaffirmed the movement's firm conviction that "the Muslims are all one nation [*umma wahida*] and that the Muslim homeland is one homeland [*watan wahid*]." Banna went on to explicitly criticize "fanaticism of race and color [*al-ta'asub li al-ajnas wa al-alwan*]" and "racist nationalism [*al-qawmiyya al-jinsiyya*]" as misguided and destructive forms of group identity, ones that were producing "quarrels, strife, and destruction" among the peoples of the world. True to his Islamic orientation, the general guide maintained that only Islam, with its uniquely universal and humane approach to solidarity, could redeem humanity from such destructive chauvinist nationalism.[20]

Referring specifically to contemporary European imperialism, Banna declared that the Muslim Brothers had a "long historical account" to settle with the European nations that had, "without any right," conquered and were still dominating areas of the Muslim world. Opposition to such foreign imperialism was a religious duty for Muslims: "Islam obliges its people, and us with them, to act to save and redeem them." The conflict in neighboring Palestine and "the deprivation of the rights of the inhabitants of Palestine" by Great Britain and Zionism was prominently noted in the address. Since "every Muslim regarded Palestine as part of the land of Islam," Banna called on Muslims to join in the struggle against British imperialism and Zionist colonialism in Palestine by supporting the Egyptian Islamic organizations currently active in assisting the Palestinian Arab cause. Banna also denounced French imperialism and its record of "persecution, exile, and arrests" of opponents of the imperialist presence in Syria and North Africa.[21]

But it was not only British and French imperialism that were denounced by Banna. The general guide's harshest anticolonial rhetoric was directed against Italian activities in Libya. "Our account with Italy is no less deep or long than our account with France," he declared. Italian imperialism as practiced in Libya was, if anything, more vicious and destructive of Islam than that being conducted elsewhere in the Arab world by Great Britain or France. In Banna's view, Italian policies of forceful repression and Italian colonial settlement aimed at turning Libya into "a part of Italy" amounted to what now would be termed "ethnic cleansing": "Arab Muslim Tripoli, the dear neighbor that is close [to Egypt]— the Duce and his men are acting to obliterate it, to pursue and harass its inhabitants, in order to wipe out any vestige or trace of their Arabism and Islam." Italian imperialism aimed at depriving Libya's population of its Muslim collective identity, reducing them to "a life of enslavement, oppression, and humiliation," a condition in which "death is preferable to life." Condemning "Mussolini's crimes" in Libya, Banna called on Muslims "always to remember and to remind your sons that Tripoli is not an Italian homeland nor will it ever be such . . . even if all of the inhabitants of Italy emigrate to there." Libya "is part of our homeland, the one Islamic homeland . . . and you [Muslims] must prepare for the time when we will redeem and save it, a time that will come very soon."[22]

Another important programmatic speech of April 1939 by the general guide, concurrent with the German absorption of the rump of Czechoslovakia and the Italian invasion of Albania that further indicated the expansionist tendencies of the European dictatorships, elaborated on the position that the general guide believed Muslims should adopt toward both Nazi Germany and Fascist Italy. Edited and reworked, the address was later published in pamphlet form as a message "To the Youth [*Ila al-Shabab*]," becoming one of the most widely circulated Muslim Brothers texts of the period.[23] Banna again denounced the "covetousness [*matma'*]" of the Western imperialists who were conquering Muslim regions and in the process undermining the unity of the "one Islamic homeland." Muslim unity overrode the artificial borders that had been carved out by imperialism: "Egypt, Syria, Iraq, Hijaz, Yemen, Libya, Tunisia, Algeria, and Morocco, and all other places where the Muslim says there is no God but God and Muhammad is His prophet, are our great Islamic homeland that we aspire to liberate and redeem so that all its parts will once again be joined together." Banna contrasted this unity based on

Islam to the ideological position of "the Third Reich that imposes itself as a protector on all those in whose arteries German blood flows" and thus was striving for Aryan racial unity. For Muslims, "the racial factor [al-'amil al-'unsuri] cannot be any stronger or more significant in forging human community than the credal factor [al-'amil al-imani]." Speaking for his movement, he again emphasized to Muslim youth that "we do not preach racial division [firqa 'unsuriyya] or sectarian fanaticism ['asabiyya ta'ifiyya]," but that Islam "respects the unity of humanity." Moving on to Fascist Italy, Banna again denounced the aggressive intentions of Italian Fascism and its aspirations to conquer and colonize Muslim lands that were properly part of the unified Muslim world. Rather than being arenas destined for Italian domination, "the Mediterranean and Red Seas are Islamic seas . . . which must be restored to the bosom of Islam." For Hasan al-Banna and the Muslim Brothers, there was a once and future empire, that of Islam, that was far nobler than the Roman Empire that Mussolini was currently aspiring to revive: "Signore Mussolini thinks it is his right to revive the Roman Empire. But that ancient empire was nothing other than a so-called empire founded on the basis of greed and passion. It is in fact our right to revive the glory of the Islamic Empire that was founded on the basis of justice and integrity to spread light among humanity."[24]

Hasan al-Banna's views of nationalism and imperialism set the conceptual and rhetorical framework within which other ideologues of the movement addressed these topics. Muhammad al-Ghazzali, then a young ideologue and later the movement's chief spokesman, similarly criticized "the nationalist tendency" within Western civilization for its destructive impact on Muslims. Nationalism as it had developed in the West was "nationalist fanaticism [ta'assub qawmi]" that, when emulated by Muslims, led to the shattering of Muslim unity and the division of the Muslim community. Using the false principle of nationalism, European imperialist governments had cynically manipulated the authentic and legitimate patriotism of Muslims, turning it into "unruly nationalism [qawmiyya jamiha]." For Ghazzali, "the splitting of humanity into races and ethnic groups battling against one another" was the negative result of modern European nationalism. The apogee of this unrestrained and pernicious nationalism was "the claim of the superiority of German and Italian nationalism" found in contemporary Nazism and Fascism. Fascism and

Nazism were the ultimate manifestation of "the [nationalist] tendency that sows destruction and ruin."[25]

Ghazzali's view of the form of nationalism being manifested by contemporary fascist movements was as negative as that of Hasan al-Banna. Like his mentor, Ghazzali viewed modern racist nationalism as a return to the paganism of the pre-Islamic *jahiliyya* and also warned Egyptians and Arabs not to be tempted into emulating Fascism or Nazism. Lamenting that "the Fascist or Nazi militarism that advocates these principles of wild, unrestrained nationalism sometimes captivates the hearts of people in Egypt" (an allusion to Young Egypt and its followers), he denounced the adoption of European fascist practices by Muslims as "foolish imitation" that Muslim youth should at all costs avoid. Muslims needed to adhere to Muslim unity and not be beguiled by "the imagined glory of nationalism." Muslim unity rather than ethnic nationalism was the bedrock of loyalty: "We must save ourselves from Muslim division on the basis of allegiance to a specific homeland, uprooting the principle of national fanaticism from the hearts [of Muslims]." For this spokesman of the Muslim Brothers, "the homeland of the Muslim is its faith and the government of Muslims is its *Shari'a*."[26]

Salih Mustafa 'Ashmawi was the editor of *al-Nadhir*, the political weekly of the Muslim Brothers that began publication in 1938 and thereafter was the most important forum for the articulation of the movement's views. In an article of 1939 entitled "Unbelief is One Community and Imperialism is One Humiliation [*al-Kufr Milla Wahida wa al-Isti'mar Dhull Wahid*]," 'Ashmawi argued that Western "infidel imperialism [*al-isti'mar al-kafir*]" was a monolithic force acting systematically to conquer the Muslim world and to annihilate Muslim identity. In 'Ashmawi's view, there was little essential difference between the imperialism of the Western democracies and that of Italian Fascism in regard to Islam: "the English, the French, and the Italians" were all "the enemies of God and His messenger and the opponents of Islam and monotheism." 'Ashmawi rejected the distinction between British and French imperialism on the one hand and Italian imperialism on the other that "some Muslims" were attempting to make: "These Muslims have forgotten that disbelief is one community and imperialism is one humiliation. All of these imperialists have one aim and that is to wipe out Islam and to debase and humiliate Muslims."[27]

'Ashmawi saw recent Italian imperialism as an equal, and in some ways even more, a threat to Islam and Muslims as the traditional European imperialism of Great Britain or France. Although the specifics of the article included the denunciation of Great Britain, particularly for its current persecution of the Muslims of Palestine and for the "Judaization of Palestine" that was taking place with the encouragement and support of the British, as well as of France for the processes of "Francization" it was carrying out in North Africa, the evil imperialism of Fascist Italy was the main focus of the article. "Italy, following in the footsteps of England and France, is trying to obliterate the Arabs and to humiliate Islam," the essay's subtitle announced. The Italian repression of Libyan resistance had been savage and brutal, including the killing of resistance leaders such as 'Umar al-Mukhtar and extending to the murder of Muslim resistors while taunting them with the jibe "Where is Muhammad to save you now?" Italy had followed its conquest of Libya by colonization, flooding the country with Italian immigrants.[28] Italy had "annexed Libya to Rome, thus severing part of the heart of the Islamic homeland and attaching it to the center of Papal Christianity." By annexing Muslim Libya, Fascist Italy was intent on eradicating the Muslim character of the indigenous population of Libya: "What sort of grace, what sort of gift is this—to deprive the Arabs of their citizenship and their Arab identity and to transfer them to Italian-Roman citizenship and identity? That indeed is the grace and the gift of Italy and Mussolini, as a first step toward stripping the Arabs of their Islamic religion and converting them to the Christian religion." 'Ashmawi ridiculed Mussolini's attempt to represent himself as "the friend of the Arabs and the protector of Islam." Islam is protected by God, he declared, and God had no need of assistance from Mussolini. On the contrary, everything that Italy had done in Libya proved the Duce to be an enemy of Islam and Muslims. Italian imperialism was a racist imperialism that regarded non-Italians as inferior races that were destined for physical and spiritual annihilation. "Today in western Tripoli the most terrible tragedy of [Muslim] life is occurring. . . . There is pressure and discrimination against Muslims in all spheres of life up to the loss of their national identity, turning them into slaves that no longer control their own destiny. They desire life but no longer find it. Death lurks at every corner, and they are dying."[29]

Thus for Muhammad al-Ghazzali and Salih Mustafa 'Ashmawi, as for Hasan al-Banna, the principle that "the enemy of my enemy is my friend" did not apply. For ideologues of the Muslim Brothers, firm critics and opponents of the British occupation of Egypt, Fascist Italy was hardly

viewed as a preferable alternative to British or French imperialism. In its
actions abroad, Fascist Italy was demonstrating a more virulent form of
imperialism, one that threatened spiritual obliteration in addition to physical domination for Muslims.

An indirect expression of the Muslim Brothers' negative view of fascism at
the close of the 1930s appears in its rivalry with and hostility toward
Young Egypt. From its formation in 1933 onwards, Young Egypt was the
Muslim Brothers' chief competitor for the allegiance of Egypt's new *effendiyya*. Both movements voiced the same disillusionment with the corrupt parliamentary order; both attempted to offer a more dynamic and
inspiring set of principles as the basis for an effective and authentic Egyptian modernity. For much of the 1930s, Young Egypt grew in popularity
and following, although not to the same extent as the Muslim Brothers.
By the close of the decade, however, Young Egypt was clearly being
eclipsed by the Muslim Brothers. The reaction of its leaders smacked of
desperation. On the one hand, they intensified the movement's militancy,
specifically on the deeply emotional issue of Palestine, through mounting
a vehement and violent anti-Jewish campaign of propaganda and boycott
that will be discussed in the following chapter; on the other, they floated
the prospect of a merger with the Muslim Brothers.[30] When the latter
failed to materialize, early in 1940 Young Egypt adopted a new name, that
of the "Islamic Nationalist Party [*al-Hizb al-Watani al-Islami*]," and pro-
mulgated a more Islamically oriented program for the renamed organization.[31]

The response of the leaders of the Muslim Brothers to the overtures
of Young Egypt is what concerns us at this point. As usual, Hasan al-
Banna set the tone. His address at the movement's Fifth Congress in
January 1939 discussed the relationship between "the Brothers and Young
Egypt." The general guide expressed a measure of resentment over Young
Egypt's previous criticisms of his movement, accusing the latter's press
outlets of having "attacked the Muslim Brothers and charging them with
baseless accusations as if they had shown animosity towards it [Young
Egypt]." He denied the claim of hostility toward Young Egypt, stating
that the majority of Muslim Brothers did not harbor any ill feelings toward Young Egypt. Indeed, Banna indicated that the idea of a union of
the two movements was receiving a positive response within some circles
and that some members of the movement he led did desire "a merger

between Young Egypt and the Muslim Brothers." For his part, the general guide rejected the possibility. The two movements were at present incompatible. Within Young Egypt, he explained, the Muslim Brothers were regarded only as a "society of preaching" lacking a political orientation, while for their part, the Brothers regarded Young Egypt as an organization in which "the true significance of Islam" had not yet "come to fruition in the souls of its members" and thus who were not capable of "preaching the authentic Islamic message." Rather than foreclosing the possibility of an eventual merger of the two movements, Banna articulated a stringent condition for its eventual realization: Young Egypt would be a candidate for merger with the Muslim Brothers "only if it declares that it is not a political party and that its acts and will continue to act in order to further the Islamic idea and the principles of Islam. Here in fact there would be a new victory for the principles of the Muslim Brothers."[32]

Banna's disciples were not as diplomatic in their attitude toward Young Egypt. Salih Mustafa 'Ashmawi charged Young Egypt with being a chauvinistic nationalist movement that failed to adhere to "pure Islamic principles." Although Young Egypt's spokesmen purported to "take pride in Islam," in actuality they did not understand its essence. The modus vivendi of the two movements was fundamentally different. The Muslim Brothers operated in a nonrevolutionary and nonmilitant manner, knowing that "the basis for the true revival of nations is to educate the people and to instill the proper consciousness in them" by means of education and cultural enlightenment. Thus the Brothers were a gradualist movement, engaged in winning hearts and minds through preaching and education in "a calm, tranquil, and disciplined environment." In contrast, Young Egypt was a movement in a hurry, a radical organization "striving to achieve its goal rapidly here and now." Hence, "they do not share the gradualist approach of the Brothers." Thus the path of Young Egypt was "not the path of the Brothers"; consequently, there was no basis for a merger of the two movements.[33]

'Abd al-Hafiz Muhammad 'Abd al-Jawad was even more forceful in his rejection of Young Egypt. In his view, Young Egypt's leader Ahmad Husayn did not understand the essential message of the Muslim Brothers. His assumption, that the Society of the Muslim Brothers was "a party with features identical to those of other parties like the Wafd or Young Egypt itself," was fundamentally flawed. 'Abd al-Jawad's essay was devoted to underscoring the differences between the two organizations. Young Egypt was primarily a nationalist movement, one that "loves Egypt and acts for the sake of Egypt"; its slogans "Egypt Over All [*Misr fawqa al-jami'*]" and "Glory to Egypt [*al-majd li Misr*]" were nationalist slogans. "But all this," 'Abd al-Jawad declaimed, "is contrary to the Islamic religion, it is unbelief and atheism [*kufr wa ilhad*]." Reiterating the Islamic ethos of the Muslim Brothers, 'Abd al-Jawad declared that "Islam does not allow this regionalism [*iqlimiyya*]. It rejects the narrow concept of nationalism [*al-nazra al-dayyiqa li al-qawmiyya*] since God, may His name be blessed, ruled that 'all believers are brothers' and he did not say 'all Egyptians. . . .'" If the Muslim Brothers were to proclaim "Egypt Over All" or "Glory to Egypt," they would be deserting "our Muslim brothers" in other Muslim countries. The glorification of narrow nationalism meant "preaching hatred and mutual antagonism," and was a defiance of God and Islam. Thus Ahmad Husayn's Egyptian nationalism, which "preaches love of only the Egyptian homeland," was un-Islamic. The Muslim Brothers were the true Egyptian nationalists because their nationalism was organically Islamic, striving for the sake of Islam. For them, "love of the homeland is not unbelief and atheism, but stemmed from the heart and soul of Islam" and thus incorporated the belief that "Islam instructs them to love also the great Islamic homeland." Young Egypt was not only unsuitable for a merger with the Brothers; it was an organization that deserved to be denounced and repudiated because of its narrow nationalist character. More clearly than Banna or 'Ashmawi, 'Abd al-Jawad's views of Young Egypt indicate the centrality of an Islamic allegiance for the Muslim Brothers and their rejection of any form of ethnocentric nationalism based on territory, ethnicity, or language.[34]

One area where the activities of the Muslim Brothers partially overlapped with, but did not necessarily derive from, those of a contemporary fascist movement was its position regarding Jews and the Jewish population in Egypt. The pro-Palestinian activism of the Muslim Brothers, a central concern of the movement in the later 1930s, eventually led it to criticize the Egyptian Jewish community for its presumed support of the Zionist enterprise in Palestine. By 1938, *al-Nadhir*'s editor Salih Mustafa 'Ashmawi was denouncing Egyptian Jews for not supporting the Palestinian Arabs in the struggle against Zionism and for their endorsement of the concept of a Jewish state in Palestine; 'Ashmawi demanded that Egyptian Jews choose "either alliance or hostility" with Egypt's Muslim majority in the latter's opposition to Zionism.[35] Other articles in *al-Nadhir* attacked the influential position held by Egyptian Jews in journalism and in the commercial and financial spheres, and asserted that Jewish prominence in the entertainment industry undermined Islamic values.[36] One warning *in al-Nadhir* to Egyptians about Jewish influence stated that "the Jewish threat to Egypt is impending, so take the initiative, boycott them and cast them out, for they have corrupted Egypt and its population."[37] Eventually the Muslim Brothers did issue a call for a commercial boycott of Jewish businesses in order to deter Egyptian Jewish support for Zionism.[38]

This anti-Jewish rhetoric and activism notwithstanding, the Muslim Brothers' hostile attitude toward Egyptian Jews did not reflect the movement's adoption of the tenets of contemporary European anti-Semitism. In theoretical terms, the movement's position was rooted in traditional Islamic teaching regarding the position of non-Muslims in Muslim society. As Hasan al-Banna put it in one of his programmatic messages to his followers, "we leave [non-Muslims] in peace as long as they leave us in peace, we wish them good so long as they refrain from hostility toward us and we believe that between us and them is the bond of the call [of Islam]."[39] As noted previously, the general guide vehemently denounced what he termed "the nationalism of aggression," the "racial self-aggrandizement" of states such as Italy and Germany, as "a reprehensible idea,"[40] and his disciple Muhammad al-Ghazzali decried "the splitting of humanity into races and ethnic groups battling one another" as "a tendency that sows destruction and ruin."[41] Abd al-Fattah Muhammad El-Awaisi's close examination of the subject came to the conclusion that the hostility of the Muslim Brothers toward Egypt's Jews was a product of the circumstances of the day, "a direct consequence of their perceived response to Zionism and to events in Palestine," and that overall "the Society emphasized the possibility of co-existing peacefully with the Jews, were it not for the events in Palestine."[42] This was a significantly different attitude toward Jews than the anti-Semitism of the Nazis. Nazi racist doctrine and practice treated Jews as an irredeemably degenerate population who must be eliminated from the German nation and eventually the world.

To situate the Muslim Brothers precisely in the context of interwar Muslim discourse, it is useful to contrast the movement's views on Fascism and Nazism with those expressed by another wing of the Islamic tendency. To do so will demonstrate that the negative attitude of the Muslim Brothers to Fascism and Nazism was not necessarily shared by all representatives of an Islamic orientation. We refer to Muhibb al-Din al-Khatib. Khatib was a prominent Islamist voice of the interwar era. Originally Syrian, but resident in Egypt since the defeat of the Arab nationalist movement in his homeland after World War I, Khatib had edited the weekly journal *al-Fath*, a central forum of Islamist discourse during the interwar era, since the mid-1920s. The journal also served as the main outlet for expressing the positions of the "Young Men's Muslim Association [*Jam'iyyat al-Shubban al-Muslimin*]," a major organizational component of the emerging Islamic tendency in Egypt.[43]

Historically an Arab nationalist as well as an advocate of Islamic revival, through the 1930s Khatib demonstrated considerable sympathy for Nazi Germany and its nationalist ambitions. Khatib admired the manner in which Nazi Germany was carrying out its plans for realizing a greater Germany, regarding the Nazi program as a role model for the Arab nationalist aim of achieving Arab unity. Thus in the wake of the Anschluss with Austria in 1938, Khatib wrote editorials expressing support for Hitler's bold move.[44] The annexation of Austria to Germany was but the latest in a succession of successful international initiatives on the part of Hitler and the Nazi regime. Considered in nationalist terms, the Anschluss was an essential step in realizing Hitler's goal of German unity. All that Hitler had done was to restore the German-speaking Austrians to their natural homeland, to a "greater Germany" based on "unity of language, unity of race, unity of culture, and unity of aspiration." The enthusiastic reception of the Anschluss among Austrians, the fact that all of Vienna had "received the successful Austrian, Herr Hitler," with cheers of "one nation, one fatherland, one leader" proved that a greater Germany was one nation. "The Austrian is not a foreigner in Germany and the German is not a foreigner in Austria," Khatib explained to his readers; rather, they were "brothers in language and race."[45] Maintaining that the boundaries between Germany and Austria were "false boundaries," Khatib argued that Hitler had been fully justified in "removing the veil of these imaginary boundaries and expunging them."[46]

Khatib was fulsome in his admiration for "the force of the German spirit" and "the passionate German faith" demonstrated by Nazi Germany. In his view, Nazi Germany was a model for Arabs to emulate. The lesson of Germany was that "faith is the secret of power and the secret of unity"; Arabs needed to copy the German model of "one homeland, one nation, one language, one race, and one leader" in order to establish an independent and unified Arab nation. The way to do so was to internalize the message of the "historical event" of Hitler's triumphant entry into Vienna: In "every Arab school" as well as in "every Arab home," teachers and parents should "instill in their children the great example of the event of the unification of Germany and Austria, so that their hearts will be filled with this exemplar of the national faith that is in the heart of every German in Germany and Austria."[47] "Arab nationalism" Khatib declared, must follow in the footsteps of "German nationalism."[48]

Khatib also endorsed Germany's anti-Jewish policies as a legitimate effort on the part of Germans to return to their authentic racial roots by purging their nation of foreign parasites. The German nation was compelled to "get rid of the mixed elements of the alien [Jewish] race that had been controlling public opinion through the press and publishing houses, had been controlling the German economy and German wealth through monopolies and manipulation of industry, banks, and markets, and had been running the public administration." Germany well understood that the prerequisite for its "achieving complete and true freedom is to rescue its nationalism from this alien racial element that had used its great influence to take over the intellectual and economic life, the administration and politics of the German nation." Jews were a "danger" to Germany; by eliminating them from its national fabric, Germany would guarantee "its freedom, power, and revival."[49]

Khatib's sympathy for Nazi Germany did not extend to Fascist Italy. As an Arab nationalist, his view of Italy and its imperial ambitions in the Mediterranean paralleled the anticolonial views expressed by the Muslim Brothers. In an article of mid-1939, on the eve of the outbreak of the war, Khatib analyzed "the position of the international blocs toward Arab nationalism." His pessimistic conclusion was that there was little difference between "the democratic bloc" and "the Berlin-Rome Axis bloc" in relation to the Arab world; both had and were acting against the national aspirations of the Arabs. While spokesmen for both blocs employed soothing rhetoric, trying to appear as enlightened nations that were sympathetic toward the desire for liberation and independence of occupied and colonized peoples, in reality both the Western democracies and the fascist dictatorships were anti-Arab, anti-Muslim imperialists. While expressing vehement criticism of the imperialist behavior of Great Britain in Palestine and France in North Africa, accusing both of wishing to divide the one Arab nation into fragments in order better to dominate and rule it, Khatib also denounced Italian imperialism in Libya. In terms quite similar to those used by 'Ashmawi of the Muslim Brothers, he mocked Mussolini's attempt to present himself as a friend of the Arabs and Islam while in fact "not one hair on his head is disturbed when each year she [Italy] settles twenty thousand Italian families on the soil of Western Tripoli in order gradually to purge it of its Arabism and Islamism and to turn it into an Italian Catholic homeland." Italy did so by brutally stripping the native Muslim Arab inhabitants of their nationalism and identity "in an effort to tear them away from the Islamic world and the Arab homeland." Thus Khatib's sympathy for the nationalist goals and actions of Nazi Germany in Europe did not extend to Fascist Italy, whose imperialist agenda threatened the aspirations and interests of Arabs and Muslims.[50]

Fully to comprehend the ideological perspective of the Muslim Brothers, it is also necessary to examine their views on the alternative set of principles represented by parliamentary democracy. It is sometimes assumed that their insistence on an Islamic ordering of society led the Muslim Brothers to reject pluralist liberal democracy and advocate an authoritarian system of rule in its place. When their position on the issue of parliamentary democracy is examined systematically, it turns out to be more nuanced.

The Brothers' attitude toward the existing Egyptian parliamentary system was a complex and in some respects contradictory one. At the movement's Fifth Congress, Hasan al-Banna's idealized view of a unitary social order led to his rejection of the divisive partisan competition inherent in parliamentary government. Branding it with the pejorative term "factionalism [*hizbiyya*]," he criticized Egypt's political parties as artificial and negative bodies that divided the nation into factions and served the interests of particular segments of society. The artificiality of the parties also stemmed from their lack of ideology or agenda beyond that of attaining power. Egypt's political parties were viewed as self-serving, corrupt organizations devoid of principles or values. *Hizbiyya* amounted to an interest-driven, opportunistic battle over positions and benefits.[51] He reiterated this view in an editorial in *al-Nadhir*, arguing that "the existence of the party system [*al-nizam al-hizbi*] has become an obstacle on the road of revival and progress and a feature that is delaying the process of regeneration."[52] Domestically, *hizbiyya* was partisan exploitation of national resources for the benefit of the national elite, to the detriment of the advancement of the nation as a whole.[53] Even more serious were its external implications: by weakening the nation vis-à-vis its foreign occupier, *hizbiyya* objectively served to perpetuate the despised British occupation of Egypt.[54] For Banna, there was only one solution to the debilitating factionalism that corrupted and weakened Egypt: the first prerequisite for improving Egyptian political life was to "totally abolish all the present political parties."[55]

What was the alternative to a political regime that allowed the evils of *hizbiyya*? The Muslim Brothers' answer to this question asserted and emphasized the primacy of social harmony and solidarity. In one major programmatic statement, his address to the movement's Fifth Congress, Hasan al-Banna vaguely suggested the institution of a nonparty system of government in which the leaders of Egypt's political parties dissolved themselves into a new "patriotic body [*hay'a wataniyya*]" of politicians, technocrats, and experts, in effect a new supreme national authority that would incorporate all sectors of Egyptian society and through consensus move the country in the direction of reform and independence.[56] Yet at the same time, Banna also acknowledged the need for the Muslim Brothers to fit into the existing political structure and to play according to the rules of the Egyptian political game in order to be able to advance their primarily religious message. Demonstrating considerable flexibility and pragmatism, Banna accepted the basic features of the constitutional parliamentary order as it had developed in Egypt by the interwar period. He accepted the legitimacy of the Egyptian monarchy as instituted in the Egyptian Constitution of 1923 (hardly a surprising stance by a movement desirous of freedom of advocacy and operation in the Egypt of the day). Banna's view of the Constitution itself was more nuanced and positive than might have been expected of the leader of an organization committed to the theoretical supremacy of the Islamic *Shari'a*. In his address to the Fifth Congress, Banna explicitly declared that the Constitution's provisions relating to personal liberties, the responsibility of the rulers to the ruled, and the limitation of government authority were fully in concert with Islam, and went on to proclaim that "of all forms of government in the world, the constitutional system of government is that which is closest to Islam. They [Muslims] will not relinquish it for another system."[57]

It was the implementation, rather than the principles, of the Egyptian Constitution that Hasan al-Banna found wanting. Rather than rejecting the Egyptian Constitution and the parliamentary system it had established, his criticism was directed at the corrupt and unrepresentative mode in which the parliamentary system operated in practice. "What the Muslim Brothers demand is rectification of the manner in which the Constitution is being implemented." Once obscure clauses in the Constitution were clarified, and when its principles were properly observed by Egypt's political class, "then we will accept and obey the basic principles of the constitutional system since we regard it as consistent with the rule of Islam, moreover as drawing upon it."[58] Pragmatic considerations undoubtedly weighed heavily in the Muslim Brothers' endorsement of the existing constitutional order: as an extraparliamentary movement, the Brothers were well aware that their freedom of expression and action were dependent on the continued existence of a pluralist parliamentary regime in Egypt.

This pragmatism had an important operational corollary. At least in the 1930s, the Muslim Brothers rejected political violence as a method for attaining their objectives. Their ideologues disavowed "revolution [*thawra*]" as a means for advancing the "message [*da'wa*]." Indeed, the general guide maintained that attaining political power was not the aim of his movement. "The Brothers are not demanding power for themselves," Banna stated at the Fifth Congress. The claim that "the Brothers are striving to launch a general revolution in the social order and the political regime in Egypt" was false, slander by their opponents employed to justify the restriction of their activities. What was required was not political power, but "faith and religious devoutness" on the part of Egyptians. If an enlightened national leadership led the country in the spirit of "the program of Islamic Qur'anic rule," then this leadership would enjoy the full support of the movement. Banna summed up his position on this issue by declaring that "revolution, the most violent manifestation of the use of force, is not the way of the Brothers. They do not consider it or base themselves upon it, because they do not believe that any benefit can be derived from it or that it will produce positive results."[59]

Banna's admonitions concerning the need for his movement to reject revolutionary political methods were articulated in the context of an internal debate within the Muslim Brothers. The movement's rapid growth by the later 1930s compelled Banna to consider the strategy his expanding movement would henceforth pursue in the public arena. In an editorial published in the first issue of *al-Nadhir* in mid-1938, Banna had spoken of the mission of the Brothers unfolding in two sequential stages; "practical struggle after verbal preaching [*al-jihad al-'amali ba'da al-da'wa al-qawliyya*]."[60] At the Fifth Congress a few months later, Banna refined the movement's strategy as consisting of three stages: first, "the stage of preaching and informing and transmitting the message"; second, "the stage of the formation and selection of supporters and of the preparations of the soldiers"; and third, "the stage of execution, operation, and results."[61] The first stage, that of preaching and disseminating its message within society, was well under way and having success; it would obviously continue. Now the movement was ready to progress to its second stage of growth, that of the formation of and training of dedicated cadres capable of eventually implementing its Islamic vision within the wider society (the movement's formation of "battalions [*kata'ib*]" date from this point onwards). By implication Banna left the third stage, that of "execution, operation, and results," meaning the actual enforcement of its program for the Islamification of Egypt, dependent on sufficient "formation" having been achieved to insure that the attempt at "execution" would be successful. In effect, Banna was postulating a gradualist approach to political involvement, one in which the attempt to change the structure of Egyptian public life was deferred to an undetermined future date.

The problem with Banna's strategy of evolutionary stages as articulated in 1938 was that it ran counter to the inclinations of part of his new *effendiyya* clientele. Militancy and a desire for direct confrontation with both imperialism and a corrupt Egyptian establishment were on the rise amongst segments of the movement's following by the later 1930s. Eventually, the new activist mood came into conflict with Hasan al-Banna's more cautious approach to political involvement. The tension between new *effendiyya* radicalization and Banna's gradualism produced serious strains within the Muslim Brothers. Frustration among some followers of the society over Banna's unwillingness to sanction immediate direct action in pursuit of the movement's goals manifested itself both in internal dissension and in unauthorized and occasionally violent demonstrations on behalf of the Palestinian Arab cause by some enthusiasts of the movement.[62] The militant mood was reinforced by Young Egypt's simultaneous adoption of a more radical and violent stance from late 1938 onward, its calls for "revolution," demands for "Islamic" reform, and undertaking of direct action on behalf of the Palestinian Arabs against the Egyptian Jewish community.[63] The organizational upshot of this desire for direct action was the defection of some of the more radicalized followers of the movement in late 1939 and their establishment of a separate and more radical Islamic movement, "The Society of Our Master Muhammad's Youth [*Jam'iyyat Shabab Sayyidina Muhammad*]."[64]

After a decade of phenomenal growth for the movement he led, Hasan al-Banna faced a tactical dilemma at the close of the 1930s. As already noted, in 1939 the movement's leadership rejected tentative feelers for the amalgamation of Young Egypt and the Muslim Brothers, criticizing both the chauvinism and the militancy of Young Egypt. Faced with both internal and external pressures to move the Brothers in a more radical direction, Banna insisted that the Muslim Brothers' approach to the public sphere would be one of moderation, gradualism, and accommodation to the existing norms of the Egyptian public sphere in the pursuit of its goals. A policy of prudence was reinforced by the problems the militancy of some of its following was producing for the movement. An internal evaluation of the movement's situation prepared by its leadership in mid-1939 elaborated on the adverse consequences likely to follow from adopting confrontational tactics. Police surveillance and administrative pressure against movement supporters in the state bureaucracy were already restricting movement activism and cutting into attendance at its meetings; Banna therefore instructed his followers to "be wise in their behavior and avoid bringing harm upon themselves."[65]

By the eve of World War II, Hasan al-Banna had opted for a gradualist and accommodationist approach to political involvement for the Muslim Brothers. By no means would the movement he led compromise or abandon its ultimate goal of the achievement of an Islamic order for Egypt; nor would it discontinue the formation and training of its cadres prepared for direct action at some future date. But what Banna would not sanction was to tempt official repression or to place his movement's legal existence in jeopardy by taking an overtly militant and confrontational stance such as that recently adopted by Young Egypt. Rather than calling for externally directed militance, an admonition by Banna in *al-Nadhir* of late 1939 enjoined the Brothers to direct their zeal toward internal spiritual struggle and purification: "Now the time for action has come! The Muslim Brothers anticipate serious action, like clashes with the government. They always express this desire to enter the battlefield. No, my dear

Brethren! Clash with ourselves first and struggle with the individual practices that are contrary to Islam."[66]

This policy of caution, a focus on internal consolidation, and the
avoidance of confrontation with the authorities, first articulated in response to the internal and external pressures for a more radical orientation
placed upon the movement's leadership in 1938–39, by and large characterized the position and behavior of the Muslim Brothers throughout
World War II. The movement's relationship with successive Egyptian governments was most tense in 1940–41, when occasional incidents of official
repression of society meetings occurred, the temporary suspension of its
publications, and the brief forced transfer of its general guide, Hasan al-
Banna, from Cairo to Upper Egypt from February until June 1941.[67] But
this fraught relationship with the authorities did not persist. In early 1942,
Banna reached an agreement with the new Wafdist ministry of Mustafa
al-Nahhas to endorse the collaboration of the Egyptian government with
the Allied war effort. Banna published a letter in *al-Ahram* to that effect
in exchange for the ministry's toleration of the movement's peaceful assembly, preaching, and publication.[68] In mid-1943, British ambassador
Lord Killearn concluded that the Wafdist ministry was currently "patron-
izing and subsidizing" the Muslim Brothers.[69]

Prudence paid off. The war years were ones of accelerated growth
and of the demonstration of an impressive operational capability by the
movement. The movement's formal status as a religious organization and
its use of mosques as the natural locales for reaching out to the public
largely prevented the authorities from prohibiting most of its meetings
and thereby impeding the grassroots dissemination of the movement's
message of reform and the expansion of its following. In addition to public meetings and the publication of periodicals and tracts disseminating
its message, the movement continued with the recruitment and indoctrination of its "battalions" of young enthusiasts that underwent rigorous
religious instruction and physical training.[70] Looking forward to the eventual stage of "execution," it was apparently in 1940 that the movement established its secret paramilitary wing of activists organized in "the special
section [*al-nizam al-khass*]" or "secret apparatus [*al-jihaz al-sirri*]."[71] By
1941, the Muslim Brothers had a network estimated at 500 branches scattered throughout Egypt, a number that may have increased to over 1,000
by 1944. The size of its following is harder to calculate, but estimates of its
membership run from 100,000 to 500,000 by war's end.[72] A Foreign

Office assessment of July 1943 gave a rough estimate of approximately a quarter of a million members of the movement by mid-1943, adding that the movement's "appeal to the younger 'intelligentsia' gives them an influence far exceeding their mere numbers."[73] By the later years of World War II, the Muslim Brothers had become "after the Wafd, the most formidable and organized society in Egypt."[74]

7

The Young Egypt Movement
An Egyptian Version of Fascism?

THE YOUNG EGYPT SOCIETY/PARTY [*Jam'iyyat Misr al-Fatah* from October 1933 to January 1937; *Hizb Misr al-Fatah* from January 1937 to March 1940] was the second-most-important organization based on and appealing to the new *effendiyya* in the 1930s. Egyptian nationalist in outlook, paramilitary in organization, militant in operation, it was a movement created by, led by, and giving voice to the aspirations of Egyptian youth. From a social standpoint, the movement grew out of the crisis of the new *effendiyya* of the interwar era. All of its leaders and activists came from this social reservoir. It differed significantly from the older nationalist parties still dominating Egyptian high politics. Claiming to represent the "new generation," the movement dichotomously separated itself from what it defined as the "old generation," meaning the Wafd and the other parliamentary parties, accusing the latter of domestic corruption and de facto collaboration with Britain's colonial domination of Egypt. Beyond nurturing this self-image as the representative of the new generation, Young Egypt also regarded itself as a popular movement representing the needs of the Egyptian people as a whole, speaking against and working for the amelioration of the impoverishment and distress afflicting the peasant and worker majority of Egyptians by the 1930s.[1] Its partial resemblance to the Muslim Brothers and other new *effendiyya* organizations elsewhere in the Arab East notwithstanding, Young Egypt was a unique phenomenon with an ideology and methodology all its own.[2]

After elaborating on the new organization's list of desired reform measures, the Young Egypt Society's initial program of October 1933 concluded as follows: "as for our means for accomplishing all this, it is not war or killing, aggression or strife, but is summarized in two words: *faith and action.*"[3] Young Egypt defined its differences from other Egyptian political organizations in terms of both ideology ["faith/*iman*"] and practice ["action/*'amal*"]. Ideologically, it was a fervently Egyptian nationalist movement preaching the necessity of uncompromising nationalist struggle against the British occupation of Egypt. Young Egypt defined the anticolonial struggle in comprehensive terms, as not just the termination of the political and military presence of a foreign occupier on Egyptian soil but also as the need totally to purge the alien economic and cultural influences that had taken root in Egypt under the umbrella of foreign occupation. Its tactics in the anticolonial struggle encompassed both legitimate forms of publicity, protest, and petition, as well as violent extraparliamentary activities intended to arouse anticolonial sentiment among the Egyptian public and to force the hand of an otherwise inert political establishment.

At least in the 1930s, Young Egypt was Egyptian territorial nationalist in ethos. Its Egyptian nationalism, however, was presented in more sweeping and visionary terms than that articulated by spokesmen for the political organizations of the older generation. The first article of the new society's program of 1933 was unambiguous about the movement's dedication to the promotion of a specifically Egyptian nationalism: "It is incumbent on us to occupy ourselves with the advancing of Egyptian nationalism [*al-qawmiyya al-misriyya*], and with filling ourselves with faith, confidence, and pride in it. It is necessary that the word 'Egyptian' become the highest ideal . . . It is necessary that Egypt become over all."[4] The slogan "Egypt Over All [*Misr fawqa al-jami'*]" implied a vision of the Egyptian past, present, and future far more ambitious and expansive than that held by Egypt's parliamentary parties. Young Egypt was committed to the revival of what it believed to be the eternal grandeur and power of the Egyptian nation. In its rhetoric, world-historical leadership was an inherent Egyptian trait. Egypt had been in the forefront of human history since the Pharaonic age, a leader of the development of civilization equally under the Pharaohs, in the long Greco-Roman era, and later within the Muslim world. Contemporary Egypt, undergoing national revival, was destined to assume a similar role in the future: "it [Egypt] shall never die, indeed it shall revive again, returning to its original position as a beacon for the world, as a crown for the East and as a leader of Islam."[5]

The movement's ultimate agenda was broader than that of merely attaining independence; it was that "Egypt become over all, a mighty empire composed of Egypt and the Sudan, allied with the Arab states, and leading Islam."[6]

Young Egypt's distinctiveness was even more marked in the sphere of "action." From its inception, the movement promoted a fiery myth of activism and militancy far more radical than that propounded by other Egyptian political bodies. Ideologically, this distinctiveness was rooted in the social Darwinist view of social dynamics held by its founder and leader Ahmad Husayn, his firm belief that "strength" or "power [*quwwa*]" was the ultimate determinant in human affairs. As he put it in a speech of 1935:

Nature teaches us that there can be no accord between the ruler and the ruled, nor between the strong and the weak. Agreement can only be reached by struggle and strife. The conqueror is the worthy one because he continues to exist; the conquered is weak, so he is exterminated. Life knows no restraint or leniency. He who is strong, lives; he who is weak, dies. In vain does a weak people imagine that they can ever reach an amicable accord with a strong people. For that is an "accord" like the "accord" of the wolf and the lamb, that always ends by the wolf eating the lamb. This is life. So, if you desire your liberty, dreaming of it and wanting to achieve it, there is but one path before you—to be strong, to be strong first and last.[7]

This belief in the efficacy of strength and power permeated the organizational structure of Young Egypt. The movement's activists were called "fighters [*mujahidun*]"; until the abolition of uniformed paramilitary organizations by the Egyptian government in March 1938, they wore the movement's distinctive uniform of green shirt and gray trousers (both made in Egypt of Egyptian materials) that gave the movement its colloquial name "the Green Shirts [*al-Qumsan al-Khadra'*]"; they were organized, at least on paper, into a hierarchy of paramilitary units ranging from "squadron/*katiba*" through "brigade/*liwa'*" to "corps/*faylaq*"; they engaged in periodic training sessions and drills, most prominently at the Great Pyramids; they took an oath in which they swore to "be subject to the military law of the society, doing honor to my leaders, executing whatever orders I may receive without debate or hesitation, within the limits of the law."[8]

The self-defined limitation on militance stipulated by the phrase "within the limits of the law" was sometimes honored more in the breach than in the observance. Throughout the mid-1930s, Young Egypt's activists engaged in periodic scuffles with the movement's opponents in the streets of Cairo and other Egyptian cities. By the end of the 1930s, Young Egypt went further, eventually jettisoning its uneasy respect for the law and coming to speak in terms of "revolution [*thawra*]" as the only way to liquidate the remnants of imperialism in Egypt as well as to achieve "social justice" in Egypt, meaning a radical redistribution of wealth within Egypt for the benefit of its oppressed and exploited peasant and working majority. Disillusioned by the manifest failures of parliamentary government in Egypt, by the end of the 1930s, Young Egypt came to view the authoritarian rule of what one of its ideologues termed the "excellent doctor" or dictator as the only cure for Egypt's many ills.[9]

Clearly, much of the foregoing description of the Young Egypt movement resembles the ideological outlook and political practice of the European fascist movements that flourished in the 1930s. Would it therefore be correct to conclude that Young Egypt was a fascist-inspired movement? The answer is complicated and by no means unequivocal. It involves making distinctions between ideology and practice, between rhetoric and agenda on the one hand and patterns of behavior and modes of action on the other, as well as between different phases in the brief history of the movement from its birth in 1933 to its wartime suppression in 1941.

A close reading of the contemporary evidence reveals a richer and more complex set of positions than is generally assumed. Again context is crucial. While the ideas and practices that characterized the leading European fascist movements of the 1930s had a definite impact and influence on Young Egypt, the adoption of fascist features by the movement was a selective process reflecting Egyptian circumstances. As Stein Ugelvik Larsen has emphasized, "fascism outside Europe was dissimilar to fascism in Europe."[10] As an ultranationalist movement emerging in a non-European country with very different conditions from interwar Europe, Young Egypt's partial emulation of fascist models was refracted through the unique context of Egypt in the 1930s. Most crucial in this respect were the anticolonial fixation that the movement's leaders and members shared with almost all politically committed Egyptians, as well as the current concern of Egyptians regarding the limitations of the existing parliamentary regime and how to make the governmental institutions of Egypt more responsive and effective. The scope of these concerns meant that a considerable degree of ambivalence, as well as occasional inconsistency, characterized the views of Young Egypt's spokesmen concerning both the question of the respective merits of democracy versus dictatorship and of the specific virtues and defects of Italian Fascism and German Nazism as possible models for modern Egypt.

The first distinction that needs to be made is between structure and ideology. In both its formal structure and its use of symbols, Young Egypt at its inception bore an unmistakable similarity to contemporary European fascist movements. The emphasis on "struggle"; its core followers being termed "fighters" and their swearing of an oath of obedience to their leader; their wearing of a distinctive uniform and their organization into "squadrons," "brigades," and "corps"; their periodic assembly in sessions for paramilitary exercises; not least their scuffles with the supporters of rival organizations: all this closely paralleled the practices of Italian Fascism, German Nazism, and the other fascist movements found on the northern side of the Mediterranean by the 1930s. Given Young Egypt's emergence after most of these had come to prominence, it is hard to avoid the conclusion that much of Young Egypt's organization and symbolism was in good part inspired by foreign examples.

Yet in substance, the differences between the paramilitarism of Young Egypt and that found in European fascist movements is equally great. First, the formal paramilitary structure of the movement was only imperfectly realized in actuality. In the movement's early years, paramilitary formations existed more on paper than as meaningful operational units, and paramilitary training sessions (conducted without arms) were occasional rather than integral features of the movement's activity. The movement could and did sustain itself in the absence of its initial paramilitary trappings; when all paramilitary formations were abolished by the Egyptian government in March 1938, Young Egypt continued to exist and indeed may have briefly reached its peak of strength as a popular movement. Sociologically, there was a massive difference between the social base of Young Egypt, drawn almost exclusively from the still relatively small cohort of educated Egyptian youth of the new *effendiyya*, and the European fascist movements who drew upon the massive pool of demobilized and demoralized war veterans present in Europe in the wake of a devastating world war. Most importantly, the scope and impact of Young Egypt's paramilitary activities pale into insignificance when compared to those of the Italian Fascists, the German Nazis, or the fascist movements of Eastern Europe. News accounts of the intermittent street clashes between the Green Shirts of Young Egypt and the Blue Shirts of the Wafd in the years of greatest urban unrest in Egypt in 1936–37 indicate occasional physical injuries, but report nothing like the sustained public intimidation and violence that were the most visible and vicious feature of European fascist paramilitarism. Largely composed of enthusiastic high school and college students devoid of either previous military experience or lethal armament, the marches and demonstrations conducted by Young Egypt's Green Shirts were a pale shadow of the urban disruption and savaging of opponents wrought by the militants of contemporary European fascist movements. Compared to the systematic violence and brutality practiced by Fascist *squadristi* or by the SA paramilitary auxiliary of the Nazis, Young Egypt was playacting at paramilitarism.

In terms of practical contact or collaboration, only circumstantial and inconclusive evidence indicates a tangible connection between Young Egypt and either Fascist Italy or Nazi Germany in the 1930s. We have found evidence of only one fleeting contact of sorts with the German government in the 1930s. In June 1934, Ahmad Husayn paid a visit to the German Legation in Cairo. According to the report of the German minister, Dr. Eberhard von Stohrer, the purpose of Husayn's visit was to "express his sympathy for the new Germany" and also to obtain a visa to travel to Germany while in Europe later in the year. The minister refused to see Husayn when the latter requested a subsequent meeting. Minister von Stohrer's evaluation of Young Egypt was that it was "extremely weak in terms of its finances" and "of no great significance."[11]

Both in the 1930s and later, Young Egypt's spokesmen denied any connection with Fascist Italy. Their denials may be less than candid. Contemporary British reports from 1935 assert that the fledging movement, in its search for financial support, accepted Italian money passed through the conduit of the *Giornale d'Oriente*, an Italian-language publication that served as a vehicle for Italian state propaganda efforts within Egypt, for the partial financing of its journals *al-Sarkha* and *Wadi al-Nil*; the British also reported Young Egypt to have taken Italian money to assist in paying for a propaganda trip to Europe taken by Ahmad Husayn and Fathi Radwan in late 1935.[12] In June 1936, Prime Minister Mustafa al-Nahhas attempted to justify a partial ban on the movement's activities on the grounds that, in the prime minister's words before the Chamber of Deputies, "the Young Egypt Society is working in the interests of a foreign power against the interests of the country."[13] Public speculation did not hesitate to identify Fascist Italy as the state Nahhas meant.[14] Young Egypt denied the charge and asked for a full investigation by the public prosecutor, which was refused on grounds that it would compromise national security; the society also attempted to bring legal action for slander against Nahhas, but the case appears never to have been heard.[15]

Again in 1939, after allegations were made in the Egyptian press that the police had uncovered documents indicating links between the movement and both Fascist and Nazi agencies, Young Egypt denied any tangible connection with the European fascist powers.[16] It is possible that a link with an anti-British movement such as Young Egypt may not have been in Italy's interest later in the decade. A subsequent account by Muhammad Subayh, one of the movement's leading prewar ideologues, implies that an approach by Young Egypt to the Italians for some sort of support in 1938–39 may indeed have been rejected by Italy because of the détente in Anglo-Italian diplomatic relations arrived at in 1938: "Mussolini refused to cooperate with the Young Egypt movement before the war out of respect for the 'Gentleman's Agreement' he had made with England in order to reduce the state of tension in Mediterranean."[17]

As members of an organization committed the realization of Egypt's national aspirations, Young Egypt's ideologues found much to admire and praise in a wide range of nationalist movements around the globe.[18] The first book written by Young Egypt's co-founder Fathi Radwan was an admiring biography of the Indian nationalist leader Mahatma Gandhi.[19] An early speech by Ahmad Husayn expressed admiration for modern Poland, emphasizing how successive generations of Poles carried the nationalist flame and Poland eventually attained her independence through perpetual struggle.[20] In 1937, Radwan produced a highly laudatory biography of Eamon De Valera in which he praised the Irish nationalist movement for "fighting a battle with the English the likes of which history has never witnessed."[21] Modern Japan and its successful course of modernization was the subject of a pamphlet in the party's Book of the Month [*Kitab al-Shahr*] series in the same year, its author Muhammad Subayh extolling Japan as a "mighty state" and noting that Japan and Egypt shared "the bond of a similar aspiration" for national rejuvenation.[22] In 1938, Husayn favorably compared Turkey's modern revival under Mustafa Kemal Ataturk to that achieved in Italy and Germany under the Fascists and Nazis. "Everything that has been said about these two states [Italy and Germany] can also be said of our sister-state Turkey," he declared; the country had been defeated in war and was on the path to imperialist subjugation until Mustafa Kemal Ataturk rallied the nation, defeated the Greek invaders, forced Britain and France to withdraw, and under his leadership "achieved its independence and is today a powerful state, one to be reckoned with, that England has to woo and court."[23] After a visit to Czechoslovakia in the summer of 1938, on the eve of the Munich crisis, Husayn attended a Czech youth rally. His conclusion about the strength of Czech national solidarity, that the Czechs had "the resolve, the will, and the determination to defend their country and to die for the sake of its glory,"[24] was tragically overstated in light of the country's subsequent dismemberment at Munich. Successful anticolonial struggle and presiding over the transformation to modernity were the main characteristics of movements anywhere in the world that resonated with the men of Young Egypt.

Ideologically, for much of the 1930s, Young Egypt's spokesmen attempted to differentiate their movement from either Italian Fascism or German Nazism. Ahmad Husayn, for one, insisted that the movement he led had both a different social basis and, as a result, a different character from both Italian Fascism and German Nazism. He was vehement about the difference in 1936: "How different is our struggle from that of Mussolini or Hitler! How great the difference between the struggle of Young Egypt and their struggle!" In terms of context, Husayn pointed out that "they [Fascism and Nazism] began their struggle by the gathering of soldiers and the unemployed, whereas Young Egypt taught the new generation and prepared it for the struggle"; in terms of outlook, he insisted that "they believe chiefly in material force, whereas we believe chiefly in spiritual force, in faith in God and in religion."[25] Husayn reiterated much the same set of distinctions in early 1938, even as his substantive view of the achievements of Fascism and Nazism was shifting: "We differ with these two states [Italy and Germany] in that the basis of our movement and our struggle is spiritual, relying on religion, morals, and faith. These other movements were founded on a material basis, which became coarse because it was based on scattered remnants of the army, or on elements of the regular army just returned from the trenches, in both countries."[26] The difference in context had profound consequences for Husayn: "As for Young

Egypt, it has no army, no remnants of one, on trenches, no spears. It is nothing but youth with faith, determination, and the desire to save their country and to build a new foundation of virtue, morals, and order."[27]

In their views of contemporary international issues, in the mid-1930s the men of Young Egypt had little that was good to say about either Fascist Italy or Nazi Germany. Italy in particular came in for strong criticism in Young Egypt's publications for its record of colonial repression and exploitation in Libya. Thus an article in *al-Sarkha* savagely satirized a "Conference of Eastern Students" held in Rome in late 1933, attacking the conference's sponsor, the Italian government, for having colonized Libya "in the most brutal manner" and for having "tyrannized its people."[28] In 1934, Fathi Radwan denounced Italy as "the worst sort of economic and cultural imperialist," and went on to accuse the regime of wishing to incorporate Egypt in her new Mediterranean Empire.[29] Ahmad Husayn paid a brief visit to Italy in 1934. His impressions of the Fascist regime were distinctly unfavorable; as he put it upon his return, "Italy has failed to live up to my impression of it, and that in only four days."[30] He had found the country still "an underdeveloped environment" with much poverty and misery. In Husayn's view, all the talk about a new Roman Empire was only "so much propaganda"; in reality, "Fascism is only the boasting of Mussolini pouring over the Italian people. The results that he has achieved for them are suspect. The privileged position that Italy assumes at the present time, or rather that it has deceived the world into believing it has assumed, will all suddenly collapse when Mussolini dies."[31] In reaction to Husayn's articles, the Italian Legation brought charges of the slandering of a friendly state against *al-Sarkha* and Husayn.[32] The case dragged on for years, apparently not being heard until after the war, when Husayn was acquitted.[33]

Young Egypt's position on the main international crisis of the mid-1930s involving a fascist power, Italy's invasion and conquest of Ethiopia in 1935, was an ambivalent one. Fathi Radwan, writing in the influential daily *al-Balagh* in August 1935, advocated Egyptian support for Ethiopia against Italy, justifying the same on the basis of the historical and cultural ties between the two African countries, but more immediately because Egypt's own desire for complete national independence compelled her to support the independence of a fellow African state.[34] One journal affiliated with the movement protested Italy's aggression against Ethiopia, accusing the Italians of brutality fueled by arrogant European racism toward "colored natives."[35] Yet Young Egypt's official position differed. In a petition to King Fu'ad in October 1935, the movement called for Egyptian neutrality in the impending war between Ethiopia and Italy. The text of the petition made it clear that the rationale for advocating neutrality as much anti-British as either anti-Ethiopian or pro-Italian: it invoked both "the necessity of Egypt taking a position of neutrality in the present conflict between Egypt and Ethiopia, and its prohibiting anything that might be taken as aid for the policy of England," and asserted "the necessity of Egypt's rejecting any protection from England in the case of aggression against her, and the necessity of entrusting the defense of Egypt to Egyptians alone."[36] The movement also used the crisis over Ethiopia to argue, as it was to do in later international crises, that greater military preparedness was an imperative for Egypt.[37]

Fathi Radwan's 1937 biography of Mussolini, published in Young Egypt's Book of the Month series of pocket-sized biographies of prominent historical and contemporary figures, provides the fullest statement of Italian Fascism offered by a spokesman of Young Egypt in the mid-1930s. Radwan was by no means an admirer of the Duce. In the work's Introduction, he admitted that when asked to write the biography, he initially hesitated while considering whether the Italian leader's positions were something he could treat with empathy.[38] After the body of the work presented a chronological account of Mussolini's career through the consolidation of Fascist power in the 1920s, the book's concluding chapter offers a highly ambivalent assessment of its subject. On the one hand, Radwan acknowledged Mussolini's historical importance: "we cannot but admit that Mussolini is a strong man, forever on the move, with far-reaching ambitions. Indeed, he is in politics what Napoleon was in war, for both of them believed in speed and surprise, and were proficient in capitalizing on every opportunity, and we can certainly say that each served his country and saved it from anarchy." On the other hand, Radwan found Mussolini to be a leader flawed by "an assemblage of contradictions and discrepancies in his words and deeds." Impetuous and opportunistic, "a powerful barrage of energy," neither his thought nor his actions were consistent. While Mussolini denounced the Soviet regime that had "suffocated freedom," he acted in a manner not dissimilar from Lenin and Stalin. Radwan's assessment of Mussolini as a thinker was dismissive: "it is impossible to find in him a solid, profound worldview. You can hear much stormy

talk from him, but he never innovates anything." This ideological poverty
meant that the historical impact of both Mussolini and the movement he
led would be a limited one: "the day when Mussolini dies, he will leave
nothing after him, no legacy. For Fascism is not a new ideology, because it
never goes beyond 'armed-to-the-teeth' patriotism, and this kind of patriotism is not beneficial for mankind."[39] In the second book he wrote for
the Book of the Month series, a laudatory biography of Eamon De Valera,
Radwan again expressed his personal dislike for the Fascist dictator: "I
did not like that my first job for Dar al-Thaqafa [Young Egypt's new publishing house] was a book about Mussolini, whom I do not care for and
whose immoderateness displeases me, indeed whose methods both inside
and outside Italy I loath."[40]

Another 1937 biography in the movement's Book of the Month series, this one of Hitler by the series' editor Muhammad Subayh, is one of
the few extended and partially sympathetic accounts of Hitler and
Nazism penned by a spokesman for Young Egypt before 1938. Much of
the work was a favorable portrait of Hitler for having "revived the power
of German youth," for having restored German self-confidence and prosperity, and for being "a great leader of the modern world" who was reasserting German prestige and power in the international arena.[41] Nonetheless, Subayh also found much to criticize in German Nazism. Prominent
in this respect was the dictatorial nature of the regime, particularly its
suppression of freedom of expression, its control over German public
opinion, and its insistence on enforcing ideological uniformity. For Subayh, spokesman for a movement that had itself frequently suffered from
press restrictions, "the existence of freedom comes before all else"; Nazi
suppression of that freedom "cannot be justified."[42] Yet what concerned
Subayh most about Nazism in 1937, and what should matter most to
Egyptians, was Nazi international aggressiveness and its expansionist ambitions. He regarded Hitler, who was on record as having said that "the
East is the granary of the West," and the Nazi regime he led as a long-term
threat to the Arab world. Subayh went on to warn the Nazis and Hitler
that "there is no one in the East, particularly in the Arab countries, who
will allow a new foreign rule to replace the old." On this cardinal matter,
Germany would be treated the same as Great Britain or France.[43] Thus
Subayh, while voicing admiration for Hitler as an historic figure and
praising the social and economic achievements of his regime, drew clear

boundaries between himself as an Egyptian activist and patriot and Nazi expansionism and imperialism.

Like all Egyptians, the attitudes of the ideologues of Young Egypt toward the European dictatorships of the 1930s were formulated in the context of their views regarding the contemporary Egyptian political system. Thus the position articulated by Young Egypt had similarities with, but eventually went much further than, that of its sibling organization based on the new *effendiyya*, the Muslim Brothers. Like the Brothers, Young Egypt consistently rejected and denounced what it regarded as the self-serving and ineffective partisanship that characterized the behavior of the political parties of the old generation. Also like the Muslim Brothers, it initially called for the restoration of national harmony and mutual collaboration of all sectors of society for the benefit of the nation. Young Egypt's primary difference from the Muslim Brothers regarding the Egyptian constitutional system was that, by the close of the 1930s, under the influence of both its own fraught history of harassment by successive governments and its favorable impressions of the effectiveness of dictatorial regimes in Europe, it eventually went much further than the Brothers in advocating the desirability of replacing a parliamentary system that it perceived to have failed by a more authoritarian system.

In its first few years of existence, Young Egypt defined itself as a "patriotic association" rather than a political party, an organization concerned with "its program, not power."[44] Through the mid-1930s, it presented itself as willing to cooperate with any individual or group it perceived to be working for the national interest. When its program of 1933 summoned Egyptians to "ten years of action," it added the qualifier "aloof from partisan squabbling."[45] This theoretical commitment to national solidarity and cooperation for the benefit of the national interest gradually frayed under the pressure of events. Continual tension with an antagonistic Wafdist government through the rest of 1936 and all of 1937 (periodic prohibition of Young Egypt's meetings; intermittent suspension or confiscation of its publications; occasional arrest and trial of its spokesmen on charges of slander), over time had a polarizing effect on Young Egypt. The conclusion of the Anglo-Egyptian Treaty of Alliance of 1936, with its legitimization of a continuing British military presence on Egyptian soil, was vehemently criticized by Young Egypt as a betrayal of the national struggle; the fact that the treaty had been negotiated and accepted by an all-party delegation led by the Wafd added to the belief that the entire Egyptian political establishment was irredeemably hopeless as a defender of Egypt's national interest.[46]

By 1937, Young Egypt's faith in the possibility of achieving national solidarity and cooperation for the sake of the common good was fading. An indication of the direction in which the Young Egypt's view of parliamentary government was evolving came in an essay of April 1937 by Hamada al-Nahil, a movement activist at the Egyptian University. Nahil's "We Believe in a Reforming Revolution" discussed the issue of democracy versus dictatorship through an analogy between the body politic and the human body.[47] Just as the human body could be afflicted by illness, so "democracy has its deadly diseases," the worst of which was "the disease of partisanship." After elaborating on the malady of partisanship, Nahil moved on to the cure. This was "the medicine of salvation as represented by discipline, and as brought by an excellent doctor. . . . This excellent doctor is the dictator." His examples of the dictator as excellent doctor were Hitler and Mussolini, each of whom had revived national confidence after a period of despair. His conclusion was that either democracy of dictatorship was could be appropriate, depending on context: "I am not among the enemies of democracy in all circumstances, not among the friends of dictatorship in all circumstances." What mattered were results: "I am rather among the believers in a national, violent, reforming revolution, swift and sudden, whoever the leaders may be. If they are democrats, as in England, because the nature of the people destines it so, then I welcome the just rulers. Or if they are dictators, as in Germany, because the nature of the people destines it so, then I welcome the noble, honorable rulers." Nahil left the nature of Egypt's reforming revolution open: "As for Egypt, which is in need of this revolution, the question of who will be its leader and how it will be accomplished is in the hands of God."[48]

The party's movement away from the acceptance of parliamentary government accelerated in 1938. The years 1938–39 were when the issue of dictatorship versus democracy became an issue of immediate and intense concern in Egypt. Growing public disillusionment with what was perceived as a factionalized, if not fractured, political structure dominated by corrupt and self-serving politicos, combined with the currency of notions of the readjustment of the institutions of the parliamentary system into a more authoritarian direction being promoted by the advisors of an enormously popular young king basking in the glow of his recent accession, seemed to indicate that the Egyptian political system established in the early 1920s might be on the cusp of major change. Apparently with the encouragement of the royal adviser Muhammad Kamil al-Bindari, the chief advocate of the ascendancy of "new men" in government,[49] Young Egypt took a leading role in the intensified debate over the respective merits of democratic versus authoritarian rule in 1938–39, articulating both some of the sharpest criticisms of the existing political order and propounding some of the most radical suggestions for its alteration in a more authoritarian direction.

After the unusually tainted parliamentary elections of March 1938, Young Egypt began to attack not only this particular election and the way it had been conducted, but also the entire parliamentary system in Egypt. Ahmad Husayn took the lead. "Elections in Egypt have not at any time revolved around principles and programs, but rather have been campaigns motivated by, and based on, partisanship for the tribe and partisanship for the family," he asserted in the wake of the elections. Egypt's electoral system had simply failed to express the popular will: "I shout at the top of my voice that all the elections that have occurred in the past, and those which are occurring today, cannot be considered as an expression of the will of the people."[50] A party petition addressed to the incoming parliament widened the critique to include the Egyptian Constitution, declaring that "all the nation is disgusted with the elections and with the present Constitution." Egyptians regarded the incoming crop of deputies with "indifference and unconcern," expecting nothing more of them but that they would "be content with the glory of being a deputy" and thus that they would unhesitatingly support the government. While the public anticipated that the new parliament would "excel in debates, arguments, and personal quarrels," what they did not anticipate was "any serious reform or saving of the country." The result of business-as-usual in parliament would be the total discrediting of the system: "all of this will, after a while, cause the nation to cry out that it does not want deputies, or a parliament, but that it wants work and bread and justice."[51]

Young Egypt's Secretary-General Fathi Radwan gave more systematic expression to this disillusionment with parliamentary government in an essay of July 1938 entitled "Are We Propagandists of Dictatorship?"[52] Radwan concurred with Husayn in believing that the existing Egyptian parliamentary system had totally failed to meet the nation's needs: "We despise the parliamentary system that prevents and hinders action, that turns the country into a stage for oratory and theatrics. The people are starving, yet the deputies wax eloquent; the country is threatened with danger from within and without, yet the minutes of the sessions contain only idle debates that delay more than they expedite affairs." What Egypt needed at the present time was "reform and renovation and bold undertakings; Parliament does not advance this need, nor does it gratify it." The essay concluded with a series of rhetorical questions that left no doubt that, for Fathi Radwan at least, practical results took priority over constitutional niceties:

If it is dictatorship that will place a limit on the anarchy that has been disclosed about our high officials, then we will be among the supporters of dictatorship, believers in it and propagandists for it. . . . If it is dictatorship that can instill the youth with strength [*quwwa*] and the nation with a militant spirit, filling the people with electricity, vigor, and dynamism, then we will be dictators to the bone.

In the same essay, Radwan had asked: If Egypt's dysfunctional political system was broken, what was required to fix it? In considering possible models for a more efficient and equitable political structure, the men of Young Egypt now looked abroad. In the context of the movement's profound frustration with the status quo, Young Egypt in 1938–39 became more openly sympathetic to the European fascist regimes and more willing to acknowledge the potential relevance of fascist principles and methods for Egypt than had been the case previously. Young Egypt's spokesmen now expressed admiration for what Mussolini and Hitler had achieved in Italy and Germany, and came to argue that Fascist Italy and Nazi Germany were models for the construction of a stronger and more dynamic Egypt.

Ahmad Husayn's speeches of 1938 offer repeated examples of this revised assessment of Fascism and Nazism. As early as January 1938, Husayn was referring to "the miracle of the Italians" and "the miracle of Germany" in positive terms.[53] Before World War I the greatest power in Europe, Germany came out of that conflict a defeated nation, its self-confidence shattered and a prey to "communist anarchy." What a change under Hitler! "Germany, which it was thought would never rise again, has today regained its dignity and become absolutely the strongest state in Europe."[54] Husayn offered a similarly glowing assessment of Italian Fascism in April when he declared that under the Fascist regime Italy, "which had been a symbol of anarchy, has now become among the greatest states in Europe." Domestically, among other things Mussolini had "made the trains respect a fixed schedule"; he had suppressed and eliminated crime, which had previous been widespread in the country; he was realizing a revolution in the agrarian economy and was industrializing Italy. On the world stage, Italy under the Fascists had become a nation "armed to the teeth" and thus capable of standing up even to Great Britain in international politics. Within a decade of the Fascists assuming power, "Italy has become undoubtedly the greatest state in the Mediterranean, a model and an example to be imitated."[55]

What accounted for these dramatic national success stories? Now ignoring the sociological differences he had previously emphasized, Husayn argued that Fascism and Nazism were the bearers of much the same values as those that Young Egypt was trying to instill in the Egyptian people—faith and action. The Italian and German "miracles" had been achieved because of "a creed, a faith, a belief in themselves; this is what Young Egypt summons you [young Egyptians] to emulate."[56] It was faith that had enabled a "little man" like Mussolini and an even lesser figure, Hitler ("only a sergeant" [sic]), to rise to a position of national leadership and to launch their respective revolutions.[57] The secret of the contemporary greatness of Fascist Italy and Nazi Germany was the "deep faith" found in each, "a faith that first fills one heart, then spreads from it to brothers and colleagues, then passes from them to an organization, and the faith of the organization spreads to the people until the whole nation becomes permeated with the new faith." Faith in turn was the motor producing action, the impetus to undertake the ceaseless effort and striving that were necessary to "the working of miracles."[58]

By 1938, Young Egypt's propaganda was presenting the movement, now a formal political party, as destined to follow a similar political trajectory as that followed by the Fascists in Italy and the Nazis in Germany. The caption of a picture of one of the Nazi Nuremberg rallies in *Jaridat Misr al-Fatah* in February proclaimed that "Young Egypt, which calls for order and the dissemination of the military spirit through all classes, hopes to achieve such as this which the Nazis have achieved in their rallies. We whisper—nay, we shout—in the ear of every Egyptian: Order, Order, if you desire peace for every individual and security for every human being."[59] Fathi Radwan pointed out the parallels between the history of the Nazi Party that had suffered persecution at the hands of various German governments because of its uniformed militants, and that of Young Egypt that had experienced repression because of the activities of its paramilitary formations. Despite these bouts of official repression, Radwan was confident that the future belonged to Young Egypt. Just as the Nazi Party had eventually ascended to power, so Young Egypt would do the same. When it did so, as in Germany there would be a day of reckoning: "we say to the enemies of Young Egypt—watch out!"[60] The implication of such comparisons was to highlight the similarity between the dynamism driving the Fascist and Nazi movements on the one hand and Young Egypt on the other. Like Young Egypt, both European movements had begun as marginal opposition groups; Young Egypt could do as they had, moving from the periphery to the center and eventually rise to a position of state power.

In the summer of 1938, Ahmad Husayn visited several European countries. His brief visits to Germany and Italy generated some of his most effusive praise for the perceived domestic achievements realized under Fascist and Nazi rule. In contrast to his Italian visit of 1934, when he came away unimpressed by the Fascist record in power, now he claimed to have found abundant evidence of Fascist domestic progress. Through industrialization, Mussolini was credited with having tripled Italian economic productivity and with doing so while nonetheless "enabling the worker and the farmer in Italy to take first place in the honor of the state."[61] In Germany, Husayn was particularly impressed with the success of Nazis in fostering a beneficial work ethic. Under the Nazis "work is an honor for the Germans, and the German who does not work has no honor." He portrayed German industriousness under the Nazi regime as fueled by national rather than individual motives; Hitler had succeeded in instilling the belief in Germans that "Germany is the homeland of everyone and hence that every individual must work for the good of all." Work was now almost a national religion in Germany; all fractions of society—young and old, rich and poor, men, women, children—all were committed to working for the benefit of the German nation's welfare and greatness. Husayn had no doubt that Egypt "must imitate the German example, so that all work together in all types of work for the good the country."[62]

What he had observed in Italy and Germany led Ahmad Husayn to blur the line between democratic and despotic government. Like his colleague Fathi Radwan, what mattered most to Husayn was results. In one statement when in Italy, Husayn was not hesitant in declaring that "the principles of his party are compatible with the principles of Rome and Berlin, and that he does not consider Mussolini and Hitler to be dictators, but rather that they are the reflection of their peoples, of their life and greatness, and that Italy and Germany are the two democratic states in Europe, the other states being capitalistic-parliamentary organizations." By "working night and day for the interests of the people as a whole," Mussolini and Hitler had succeeded in transcending social and economic divisions in their countries; as a result, their respective systems represented "the genuine rule of the people for the sake of the people."[63]

In a speech at a party rally in Alexandria upon his return to Egypt in August 1938, Ahmad Husayn expressed the view that the structural differences between democracy and dictatorship were immaterial: "I don't know what democracy is, and I don't know what dictatorship is. I know only one thing, and that is sound government." Young Egypt's leader went on to define "sound government [al-hukm al-salih]" as a system of rule "that is based on the service of the people and the raising of the living standard of the working classes. Any rule that augments the sovereignty of the people, any rule that concerns itself with the living standards of the people, any rule that advances the health of the people, is sound government, and thus is that to which I give allegiance." By August 1938, Husayn was viewing labels such as "democracy" and "dictatorship" as meaningless: "As for the words democracy and dictatorship, they are political expressions used for political purposes, to propagandize against one state in the service of another."[64]

The bulk of the Alexandria speech was devoted to spelling out the urgent need for sweeping domestic reform that had progressively come to predominate in Young Egypt's rhetoric of 1938. In the course of expounding at length on the poverty and misery that characterized the life of the majority of Egyptians and the determination of Young Egypt to work for the betterment of the living conditions of Egypt's oppressed masses, Husayn repeatedly declared his willingness to jettison both the Egyptian Constitution and the country's parliamentary system if they proved to be barriers to the achievement of Young Egypt's demand for a more just social order. As far as Egypt's Constitution was concerned, Husayn made it clear that "if the Constitution and the Parliament are able to achieve this result [social justice] for us, then I will be content. Otherwise, say of me that I am an aggressor against the Constitution." Much the same went for Parliament: "If Parliament aids us in the achievement of this program, we shall be content. If it does not contribute to it, and stands as an obstacle in the way of the achievement of this program—then say of me that I am an aggressor against Parliament, and that I will fight it and get rid of it."[65] By late 1938, Ahmad Husayn and Young Egypt had come a long way from their earlier acceptance of parliamentary government and their declarations of support for the existing constitutional order in Egypt.

The most elaborate endorsements of fascist ideology written by a representative of Young Egypt during the late 1930s came from the pen of ʿAbd al-Rahman Badawi, in 1938 head of the party's newly established "Office of External Affairs [*Maktab al-Shuʾun al-Kharijiyya*]." The office was established in March 1938 to track international developments and to suggest options and possible scenarios for the party's leadership.[66] A younger enthusiast of Young Egypt (b. 1917), subsequently a noted scholar of philosophy,[67] in 1938 Badawi published several substantial translations of documents and analytical essays concerning Fascism and Nazism in the party's newspaper. The series "The School of Fascism [*Madhhab al-Fashiyya*]" consisted of Badawi's translations of Mussolini's writings that expounded on the principles underlying Italian Fascism.[68] A subsequent translation by Badawi was of the 1920 program of the Nazi Party.[69] Badawi's major contribution to the articulation of Young Egypt's view of Nazism in particular came in a series of lengthy analytical articles he published in *Jaridat Misr al-Fatah* in August and September 1938. Whereas Ahmad Husayn's recent reports from Germany had focused primarily on what he perceived as social and economic efficacy of Nazism, Badawi attempted to provide a philosophical understanding of the fundamental principles upon which the Nazi system of rule was based and which accounted for its success. Badawi's essays are a prime example where an Egyptian analyst attempted to come to grips with the fundamental principles of Nazism.

The most notable feature of the first two essays in the series is the extent to which Badawi explicitly endorsed the Nazi theory of race. Badawi's first article dealt with the Nazi approach to labor, an aspect of Hitler's regime that had generated admiration from Ahmad Husayn on his European trip. Badawi accepted the Nazi claim that the regime's control and coordination of the German labor force was a success because, unlike the rival ideology of socialism, their approach derived from a "racial mysticism" that transcended the solely material: "while Marxist socialism is based on material pleasure, a selfish materialistic view of life whose object is to achieve the maximum material happiness for individuals, the Nazis believe that the individual is subject to a lofty mystical reality that towers above all individuals or any group." Race was indeed "a reality that imposes itself on all individuals, and the individual has no choice but to sacrifice himself for its sake."[70] The second essay in the series, "Racism in Nazi Philosophy," directly analyzed the historical development of racist ideology in Europe from Joseph-Arthur de Gobineau and Houston Stewart Chamberlain to contemporary Nazi theorists such as Alfred Rosenberg. Like Husayn's more descriptive reports stressing the practical effectiveness of the Nazis in mobilizing the population of Germany for national purposes, Badawi emphasized the nationalist utility of racism as practiced by the Nazis: "Hitler could not have found a better way than racism [al-'unsuriyya] to revive the spirit of the people again." This revival was possible because race was an inherent and indelible characteristic of human beings: "the individual is an indivisible part of the race and is incapable of separating himself from it. . . . There is no life for the individual outside of the race." Race was indeed the "synthesis" that erased "the contradiction between thesis [individual] and antithesis [society]" and thus could "resolve the great questions of life, that is questions of the interaction between the individual and society."[71]

After having accepted the Nazi view of the centrality of race in human affairs, Badawi's third and fourth articles in the series discussed and endorsed as equally valid the Nazi positions concerning the necessity of submission to the leadership of Adolf Hitler and the leading role of the Nazi Party in Germany. For its part the effectiveness of the führer principle in revivifying Germany derived from its being suited to the specific racial character of the German people: "this theory of leadership that the Nazis have brought to Germany and that the Nazi state adheres to in its rule is the one system that is compatible with the spirit of the German people because it is based on the two factors of unlimited obedience and absolute responsibility, and these two attributes are peculiarities that fit the German race perfectly." Badawi went as far as to insist that, based as it was on the unchangeable racial essence of the German people, the dictatorial leadership of the Führer should be regarded as "true democracy, rather than these parliamentary comedies that the so-called democratic states boast about, states in which the fancy traders in words and the capitalists dominate the state."[72] The essay on the role of the party in Germany justified the

Nazi dictatorship by returning to the construct of thesis-antithesis-synthesis, in this case applied to the three elements of people-state-party: "the Nazis have been able to eliminate friction between the people and the state, and to link the two indissolubly, by means of the third factor they have created. It is the point where the original bodies [people and state] meet, and it joins them together. It is the synthesis in which the thesis and antithesis are sublimated. This third element is the party."[73]

Badawi's analysis of racist ideology in his essays on the principles of Nazism were prologue to a brief period in which Nazi racist thought in general and its antipathy to Jews in particular found parallels in the rhetoric and activism of Young Egypt. Racism and anti-Semitism had not been a major subject of discussion in the views of the Nazi regime expressed by spokesmen of Young Egypt through most of the 1930s; what drew their attention were the manifestations of national revival and strength that they believed could be credited to Nazism. Movement leaders sometimes expressed a degree of sympathy for the plight of Jews in Germany: as late as August 1938, Ahmad Husayn was referring to Nazi persecution of German Jews as "an excess that does not agree with human progress" in addition to its being a policy for which "Palestine is paying the price."[74] The movement's physical involvement in the Palestine question was relatively muted prior to 1939. In November 1938, the movement instructed its followers not to participate in a student protest strike on the anniversary of the Balfour Declaration.[75] It was only in 1939 that Young Egypt turned its sights on the Egyptian Jewish community for their alleged support for Zionist aspirations in Palestine.

When Young Egypt did take up the anti-Jewish theme, it did so with a vengeance. Articles in *Jaridat Misr al-Fatah* now presented the struggle against Jews in a global context by mid-1939, warning "all Muslims in all parts of the world" that Jews were "the secret of this decline and decay that afflicts the whole Islamic world" and calling all Muslims to rally in support of the Palestinian Arabs since "the success of the Palestinian revolution is the key to success for all Islamic nations, the corner-stone of the building of their unity."[76] Other articles claimed Jewish responsibility for various anti-Egyptian, anti-Arab, and anti-Muslim "plots": a plot to cut off all advertising from any journal critical of Zionism and Jewry;[77] an economic conspiracy by which "Jews have come to dominate the arteries of life in Egypt and to direct these to serve their own ends and goals";[78] finally a

plot, reminiscent of the Protocols of the Elders of Zion, that had been recently revealed in "special Jewish documents . . . that prove their designs
upon the Arabs: it says 'verily, we have turned our guns upon the Arabs.'"[79]
Young Egypt's anti-Jewish activism went beyond rhetoric in mid-1939. The
movement attempted to organize a boycott of Egyptian Jewish merchants,
establishing a "Committee for the Boycott of Jewish Commerce," sending
activists to preach in mosques in support of the campaign, publishing lists
of Jewish Cairo merchants to be boycotted, and distributing anti-Jewish
literature in provincial cities.[80]

The hostility to Zionism sparked by the Palestine issue in time worked
itself into attacks on Jews that resemble the venomous anti-Semitism inherent in Nazism. The height of vitriolic journalism on the part of Young
Egypt came in an article entitled "A Letter from a Jew," in which Husayn
elaborated on an anonymous derogatory letter from a Jew he said he had
received in the mail. The fact that the letter was unsigned was for Husayn
"a mark of the cowardice of all Jews, who work in the dark, behind a cur-
tain." The "obscene expressions" found in the letter's text were "a model of
the literature of the Jews itself, and a picture of the destructive nature of
their character." The article echoed the standard anti-Semitic trope of the
Jews being responsible for the spread of "destructive principles like anar-
chism and communism" and went on to place collective responsibility for
the all the ills of the Arab and Muslim worlds on their Jewish minorities:
"They are the secret of this moral desolation that has become prevalent in
the Arab and Islamic worlds. They are the secret of this cultural squalor
and these filthy arts. They are the secret of this religious and moral decay,
up to the point where it has become correct to say 'search for the Jew behind every depravity.'" Despite his concluding the article with verbal acro-
batics in which he attempted to deny that he and his movement were racist
("If we fight the Jews, and if we will continue to fight them, we do not do
that because we despise them as Jews. We do not fight them as Italy and
Germany do. We despise racial discrimination. What we do is a defense of
ourselves and our Palestinian brothers"), the influence of anti-Semitic
ideology on the rhetoric of Young Egypt by the eve of World War II is
unmistakable.[81]

Ahmad Husayn's open admiration for the domestic achievements of
Fascism and Nazism, 'Abd al-Rahman Badawi's more philosophically
phrased essays endorsing the totalitarian and racist principles that were

responsible for the success of Nazism, and Young Egypt's denunciations of and campaign against Jews mark the apex of Young Egypt's infatuation with contemporary European fascism. But they represent only one dimension of Young Egypt's complex position regarding the European dictatorships in the late 1930s. They were accompanied and tempered by increasing concern regarding the regional and international implications of the growth of Fascist and Nazi power.

Young Egypt's overall perspective vis-à-vis Fascism and Nazism was marked both by attraction and repulsion, admiration and fear. This ambivalence was rooted in the dilemma of being pulled in one direction by their nationalism, yet in another by their anticolonialism. On the one hand, as an ultranationalist organization Young Egypt was greatly impressed to the success of the "revolutions" under way in Fascist Italy and Nazi Germany and what the success of both regimes meant for Italy's and Germany's stature and influence in international affairs. Yet, as a fiercely nationalist organization with an anti-imperialist agenda, Young Egypt was led to reject and to object to the unquestioned imperialist ambitions manifested by both Fascism and Nazism. Whereas Young Egypt admired Italy and Germany for having achieved national "miracles," it simultaneously criticized their having made their successful revolutions the launching pad for territorial expansion and imperial conquests abroad. Whereas Egypt's liberal intellectuals on the whole understood and related primarily to the totalitarian threat of fascism to fundamental liberal values such as individualism and freedom of expression, for the younger ideologues and adherents of both Young Egypt and the Muslim Brothers totalitarianism was not the central issue; their primary concern was fascist imperialism.

Fascist Italy and its regional ambitions in the Mediterranean clearly were a subject of concern on the part of Young Egypt in the later 1930s. The potential implications of an Anglo-Italian diplomatic agreement regarding their respective interests in the Mediterranean, eventually concluded in April 1938, aroused apprehensive speculation on the part of Young Egypt's spokesmen. Ahmad Husayn voiced his concern about Italy's intentions in the Mediterranean, viewing the possibility of British concessions to Italy in order to achieve Anglo-Italian detente as a direct threat to the Suez Canal. Afraid that Britain would sacrifice Egyptian interests in order to buy agreement with Italy, Husayn argued that "we in Egypt are obliged to define our position quickly and to find a way to defend our sovereignty and honor that Mussolini wishes to destroy by either peaceful or warlike means." He went on to ask "what can we do to prevent this out-rageous situation? What can we do to declare to England and to Italy that Egypt, an independent nation, will not accept to be the subject of haggling and negotiations, and that it alone can assume the defense of the Suez Canal?" There was "only one effective answer" to this threat, an increase of the size of the Egyptian military to 50,000 men and of its air force to 200 planes.[82]

Both Italy's colonial occupation of Libya and the presence of a large Italian military force on the Egyptian border generated criticism on the part of Young Egypt in 1938–39. In April 1938, an article in *Jaridat Misr al-Fatah* criticized a recent speech by Mussolini in which he had expounded on the strength of Italian armed forces and his country's preparedness for war. Noting the movement's previous admiration for Mussolini's achieve-ments in Italy, the newspaper stated that "we in Egypt cannot praise Mus-solini when we fear his expansionism and his policies. . . . Everything in Mussolini's speech practically announces that he is considering aggression against Egypt, and that these huge forces [in Libya] of which he has spo-ken so proudly have but one object, and that undoubtedly is to attack Egypt."[83] In June Fathi Radwan, while admitting his admiration of Mus-solini for "having built Italy into a great power," was nonetheless unable to ignore the potential threat to Egypt posed by the imperial aspirations of Italian Fascism: "what does Italy wish except a new Empire, the revival of the old Roman Empire of which Egypt was a part?"[84] In December, *Jaridat Misr al-Fatah* printed a series of protests by exiled Libyans against the recent decision of the Italian government to impose Italian citizenship on the indigenous population of Libya. Like the Muslim Brothers, Young Egypt denounced this attempt "to turn Libya into a part of Italy" and its commitment to the maintenance of "Libya as an Arab country."[85] Criti-cism of Italy's anti-Islamic policies in Libya continued into 1939.[86]

Germany's expansionist aspirations and actions of the late 1930s were a more remote but nonetheless globally more significant subject of concern for Young Egypt. From their nationalist perspective, Young Egypt's publicists by and large endorsed Germany's incorporation of Austria into the Third Reich in the Anschluss of March 1938. In an article entitled "Frederick the Great Rises Again," party spokesman Mustafa al-Wakil evaluated the Anschluss as a justifiable effort on the part of Germany to reassert its proper position in the world, a major step in the campaign Hit-ler had marked out in *Mein Kampf* to overturn the unfavorable settlement imposed on Germany after World War I. He also saw the event as a hopeful parallel for Egypt, specifically with reference to Egyptian aspirations for eventually regaining control of the Sudan.[87] Fathi Radwan similarly took encouragement from Germany's successful challenge to an unfavorable international status quo. Like Wakil, Radwan viewed this realization of a long-standing German nationalist aim as indicating that Young Egypt, inspired by a similar faith in its mission, would triumph in the end.[88] Ahmad Husayn saw the Anschluss as a clear confirmation of his and his movement's belief that "the world today respects only one law, and that is the law of power, organized power." To Husayn the lesson Egyptians should learn from the Anschluss was obvious: "the example [of the Anschluss], oh youth, should be sufficient to awaken you finally from your long slumber, and prompt you to form one rank under one banner, the banner of Young Egypt, which desires glory based on power and organization for this country."[89]

The extended crisis over Czechoslovakia that culminated in the Munich Conference of September 1938 was a turning point in Young Egypt's view of Nazi Germany and its potential for producing international tension. As Germany ratcheted up its threats of military action over the Sudetenland in the late summer of 1938, Egyptian apprehension turned to panic over the prospect of the outbreak of a wider war that might draw Egypt into the maelstrom. With the exception of the victim Czechoslovakia, Young Egypt's spokesmen found plenty to criticize in the behavior of all the major participants in the Munich crisis. Responsibility for bringing the world to the edge of the precipice of war was indisputably Hitler's. "If war occurs now, Hitler is responsible and by this will deserve the loathing of the world," was the title of a commentary by Young Egypt's "political correspondent" in late September.[90] Ahmad Husayn was as usual more vehement: "if war breaks out now, after all the efforts and sacrifices that England and France have made and that Czechoslovakia was accepted, the meaning of that is that Hitler is a madman who wishes to destroy the world to satisfy his arrogance and his lusts."[91] Yet the Western democracies were not held blameless in the rape of Czechoslovakia. One clear conclusion drawn from the eventual British and French acquiescence to German demands at Munich was the weakness of political will demonstrated by the Western democracies. For Young Egypt, substantial responsibility for the partial dismemberment of Czechoslovakia lay with Great Britain and France. The Western powers were accused of deserting Czechoslovakia, "which is going the way of Ethiopia, after having promised to protect it . . . and to defend its existence against any aggressor." Their treacherous abandonment of Czechoslovakia "at the last moment," sacrificing it to Germany for the sake of preserving peace, was abominable.[92] The title of a later retrospective on the Munich crisis summarized what it had demonstrated about the decline of the Western democracies: "Have Britain and France Reached the Stage of Senility and Impotence? All the Indications Say Yes."[93]

Beyond the disgraceful behavior of all the powers at Munich, for Young Egypt the crisis as a whole reinforced a fundamental tenet of the movement; that might makes right and that, if Egypt wanted to protect itself in a brutal world of dog-eat-dog, it had best be ready to defend itself. Munich proved again that power ruled in international affairs and that "weakness deserves only contempt and denunciation."[94] However lamentable its consequences, what Hitler had achieved at Munich was further proof that "politics is a swindle and a double-cross."[95]

In the wake of the Munich crisis, national defense became a major concern for Young Egypt. The movement repeatedly called upon the Egyptian government to undertake a program of strengthening Egypt's defense capabilities by introducing compulsory conscription, expanding the armed forces, and establishing munitions factories on Egyptian soil. For its part, the party attempted to mobilize Egyptians for war by encouraging its followers to register for military service and by offering civil defense lectures and classes.[96] From late 1938 onward, the imperative of preparing Egyptians to participate in national defense was used by Young Egypt to partially subvert the government's previous ban on paramilitary organizations. Thus the party enjoined its student followers to participate in classes in military training instituted by the Ministry of Education for secondary school and university students, and some party branches began holding their own classes in military training for party members.[97]

From Munich until the outbreak of war in September 1939, Young Egypt's general attitude to the international position of the Axis powers was one of hostility. In the eyes of Young Egypt, the most egregious acts of Fascist and Nazi imperialist aggression prior to World War II came in the spring of 1939, when Germany annexed the rump of Czechoslovakia and Italy invaded Albania. Germany's incorporation of what had remained of Czechoslovakia after Munich was defined as "undoubtedly a blatant step of aggression," while Italy's "conquest of Albania with fire and sword" drew similar denunciation by Young Egypt.[98] For his part Ahmad

Husayn, who had been effusive in his praise of the young Czech state upon his visit there in 1938, lamented that "this splendid state was obliterated in the twinkling of an eye, without the firing of a shot and without the shedding of a drop of blood." Again Husayn found plenty of blame to go around: finding Germany's justification of the annexation as one of self-defense in the face of Czech hostility a dubious claim, he also denounced France and Great Britain for refusing the support Czech territorial integrity from Munich onward.[99]

The actions of the Axis powers in the spring of 1939 served to reinforce Young Egypt's long-standing conclusions about the nature of international politics: "all this is but another proof that there is no international law now except the law of power according to which the strong subjugate the weak," another indisputable indication of "the hysteria of conquest and aggression that has become prevalent in Germany and Italy, and Japan as well," and of "the negligence of the democracies and their submission to the conquest of others."[100] In his bitter commentary on the events of the spring of 1939, Ahmad Husayn went as far as to "praise the Lord for Italy, the other member of the Axis, for she has erased the last doubt and confirmed the glaring, screaming reality—that powerful states are not prepared to respect treaties or agreements, and that they have begun taking over and gobbling up weak states." From Husayn's cynical perspective, Italy's aggression in Albania was "a lucky blow, for it has awakened the world from its slumber. It is a blessed moment, for it has eliminated every hesitation and every attachment to dreaming—to the dream of treaties and friendship and brotherhood and cooperation."[101]

By mid-1939, the eve of World War II, Young Egypt was clearly trying to distance itself from the European fascist movements that it had previously emulated. It did so most definitively in Ahmad Husayn's "Message to Hitler! [*Risala Ila Hitlar!*]," an open letter to the Nazi leader published in *Jaridat Misr al-Fatah* in July 1939.[102] The message appears to have been written largely for domestic consumption, to impress Egyptians with Husayn's devotion to Islam as well as to disassociate Young Egypt from European fascism. The first half of the document is a comparison between Islam and German National Socialism, emphasizing the egalitarian and nondiscriminatory nature of the former and defining "the Islamic spirit" as "democracy without looseness; freedom without anarchy or recklessness, and without extreme communism or nihilism; cooperation between rich and poor and charity regulated by religion without extreme socialism or the dictatorship of one class over other classes of people."[103] The second half of the message contrasted National Socialism, its foreign policy in particular, to this vision of Islam and found it sorely lacking:

Neither you nor the German people carry to the world a new message or present humanity with anything that would lighten its misery and woes. . . . So what have you prepared for the other nations and what is your message for their happiness? Nothing! Nothing! Your program contains nothing. Since no one who is not a German can ever become a German. And woe to anyone who is not a German! You will tread on him with your feet. This is what is prompting the world, sooner or later, to rise as one in defense of itself against a master who wants nothing but domination over it and its conquest; against a master who will not present to it a remedy for its spiritual ailments and for its material sufferings.[104]

The message concluded with an appeal for Hitler to "adopt Islam," or at least to "study Islam" in the hope that its truths would have a mitigating effect upon the National Socialist agenda.

When world war did break out in September 1939, Young Egypt's position on Egypt's possible participation in the hostilities was remarkably convoluted. Ahmad Husayn took the lead in formulating Young Egypt's public stance regarding the war. In an editorial of August 31, as war appeared imminent, Husayn analyzed the dilemma facing Egypt should war erupt. Both the possible alternative outcomes of war were unappealing for an Egyptian nationalist like Husayn. If Great Britain emerged victorious, she was unlikely to relinquish her hold on Egypt. On the other hand, if the Axis emerged triumphant, the country would be in an equally unenviable situation: "Let us imagine now the opposite picture, that is that the other side, Rome and Berlin, win. What will be our fate in this case, except to be the spoils of victory? They will take us by right of conquest, considering that we were subordinates of the defeated powers."[105]

Since war carried the prospect of postwar subjugation regardless of who won, Husayn now argued that only Egyptian participation in war as a belligerent on the side of Great Britain held out hope for Egypt. He justified the same on two grounds. The first reflected the social Darwinist perspective that had inspired much of Young Egypt's activism throughout the 1930s. For Husayn, war was the crucial arena for demonstrating national vigor and resolve. War would prove to the world the national worthiness of Egyptians:

It is the duty of peoples, if they find themselves participants in a war, that they enter into it wholeheartedly, defying death. . . . This is what all living peoples do in order to achieve victory. For our part we are no less in faith in our country, in understanding of the reality of the struggle, than those Europeans, and we are not less than they in bravery and courage.

The second was strictly pragmatic; by assisting Great Britain in its war effort, Egypt would be in a position to argue more effectively for British concessions to Egypt's nationalist demands after the war. Husayn thus called on the newly installed Egyptian government headed by 'Ali Mahir to make it clear to the British that "when the war ends in favor of England and Egypt," Egypt would not retreat from her nationalist claims to full independence and sovereignty.[106]

Husayn's article of August 31 elaborating on Egypt's options in case of war provided the rationale for a set of resolutions issued on the same day by Young Egypt's Administrative Council. The first resolution was the crucial one: "The Party declares the absolute necessity that, in case of the outbreak of war, it is incumbent upon Egypt to take upon itself the burden of defending its borders from outside aggression, and to stand at the side of England until final victory is achieved, in order that that may be the basis for building a glorious future for Egypt and for liberating the Arab states."[107]

Young Egypt's advocacy of Egyptian entry into war alongside Great Britain was based on the expectation that Italy would join Germany once war began. When at the start of September 1939 Italy did not do so, Young Egypt's position on the war immediately shifted. A statement issued in the name of the party by Ahmad Husayn on September 2 significantly revised the movement's official position on the war. Italy's unexpected abstention from the war changed everything. Italy's decision had lifted the threat of immediate invasion from Egypt. In this circumstance, Husayn argued that "if there is no aggression against us, it is not possible for us to participate in a war which had nothing to do with us. This became obvious to us as soon as Italy declared her neutrality. Egypt's duty in this situation is sleeplessly to preserve the integrity of her borders and to complete her preparations for war."[108] Husayn's new position on Egypt and the war paralleled that being adopted by the new Egyptian ministry of 'Ali Mahir, which in early September split on the question of Egyptian entry into the war and on September 4 informed the British that Egypt was adopting a position of formal nonbelligerence.

Resonating throughout Ahmad Husayn's commentaries as war began, but contrasting with the prudence he eventually came to express concerning Egypt's possible participation, was the theme of war as the true test of national vigor and worth. While war would undoubtedly bring destruction and suffering for Egypt, war also offered unparalleled opportunities for the nation to assert its proper place in the world: "If the fires of war erupt, this country will face them in one rank, with a firm faith and hearts of iron. We will defend our existence and our future, and will come out of it winners, victors. We shall carry out our mission to lead the Arabs, to be a leader of Islam, and to be a guide for the two worlds."[109] Husayn's most bellicose statement preceding the war came on August 28, when he declared that "it is inevitable for us to participate wholeheartedly in the coming war, for our glorious future and our chance of dazzling the two worlds is conditional on success in this war. So be prepared, oh soldiers of Young Egypt, to sacrifice your spirit in order to lead your country through your resolution."[110] A proclamation by Husayn addressed to Egyptian youth that accompanied his September 2 statement revising Young Egypt's position on the war reached new lyrical heights. At the same time as arguing that the present circumstances necessitated Egyptian abstention from the war, Husayn nonetheless exulted that the cataclysm about to begin would eventually provide the generation in whose name he spoke the opportunity to demonstrate their willingness to struggle and sacrifice for the greater glory of Egypt:

How long have we hoped from God that the opportunity would be given to us, the opportunity to sacrifice for the sake of the homeland so worthy of sacrifice and for the sake of exalted principles. How long have we looked with an eye of envy and jealousy at the youth of those countries who know how to defend their country and to die for the sake of it. . . . How long have we prayed to God that He will prepare for us a trial by which we will test our patience and our faith and our readiness to die for the sake of God and the homeland. And now the hour has come, the hour in which we will affirm our manhood and our strength and that we are not less in determination, on the contrary that we surpass other peoples in love of our country and the desire to struggle for the sake of high ideals. The hour has come in which Egypt will astonish the worlds with miracles that will astonish Egyptians themselves before it astonishes their adversaries.[111]

For Ahmad Husayn, World War II would be the ultimate arena for Young Egypt's followers to demonstrate the power of their faith though action.

Once war was a reality, Young Egypt's trajectory took a radically different course from that of its chief competitor for the loyalties of the new *effendiyya*, the Muslim Brothers. As we have seen, save for the occasional but never sustained harassment of its leadership and publications by apprehensive Egyptian governments in 1940–41, the Muslim Brothers continued to function and to grow during the war years. In contrast, Young Egypt's prewar verbal and physical militance, as well as suspicions of its involvement in wartime anti-British activity, brought the constraint of its public activities in the first few years of the conflict and by mid-1941 its complete suppression.

The outbreak of the war and the immediate emergency measures enacted by the Egyptian government (the declaration of a state of siege and the institution of press censorship) restricted but did not totally eliminate Young Egypt's ability to operate in the public sphere. Its physical campaign of anti-Jewish incitement and the boycott of Jewish merchants that it had attempted to organize in the summer of 1939 effectively ceased with the outbreak of war and the stricter public security enforced under the state of siege. As Ahmad Husayn wryly explained to his supporters shortly after the start of the war, the imperative of national unity in wartime meant that "we are compelled to desist from our struggle against some things."[112] The less disruptive forms of activity that characterized the movement, on the other hand, continued through the first year and a half of the war. Party clubhouses continued to function; party branches continued to hold meetings; both in 1940 and 1941, the movement was allowed to hold its annual rally at the Pyramids.[113] *Jaridat Misr al-Fatah*, Young Egypt's newspaper, continued to appear until May 1941, but its size, content, and frequency of appearance were all adversely affected by the censorship in effect in Egypt as well as by the wartime shortage of newsprint that constrained all Egyptian publications. The paper operated as a daily until November 1939, as a biweekly thereafter; by early 1941, only a reduced-in-size issue was appearing irregularly.

The main institutional development affecting Young Egypt during the war was a formal change of name and the adoption of a new program. In competition with the surging Muslim Brothers, from late 1938 onward, Young Egypt's rhetoric had taken a more Islamic coloration, its demands for greater social justice in Egypt now being articulated as the realization of authentic Islamic values. The party formalized its movement in a more Islamic direction in March 1940, when it changed its name from "the Young Egypt Party [*Hizb Misr al-Fatah*]" to "the Islamic Nationalist Party [*al-Hizb al-Watani al-Islami*]," and when it issued a new party program that simultaneously called for the enforcement of Islamic mores in Egypt and for a closer Egyptian orientation with the neighboring Arab and Muslim countries.[114]

Young Egypt's public activity and publication came to an end in the spring of 1941, at the time of the anti-British uprising in Iraq. Wishing to preempt any similar anti-British uprising in Egypt and suspecting Young Egypt of being responsible for the recent distribution of "inflammatory anti-British pamphlets" calling for Egyptians to prepare themselves for "revolution" and for the sabotage of communications facilities should the Axis force a British retreat in the desert war,[115] the authorities cracked down on Young Egypt. *Jaridat Misr al-Fatah* was closed by order of the censorship; party meetings were prohibited; numerous members of the party were taken into custody (some 300 initially); and the party's leaders Fathi Radwan and Ahmad Husayn were apprehended. Until the gradual release of its most prominent detainees from late 1944 onward, when the war was almost over, Young Egypt/The Islamic Nationalist Party ceased to exist as an organized movement.[116] In contrast to the policy of gradualism and accommodation adopted by the Muslim Brothers during the war, the movement's prewar adoption of a more radical ideological stance and its suspected wartime involvement in activities that were simultaneously subversive of public order and a threat to the stability of the Egyptian domestic scene led to its eventual repression and marginalization as a movement appealing to and speaking for Egypt's new *effendiyya*.

Conclusion
Shifting Narratives

FASCIST AUTHORITARIANISM'S CHALLENGE to liberal democracy received intensive attention in Egyptian public discourse in the 1930s. A number of Egyptians—politicians, journalists, public intellectuals—made a point of visiting Fascist Italy or Nazi Germany on their visits to Europe, and on their return reported their impressions at length. A much larger body of Egyptians, well informed regarding the European scene from both the local and international press, did not hesitate to interpret and comment on various aspects of fascist ideology and policy as they took shape in Italy and Germany. Discussions and evaluations of the polar ideological systems of authoritarian fascism versus liberal democracy proliferated in the Egyptian print and visual media, increasing in frequency as the ideological and political confrontation between the two accelerated over the course of the decade.

This profound Egyptian interest in contemporary fascism was spurred by both external and internal stimuli. Externally, the growth of fascist movements in various European countries; their rise to power in two major European states, Italy and Germany; and the challenge that fascist aggressiveness and expansionism posed to the post–World War I international order, eventually culminating in world war—all these events made contemporary fascism an unavoidable topic of concern for Egyptians interested in world affairs. This externally driven impetus was overlaid and reinforced by an equally or more important set of domestic circumstances that made fascism a subject of attention by the 1930s. On the popular level, Egyptians came to perceive and fear that fascist ideas, as manifested in the emergence of youth, militant and paramilitary movements that appeared to parrot fascist rhetoric and emulate fascist practices, were increasing in appeal among the Egyptian younger generation in particular and as such represented a threat to the existing constitutional and parliamentary order erected in the 1920s. On the level of high politics, the emergence of a young and initially popular monarch in the person of King Faruq was perceived as a potential threat to the existing parliamentary system of government. In 1936–37, Faruq successfully challenged and ousted the popularly elected ministry of the Wafd; in 1938–39, the fear that the king and his advisers entertained hopes of restructuring the constitutional and parliamentary order in a more autocratic fashion that might echo fascist concepts of leadership and efficiency was an additional incentive for Egyptians to concern themselves with the possible relevance of contemporary authoritarian ideas and practices.

As the preceding chapters have demonstrated, Egyptian attitudes toward authoritarian fascism and liberal democracy were neither uniform nor static. Nonetheless, a definite weight of public opinion can be identified. In terms of time, some Egyptians were initially open to the possibility that fascist organizational strength, socio-economic restructuring, psychological self-confidence, and success in apparently achieving national revival all represented a positive model that Egypt might emulate. Gradually, this openness gave way to the perception that these aspects of fascism were outweighed by the adverse effects of totalitarian rule and aggressive chauvinist nationalism. In terms of substance, the earlier receptivity to the possibility that fascist principles of domestic organization were a viable alternative to liberal democracy largely evaporated once Fascist Italy and Nazi Germany had demonstrated the pernicious consequences that flowed from internal dictatorship and external aggression. By the eve of World War II, the bulk of informed Egyptian opinion had come to the consensus that fascist totalitarianism, racism, and imperialism represented a manifest threat to Egypt, the Middle East, and the rest of the world.

In summarizing differences in the views of individuals and in the orientation of publications concerning the issue of fascism versus democracy, certain cleavages can be identified. One line of cleavage in Egyptian opinion was not according to religious background. Positive and negative views of fascism crossed religious boundaries. One of the few Egyptian commentators who expressed wholehearted enthusiasm for Nazi principles at one point or another in the 1930s was the Coptic Christian Salama Musa of *al-Majalla al-Jadida* (although Musa substantially revised his opinion later in the decade); conversely, a staunchly Islamic-oriented commentator such as Ahmad Hasan al-Zayyat, the editor of *al-Risala*, was an early and vitriolic critic of fascist totalitarianism, racism, and imperialism. In the intellectual press, it was Musa's vigorously modernist and secularist *al-Majalla al-Jadida* that published the most positive assessments of fascism's domestic achievements in the mid-1930s, while the more Islamic and Arab-oriented *al-Risala* was the Egyptian publication that took the lead in defining fascism as totalitarian and in denouncing fascist principles almost from the journal's inception in 1933. For their part, the explicitly Islamic *salafi*-oriented messages of Hasan al-Banna and the publications of the Muslim Brothers expressed little sympathy for either alien fascist ideology or repressive fascist practice. The Muslim Brothers rejected Nazi racist doctrine, and viewed Fascism and Nazism as a new mode of Western expansionism and imperialism that was no less and perhaps even more threatening than existing forms of French and British colonialism. Egyptian evidence from the 1930s does not indicate any inherent Muslim predisposition toward authoritarianism underpinning Egyptian interpretations of fascism.

If religious background was not an important criterion for distinguishing among different views regarding fascism, what was? Far more significant in leading an Egyptian of the 1930s to take a favorable view of (some aspects) of fascism was one's conviction of the necessity for rapid and sweeping change in order to usher Egypt into the modern age. The odd couple of the Fabian socialist Salama Musa and radical youth leader Ahmad Husayn of Young Egypt illustrate the point: despite substantial differences in their analyses of the ills of contemporary Egypt, it was the fervent conviction of both commentators that Egyptian society and politics required drastic transformation. This conviction led them to praise the dynamism, organizational strength, and apparent success of Nazism in realizing such a transformation in a short period of time in Germany. At least for a time, both Musa and Husayn viewed fascism as the road to modernity. However, contributors to a venerable establishment publication such as *al-Hilal*, or somewhat differently in the case of the newer journals *al-Risala* and *al-Thaqafa*, found little of appeal in the polarizing ideology and immoderate behavior of European fascists. For most voices writing in these Egyptian intellectual periodicals, Fascism and Nazism were viewed as antimodernist and antiprogressive reactionary movements that subversively undermined Enlightenment ideas and principles. They represented an antihumanist trend, which seriously endangered human freedom, equality, and solidarity.

Anticolonialism was the most important factor shaping the negative Egyptian consensus regarding fascism and Nazism in the 1930s. As first Fascist Italy and then Nazi Germany expressed their nationalist dynamism through external aggressiveness and expansion, Egyptians of virtually all ideological inclinations came to view contemporary fascism as a potential threat to "small states" and "weak nations," to world stability and peace, and eventually to the independence and sovereignty of Egypt itself. Among fascist regimes the imperialist label was applied first to Fascist Italy. Italy's imperialist expansion into neighboring Libya had been a matter of long-standing Egyptian concern; it accelerated in the 1930s as a result of Italy's ruthless policies of colonization in its Libyan colony. Apprehension about Italian imperialism was greatly reinforced in the course of Italian expansion in East Africa in the mid-1930s, and perpetuated thereafter by periodic Italian bluster about the Mediterranean as a "Roman Sea" and most directly by the fear of an Italian threat to Egyptian control of the Suez Canal.

Initially over the horizon for Egyptians, Nazi Germany's more sweeping aspirations for territorial aggrandizement were slower to materialize and to have an impact on public discourse. By 1938–39, however, Germany's aggressive expansion in central Europe, its obliteration of the independent existence of small states such as Austria and Czechoslovakia, its intention of doing the same to Poland (all three of which, like Egypt, owed their independence to the post–World War I settlement), and the threat of general war represented by Germany's unrelenting drive for *lebensraum* united the entire spectrum of Egyptian public opinion in opposition to Nazism and German foreign policy. It was primarily nationalism and anticolonialism that accounted for the hardening of antifascist opinion over time; as first the Italian Fascist and subsequently the German Nazi threat to the international order became increasingly evident, Egyptians joined forces in warning against fascist imperialism and the threat it posed to small states as well as to world peace.

Egyptian aversion to fascist imperialism was primarily a political, rather than an ideological, response. But it had ideological consequences. A limited number of commentators—Ahmad Husayn of Young Egypt is the prime example—retained an admiration for fascist principles of political organization and leadership even as they became aware of the potentially negative consequences of fascist imperialism. But most Egyptian observers regarded fascism as a seamless whole, a phenomenon in which the ruthless disrespect for international norms of the Fascists and the Nazis when in power was part and parcel of their general contempt for the standards and expectations of liberal bourgeois culture. For commentators as diverse as ʿAli Adham, ʿAbbas Mahmud al-ʿAqqad, Ahmad Hasan al-Zayyat, Muhammad ʿAbdalla ʿInan, and eventually Salama Musa, fascist imperialism was inseparable from fascist totalitarianism and racism. Fascist dedication to the elevation of a specific national community or "race" fueled fascist expansionism and imperialism; fascist totalitarianism provided the organizational strength that made first Italian and later German aggression a manifest international threat.

A powerful arena for representing Fascism and Nazism as an arch imperialist force whose main victims were small nations was Egypt's illustrated weeklies. Anti-Fascist caricature employed vivid images to present a thoroughly negative portrait of Hitler and Mussolini and more generally of Nazi Germany and Fascist Italy. Hitler and Mussolini were invariably portrayed as power hungry warmongers with an insatiable appetite for "living spaces," colonies acquired through military expansion and occupation. The message presented in visual imagery was one of the ugliness, the brutality, and the inherent evil of Fascism and Nazism. Assuming that these images were accessible to a nonliterate as well as a literate readership and thus that they reached broad sectors of society, visual imagery may be credited with playing a crucial role in creating and disseminating an anti-Fascist and anti-Nazi public mood.

Our case study of Egyptian attitudes regarding fascism versus democracy in the 1930s carries implications for understanding of both modern Egyptian history and the trajectory of political and ideological evolution in the Arab Middle East generally. Contrary to the conventional interpretation of the course of Egyptian political and intellectual history over the early decades of the twentieth century, the material we have examined does not bear out the prevalence of a general "crisis of orientation" or "the failure of the liberal experiment" that saw educated Egyptians abandon their earlier belief in the values of liberal society or accused them of applying these values with an insufficient awareness of their possible relevance to their social environment and local culture. The "crisis of orientation"/"failure of the liberal experiment" interpretation relies on too narrow a range both of intellectuals (several of Egypt's leading Muslim men of letters) and of publications (some of their books addressing the specific topic of early Islamic history). When the canvas is broadened to consider a wider range of commentators (secondary intellectuals, journalists, political and religious activists) and the views specifically related to the subject of fascism versus democracy that they voiced in a number of the daily, weekly, and monthly publications that shaped and expressed public discourse in the later 1930s, quite a different picture of the state of Egyptian opinion regarding the contemporary confrontation between fascism and democracy emerges. The vast majority of articulate Egyptian observers, while often lamenting the erratic performance of the existing Egyptian parliamentary system, nonetheless did not retreat from their ultimate faith in liberal values or abandon their democratic *weltanschauung*. As the evils of Fascist and Nazi totalitarianism, racism, and imperialism became increasingly apparent, they certainly did not promote fascism as an alternative to liberal democracy. The preponderance of the testimony presented in contemporary British assessments of the Egyptian scene largely corroborates this reading of the prewar Egyptian press: Fascist and Nazi propaganda efforts in Egypt were both limited in scope and had a limited impact on Egyptian opinion prior to the outbreak of World War II.

In our opinion, too much attention and meaning has been given to the intermittent and largely unproductive contacts of Egyptians with the Axis powers once the war was under way. The abortive efforts of a handful of Egyptians (the king and his associates; some army officers; the anti-imperialist activists of Young Egypt) to collaborate with the Axis powers cannot be extended to generalize that most Egyptians were *ideologically* disposed toward fascism. Viewing the global struggle between the two ideologies primarily through anti-imperialist lenses, some Egyptians did perceive wartime Axis advances in the Middle East as a potentially useful lever for ending the British occupation of Egypt. But this was a purely political calculus, one that should not carry ideological weight. It stands in sharp contrast to the position of the majority of Egyptian commentators toward fascism in the years immediately preceding the war. Thanks to the freedom of expression that made for a vigorous press, and before wartime censorship made the evaluation of the state of public opinion from published sources precarious, with few exceptions politically involved Egyptians were repulsed by fascism and remained faithful to liberalism. The cliché "the enemy of my enemy is my friend" does not represent mainstream Egyptian public opinion before World War II. When deliberating between the new and apparently insatiable imperialism of Italy and Germany, and the familiar and satiated imperialism of Great Britain or France, Egyptians almost always preferred the latter.

Our rereading of Egyptian history in the 1930s forms part of an emerging alternative narrative concerning the relationship of the Arab world to fascism. Similar to Egypt where, based on a historical narrative that reflected both Western anti-Arab polemics of the 1950s and 1960s and a rereading of the war years by a new military regime anxious to prove its anti-imperialist credentials, ideological sympathy with fascism was assumed to have been widespread, older historiography on the Arab Fertile Crescent (Iraq, Syria, Lebanon, Palestine) often posited the prevalence of an ideological orientation toward fascism on the part of Arabs generally. The grounds for doing so were similar to those as relied upon in the case of Egypt.

In Iraq, a commonly held narrative underscores the rivalry between the mostly pro-British Hashemite camp on the one hand, and a variety of radical and pro-Nazi forces that challenged the political establishment on the other. The narrative stresses the ideological attraction of Nazism to a network of individuals and groups. From a political and strategic perspective, this narrative suggests that Germany appeared to be the only power capable of challenging British colonial hegemony in Iraq and in the Arab Middle East. Practically speaking, Rashid ʿAli al-Kaylani's pro-Nazi coup d'état, in April–May 1941, is presented as demonstrating the strong support for Nazi Germany among the Iraqi military elite, especially younger officers desirous of liberating their country from the yoke of British colonialism. Leading Iraqi educators, most prominently Sami Shawkat, are viewed as having been fascinated by the winning combination of patriotism, militarism, and physical education in Nazi schools. The activities of the radical youth organization *al-Futuwwa* are considered a manifestation of Nazi youth indoctrination practices, and speeches supporting Nazism delivered in Baghdad's Pan-Arab *al-Muthanna* Club perceived as reflecting popular support for Nazi Germany among the Iraqi *effendiyya*.[1] In Syria, studies analyzing the process of radicalization in the 1930s often highlight pro-fascist tendencies among various newly created nationalist organizations. These tendencies are seen as having manifested themselves particularly in the mushrooming of new radical youth organizations such as the League of National Action, the Lion Cubs of Arabism, the Syrian Social Nationalist Party led by Antun Sa'ada, the Arab Club, the Steel Shirts, the early Ba'ath movement, and various radical Islamic organizations. In Lebanon, the White Shirts, the *Najjada*, and the Phalanges/ *Kata'ib* led by Pierre Gemayel are viewed as having been inspired by Nazi or Fascist ideology and forms of organization.[2] In regard to Palestine, scholarship has concentrated on the pro-Nazi activities of the exiled Mufti al-Hajj Amin al-Husayni, the leader of the Palestinian national movement. A supporter of Kaylani's 1941 coup d'état in Iraq, Amin al-Husayni subsequently fled to Nazi Germany, collaborated with the Nazi regime, and actively assisted the German war effort.[3]

Studies dealing with the Arab region as a whole follow the same historiographic pattern. These studies tend to emphasize the great allure that Nazism held for various official and nonofficial Arab groups, organizations, parties, and young military officers. They explain their motives and describe their ideology, style, and patterns of behavior as modeled after Fascist and Nazi ideas and actions.[4] The growth of Pan-Arab nationalist ideology in Egypt, Iraq, Syria, Lebanon, and Palestine is sometimes portrayed as reflecting the growing power of German National Socialism.[5]

Conclusions regarding Arab pro-Axis sympathies in these established narratives are based on a limited sample of the primary Arab sources and are usually informed by a Eurocentric perspective that portrays Arab responses to fascism through the eyes and voices of contemporary British, French, or German officials. Only rarely is what has been termed the "ideological and strategic incompatibility" between Nazi efforts to influence the Arab Middle East and the poor results in terms of the Arab public receptiveness to Nazi ideas and practices noted.[6] The rich repertoire of materials relevant to comprehending Arab views of fascism is only infrequently tapped, the extensive and sustained local public discourses relating to fascism only minimally reflected. On the whole, older scholarship about the Arab Fertile Crescent either ignores or is completely unaware of the substantial anti-Fascist and anti-Nazi voices and forces present in the region.

This narrative emphasizing Arab sympathy and collusion with the Axis powers has recently been overlaid by a newer narrative using a much wider range of sources and with a more Arab-oriented perspective. Recent studies have revisited the subject of Fascist Italy and Nazi Germany's presence and influence in the Arab Middle East by intensively scrutinizing the print media as well as Western and Arab archival material of the period in order to reconstruct local public discourses. As a result, an alternative narrative is taking shape. These studies demonstrate that the growing global importance of Nazi Germany triggered lively public debates on the same crucial issues we have witnessed under discussion in Egypt: democracy versus dictatorship, liberalism versus authoritarianism, pluralism versus totalitarianism. These new studies reveal that the public discourses of the era contained many voices that supported liberal democracy and rejected fascist totalitarianism and imperialism. Germany's racist theories and anti-Semitic ideology gave rise to controversial debates about the very concept of the nation, the status of ethnic and religious minorities among an Arab-Islamic majority, as well as about the relations between the individual and his assumed primordial community. Recent scholarship, while documenting the influence of contemporary fascism on specific Arab organizations and individuals (particularly in greater Syria), on the whole indicates the difficulty in simply applying the label "fascist" in the Arab environment.[7]

In Iraq, studies by Peter Wien and Orit Bashkin have challenged the established narrative by showing that the scholarly focus on pro-Nazi voices and forces ignores numerous liberal and democratic spokesmen present in the Iraqi print media. The substantial criticism of Nazism, expressed particularly by the *al-Ahali* group that espoused a Fabian social-democratic worldview, has been analyzed by Bashkin, as have the views of the communist-inclined individuals and publications that attacked Germany's imperialist policies in Europe. The presence of Jewish writers in the local media also influenced Iraqi rejection of Nazism.[8] Based on his intensive examination of Iraqi publications in the years from 1932 to 1941, Peter Wien states that "British complaints about a general pro-Nazi stance of the Iraqi press seem quite unjustified," and has concluded that "[a]n analysis of the discourse of the 1930s and early 1940s therefore does not support the 'single-thread narrative' of Iraqi pro-Nazi tendencies. . . . [A] proper term for the references to authoritarian, totalitarian, or fascist principles is 'flirting with fascist imagery.' There was no direct adoption of fascist thought."[9]

A similar narrative is emerging regarding Syria, Lebanon, and Palestine. Recent studies by several authors demonstrate the continuing presence and power of liberal democratic forces both on the political level and within civil society. Support for the French model of parliamentary government and a commitment to a representative constitutional regime have been shown to have persisted in both Lebanon and Syria throughout the interwar years,[10] just as Sami al-Kayyali's journal *al-Hadith* was a vigorous proponent of a liberal democratic orientation.[11] Politically, individual establishment politicians such as Jamil Mardam and ʿAbd al-Rahman Shahbandar in Syria and Emile Eddé in Lebanon continued to articulate a liberal political outlook. The National Bloc, the hegemonic political force in interwar Syria, maintained a pro-democratic position.[12] Arguing from a religious perspective, the Maronite Patriarch Antoine Pierre ʿArida openly criticized Nazism and expressed sympathy for the Jews persecuted by Nazi Germany.[13] Most recently, René Wildangel's detailed examination of the Palestinian press demonstrates widespread anti-fascist sentiment among Palestinians, an attitude that indeed increased once the war was under way and fascist mistreatment of conquered peoples became apparent. Wildangel's study is a corrective to the conventional assumption that the pro-Nazi activities of Amin al-Husayni represented the prevailing Palestinian view of fascism.[14]

Beyond the political establishment, a new variety of left-wing organizations reinforced anti-Fascist democratic principles.[15] The League Against Nazism and Fascism in Syria and Lebanon represented a broad progressive spectrum of intellectuals and political activists, bringing together communists and members of the National Bloc, women's groups and trade unions, Armenians and moderate Arab nationalists. As Götz Nordbruch has demonstrated, the Conference Against Nazism and Fascism, organized by the League in early May 1939, adopted a well-defined anti-Fascist agenda. The conference highlighted the prevailing mood of the French-Syrian and French-Lebanese partnerships, and the position that support for France and its democratic allies continued to be the only viable option for Syrians and Lebanese, and the Arab Middle East in general. With over 200 participants, the conference attracted support from dozens of organizations and several important Syrian and Lebanese politicians and men of letters.[16]

During the conference, a powerful public statement was made by Raʾif Khuri, a major Lebanese intellectual and leading figure in leftist circles. In his address, he expressed a strong anti-Fascist position, declaring:

Our conference shows that we are a people that is confident in democracy and its strength. We believe in a cooperation with democracies and democrats. Our people knows that neutrality is a joke in a struggle between fascism and democracy, for fascism will not let them stay neutral. They are aware that it is impossible to gain fascism's friendship by staying aside, for fascism is no friend of small and weak peoples. Finally, our people are confident that the noble and beautiful face of democracy that is shining on us through the flame of the great French Revolution will not be defaced by false democrats, neither here nor there. Our slogan is: We are part of the democratic front![17]

Götz Nordbruch emphasizes that for Khuri, neither Italian Fascism nor German Nazism was an option for the Arab world.[18] The anti-Fascist stand of the secretary general of the Communist Party, Khalid Bakdash, was another noteworthy example. Already in the late 1930s, Bakdash declared that "if Fascism will be victorious, we will be deprived of everything, even the air of our country."[19] Thus our work on Egypt does not stand alone, but joins a body of new scholarly literature that presents a more complex, historically grounded, and less politicized picture of the Arab world in the 1930s and 1940s.

This new body of scholarship should also serve as a contribution to discussions regarding the global influence of European fascism as well as to the contemporary debate concerning the presumed authoritarian inclinations imbedded in Arab and Muslim culture. Histories of fascism frequently present an incomplete and misleading picture of the general impact of fascism, and of Nazi Germany in particular, on the Arab world. Privileging and highlighting the organizational and ideological pro-Fascist and pro-Nazi tendencies manifested by particular youth movements and specific intellectuals, generalizations about the Middle East in histories of European fascism tend to ignore or marginalize antifascist currents and voices. The few pages devoted to the Middle East in Stanley Payne's authoritative *A History of Fascism, 1914–1945*, represent this perspective. In Payne's view, in the Middle East "the radical Arab nationalist groups of the 1930s and after were at least as much influenced by European fascism as movements in any other part of the world."[20] Payne goes on to list various examples of fascist outreach and influence in the region: Italian and German diplomatic contacts and propaganda efforts, translations of *Mein Kampf* into Arabic, visits of Arab political figures to

Nazi Germany, "the violently anti-Jewish" Amin al-Husayni's collusion with the Germans, and most prominently, the emergence of a number of youth movements influenced by fascist organizational principles and ideology (although he does conclude that "none of these were developed fascist movements, and none reproduced the full characteristics of European fascism").[21] With specific reference to Egypt, Payne's view is that "there was much pro-German sentiment in Egypt."[22]

With the exception of this last generalization, all of the foregoing have some validity. Yet these slices of historical reality amount to considerably less than half the loaf. Contemporary British assessments prior to World War II concluded that Axis propaganda efforts in Egypt (and other parts of the Arab Middle East) were largely ineffective. Arab visits to Fascist Italy or Nazi Germany, such as those of Ahmad Husayn in 1934 or Mustafa al-Nahhas in 1936, did not always result in a positive impression of fascism and its leaders. As Payne correctly notes, Arab youth organizations of the 1930s, while influenced by aspects of fascism, did not develop into full-fledged fascist movements. Most importantly, the vigorous antifascist public discourse of the later 1930s, in which most participants rejected both fascist ideology and practice, is totally ignored. As we have shown, the generalization that "there was much pro-German sentiment in Egypt" is an incorrect characterization of Egyptian public discourse in the later 1930s, when the bulk of public opinion turned against fascist totalitarianism, racism, and imperialism.

The new scholarship on fascism's ambiguous impact on Arab thought and behavior may also have a contribution to make to the contemporary debate (more political and journalistic than academic) over presumed Arab and Muslim "Islamo-Fascism." The conclusions of several adjacent but eventually intersecting Western historiographies—the "crisis of orientation"/"failure of the liberal experiment" school discussed in our Introduction; the old narrative emphasizing Arab sympathy for the Axis powers; histories of European fascism that draw on the latter in reaching their generalizations—have also percolated into the large body of current political and policy-oriented writing discussing Arabs, Muslims, and the West. They have combined to produce the frequently voiced opinion that Muslims and in particular Arab Muslims are inclined to a complex of ideological predispositions resembling those of historic fascism: authoritarianism, extreme ethnocentrism, and anti-Semitism.

The tragedy of 9/11 gave renewed impetus to this viewpoint. A large number of scholarly as well as nonscholarly works have invested great effort in finding similarities and links between past and present radical Islamism and historical fascism. A case in point is Matthias Küntzel's *Jihad and Jew-Hatred: Islamism, Nazism and the Roots of 9/11* (German version 2002, English translation, 2007), a work that has enjoyed a warm welcome in the media.[23] One of Küntzel's major arguments is that the origins of radical jihadist Islam, expounded in embryo in the 1950s and 1960s by Sayyid Qutb and culminating in today's Usama bin Laden and al-Qaʻida, can be traced to the ideology and activities of the Egyptian Muslim Brothers in the 1930s and 1940s. As the author summarized his work's central point, "[m]y book demonstrates that al-Qaʻida and the other Islamist groups are guided by an antisemitic ideology that was transferred to the Islamic world in the Nazi period."[24] The book's lengthy first chapter is devoted to developing the thesis that "the Muslim Brothers were inspired not by the Nasserism of the 1960s, but by the European fascism of the 1930s."[25] Relying heavily on secondary sources, particularly on Abd al-Fattah Muhammad El-Awaisi's detailed study on *The Muslim Brothers and the Palestine Question, 1928–1947*, Küntzel's analysis emphasizes the centrality of the concept of jihad in the ideology of the Muslim Brothers, its pro-Palestinian and anti-Zionist activism of the later 1930s, its prewar links with the Mufti al-Hajj Amin al-Husayni of Palestine as well as the Mufti's intensive wartime collaboration with the Nazis, and the movement's physical involvement in the Palestine conflict after World War II.[26] In Küntzel's view, it was not the escalating anticolonial struggle against the British Mandate and Zionism of the late 1930s, together with the consequent growing Arab sympathy for the Palestinian national struggle and the identification with its national goals and naturally also with Amin al-Husayni, president of the Palestinian Higher Committee, that explained the anti-Zionist and sometimes anti-Jewish positions adopted by the Muslim Brothers during the 1930s and 1940s (the causal factor usually emphasized in both older and newer research on the early history of the movement); rather, it was Nazi-inspired anti-Semitism which was appropriated from Nazi Germany.[27]

In our view, this claim of the central importance of Nazi racism and anti-Semitism on the pre–World War II ideas and activities of the Muslim Brothers is mistaken. Küntzel's analysis suffers from several flaws. It relies heavily on guilt by association, using al-Hajj Amin al-Husayni's well-documented links with the Nazis as a blanket indictment of the Muslim Brothers because they were in contact with the Mufti in the later 1930s and supported his being given refuge in Egypt after the war.[28] Küntzel emphasizes what he describes as "the alliance between al-Banna and el-Husseini," an alliance which "had disastrous consequences for both the Jews and the Arabs of Palestine."[29] In his narrative, the Mufti is the embodiment of the general Arab "sympathy" and "enthusiasm" toward German National Socialism.[30]

The fact that Amin al-Husayni collaborated with the Nazi regime during World War II is irrelevant for understanding the Muslim Brothers' ideological position regarding Nazism and anti-Semitism. Any effort to show a similarity between Nazi racism and the ideas expressed by the Muslim Brothers must be rooted in the texts produced by the movement's spokesmen. This is not done in *Jihad and Jew-Hatred*. The book fails to take account of Muslim Brothers texts of the 1930s that speak directly and critically to the issue of contemporary Fascism and Nazism, such as Hasan al-Banna's explicit rejection of what he termed the "nationalism of aggression," meaning "racial self-aggrandizement to a degree which leads to the disparagement of other races, aggression against them, and their victimization for the sake of the nation's glory and its continued existence, as preached for example by Germany and Italy," in his treatise *Daʿwatuna* ["Our Mission"] of 1937.[31] This oversight is reflective of a general failure to identify or cite ideological similarities between Nazi racism and the ideas being articulated by the Muslim Brothers. Indeed, at one point the work acknowledges the absence of ideological influence between Nazism and the Muslim Brothers: contradicting its earlier assertion that the alleged "transfer" of Nazi racism to the Arab and Muslim world occurred through the agency of the Muslim Brothers in the 1930s and 1940s, it states that "it would be wrong to characterize the Muslim Brothers as ardent followers of the Nazis. The Brotherhood rejected the Nazis' race policies and German supremacist nationalism, since both were at odds with their concept of the *umma* as the universal Islamic brotherhood. Moreover, al-Banna was far too religious a man to accept a non-Muslim leader such as Hitler as his model."[32]

Most important, *Jihad and Jew-Hatred* makes no mention of the considerable antipathy to Nazi racism and the sympathy with Jewish suffering expressed in the Arab world in the era of Nazism. As we attempted to show in our study, and as is being increasingly demonstrated by the new narrative concerning the relationship of the Arab world to historical fascism, the effort to trace the later Islamicist radicalism of Sayyid Qutb and Usama bin Laden to a purported origin in the Arab world of the 1930s and 1940s is unjustified. Perhaps there are valid reasons for characterizing certain aspects of the militant Islamism that developed in the second half of the twentieth century and is unfolding with such violent results early in the twenty-first as a type of "fascism." An answer to this question is beyond the scope of this work.[33] However, the effort to locate origins of 9/11 in the early ideology and activities of the Muslim Brothers is mistaken. Only the most peripheral connection exists between the Muslim Brothers' critique and campaign directed against the British Mandate and Zionism in Palestine in the later 1930s and the ideological and practical "redemptive anti-Semitism" of Nazi Germany, to use the characterization of Saul Friedländer.[34] The attempt to appropriate the Islamic *salafi* ideology and activism that developed in the first half of the twentieth century to contemporary militant Islamism is an anachronistic search for false roots. The advocates of this ahistorical approach seem to have forgotten Marc Bloch's warning that "history oriented towards origins was put to the service of value judgments. . . . [I]n many cases the demon of origins has been, perhaps, only the incarnation of that other satanic enemy of true history: the mania for making judgments."[35]

To sum up, the new body of historical research of which our study is a part raises serious questions about an origin-searching approach. Drawing conclusions about the contemporary world from past patterns is always problematic; both circumstances and men, thoughts and actions, change, sometimes dramatically. The new and more extensive research into the inner history of the Arab world in the era of fascism (the 1930s and 1940s) indicates that educated Arabs were familiar with but by and large rejected the fundamental ideological components and practices of Fascism and Nazism. As we have shown, totalitarianism was viewed as a threat to the pluralist political culture and the civil society that had begun to flourish in the more advanced countries of the Arab world; under the impact of the conflict in Palestine, Nazi racism and anti-Semitism were endorsed by a minority of voices but denounced by the majority both in philosophical terms and because of their inclusion of Arabs in the despised Semitic category; and Fascist and Nazi expansionism were overwhelmingly seen as a new and more pernicious form of imperialism. Rather than arousing latent authoritarian and racist impulses imbedded in the Egyptian character, culture, or history, the encounter with historic fascism produced a reaction against what fascism meant for the present and future.

Reference Matter

Notes

Introduction

1. For this interpretation, see Nadav Safran, *Egypt in Search of Political Community* (Cambridge, MA, 1961), 187–193; P. J. Vatikiotis, *The Modern History of Egypt* (New York, 1969), 315–324; Afaf Lutfi al-Sayyid-Marsot, *Egypt's Liberal Experiment, 1922–1936* (Berkeley, CA, 1977), 227–231.

2. This interpretation of Egyptian history is part of a broader narrative concerning the history of the modern Arab world. The dominant historical interpretation of the political history of the Arab countries of the Fertile Crescent similarly emphasizes the popularity and spread of pro-fascist trends in the 1930s, giving prominence to the thought and activities of individuals and forces in Iraq, Syria, Lebanon, and Palestine who were attracted to fascist principles and practices and some of whom engaged in practical collaboration with the fascist powers during the war. We discuss this broader historiography in our Conclusion.

3. British speculation about pro-Axis inclinations in political and Palace circles prior to World War II is discussed in Chapter 1.

4. E.g., The Nation Associates, *The Record of Collaboration of King Farouk of Egypt with the Nazis and Their Ally, the Mufti* (New York, 1948), which published a selection of captured German documents from 1941–43 in an effort to prove "Farouk's alliance with the Nazi High Command" (p. 1). For a similar indictment of Egyptian wartime activities, see American Christian Palestine Committee, *The Arab War Effort: A Documented Account* (New York, [1946?]).

5. George Kirk, *Survey of International Affairs, 1939–1946*, vol. 2, *The Middle East in the War* (London, 1952), 31–41, 193–228, 255–272.

6. For the most important statements of the self-narrative as expounded in the 1950s, see Jamal 'Abd al-Nasir, *Falsafat al-Thawra* (Cairo, 1954), translated as Gamal Abdel Nasser, *The Philosophy of the Revolution* (Buffalo, 1959); Anwar al-Sadat, *Qissat al-Thawra Kamilatan* (Cairo, 1956); and al-Sadat, *Asrar al-Thawra al-Misriyya* (Cairo, 1957),

partially translated as Anwar El Sadat, *Revolt on the Nile* (New York, 1957). Other early statements of the self-narrative include ʿAbd al-Latif al-Baghdadi, "Ma Qabla al-Dubbat al-Ahrar," in *Hadhihi al-Thawra* (Cairo, 1953), 188–189; and the symposium on "Lau Kana Hitlar Hayyan Madha Turidu ʿan Taqulu Lahu?" *MSR*, Sept. 18, 1953, 10, 32–33. A later and somewhat different account of the genesis of the Revolution can be found in Anwar el-Sadat, *In Search of Identity: An Autobiography* (New York, 1977).

7. See John W. Eppler, *Rommel Ruft Kairo: Aus dem Tagebuch eines Spions* (Gutersloh, 1959); Hans von Steffens, *Salaam: Geheimcommando zum Nil, 1942* (Neckargemund, 1960); Alfred William Sansom, *I Spied Spies* (London, 1965). For more recent Egyptian accounts of wartime collaboration, see Wajih ʿAtiq, *al-Malik Faruq wa Almaniya al-Naziyya: Khams Sanawat min al-ʿAlaqat al-Sirriyya* (Cairo, 1992); and ʿAtiq, *al-Jaysh al-Misri wa al-Alman fi Athnaʾ al-Harb al-ʿAlamiyya al-Thaniyya* (Cairo, 1993).

8. For example, see Jean and Simonne Lacouture, *Egypt in Transition* (1956; repr., New York, 1958), 125–136; Georges Vaucher, *Gamal Abdel Nasser et son Equipe* (Paris, 1959), 1:116–138; Robert St. John, *The Boss: The Story of Gamal Abdel Nasser* (New York, 1960), 35–57; Wilton Wynn, *Nasser of Egypt: The Search for Dignity* (Cambridge, MA, 1960), 32–33; Keith Wheelock, *Nasser's New Egypt* (New York, 1960), 4–6; Peter Mansfield, *Nasser's Egypt* (Baltimore, 1965), 36–38; Eliezer Beʾeri, *Army Officers in Arab Politics and Society* (Tel Aviv, 1966 [Hebrew]; Eng. trans., New York, 1970), 41–49.

9. Heinz Tillmann, *Deutschlands Araberpolitik im Zweiten Weltkrieg* (Berlin, 1965); Lukasz Hirszowicz, *The Third Reich and the Arab East* (London, 1966), 152, 232–243; Bernd Philipp Schröder, *Deutschland und der Mittlere Osten im Zweiten Weltkrieg* (Göttingen, 1975), 59–62, 181–183, 190–198, 239–240.

10. For incorporation of the narrative of Egyptian-Axis collusion into prominent biographies of Nasser written after his death, see Anthony Nutting, *Nasser* (New York, 1972), 19–21; Robert Stephens, *Nasser: A Political Biography* (New York, 1972), 49–62; Jean Lacouture, *Nasser: A Biography* (New York, 1973), 46–50.

11. Nadav Safran, *Egypt in Search of Political Community* (Cambridge, MA, 1961).

12. "Progressive phase," "crisis of orientation," and "reactionary phase" are the titles of chapters 10, 11, and 13 of *Egypt in Search of Political Community*. The section in which the three chapters appear is entitled "The Progress and Decline of Liberal Nationalism."

13. Ibid., 192.

14. See Charles D. Smith, "The 'Crisis of Orientation': The Shift of Egyptian Intellectuals to Islamic Subjects in the 1930s," *International Journal of Middle East Studies*, 4 (1973), 382–410; Smith, *Islam and the Search for Social Order in Modern Egypt: A Biography of Muhammad Husayn Haykal* (Albany, NY, 1983).

15. Vatikiotis, *Modern History of Egypt*, 292–342. For a subsequent elaboration, see his *Nasser and His Generation* (New York, 1978), 26–35, 50–53. Later editions of *The Modern History of Egypt* published in the 1970s, 1980s, and 1990s retained the interpretation unchanged.

16. Ibid., 315.

17. al-Sayyid-Marsot, *Egypt's Liberal Experiment*, 229. See also ʿAbd al-ʿAzim Muhammad Ramadan, *Tatawwur al-Haraka al-Wataniyya Fi Misr, 1937–1948* (Cairo, 1972),

1:5–14. For a recent restatement of "the failure of the liberal experiment" in interwar Egypt and of the view that "the movement of Islamic revivalism as a whole signaled a rejection of Western constitutionalism on cultural grounds" in a study that otherwise demonstrates more profound contradictions within interwar Egyptian liberalism, see Abdeslam M. Maghraoui, *Liberalism Without Democracy: Nationhood and Citizenship in Egypt, 1922–1936* (Durham, NC, 2006), 52, 132.

18. For relevant material from earlier English-language studies, see Richard Mitchell, *The Society of the Muslim Brothers* (London, 1969), 218–220, 260–263; James Jankowski, *Egypt's Young Rebels: "Young Egypt," 1933–1952* (Stanford, 1975), 60–64.

19. On Young Egypt's attitude toward fascism in the 1930s, see Jankowski, *Egypt's Young Rebels,* 14–18, 58–60; Vatikiotis, *Nasser and His Generation,* 50–54, 78–80. On militarism in the Muslim Brothers, see Mitchell, *Muslim Brothers,* 30–32; Brynjar Lia, *The Society of the Muslim Brothers in Egypt: The Rise of an Islamic Mass Movement, 1928–1942* (Reading, UK, 1998), 166–181; Abd Al-Fattah Muhammad El-Awaisi, *The Muslim Brothers and the Palestine Question, 1928–1947* (London, 1998), 105–131.

20. "Fundamental reforms" is Jacques Berque's term; see his *Egypt: Imperialism and Revolution* (London, 1972), 561–564.

21. Safran, *Egypt in Search of Political Community,* 210. For a similar evaluation, see Vatikiotis, *Modern History of Egypt,* 323–324.

22. For an earlier statement of this position, see Israel Gershoni, "Egyptian Liberalism in an Age of 'Crisis of Orientation': *al-Risala's* Reaction to Fascism and Nazism, 1933–1939," *International Journal of Middle East Studies,* 31 (1999), 551–576.

23. For earlier but less comprehensive studies of the discourse that largely concur with our assessment, see Ami Ayalon, "Egyptian Intellectuals versus Fascism and Nazism in the 1930s," in *The Great Powers in the Middle East, 1919–1939,* ed. Uriel Dann, 391–404 (New York, 1988); Haggai Erlich, "Periphery and Youth: Fascist Italy and the Middle East," in *Fascism Outside Europe,* ed. Stein Ugelvik Larsen, 393–423 (New York, 2001).

Chapter 1

1. Manuela A. Williams, *Mussolini's Propaganda Abroad: Subversion in the Mediterranean and the Middle East, 1935–1940* (London, 2006), 35. See also Claudio G. Segrè, "Liberal and Fascist Italy in the Middle East, 1919–1939: The Elusive White Stallion," in Dann, *The Great Powers in the Middle East,* 199–212, esp. 204–205.

2. Williams, *Mussolini's Propaganda,* 52–53; Erlich, "Periphery and Youth," 402; Callum A. MacDonald, "Radio Bari: Italian Wireless Propaganda in the Middle East and British Countermeasures," *Middle Eastern Studies,* 13 (1977), 195–207.

3. Williams, *Mussolini's Propaganda,* 66, 109–113.

4. Ibid., 131–134. On Ugo Dadone, see the "Egyptian Personalities Report" (1938); repr. in *British Documents on Foreign Affairs: Reports and Papers from the Foreign Office Confidential Print* [henceforth *BDFA*], general ed. Kenneth Bourne, D. Cameron Watt, and Michael Partridge, Part II, Series G, *Africa, 1914–1939: Egypt and the Sudan,* ed. Peter Woodward (Lanham, MD, 1994–1995), 19:202.

5. Undated memorandum on the Egyptian press, *BDFA,* 17:271–274.

6. Kelly to Hoare, Sept. 12, 1935, *BDFA*, 17:11; see also Kelly to Hoare, Sept. 2, 1935, *BDFA*, 17:73–74.

7. Note on the student movement in Egypt, Jan. 23, 1936, *BDFA*, 17:245–252.

8. Undated memorandum on the Egyptian press, *BDFA*, 17:271–274.

9. Kelly to Hoare, Aug. 12, 1935, *BDFA*, 17:71–73.

10. Lampson to Eden, May 21, 1936, *BDFA*, 17:295–297.

11. Memorandum on the Egyptian press, June 2 to July 2, 1937, *BDFA*, 18:365; Memorandum on the Egyptian press, Aug. 3 to Sept. 1, 1937, *BDFA*, 18:370.

12. Memorandum on the Egyptian press, Mar. 27 to Apr. 10, 1937, Great Britain, Public Record Office, Foreign Office [henceforth FO], 371:20903, J 1978:148:16.

13. Memorandum on the Egyptian press, Oct. 5 to Nov. 2, 1937, *BDFA*, 18:380.

14. Memorandum on the Egyptian press, Sept. 2 to Oct. 1, 1937, *BDFA*, 18:376. The content of Egyptian caricatures is discussed in Chapter 3.

15. See Williams, *Mussolini's Propaganda*, 53, 87–88.

16. Lampson to Halifax, Jan. 16, 1939, *BDFA*, 20:111–117.

17. According to a May 1939 interview of Lampson with the university's rector, *BDFA*, 20:125–127.

18. For instance, see Memorandum on the Egyptian Press, Oct. 7 to Dec. 7, 1938, *BDFA*, 19:364–367; Memorandum on the Egyptian press, Feb. 2 to May 2, 1939, FO 371:23364, file J 1973:774:16.

19. Williams, *Mussolini's Propaganda*, 185; Segré, "Liberal and Fascist Italy in the Middle East," 208.

20. "Notes on a Visit to Upper Egypt," Mar. 3–8, 1939, *BDFA*, 20:121–122.

21. "Notes on a Visit to Delta," May 3–5, 1939, *BDFA*, 20:127–129.

22. Williams, *Mussolini's Propaganda*, 185.

23. Nir Arielli, "Fascist Italy in the Middle East, 1935–1940," PhD. diss., University of Leeds, 2008, 294–297.

24. The Earl of Perth to Viscount Halifax, Mar. 31, 1938, *BDFA*, 19:224–225.

25. Stefan Wild, "National Socialism in the Arab Near East Between 1933 and 1939," *Die Welt des Islams*, 25 (1985), 126–173, esp. 147–152.

26. Ibid., 153–170.

27. Ahmad Mahmud al-Sadati, *Adulf Hitlar, Za'im al-Ishtirakiyya al-Wataniyya ma'a Bayan al-Mas'ala al-Yahudiyya* (Cairo, 1934), intro., 39–41, 48–52, 63–71, 77–111, 118–155, 161–166.

28. German Foreign Ministry, letter from Sadati to Goebbels, Aug. 2, 1934 (copy); U.S. National Archives, Microfilm Series T-120 (Deutsches Auswärtiges Amt), roll 4873, frames L310771–310774.

29. Discussed in Wild, "National Socialism in the Arab Near East," 156–157; Israel Gershoni, *Light in the Shade: Egypt and Fascism, 1922–1937* (Tel Aviv, 1999), 127–129 [in Hebrew]. By his own testimony an employee of the Egyptian National Library (Dar al-Kutub), Sadati was a relative unknown; we have found no other works written by him in the 1930s.

30. See Wild, "National Socialism in the Arab Near East," 157–162. We have not seen this work.

31. Discussed in Williams, *Mussolini's Propaganda*, 101–105. See also Hirszowicz, *The Third Reich in the Arab East*, 27, 41; Andreas Hillgruber, "The Third Reich and the Near and Middle East, 1933–1939," in Dann, *The Great Powers in the Middle East*, 274–282, esp. 276–279.

32. Memorandum on the Egyptian press, Oct. 7 to Dec. 4, 1937, *BDFA*, 19:364–367.

33. Lampson to Halifax, Jan. 16, 1939, *BDFA*, 20:111–117.

34. Williams, *Mussolini's Propaganda*, 101–102.

35. "Notes on Wilhelm Stellbogen," Oct. 23, 1939, in Great Britain, Public Record Office, War Office 208:502, as cited in Lia, *Society of the Muslim Brothers in Egypt*, 179–180.

36. Memorandum on the Egyptian press, Feb. 2 to May 2, 1939, FO 371:23364, J 1973:774:16.

37. For studies of the movement, see James Jankowski, "The Egyptian Blue Shirts and the Egyptian Wafd, 1935–1938," *Middle Eastern Studies*, 6 (1970), 77–95; Haggai Erlich, *Students and University in Twentieth Century Egyptian Politics* (London, 1989), 123–133.

38. Mustafa al-Nahhas, *Mudhakkirat Mustafa al-Nahhas: Rabʿ Qarn min al-Siyasa fi Misr, 1927–1952*, ed. Ahmad ʿIzz al-Din (Cairo, 2000), 1:177–178; for further details on the trip, see ibid., 190–191; also the enclosure in Kelly to Eden, Oct. 24, 1936, *BDFA*, 17:368; *MQ*, Oct. 7, 1936, 7.

39. See Lampson to Eden, Feb. 16, 1937, *BDFA*, 18:133–137.

40. Lampson to Eden, Mar. 25, 1937, *BDFA*, 18:223–225.

41. Interview with Kelly, May 2, 1938, *BDFA*, 19:137. Nahhas repeated the accusation to Bateman in August 1938: see *BDFA*, 19:285.

42. Nahhas, *Mudhakkirat*, 1:233–234, 237, 252–253, 267.

43. Lampson to Eden, Jan. 1, 1938, *BDFA*, 19:98.

44. Lampson to Halifax, May 6, 1938, *BDFA*, 19:136.

45. Lampson to Halifax, Sept. 27, 1938, *BDFA*, 19:319.

46. Lampson to Halifax, Nov. 7, 1937, *BDFA*, 19:325–329.

47. Lampson to Halifax, Jan. 16, 1939, *BDFA*, 20:111–117.

48. Lampson to Halifax, Feb. 3, 1939, *BDFA*, 20:117–119.

49. Lampson to Halifax, Oct. 2, 1939, *BDFA*, 20:248–249.

50. Lampson to Halifax, Nov. 8, 1939, *BDFA*, 20:253–258.

51. See Lampson to Eden, May 7, 1936, *BDFA*, 17:295–297.

52. "Local Reaction to Italy's Success in Abyssinia," enclosed in Lampson to Eden, May 28, 1936, *BDFA*, 17:300–302.

53. From a December 1937 report on political sentiment in Lower Egypt, *BDFA*, 19:104–105.

54. Memorandum on the Egyptian press, Mar. 11 to Apr. 15, 1938, *BDFA*, 19:237.

55. Bateman to Halifax, Sept. 25, 1938, *BDFA*, 19:318.

56. Memorandum on the Egyptian press, Oct. 7 to Dec. 4, 1938, *BDFA*, 19:364–367.

57. Lampson to Halifax, Dec. 6, 1938, *BDFA*, 19:344–346.

58. Lampson to Halifax, May 12, 1939, *BDFA*, 20:129–133.

59. Memorandum on the Egyptian press, Feb. 2 to May 2, 1939, FO 371:23364, J 1973:774:16.

60. Lampson to Halifax, July 13, 1939, *BDFA*, 20:150–154.

61. Lampson to Halifax, Sept. 29, 1938, *BDFA*, 19:319–320.

62. Lampson to Halifax, Nov. 7, 1938, *BDFA*, 19:325–329.

63. Memorandum on the Egyptian press, Sept. 1 to Oct. 7, 1938, *BDFA*, 19:360–364.

64. Lampson to Halifax, Dec. 13, 1938, *BDFA*, 19:334–335.

65. Lampson to Halifax, Dec. 22, 1938, *BDFA*, 20:106–108; memorandum on the Egyptian press, Dec. 6, 1938 to Feb. 1, 1939, FO 371:23364, J 774:16.

66. Lampson to Halifax, Dec. 22, 1938, *BDFA*, 20:106–108.

67. Lampson to Halifax, Jan. 16, 1939, *BDFA*, 20:111–117.

68. Ibid.

69. Ibid.

70. Lampson to Halifax, May 12, 1939, *BDFA*, 20:129–133. This remained the Wafdist position through the early years of the war.

71. Lampson to Halifax, Jan. 16, 1939, *BDFA*, 20:111–117.

72. Galeazzo Ciano, *Diary, 1937–1943* (New York, 2002), 193. In May 1940, on the eve of Italy's entry into the war, the Egyptian minister in Rome similarly discussed the possibility of a declaration of Egyptian neutrality with Ciano; ibid., 357.

73. Lampson to Halifax, July 13, 1939; *BDFA*, 20:150–154.

74. For British requests for, and Egyptian evasion of, a declaration of war in September 1939, see Lampson to Halifax, Sept. 4, 1939, *BDFA*, 20:240; Lampson to Halifax, Sept. 7, 1939, *BDFA*, 20:245; Halifax to Lampson, Sept. 8, 1939, *BDFA*, 20:246.

75. Lampson to Halifax, Nov. 8, 1939, *BDFA*, 20:253–258.

76. Ibid.

77. For Lampson's evaluations concerning Egypt's satisfactory fulfillment of specific obligations in the early months of the war, see Lampson to Halifax, Oct. 2, 1939, *BDFA*, 20:248–249; Lampson to Halifax, Nov. 8, 1939, *BDFA*, 20:253–258.

78. Lampson to Eden, May 8, 1936, *BDFA*, 17:284–285; see also Nahhas, *Mudhakkirat*, 1:170, 180.

79. Lampson to Eden, May 16, 1936, *BDFA*, 17:281; Nahhas, *Mudhakkirat*, 1:170; see also 'Abd al-Rahman al-Rafi'i, *Fi A'qab al-Thawra al-Misriyya* (Cairo, 1947–1951), 3:15; Ramadan, *Tatawwur*, 1:57–61, 130–133; Ramadan, *al-Sira' bayna al-Wafd wa al-'Arsh, 1936–1939* (Cairo, 1979), 23–25.

80. For the results, see Lampson to Eden, May 20, 1936, *BDFA*, 17:288; Lampson to Eden, Feb. 16, 1937, *BDFA*, 18:133–137; Ramadan, *Tatawwur*, 1:123–129.

81. Lampson to Eden, Feb. 16, 1937, *BDFA*, 18:133–137.

82. Descriptions in Kelly to Eden, Aug. 12, 1937, *BDFA*, 18:309–311; Nahhas, *Mudhakkirat*, 1:207–208; Rafi'i, *Fi A'qab*, 3:40–43.

83. See Nahhas, *Mudhakkirat*, 1:201–202; Ramadan, *Tatawwur*, 1:61–65; Ramadan, *al-Sira'*, 36–39, 79; Elie Kedourie, "Egypt and the Caliphate, 1915–52," in *The Chatham House Version and Other Middle-Eastern Studies* (London, 1970), 199.

84. Kelly to Eden, Aug. 12 1937, *BDFA*, 18:309–311.

85. For details on the schism, see Nahhas, *Mudhakkirat*, 1:140–153, 158–164, 173–176, 200–210; Muhammad Husayn Haykal, *Mudhakkirat fi al-Siyasa al-Misriyya* (Cairo, 1951, 1953), 2:35–36; Rafiʿi, *Fi Aʿqab*, 3:46–51; Ramadan, *Tatawwur*, 1:73–120; Ramadan, *al-Siraʿ*, 40–48.

86. Kelly to Eden, Oct. 9, 1937, *BDFA*, 18:322–323; see also Rafiʿi, *Fi Aʿqab*, 3:52–53; Haykal, *Mudhakkirat*, 2:51–52.

87. Kelly to Eden, Sept. 16, 1937, *BDFA*, 18:316–317.

88. Kelly to Eden, Oct. 28, 1937, *BDFA*, 18:330.

89. Details in Kelly to Eden, Aug. 7, 1937, *BDFA*, 18:308–309; Lampson to Eden, Dec. 9, 1937, *BDFA*, 18:341–342; Nahhas, *Mudhakkirat*, 1:208–212; Haykal, *Mudhakkirat*, 2:54–55; Ramadan, *Tatawwur*, 1:139–144; Marius Deeb, *Party Politics in Egypt: The Wafd and Its Rivals, 1919–1939* (London, 1979), 336.

90. Nahhas, *Mudhakkirat*, 1:211; Ramadan, *al-Siraʿ*, 91–93.

91. Kelly to Eden, Sept. 2, 1937, *BDFA*, 18:311–313.

92. Ramadan *Tatawwur*, 1:135–136.

93. See the memoranda on the Egyptian press contained in *BDFA*, 18:371, 373, 375, 386; also Rafiʿi, *Fi Aʿqab*, 3:53–54; Haykal, *Mudhakkirat*, 2:37–39, 49–50; Ramadan, *Tatawwur*, 1:136–139;Ramadan, *al-Siraʿ*, 52–55, 106–107.

94. Kelly to Eden, Oct. 2, 1937, *BDFA*, 18:320–322; Rafiʾi, *Fi Aʿqab*, 3:54–55.

95. Ramadan, *Tatawwur*, 1:135. Nahhas's diary similarly refers to the conflict between ministry and monarchy as "the war between the Palace and the Wafd"; Nahhas, *Mudhakkirat*, 1:211.

96. Kelly to Eden, Oct. 20, 1937, *BDFA*, 18:320; Kelly to Eden, Oct. 22, 1937, *BDFA*, 18:324–325; see also Ramadan, *Tatawwur*, 1:139–144.

97. Lampson to Eden, Dec. 29, 1937, *BDFA*, 18:354; Lampson to Eden, Dec. 29, 1937, *BDFA*, 18:355; Lampson to Eden, Dec. 31, 1937, *BDFA*, 19:99–104; Ramadan, *Tatawwur*, 1:153–155; Ramadan, *al-Siraʿ*, 146–150.

98. Ramadan, *Tatawwur*, 1:139–144, 148.

99. Kelly to Eden, Oct. 7, 1937, *BDFA*, 18:320–322.

100. Ibid.

101. Lampson to Eden, Nov. 23, 1937, *BDFA*, 18:335.

102. Lampson to Eden, Nov. 2, 1937, *BDFA*, 18:328–329. Nahhas's raising the issue of the king's possible ouster was echoed a day later, in more indirect form, by Foreign Minister Makram ʿUbayd; see Ramadan, *al-Siraʿ*, 61–63.

103. Text in Haykal, *Mudhakkirat*, 2:58; Lampson to Eden, Dec. 30, 1937, *BDFA*, 18:355.

104. Ramadan, *al-Siraʿ*, 141.

105. For accounts of election manipulation, see *BDFA*, 19:122, 125, 127–128; Haykal, *Mudhakkirat*, 2:70–84; Nahhas, *Mudhakkirat*, 1:224–228; Deeb, *Party Politics in Egypt*, 337–338.

106. See Haykal, *Mudhakkirat*, 2:86–89; Ramadan, *Tatawwur*, 1:217–219, 251–253; Ramadan, *al-Siraʿ*, 198–201; Berque, *Egypt*, 561–563; Deeb, *Party Politics in Egypt*, 338–341.

107. Lampson to Halifax, May 6, 1938, *BDFA*, 19:134–136.

108. Haykal, *Mudhakkirat*, 2:155; Ramadan, *Tatawwur*, 1:252.

109. See Lampson to Halifax, May 6, 1938, *BDFA*, 19:134–135; Bateman to Halifax, Aug. 30, 1938, *BDFA*, 19:310–313.

110. On the decay of Muhammad Mahmud's ministries, see Haykal, *Mudhakkirat*, 2:160–162.

111. Ramadan, *al-Sira*, 194–197; Charles Tripp, "Ali Mahir and the Politics of the Egyptian Army, 1936–1942," in *Contemporary Egypt: Through Egyptian Eyes. Essays in Honour of P. J. Vatikiotis*, ed. Charles Tripp (London, 1993), 50–53.

112. According to his testimony in a 1969 interview with Ramadan; Ramadan, *Tatawwur*, 1: 221.

113. Ibid., 221–224.

114. See his conversation with Muhammad Husayn Haykal in Haykal, *Mudhakkirat*, 2:156–157; quoted in Kedourie, "Caliphate," 205.

115. The terms are those of the journalist Fikri Abaza, writing in 1939; see Ramadan, *al-Sira*, 210–211.

116. See Haykal, *Mudhakkirat*, 2:87–91; Ramadan, *Tatawwur*, 1: 224–227; Ramadan, *al-Sira*, 211–213.

117. Bateman to Halifax, Aug. 30, 1938, *BDFA*, 19:310–313.

118. Lampson to Halifax, Nov. 7, 1938, *BDFA*, 19:325–329.

119. "Notes on a Visit to Upper Egypt," Mar. 3–8, 1939, *BDFA*, 20:121–122.

120. "Notes on a Visit to Delta," May 3–5, 1939, *BDFA*, 20:127–129.

121. From a December 1937 report on political opinion in Lower Egypt, *BDFA*, 19:104–105.

122. See Bateman to Halifax, Aug. 30, 1938, *BDFA*, 19:310–313.

123. Lampson to Halifax, Nov. 7, 1938, *BDFA*, 19:325–329.

124. Lampson to Halifax, Jan. 16, 1939, *BDFA*, 20:111–117.

125. Lampson to Halifax, May 12, 1939, *BDFA*, 20:129–133.

126. Heathcote-Smith to Lampson, Feb. 14, 1938, *BDFA*, 9:115–117.

127. Lampson to Halifax, July 13, 1938, *BDFA*, 19:272.

128. Memorandum on the Egyptian press, June 28 to July 27, 1938, *BDFA*, 19:350–353.

129. Memorandum on the Egyptian press, July 28 to Aug. 31, 1938, *BDFA*, 19: 353–359.

130. Lampson to Halifax, May 6, 1938, *BDFA*, 19:134–136; reiterated in Lampson to Halifax, Nov. 7, 1938, *BDFA*, 19:325–329.

131. For details, see James Jankowski, "Egyptian Regional Policy in the Wake of the Anglo-Egyptian Treaty of Alliance of 1936: Arab Alliance or Islamic Caliphate?" in *Britain and the Middle East in the 1930s: Security Problems, 1935–39*, ed. Michael J. Cohen and Martin Kolinsky (London, 1992), 89–90.

132. Ibid., 90; Kedourie, "Caliphate," 201–204.

133. Lampson to Eden, Feb. 17, 1938, FO 371:21838, E 1114:1034:16.

134. Memorandum on the Egyptian press, Jan. 6 to Feb. 14, 1938, *BDFA*, 19:229–232; Ramadan, *al-Sira*, 196.

135. Lampson to Eden, Feb. 17, 1938, FO 371:21945, J 893:6:16; see also Kedourie, "Caliphate," 201–202.

136. *JMF*, June 6, 1938, 9; ibid., Jan. 25, 1939, 3; see also Ramadan, *al-Sira'*, 196–197.

137. *BL*, Oct. 8, 1938, 9–10; *Khutub Haflat al-Iftitah al-Kubra li al-Mu'tamar al-Barlamani al-'Alami li al-Bilad al-'Arabiyya wa al-Islamiyya li al-Difa' 'an Filastin wa Qararat al-Mu'tamar wa A'da' al-Wufud* (Cairo, 1938). See also Kedourie, "Caliphate," 204.

138. *BL*, Oct. 16, 1938, 8.

139. Lampson to Halifax, Jan. 25, 1939, FO 371:23304, J 358:1:16.

140. Ibid.

141. *AH*, Feb. 9, 1939, 9; see also Kedourie, "Caliphate," 204–205.

142. According to Bindari's later testimony; see Ramadan, *al-Sira'*, 261.

143. Quoted in Ramadan, *Tatawwur*, 1: 254; see also Haykal, *Mudhakkirat*, 2:157.

144. Ramadan, *Tatawwur*, 1:254–257.

145. Lampson to Halifax, Apr. 4, 1939; *BDFA*, 20:124–125. Bindari himself assured Muhammad Husayn Haykal that he had not attempted to undermine Mahir's position with the king during the latter's absence in London; Haykal, *Mudhakkirat*, 2:157.

146. Lampson to Halifax, May 12, 1939, *BDFA*, 20:129–133; Haykal, *Mudhakkirat*, 2:157–159; Ramadan, *Tatawwur*, 1:262–265.

147. For an example, see n. 157.

148. Lampson to Halifax, May 12, 1939, *BDFA*, 20:129–133.

149. Memorandum on the Egyptian Press, Jan. 6 to Feb. 14, 1938, FO 371:22000, J 748:264:16.

150. See Lampson to Halifax, July 4, 1938, FO 371:22004, J 2691:2014:16; Lampson to Halifax, July 9, 1938, FO 371:22004, J 2792:2014:16.

151. *BL*, Oct. 16, 1938, 8; *al-Dustur*, Jan. 26, 1938, 1.

152. Lampson to Halifax, Feb. 6, 1939, *BDFA*, 20:138.

153. Lampson to Halifax, July 4, 1938, FO 371:22004, J 2691:2014:16.

154. Lampson to Eden, Feb. 17, 1938, FO 371:21838, E 1114:1034:16.

155. Interview with 'Azzam as cited in Ralph Coury, "Who 'Invented' Egyptian Arab Nationalism?" *International Journal of Middle East Studies*, 14 (1982), pt. 1:261.

156. See Lampson to Eden, Feb. 17, 1938, FO 371:21838, E 1114:1034:16; Baggallay to Lampson, Apr. 4, 1938, FO 371:21838, E 1527:1034:16; note by Cavendish-Bentnick, May 9, 1938, FO 371:22004, J 2014:2014:16.

157. Lampson to Halifax, Feb. 3, 1939, FO 371:23361, J 564:364:16.

158. Ibid.

159. Extract from *The Times*, Jan. 25, 1939, as contained in FO 371:23361, J 364: 364:16.

160. Lampson to Halifax, Feb. 3, 1939, FO 371:23361, J 564:364:16.

161. See Lampson to Halifax, Jan. 16, 1939, *BDFA*, 20:111–117; Lampson to Halifax, May 12, 1939, *BDFA*, 20:129–133.

162. Bateman to Halifax, Aug. 25, 1939, *BDFA*, 20:241–245.

163. From the Saʿdist newspaper *al-Dustur*, June 15, 1939, as quoted in Deeb, *Party Politics in Egypt*, 366.

164. Ibid., 342.

165. Lampson to Halifax, Dec. 2, 1939, *BDFA*, 20:293–294.

166. See Berque, *Egypt*, 559–563; Deeb, *Party Politics in Egypt*, 311–344; Ramadan, *Tatawwur*, 1:216–267;Ramadan, *al-Siraʿ*, 153–300.

167. Especially in Ramadan, *Tatawwur*, 1:227, and Ramadan, *al-Siraʿ*, 214.

168. In his 1969 interview with ʿAbd al-ʿAzim Muhammad Ramadan; Ramadan, *Tatawwur*, 1:241.

Part II Prologue

1. Jürgen Habermas, *The Structural Transformation of the Public Sphere: An Inquiry into a Category of Bourgeois Society*, trans. Thomas Burger (1962; repr., Cambridge, MA, 1989), 27.

2. Ibid., 5–56.

3. Ibid., 4, more broadly, 141–235.

4. Ibid., 159–180.

5. See in particular *Habermas and the Public Sphere*, ed. Craig Calhoun (Cambridge, MA, 1992), and the essays contained therein. For a discussion of the concept within Habermas's general philosophy, see Robert C. Holub, *Jürgen Habermas: Critic in the Public Sphere* (London, 1991); and Andrew Edgar, *The Philosophy of Habermas* (Montreal, 2005). The following have also informed our approach to the subject: Keith Michael Baker, "Politics and Public Opinion under the Old Regime: Some Reflections," in *Press and Politics in Pre-Revolutionary France*, ed. Jack R. Censer and Jeremy D. Popkin, 204–246 (Berkeley, CA, 1987); Margaret R. Somers, "What's Political or Cultural about Political Culture and the Public Sphere? Toward an Historical Sociology of Concept Formation," *Sociological Theory*, 13, no. 2 (July 1995), 113–144; Brian Cowan, "Mr. Spectator and the Coffeehouse Public Sphere," *Eighteenth Century Studies*, 37, no. 3 (Spring 2004), 345–366; Michael McKeon, "Parsing Habermas's 'Bourgeois Public Sphere,'" *Criticism*, 46, no. 2 (Spring 2004), 273–277; David Norbrook, "Women, the Republic of Letters, and the Public Sphere in the Mid-Seventeenth Century," *Criticism*, 46, no. 2 (Spring 2004), 223–240; Kevin Pask, "The Bourgeois Public Sphere and the Concept of Literature," *Criticism*, 46, no. 2 (Spring 2004), 241–256; Alan G. Gross, "Habermas, Systematically Distorted Communication, and the Public Sphere," *Rhetoric Society Quarterly*, 36, no. 3 (Summer 2006), 309–330.

6. Nancy Fraser, "Rethinking the Public Sphere: A Contribution to the Critique of Actually Existing Democracy," in Calhoun, *Habermas and the Public Sphere*, 110–111.

7. For attempts to use the public sphere as a conceptual framework for the study of Middle Eastern and Islamic societies, see Miriam Hoexter, Shmuel N. Eisenstadt, and Nehemia Levtzion, eds., *The Public Sphere in Muslim Societies* (Albany, NY, 2002). For recent studies employing the concept in the analysis of specific Middle Eastern societies, see Elizabeth Thompson, *Colonial Citizens: Republican Rights, Paternal Privilege, and Gender in French Syria and Lebanon* (New York 1999), 172–173; Keith David Watenpaugh, *Being Mod-

ern in the Middle East: Revolution, Nationalism, Colonialism, and the Arab Middle Class (Princeton, NJ, 2006), 64, 78–81, 303–304; Weldon C. Matthews, *Confronting an Empire, Constructing a Nation: Arab Nationalists and Popular Politics in Mandate Palestine* (London, 2006), 136–137, 146–147.

8. For the evolution of the term *effendi*, see Lucie Ryzova, "Egyptianizing Modernity through the 'New Effendiya': Social and Cultural Constructions of the Middle Class in Egypt under the Monarchy," in *Re-Envisioning Egypt, 1919–1952*, ed. Arthur Goldschmidt, Amy J. Johnson, and Barak A. Salmoni, 124–163 (Cairo, 2005); and Lucie Ryzova, *L'effendiyya ou la modernité contestée* (Cairo, 2004).

9. See Ryzova, "Egyptianizing Modernity," 131–133, 141.

10. Fraser, "Rethinking the Public Sphere," 116–126.

11. Habermas, *Structural Transformation of the Public Sphere*, 181.

12. Ibid., 184.

13. See ibid., 141ff. (term from 142).

14. Anwar al-Jundi, *al-Ma'arik al-Adabiyya fi al-Shi'r wa al-Nathr wa al-Thaqafa wa al-Lugha wa al-Qawmiyya al-'Arabiyya* (Cairo, 1961); revised and expanded as *al-Ma'arik al-Adabiyya fi Misr, 1914–1939* (Cairo, 1983). For an excellent presentation of Habermas's concepts of the literary and the political public spheres, see Edgar, *Philosophy of Habermas*, 34–39.

Chapter 2

1. Memorandum on the Egyptian Press, Sept. 2 to Oct. 1, 1937; FO 371:20903, J 4334:148:16.

2. For the 1937 estimate, see the table in Ami Ayalon, *The Press in the Arab Middle East: A History* (New York, 1995), 149–150; for that of 1944, see "Note sur la presse égyptienne et la presse palestinienne à la fin de 1944," *Cahiers de l'Orient contemporaine*, 1 (1944–45), 124–127.

3. See Ayalon, *Press*, 56–57, 149–150.

4. Memorandum on the Egyptian Press, Feb. 15 to Mar. 10, 1938; FO 371:22000, J 1080:264:16.

5. See FO 371:22000, J 3628:264:16; FO371:22000, J 3978:264:16.

6. Memorandum on the Egyptian Press, Feb. 15 to Mar. 10, 1938; FO 371:22000, J 1080:264:16.

7. Ayalon, *Press*, 149–150; "Note sur la presse égyptienne et la presse palestinienne," 124.

8. Sir Miles Lampson put it more cynically: "The fact is that in Egypt—as in most other countries—the editorial policy of a paper must inevitably be guided by considerations of finance." Memorandum on the Egyptian Press, Jan. 29 to Feb. 24, 1937; FO 371:2093, J 1021:148:16.

9. See the editorials "Bayna Italiya wa al-Habasha," *MQ*, Oct. 8, 1934, 1; "Bayna Italiya wa al-Habasha," *MQ*, Nov. 29, 1934, 1, 10; "al-Habasha Talja'u ila Jama'at al-Umam," *MQ*, Dec. 17, 1934, 1.

10. "Sir Musulini," *MQ*, Jan. 19, 1935, 1; "Italiya fi al-Bahr al-Ahmar wa al-Habasha," *MQ*, Jan. 19, 1935, 5; "Bayna Italiya wa al-Habasha," *MQ*, Feb. 13, 1935, 4; "Idha Waqaʿat al-Harb bayna Italiya wa al-Habasha," *MQ*, Feb. 26, 1935, 4; "Bayna Italiya wa al-Habasha," *MQ*, Apr. 15, 1935, 4.

11. "Misr wa al-Habasha wa Italiya," *MQ*, Feb. 28, 1935, 12; "Wa Tanshub al-Harb bayna Italiya wa al-Habasha," *MQ*, Apr. 4, 1935, 1; "Urubba wa al-Silah wa al-Salam," *MQ*, Apr. 13, 1935, 4; "Bayna Italiya wa al-Habasha," *MQ*, Apr. 15, 1935, 4.

12. "Ayy al-Duwal Yuwali Italiya al-An," *MQ*, July 24, 1935, 4.

13. "al-ʿAwamil al-Khafiyya fi al-Mushkila al-Habashiyya," *MQ*, Oct. 16, 1935, 1, 4.

14. See "Nawahi al-Mushkila al-Habashiyya al-Italiyya," *MQ*, Oct. 6, 1935, 1, 4; "al-Asbab al-Zahira wa al-Khafiyya fi al-Nizaʿ al-Habashi al-Itali," *MQ*, Oct. 10, 1935, 1, 4.

15. "Nawahi al-Mushkila al-Habashiyya al-Italiyya," *MQ*, Oct. 6, 1935, 1, 4.

16. For examples see *MQ*, Oct. 1, 1935, 5; *MQ*, Oct. 10, 1935, 1,4; *MQ*, Oct. 16, 1935, 1; *MQ*, Oct. 29, 1935, 7.

17. "Misr wa al-ʿUqubat," *MQ*, Nov. 2, 1935, 7; "Misr wa al-ʿUqubat," *MQ*, Nov. 24, 1935, 4, 7.

18. "Bayna Misr wa Italiya," *MQ*, Jan. 26, 1936, 1, 4; see also "al-Khilaf bayna Italiya wa al-Habasha," *MQ*, Jan. 9, 1936, 1, 4; "Istiʿdad Misr li Muwajahat al-Ghazat al-Samma," *MQ*, Feb. 6, 1936, 4.

19. "al-ʿUqubat al-Iqtisadiyya ʿala Italiya," *MQ*, Mar. 24, 1936, 7; "Bayna Misr wa Italiya," *MQ*, Apr. 1, 1936, 6; "Italiya wa Maʾ al-Nil li Misr wa al-Sudan," *MQ*, Apr. 4, 1936, 1, 4; "Italiya wa Bahirat Tana," *MQ*, Apr. 9, 1936, 1; "Misr wa Italiya wa Bahirat Tana," *MQ*, Apr. 21, 1936, 1, 4.

20. "Bayna Misr wa Italiya," *MQ*, May 5, 1936, 4; "Bayna Misr wa Italiya," *MQ*, May 8, 1936, 1, 4; "Qunsul Misr fi al-Habasha wa Mawqifuhu Tijah Italiya," *MQ*, June 22, 1936, 6.

21. "Bayna Misr wa Italiya baʿda Ihtilal al-Habasha," *MQ*, Aug. 7, 1936, 1, 4.

22. "Ilghaʾ al-ʿUqubat ʿala Italiya," *MQ*, July 14, 1936, 7; see also *MQ*, July 16, 1936, 5.

23. "Baʿda Imdaʾ al-Muʿahada," *MQ*, Aug. 28, 1936, 1, 5; "Italiya wa al-Muʿahada al-Misriyya: Awham la Haqiqa Laha," *MQ*, Sept. 25, 1936, 5; "al-Ittifaq al-Itali al-Biritani," *MQ*, Jan. 4, 1937, 4.

24. Thabit's articles on "Italy Today" ("Italiya al-Yawm") appeared in *MQ* between Oct. 20 and Nov. 26, 1936.

25. "Tajaddud al-Qital fi al-Habasha," *MQ*, Jan. 22, 1937, 4; "Hadith al-Habasha al-Akhir," *MQ*, Feb. 23, 1937, 4; "al-Madaniyya al-Athyubiyya wa al-Fath al-Itali," *MQ*, Apr. 9, 1937, 1, 5.

26. For examples see "Italiya wa Misr," *MQ*, Jan. 5, 1937, 6; "Italiya wa Misr," *MQ*, Jan. 6, 1937, 6.

27. See "Hadith al-Habasha," *MQ*, Feb. 23, 1937, 4; "Tahdid Bab al-Mandab wa Khalij ʿAdn," *MQ*, Feb. 23, 1937, 1, 5; "Misr wa Mustaqbaluha fi al-Bahr al-Abyad al-Mutawassit," *MQ*, Aug. 27, 1937, 1, 4.

28. See *AH*, Apr. 8, 1935, 1,10; *AH*, Apr. 15, 1935, 3; *AH*, May 23, 1935, 2; *AH*, June 3, 1935, 1; *AH*, July 22, 1935, 1; *AH*, July 31, 1935, 1; *AH*, Aug. 1, 1935, 1–2; *AH*, Aug. 30, 1935, 3; *AH*, Sept. 14, 1935, 3.

29. "Ibtida' al-Harb bayna Italiya wa al-Habasha," *AH*, Oct. 4, 1935, 4; "al-Harb al-Habashiyya wa al-Mashakil al-Dawliyya," *AH*, Oct. 5, 1935, 4; "al-Harb fi al-Habasha," *AH*, Oct. 7, 1935, 6; "Fi al-Hala al-Siyasiyya," *AH*, Oct. 12, 1935, 9; "Risalat al-Habasha: Ibtida' al-Qital," *AH*, Oct. 16, 1935, 1; Tadrus Mikha'il Tadrus, "Hawla al-Harb fi al-Habasha," *AH*, pt. 1, Oct. 16, 1935, 1–2, and pt. 2, Oct. 22, 1935, 1; "Fi Sabil al-Habasha," *AH*, Oct. 28, 1935, 1.

30. "Tatbiq al-ʿUqubat ʿala Italiya," *AH*, Nov. 2, 1935, 1.

31. Ibid.; "al-Azma al-Dawliyya," *AH*, Nov. 2, 1935, 4; "Ishtirak Misr fi Tawqiʿ al-ʿUqubat," *AH*, Nov. 2, 1935, 9; Muhammad Ahmad, "Usbat al-Umam wa al-Nizaʿ bayna al-Duwal," *AH*, Nov. 4, 1935, 2; Tadrus Mikha'il Tadrus, "Hawla al-Harb fi al-Habasha," *AH*, pt. 3, Nov. 6, 1935, 1, 12.

32. See "al-Saʿat al-Fadila fi al-Ta'rikh," *AH*, Jan. 9, 1936, 4; "al-Azma al-Dawliyya," *AH*, Jan. 11, 1936, 4; also *AH*, Jan. 22, 1936, 1–2; *AH*, Feb. 22, 1936, 4; *AH*, Mar. 8, 1936, 1, 4, 7.

33. "Harb al-Habasha wa Mashakil Urubba," *AH*, Mar. 31, 1936, 4.

34. See "al-Azma al-Dawliyya," *AH*, Jan. 11, 1936, 4; "al-Harb al-Habasha wa Mashakil Urubba," *AH*, Mar. 31, 1936, 4.

35. "Inhiyar al-Habasha," *AH*, May 4, 1936, 4.

36. "Bayna al-Harb wa al-Salam," *AH*, May 7, 1936, 4; "Mushkilat al-Habasha wa Mawqif al-Duwal," *AH*, May 8, 1936, 4; "al-Mushkila al-Habashiyya," *AH*, May 12, 1936, 4; "al-Azma al-Dawliyya," *AH*, June 2, 1936, 4; "Haraka Jadida fi Bilad al-Habasha," *AH*, Aug. 1, 1936, 1.

37. "Tafaqum al-Hala al-Dawliyya," *AH*, 6 Nov. 1936, 4; "Mushkilat al-Bahr al-Mutawassit," *AH*, 11 Nov. 1936, 4; "Misr fi al-Bahr al-Mutawassit," *AH*, 30 Dec. 1936, 1.

38. "Ittifaq al-Jantalman," *AH*, Jan. 3, 1937, 4; "al-Azma al-Dawliyya," *AH*, Jan. 5, 1937, 4; "Ittifaq al-Karam bayna Injiltara wa Italiya," *AH*, Jan. 12, 1937, 1.

39. See "Thawrat Isbaniyya wa Khataruha ʿala Urubba," *AH*, Aug. 5, 1936, 4; "Hadhithan Khatiran fi Urubba," *AH*, Nov. 16, 1936, 4; "Ishtidad al-Azma al-Dawliyya," *AH*, Nov. 20, 1936, 4; "Muʿahadat Firsay wa Ma Alladhi Baqa Minha?" *AH*, Feb. 8, 1937, 6; "al-Hala al-Dawliyya," *AH*, Aug. 22, 1937, 4.

40. "Tafaqum al-Hala al-Dawliyya," *AH*, Nov. 6, 1936, 4.

41. See "Mushkilat al-Bahr al-Mutawassit," *AH*, Nov. 11, 1936, 4; "Misr fi al-Bahr al-Mutawassit," *AH*, Dec. 30, 1936, 1; "Mashruʿ al-Mithaq al-Gharbi," *AH*, Mar. 19, 1937, 6; "Idtirab al-Hala al-Dawliyya: Urubba wa Shabah al-Harb," *AH*, Mar. 27, 1937, 6; "Ittifaq ʿAdam al-Tadakhul fi Shu'un Isbaniyya," *AH*, May 5, 1937, 4; "al-Azma al-Dawliyya: Siyasat Italiya wa Ittijahaha al-Jadid," *AH*, Aug. 20, 1937, 4.

42. "Italiya wa al-ʿArab: Ittijah Jadid fi al-Siyasa al-Fashistiyya," *AH*, Apr. 12, 1937, 4.

43. For example, see "Hal Tastaʿidu Almaniya li al-Harb," *MQ*, Nov. 21, 1934, 4; "al-Tajnid al-Lizami al-ʿAmm fi Almaniya," *MQ*, Mar. 20, 1935, 1; "Tanzim al-Jaysh al-Almani al-Jadid," *MQ*, Apr. 12, 1935, 5; "Almaniya wa al-Duwal al-Ukhra," *MQ*, May 11,

1935, 4; "al-Har Hitlar Yasifu Siyasat Dawlatihi," *MQ*, May 23, 1935, 4; "Almaniya Tatlubu Mustaʿmarat," *MQ*, July 2, 1935, 5; "al-Mustaʿmarat: bayna Britaniya wa Almaniya," *MQ*, Feb. 14, 1936, 4.

44. "Almaniya wa al-Duwal al-Ukhra," *MQ*, May 11, 1935, 4.

45. See "Bayna Misr wa Almaniya," *MQ*, Oct. 19, 1936, 1, 4; "Almaniya Taduʿ ila Tafahum wa Tafrij al-Azamat," *MQ*, Mar. 3, 1936, 1, 4; "Bayna al-Nuzum al-Naziyya wa al-Nuzum al-Balshafiyya," *MQ*, Nov. 18, 1936, 2; "al-Taʾmim al-Sihhi fi Almaniya," *MQ*, May 11, 1937, 1.

46. "Nahnu La Nuridu al-Harb: Hakadha Yaqul Musaʿid al-Har Hitlar" (citing a press interview in which Nazi Party official Rudolf Hess maintained Germany's peaceful intentions), *MQ*, Dec. 11, 1934, 5.

47. Thabit Thabit, series on "Almaniya al-Yawm," *MQ*, Aug. 7 to Sept. 5, 1936.

48. Thabit Thabit, "Almaniya al-Yawm: Barlin fi ʿId," *MQ*, Aug. 7, 1936, 1;Thabit, "Fi al-Alʿab al-Ulimbiyya: Barlin fi ʿId," *MQ*, Aug. 10, 1936, 5.

49. See "al-Nizaʿ al-Dini fi al-Raykh," *MQ*, Oct. 15, 1934, 5; "al-Haraka al-Diniyya fi Almaniya," *MQ*, June 8, 1935, 2; "Almaniya wa al-Ittihad al-Dini," *MQ*, July 23, 1935, 4.

50. See "Qanum al-Taʿqim fi Almaniya," *MQ*, Apr. 25, 1935, 2; "Almaniya wa al-Kathulik wa al-Yahud," *MQ*, Aug. 17, 1935, 4; "Bayna al-Yahud wa al-Alman," *MQ*, Aug. 22, 1935, 8; "Bayna al-Bid wa Ghayr al-Bid," *MQ*, Jan. 30, 1936, 1; "al-Shiʿar al-Nazi fi al-Zawaj," *MQ*, Apr. 21, 1936, 2; "Li man Yasmah bi al-Zawaj fi Almaniya?," *MQ*, Apr. 30, 1937, 2; "Hukumat al-Nazi wa al-Usra," *MQ*, June 15, 1937, 2.

51. "Almaniya Tatrudu Ashab al-Unuf al-Maʿkufa," *MQ*, Aug. 26, 1937, 2.

52. Quotation from "Li Sawn al-Damm al-Almani," *MQ*, Mar. 13, 1935, 5.

53. "Qanun Nurmburj wa Ibtal al-Zawaj," *MQ*, June 18, 1936, 1.

54. Reported in "al-Misriyyun wa al-Jins al-Ary," *MQ*, June 19, 1936, 7.

55. "al-Aryyun wa Ghayr al-Aryyin," *MQ*, June 20, 1936, 4. The issue became a diplomatic one. When the Egyptian Legation in Germany demanded clarification regarding the reported ban on Egyptian-German marriage, the German Foreign Ministry responded with a statement to the effect that "German law allows Egyptian men who are not Jews to marry German women with no constraints. These laws also allow non-Jewish Egyptian women to marry German men"; "al-Misriyyun wa al-Jins al-Ary," *MQ*, June 22, 1936, 5.

56. See "al-Hala al-Jadida fi Urubba," *AH*, July 15, 1936, 4; "Mawqif Almaniya," *AH*, Nov. 11, 1935, 4; "Masaʿi al-Siyasa al-Almaniyya li al-Taqarub min Injiltara," *AH*, Nov. 5, 1936, 4; "al-ʿAmil al-Almani," *AH*, July 17, 1937, 1.

57. "Wusul al-Fariq al-Misri li Aʿlab al-Ulimbiyya ila Barlin," *AH*, July 15, 1936, 9; "al-Misriyyun fi Almaniya," *AH*, Aug. 6, 1936, 8.

58. For critiques of German foreign policy in 1936, see "Alamiya Tahtallu ʿAskariyan Mantiqat al-Rayn," *AH*, Mar. 8, 1936, 5; "Baʿda Hubut al-ʿAsifa: al-Hala fi Urubba," *AH*, Mar. 10, 1936, 4; "Bayna al-Harb wa al-Silm: al-Hala al-Dawliyya," *AH*, May 7, 1936, 4; "al-Hala al-Dawliyya," *AH*, May 9, 1936, 4; "Almaniya wa Bulanda wa Mushkilat

Danzij," *AH*, July 9, 1936, 4; "al-Inqilab al-Khatir fi al-Mawqif al-Dawli," *AH*, July 14, 1936, 4; "al-Hala al-Jadida fi Urubba: al-Ittifaq al-Alamni al-Nimsawi," July 15, 1936, 4; "al-Thawra al-Isbaniyya," *AH*, July 27, 1936, 9; "Thawrat Isbaniya wa Khataruha ʿala Urubba," *AH*, Aug. 5, 1936, 4; "Alamiya wa Mashruʿatuha fi al-Dakhil wa al-Kharij," *AH*, Nov. 18, 1936, 4; "Ishtidad al-Azma al-Dawliyya," *AH*, Nov. 20, 1936, 4; "al-Azma al-Dawliyya," *AH*, Jan. 5, 1937, 4.

59. "Khutbat al-Ra'is Hitlar fi al-Raykhstag: Tatawwur al-Thawra al-Almaniyya fi Arbaʿ Sanawat," *AH*, Jan. 31, 1937, 1, 4–5; "Kayfa Turidu Almaniya an Yakun al-Salam fi al-ʿAlam," *AH*, Feb. 1, 1937, 4; "Mutalabat Almaniya bi Mustaʿmaratiha," *AH*, Feb. 5, 1937, 4; "Mas'alat al-Mustaʿmarat: Matalib Almaniya wa Khataruha," *AH*, Feb. 11, 1937, 4.

60. For assertions of this position, see "Bayan li al-Nas," *AH*, Nov. 16, 1935, 1; "al-Tatawwurat al-Muntazara fi al-Azma al-Dawliyya," *AH*, Jan. 15, 1936, 6; "Ittifaq al-Karam bayna Injiltara wa Italiya," *AH*, Jan. 12, 1937, 1; "al-Azmat al-Ijtimaʿiyya baʿda al-Azmat al-Siyasiyya," *AH*, May 5, 1937, 4; " ʿId al-Insaniyya," *AH*, July 14, 1937, 1, 15; "Misr fi Jinif," *AH*, Aug. 29, 1937, 1.

61. "Ishtidad al-Azma al-Dawliyya: Ansaruha Yuridunaha li al-Fath wa al-Istiʿmar," *AH*, Aug. 30, 1937, 4.

62. Salah al-Din al-Sharif, "al-Makyafiliyya Tasaytaru ʿala al-ʿAlam," *AH*, Sept. 5, 1937, 3.

63. "Qawanin Nurmburj fi Almaniya," *AH*, Jan. 3, 1936, 4.

64. "al-Hala fi Almaniya," *AH*, Jan. 11, 1936, 7.

65. "Almaniya wa al-Fatikan: Ishtidad al-Khilaf Baynahuma," *AH*, Apr. 1, 1937, 6.

66. See *AH*, Feb. 6, 1938, 4; *AH*, Feb. 17, 1938, 1; *AH*, Feb. 21, 1938, 7; *AH*, Feb. 22, 1938, 1.

67. *AH*, Mar. 16, 1938, 1; *AH*, Mar. 18, 1938, 1.

68. "Barnamij Hitlar wa Tanfizuhu: Hawla Damm al-Nimsa ila Almaniya," *AH*, Mar. 16, 1938, 1.

69. Muhammad Zaki ʿAbd al-Qadir, "Damm al-Nimsa li Almaniya," *AH*, Mar. 14, 1938, 1.

70. Editorial, "Min Srayifu Sanat 1914 ila Fina Sanat 1938," *MS*, June 4, 1938, 4.

71. "Kayfa Tadaraja Hitlar," *MS*, July 11, 1938, 3, 11.

72. "al-Imbiraturiyya al-Almaniyya fi Nazar al-Naziyyin," *MS*, July 19. 1938, 3.

73. "Mu'tamar Ifyan wa al-Laji'un al-Yahud," *MS*, July 15, 1938, 4,

74. Ibid.

75. For example, see *MS*, May 23, 1938, 7; *MS*, June 16, 1938, 1; *MS*, July 7, 1938, 1–2; *MS*, Feb. 25, 1939, 6; *MS*, Mar. 3, 1939, 6.

76. See *MS*, May 28, 1938, 4; *MS*, June 26, 1938, 3.

77. For representative reports, see *MS*, May 23, 1938, 4; *MS*, June 14, 1938, 4; *MS*, June 20, 1938, 4–6; *MS*, July 10, 1938, 4; *MS*, July 19, 1938, 3.

78. "Hal Taʿnu Tshikuslufakiya li al-Daght al-Iqtisadi?" *MS*, June 26, 1938, 4. See also *MS*, May 23, 1938, 4; *MS*, July 7, 1938, 4; *MS*, July 11, 1938, 4.

79. "Qawa'id Siyasat Tshambarlin," *MS*, June 19, 1938, 4.

80. "Al-Salam bi Ayy Thaman: Hakadha Tusaf Siyasat Tshambarlin," *MS*, July 12, 1938, 4.

81. "Khatar Azmat Tshikuslufakiya 'ala al-Salam al-Urubbi," *JH*, Aug. 31, 1938, 3.

82. "Hitlar wa al-Ghazw al-Urubbi," *JH*, Aug. 31, 1938, 1, 5.

83. See *JH*, Sept. 2, 1938, 3–5; *JH*, Sept. 3, 1938, 3–4; *JH*, Sept. 4, 1938, 1–4.

84. "Azmat al-Dimuqratiyya wa Wajibuna fi Dar' Akhtariha," *AH*, Sept. 2, 1938, 1.

85. Muhammad Zaki 'Abd al-Qadir, "al-Qawmiyya wa al-Harb," *AH*, Sept. 27, 1938, 1.

86. "'Ibrat al-Azma al-Dawliyya," *AH*, Oct. 4, 1938, 1.

87. 'Abdalla Husayn, "Khata' al-Diblumasiyya al-Dimuqratiyya fi Sabagha al-Mushkila al-Tshikiyya bi al-Sibgha al-Dawliyya," *AH*, Oct. 14, 1938, 1.

88. "Asbab wa Nata'ij: Almaniya wa Italiya Tu'alifan Jabha Wahida: 'Alam Jadid," *AH*, Nov. 4, 1938, 1–2.

89. Ibid.

90. "al-Mawqif al-Dawli wa Khuturatuhu," *AH*, Nov. 14, 1938, 4.

91. "Siyasat al-Quwwa wa al-'Unf fi al-'Alam: Idtihad al-Yahud fi Almaniya," *AH*, Nov. 15, 1938, 4.

92. Muhammad Zaki 'Abd al-Qadir, "Najah al-Diktatur," *AH*, Nov. 22, 1938, 1; for the same theme, see 'Abd al-Qadir's earlier article entitled "Kalimat Diktatur," *AH*, Oct. 13, 1938, 1.

93. "Hal Kana Ittifaq Munikh Khatima aw Fatiha?" *AH*, Feb. 10, 1939, 1–2, 6.

94. "Ba'da Sukut Barshaluna," *MS*, Jan. 29, 1939, 4–5; for a similar analysis, see *MS*, Jan. 24, 1939, 3, 5.

95. "Amal Almaniya al-Fuja'i—Hitlar fi Bragh la fi Fina," *AH*, Mar. 17, 1939, 4.

96. "Jabha Qawiyya didda al-Saytara bi al-Quwwa," *MS*, Apr. 28, 1939, 1.

97. For example, see *MS*, Jan. 21, 1939, 3; *MS*, Jan. 22, 1939, 7; *MS*, Jan. 31, 1939, 4–5; *MS*, Feb. 5, 1939, 7; *MS*, Feb. 22, 1939, 4; *MS*, Feb. 25, 1939, 3.

98. "Nakbat al-Sihafa wa Hurriyyat al-Ra'y: Inhiyar al-Rukn al-Asasi li al-Dustur wa al-Dimuqratiyya," *MS*, Mar. 7, 1939, 1–2. See also *MS*, Feb. 26, 1939, 1; *MS*, Mar. 3, 1939, 6–7.

99. "Ghazwat Italiya li Albaniya," *AH*, Apr. 8, 1939, 4.

100. Muhammad Zaki 'Abd al-Qadir, "Musulini fi Albaniya," *AH*, Apr. 9, 1939, 1.

101. "Hawla Khitab Musulini," *AH*, Apr. 1, 1939, 2.

102. For mid-1939 assessments of the global situation, see "al-Azma al-Hadira wa Tatawwuratuha," *AH*, June 19, 1939, 4; "al-'Alam bayna al-Tafa'ul wa al-Tasha'um," *AH*, Aug. 1, 1939, 4; "Ishtidad al-Azma fi al-Gharb wa al-Sharq," *AH*, Aug. 15, 1939, 4.

103. "Hal Tadumu Isbaniya ila Dawlatay al-Mihwar?" *AH*, July 17, 1939, 4.

104. See editorials in *AH*, Aug. 1, 1939, 4; *AH*, Aug. 16, 1939, 4; *AH*, Aug. 17, 1939, 4; *AH*, Aug. 21, 1939, 4.

105. For reports on the Mediterranean situation in the summer of 1939, see "Italiya wa Mushkilat al-Bahr al-Mutawssit," *AH*, July 2, 1939, 4; "Idha Waqa'at al-Harb," *AH*, Aug. 6, 1939, 4; "al-Hala fi al-Bahr al-Mutawassit," *AH*, Aug. 8, 1939, 4; "al-Hawd al-Sharqi li al-Bahr al-Mutawassit," *AH*, Aug. 10, 1939, 4.

106. For early reports on the Danzig issue, see *AH*, May 5, 1939, 4; *AH*, May 10, 1939, 4; *AH*, May 24, 1939, 4; *AH*, May 26, 1939, 4.

107. "Danzij Tahazzu al-ʿAlam," *AH*, July 20, 1939, 4.

108. "Shabah al-Harb fi Urubba: Mushkilat Danzij wa Mawqif al-Duwal Minha," *AH*, July 3, 1939, 4.

109. "Mushkilat Danzij wa Khuturatuha," *AH*, July 12, 1939, 4; see also *AH*, July 20, 1939, 4.

110. "Danzij bayna Almaniya wa Bulanda," *AH*, July 28, 1939, 4. See also "Mushkilat Danzij wa Akhtaruha al-Qariba," *AH*, Aug. 22, 1939, 4.

111. First quotation from "Khutbat al-Har Hitlar," *MS*, Apr. 29, 1939, 1; second from "Faransa Tusaʿidu Buluniya fi Halat al-Harb," *MS*, May 6, 1939, 1–3. For the same opinion, see *MS*, May 3, 1939, 4.

112. "Buluniya Laysat Mithl Tshikuslufakiya," *MS*, July 4, 1939, 4.

113. "al-Harb Waqiaʿh wa Sataqʿu ʿAjilan," *MS*, June 29, 1939, 1, 4; and reiterated in "La Mafar min Iʿlan al-Harb," *MS*, June 30, 1939, 1.

114. "Nushub al-Harb," *MS*, July 2, 1939, 1–2.

115. "Tafawwuq Almaniya al-Harbi ʿala Buluniya," *MS*, Aug. 21, 1939, 4.

116. "al-Nishat al-Harbi fi Buluniya wa Danzij," *MS*, July 24, 1939, 3.

117. "Mashruʿ li Taswiyat Mushkilat Danzij," *MS*, Aug. 14, 1939, 4.

118. "al-Wajib ʿala Baritaniya an Tatasalahu," *MS*, June 28, 1939, 3.

119. "Mufakharat al-Alman bi Quwwatihim al-Harbiyya," *MS*, June 29, 1939, 5.

120. "Aghustus 1914 wa Aghustus 1939," *AH*, Aug. 8, 1939, 1.

121. "Urubba bayna al-Harb wa al-Silm: 12 Malyun Jundi tahta al-Silah fi Urubba," *AH*, Aug. 21, 1939, 4.

122. "Mushkilat Danzij wa Akhtaruha al-Qariba," *AH*, Aug. 22, 1939, 4.

123. See *MS*, July 31, 1939, 5; *MS*, Aug. 4, 1939, 1–5; *MS*, Aug. 13, 1939, 5; *MS*, Aug. 16, 1939, 1–2.

124. "Danzij Multaqan al-Anzar," *MS*, Aug. 19, 1939, 4–5.

125. See *MS*, Aug. 21, 1939, 3; *MS*, Aug. 22, 1939, 4; *MS*, Aug. 23, 1939, 3–4.

126. "al-Hadith al-Khatir fi Urubba: al-Ittifaq bayna Almaniya wa Rusiya," *AH*, Aug. 23, 1939, 4; see also "Saʿat al-Qalaq wa al-Intizar," *AH*, Sept. 1, 1939, 4.

127. "Hadath Mufajiʾ fi al-Mawqif al-Dawli: Rusiya Taʿqidu Mithaqan bi ʿAdam al-Iʿtidaʾ Maʿa Almaniya!," *MS*, Aug. 23, 1939, 4–6, 11; see also *MS*, Aug. 24, 1939, 3–6.

128. "Tadwij al-ʿAsabat," *AH*, Aug. 28, 1939, 1.

129. "Wataniyyat al-Diktaturiyya wa Wataniyyat al-Dimuqratiyya," *AH*, May 23, 1939, 1.

130. Ibid.

131. Ibid.

132. Ibid. For further critiques of the expansionist dynamic in Nazi racism, see "Masʾalat al-ʿUnsuriyya," *AH*, July 30, 1938, 4; "al-Mada al-Hiyawi wa Mukafahat al-Iʿtidaʾ," *AH*, Aug. 13, 1939, 4.

133. "Duwal al-Sharq bayna al-Dimuqratiyya wa al-Diktaturiyya," *MS*, July 23, 1939, 1–2.

134. Ibid.

135. "Fi Sabil al-Dimuqratiyya Yakhudu al-Misriyyun Ghimar al-Harb," *MS*, Sept. 14, 1939, 6.

Chapter 3

1. Egyptian illustrated weeklies often included a list of the price of the publication in other Arab countries. For the role of the political cartoon in shaping public opinion in Egypt and the Middle East, see Afaf Lutfi al-Sayyid Marsot, "The Cartoon in Egypt," *Comparative Studies in Society and History*, 13 (Jan. 1971), 2–15; Fatma Müge Göçek, ed., *Political Cartoons in the Middle East* (Princeton, NJ, 1998).

2. Ayalon, *Press*, 78, 149.

3. Ibid., 150; "Note sur la presse égyptienne et la presse palestinienne," 125.

4. Ayalon, *Press*, 150; "Note sur la presse égyptienne et la presse palestinienne," 125.

5. Ibid.

6. *MSR*, Sept. 6, 1935, front page.

7. *ITH*, Nov. 11, 1935, front page.

8. *RUY*, Nov. 18 1935, 7.

9. *ITH*, Jan. 13, 1936, front page.

10. *ITH*, Apr. 13, 1936, front page.

11. *MSR*, Jan. 22, 1937, 37.

12. *MSR*, Mar. 26, 1937, 12.

13. *ITH*, Jan. 3, 1938, front page.

14. *RUY*, Jan. 3, 1938, back page.

15. *ITH*, Mar. 21, 1938, 5.

16. *ITH*, Sept. 5, 1938, 2.

17. *ITH*, Sept. 26, 1938, front page.

18. *ITH*, Oct. 3, 1938, front page.

19. *ITH*, Oct. 3, 1938, 3.

20. *ITH*, Oct. 10, 1938, front page.

21. *RUY*, Aug. 22, 1938, 15.

22. *RUY*, Sept. 18, 1938, 13.

23. *RUY*, Oct. 2, 1938, front page.

24. *RUY*, Oct. 2, 1938, 10.

25. *RUY*, Oct. 2, 1938, 11.

26. *RUY*, Oct. 9, 1938, front page.

27. *RUY*, Dec. 11, 1938, back page.

28. *RUY*, Dec. 4, 1938, front page.

29. *RUY*, Dec. 25, 1938, front page.

30. *ITH*, Dec. 26, 1938, front page.

31. *ITH*, Jan. 9, 1939, front page.

32. *RUY*, Jan. 1, 1939, back page.

33. *MSR*, Jan. 20, 1939, 13.

34. *RUY*, Mar. 17, 1939, 9.

35. *RUY,* Apr. 2, 1939, 7.
36. *RUY,* Apr. 2, 1939, back page.
37. *RUY,* Apr. 9, 1939, front page.
38. *ITH,* Apr. 3, 1939, 3.
39. *ITH,* Apr. 17, 1939, front page.
40. *ITH,* Apr. 24, 1939, 18.
41. *RUY,* May 7, 1939, back page.
42. *RUY,* Apr. 30, 1939, front page.
43. *ITH,* Apr. 24, 1939, 3.
44. *ITH,* May 1, 1939, front page.
45. *ITH,* Apr. 24, 1939, front page.
46. *ITH,* May 29, 1939, front page.
47. *MSR,* July 7, 1939, front page.
48. *MSR,* July 28, 1939, 20.
49. Ibid.
50. See "Danzij: Mawtin al-Khatar fi Urubba," *ITH,* July 10, 1939, 25.
51. *ITH,* July 10, 1939, 3.
52. *ITH,* July 17, 1939, 3.
53. *ITH,* July 3, 1939, 3.
54. *MSR,* Sept. 22, 1939, 8.
55. *ITH,* Oct. 16, 1939, front page.
56. *RUY,* Sept. 9, 1939, front page.
57. *ITH,* Sept. 4, 1939, 3.
58. *ITH,* Sept. 18, 1939, front page.

Chapter 4

1. A special issue of the publication on "The Arabs and Islam in the Modern Age" of April 1939 reported a press run of 40,000 copies. From this figure, we infer a somewhat smaller but still significant regular circulation.

2. *Al-Hilal*'s origins are discussed in Thomas Philipp, *Gurgi Zaidan: His Life and Thought* (Beirut, 1979), 229–234; for its publishing history, see Ayalon, *Press,* 53–54, 76–78, 192, 197.

3. See Ayalon, *Press,* 81; J. Brugman, *An Introduction to the History of Modern Arabic Literature in Egypt* (Leiden, 1984), 381–384; Gershoni, "*Al-Risala*'s Reaction to Fascism and Nazism," 555–556; Ni'mat Ahmad Fu'ad, *Qiman Adabiyya: Dirasat wa Tarajim li al-A'lam al-Adab al-Misri al-Hadith* (Cairo, 1966), 175–232; Muhammad Sayyid Muhammad, *al-Zayyat wa al-Risala* (Riyadh, 1982).

4. Muhammad, *al-Zayyat,* 190; Fu'ad, *Qimam Adabiyya,* 177–178.

5. Ahmad Amin, "al-Thaqafa fi 'Ammiha al-Thani," *TQ,* Jan. 2, 1940, 1. For its orientation, see also Ayalon, *Press,* 81; Brugman, *Literature,* 388–389.

6. *Al-Thaqafa*'s circulation figure is based on reviews of its first year of publication that appeared in *TQ* in late 1939 and early 1940.

7. For its publishing history, see Salama Musa, *The Education of Salama Musa*, trans. L. O. Schuman (Leiden, 1961), 130–131; Vernon Egger, *A Fabian in Egypt: Salamah Musa and the Rise of the Professional Classes in Egypt, 1909–1939* (Lanham, MD, 1986), 171, 178, 180, 221–222; Ayalon, *Press*, 239; Brugman, *Literature*, 394.

8. See Brugman, *Literature*, 382, for testimony as to its impact on younger modernist writers.

9. ʿAli Adham, "Bayna Karlayl wa Nitsha: al-Batal wa al-Insan al-Aʿla," *HL*, Apr. 1938, 623–630.

10. Ibid.

11. ʿAli Adham, "Asatidha Musulini wa Hitlar: al-Mufakkirun alladhina Mahadu li al-Diktaturiyya al-Haditha," *HL*, Nov. 1938, 28–32.

12. Ibid.

13. Ibid.

14. ʿAbd al-Rahman Sidqi, "al-Jamahir Ka al-Atfal," *HL*, May 1938, 777–780.

15. Ibrahim al-Misri, "Li man Yaktubu al-Katib fi Misr: al-Jumhur La Yaktarithu fi al-Haraka al-Fikriyya," *HL*, July 1938, 987–991.

16. Muhammad Husayn Haykal, "Athr al-Siyasa fi Akhlaq al-Mujtamaʿ," *HL*, Mar. 1936, 485–488.

17. Niqula al-Haddad, "Bayna al-Hurriyya wa al-Diktaturiyya," *HL*, Nov. 1936, 33–38.

18. ʿAbd al-Rahman Sidqi, "Tahlamu bi Rijal al-Aqdar," *HL*, Dec. 1938, 158–162.

19. Ibid.

20. "al-Thawra al-Fashistiyya min Sanat 1919 ila Sanat 1939," *HL*, Mar. 1939, 553–556.

21. For one discussion, see ʿAbd al-Rahman Sidqi, "Almaniya al-Naziyya Tuqimu Nahdataha ʿala al-ʿUnsuriyya," *HL*, June 1939, 741–744. Egyptian views of German racism are discussed later in this chapter.

22. ʿAli Adham, "al-Harb wa Nazʿat al-Fikr al-Almani," *HL*, Nov. 1939, 59–64.

23. Ibid., 61–63; see also his earlier "al-Batal wa al-Insan al-Aʿla," *HL*, Apr. 1938, 629–630.

24. ʿAli Adham, "al-Harb wa Nazʿat al-Fikr al-Almani," *HL*, Nov. 1939, 59–60, 64.

25. For one example, see Salama Musa, "Almaniya wa al-Islah al-Ijtimaʿi," *MJ*, Nov. 1936, 10–11; for a broader discussion, see Egger, 169–217.

26. Salama Musa, *al-Dunya baʿda Thalathin Sana* (Cairo, 1936). This extended essay first appeared as a special supplement to *MJ*, Feb. 1936.

27. Editorial, "Almaniya wa al-Islah al-Ijtimaʿi," *MJ*, Nov. 1936, 10–11.

28. Salama Musa, "al-Jadid fi Almaniya," *MJ*, Sept. 1935, 30–32; Musa, "Almaniya wa al-Islah al-Ijtimaʿi," *MJ*, Nov. 1936, 10–11.

29. Salama Musa, "Almaniya Tastaghni al-ʿAlam," *MJ*, Dec. 1936, 5–7; see also Musa, "al-Jadid fi Almaniya," *MJ*, Sept. 1935, 30–32; Musa, *al-Dunya*, 35–37.

30. Salama Musa, "al-ʿAlam Yastayqizu wa Nahnu Niyam," *MJ*, Jan. 1935, 7; Musa, "Fi al-Duwal al-Diktaturiyya," *MJ*, Nov. 1936, 7–8; Musa, "Almaniya Tastaghni al-ʿAlam," *MJ*, Dec. 1936, 5–7.

31. Salama Musa, "al-Jadid fi Almaniya," *MJ*, Sept. 1935, 30–32; Musa, "Fi al-Duwal al-Diktaturiyya," *MJ*, Nov. 1936, 8; "Harakat al-Shabab al-Hitlari," *MJ*, July 1937, 9–12.

32. Editorial, "al-Al'ab al-Ulimbiyya," *MJ*, Jan. 1936, 94–95.

33. Salama Musa, "Fi al-Duwal al-Diktaturiyya," *MJ*, Nov. 1936, 7–8.

34. Musa, *al-Dunya*, 5–6, 35–37.

35. Salama Musa, "al-Hukumat al-Hadira wa Mustaqbaluha," *MJ*, Mar. 1936, 17–22.

36. Salama Musa, "Almaniya wa al-Islah al-Ijtima'i," *MJ*, Nov. 1936, 11.

37. Salama Musa, "Almaniya ba'da Khams Sanawat," *MJ*, Mar. 1938, 6–13.

38. Ibid., 6–7.

39. Ibid., 7–8.

40. Salama Musa, "Masa'il al-Shabab al-Misriyyin," *MJ*, Apr. 1938, 80–87.

41. Ibid., 83–86.

42. Salama Musa, "al-Dawla al-Jami'a wa al-Dawla al-Dimuqratiyya," *MJ*, Dec. 1938, 65–66.

43. Ibid.

44. Ibid.

45. Rushdi Sa'id, "al-Dimuqratiyya wa al-Diktaturiyya," *MJ*, Aug. 1938, 61–75.

46. Ibid., 73.

47. Ibid., 69–71.

48. 'Ali Adham, "al-Siyasa wa al-Akhlaq: Khatar al-Makyafiliyya fi al-'Asr al-Hadith," *HL*, July 1936, 977–983.

49. Ibrahim al-Misri, "Nazariyyat Siyadat al-Dawla wa Atharuha fi Taqahaqur al-Fikr al-Urubbi al-Yawm," *HL*, Dec. 1937, 158–161.

50. "Ma'asi al-Hurriya fi al-'Asr al-Hadith: Ahrar al-Fikr fi al-Manfa," *HL*, Dec. 1938, 194–198.

51. For the use of the term, see Muhammad 'Abdalla 'Inan, "al-Sira' bayna al-Tughyan wa al-Dimuqratiyya," *RS*, Nov. 25, 1935, 1887–1889.

52. Editorial, "Mihnat al-Sihafa al-Almaniyya fi Dhill al-Irhab al-Hitlari," *RS*, Nov. 4, 1935, 1797–1798.

53. Muhammad 'Abdalla 'Inan, "Masra' al-Sihafa al-'Azima fi Dhill al-Nuzum al-Taghiyya," *RS*, May 20, 1935, 809–812.

54. Editorial, "Diktaturiyyat Hitlar," *RS*, Apr. 24, 1939, 836; see also *RS*, May 22, 1939, 1028.

55. See the editorials "al-Wataniyya wa Isti'bad al-Fikr," *RS*, Nov. 2, 1936, 1816, and "Nazariyyat Jadida fi al-Fann wa al-Naqd," *RS*, Nov. 21, 1936, 2095.

56. Editorial, "al-Di'aya fi Almaniya," *RS*, May 15, 1939, 983; editorial, "al-Dimuqratiyya wa al-Idha'a," *RS*, June 19, 1939, 1221–1222.

57. Ibid.

58. Editorial, "al-Di'aya fi Almaniya," *RS*, May 15, 1939, 983.

59. Taha Husayn, "Ba'd Wujhat al-Tafkir al-Hadith," *HL*, Feb. 1937, 361–366.

60. Ibid.

61. Salama Musa, "al-Dawla al-Jamiʿa wa al-Dawla al-Dimuqratiyya," *MJ*, Dec. 1938, 65–66.

62. Editorial, "al-Marʾa fi Zill al-Diktaturiyya," *RS*, May 1, 1939, 886–887.

63. Ibid. See also al-Barid al-Adabi, "al-Haraka al-Nisawiyya fi Almaniya," *RS*, Oct. 3, 1938, 1635–1636; "al-Nazi wa Tabiʿat al-Marʾa," *RS*, Sept. 25, 1939, 1877–1878.

64. ʿAbd al-Razzaq al-Sanhuri, "al-Taʿbir ʿan Rayʾ al-Umma," pt. 1, *HL*, Apr. 1938, 601–606; pt. 2, *HL*, May 1938, 734–739.

65. ʿAbd al-Razzaq al-Sanhuri, "al-Taʿbir ʿan Rayʾ al-Umma," *HL*, Apr. 1938, 601–606.

66. Ibrahim al-Misri, "Wahy Sbarta al-Diktaturiyya," *HL*, Jan. 1939, 280–283.

67. Ibid., 281–283.

68. Ibid., 283.

69. Muhammad Lutfi Jumʿa, "Tatawwurat al-ʿAsr al-Hadith fi al-Khuluq al-Siyasi," *RS*, Mar. 16, 1939, 108–110.

70. Ibid.

71. "al-Thawra al-Fashistiyya min Sanat 1919 ila Sanat 1939," *HL*, Mar. 1939, 553–556.

72. Editorial, "al-Majlis al-Fashi al-Aʿla," *HL*, May 1939, 678–680.

73. Ibid.

74. Ibid., 679–680.

75. Ibid., 678–680.

76. "Hal Tanjahu al-Diktaturiyya ʿIndana?" *HL*, Feb. 1939, 361–368.

77. Ibid., 362–363.

78. Ibid., 363–367.

79. Ibid., 367–368.

80. ʿAbd al-Rahman Shukri, "Hal Tanjahu al-Diktaturiyya ʿIndana?" *HL*, Mar. 1939, 515–517.

81. Ahmad Hasan al-Zayyat, "Hadha Rajul . . . !" *RS*, May 1, 1939, 847–848.

82. Ibid., 848.

83. ʿAbbas Mahmud al-ʿAqqad, "Masir al-Madhahib al-Ijtimaʿiyya al-Hadira idha Waqaʿat al-Harb," *HL*, June 1939, 721–725.

84. Ibid., 723–725.

85. Niqula al-Haddad, "al-Diktaturiyya Humma ʿAridatun la Khatar minha ʿala al-Dimuqratiyya," *HL*, June 1939, 753–758.

86. Ibid., 754–755, 757.

87. See Egger, 41–45, 61–62.

88. Salama Musa, "Madha Tatlubu Hadhihi al-Majalla," *MJ*, Aug. 1935, 43; Musa, "al-Wirath wa al-Wasat," MJ, Sept. 1935, 33–36; Musa, "al-Jadid fi Almaniya," *MJ*, Sept. 1935, 30.

89. Salama Musa, "al-ʿAlam Yastayqizu wa Nahnu Niyam," *MJ*, Jan. 1935, 7; idem, "al-Jadid fi Almaniya," *MJ*, Sept. 1935, 30–32.

90. Musa, *al-Dunya*, 42–43.

91. Ibid., 42–43. For similar ideas and terminology from Musa, see Musa's "al-ʿAlam Yastayqizu wa Nahnu Niyam," *MJ*, Jan. 1935, 7; editorial, "al-Taʿqim wa Sihhat al-Dhihn wa al-Jism," *MJ*, Aug. 1935, 9.

92. See Salama Musa, "al-Jadid fi Almaniya," *MJ*, Sept. 1935, 30–31; Musa, "Almaniya wa al-Islah al-Ijtima'i," *MJ*, Nov. 1936, 9; editorial, "Uqdat Filastin," *MJ*, Jan. 1937, 92.

93. Editorial, "al-Al'ab al-Ulimbiyya," *MJ*, Jan. 1936, 94.

94. See Salama Musa, "Qawmiyyatuna al-Fir'awniyya," *MJ*, June 1937, 82–85; Musa, "al-Fara'ina wa Almaniya," *MJ*, Feb. 1937, 85–87; Musa, "Tatawwur al-Wataniyya wa Qimmatuha al-Akhlaqiyya fi al-'Asr al-Hadith," MJ, May 1937, 61–69; see also Egger, 136–139.

95. Salama Musa, "Almaniya ba'da Khams Sanawat," *MJ*, Mar. 1938, 8–12.

96. Salama Musa, "Mashakil al-'Asr al-Hadith: al-Mas'ala al-Yahudiyya," *MJ*, July 1938, 3–5.

97. Ibid., 4–5.

98. Ibid.

99. Ibid., 3–4.

100. *MJ*, Sept. 1938, 93–94.

101. "Idtihad al-Yahud fi Italiya," *MJ*, Nov. 1938, 87–89.

102. "Masdar al-Hitlariyya," *MJ*, Nov. 1938, 78–80.

103. Michel 'Abd al-Lahad, "al-Yahudi al-Ta'ih," *MJ*, Feb. 1939, 38–47.

104. Ibid., 42–44.

105. Ibid., 45–47.

106. Muhammad 'Abdalla 'Inan, "al-Sira' bayna al-Tughyan wa al-Dimuqratiyya wa Mihnat al-Dimuqratiyya al-Mu'asira," *RS*, Nov. 25, 1935, 1887–1889; see also 'Inan, "Zikrayyat 'an Qadiyyat Drayfus," RS, Aug. 12, 1935, 1290–1293; 'Inan, "Riyah al-Ta'assub al-Jinsi Tahubbu 'ala Urubba," *RS*, Jan. 27, 1936, 126–128.

107. "Nazariyyat al-Jins wa al-Damm fi Almaniya," *RS*, Aug. 26, 1935, 1398.

108. "Mas'alat al-Ajnas," *RS*, Aug. 10, 1936, 1317.

109. Editorial, "Hitler wa al-Samiyya," *RS*, Oct. 31, 1938, 1795.

110. "Nazariyyat al-Jins wa al-Sulala wa al-Khusuma al-Samiyya," *RS*, Oct. 28, 1935, 1758–1759.

111. "Nazariyyat al-Jins wa al-Sulala," *RS*, Nov. 18, 1935, 1878.

112. Editorial, "Sumbart [Werner Sombart] wa al-Wataniyya al-Ishtirakiyya," *RS*, Jan. 31, 1938, 195.

113. Ahmad Hasan al-Zayyat, "Uqtulu al-Ju' Taqtulu al-Harb," *RS*, Apr. 24, 1939, 800.

114. "al-Haraka al-Fikriyya al-'Unsuriyya fi Almaniya" *RS*, Nov. 9, 1936, 1856.

115. Jawad 'Ali, "'Aqidat al-Za'ama fi al-Naziyya," *RS*, Sept. 18, 1939, 1825–1827; see also the editorial "Hitlar wa al-Samiyya," *RS*, Oct. 31, 1938, 1795; Ahmad Hasan al-Zayyat, "Uqtulu al-Ju' Taqtulu al-Harb," *RS*, Apr. 24, 1939, 799–800.

116. Ibrahim 'Abd al-Qadir al-Mazini, "Harban 'Uzayman: Tuthiruhuma Almaniya 'ala Namat Wahid," *RS*, Sept. 18, 1939, 1807–1808.

117. Al-Barid al-Adabi, "al-Haraka al-Nisawiyya fi Almaniya," *RS*, Oct. 3, 1938, 1635.

118. Editorial, "Hitlar wa al-Samiyya," *RS*, Oct. 31, 1938, 1795; see also Jawad 'Ali, "'Aqidat al-Za'ama fi al-Naziyya," *RS*, Sept. 18, 1939, 1825–1827.

119. Ahmad Hasan al-Zayyat, "Usbu' Mahmum: bayna al-Dimuqratiyya wa al-Diktaturiyya," *RS*, Sept. 26, 1938, 1561–1562.

120. See ʿAli Adham, "al-Shuʿubiyya fi al-ʿAsr al-Hadith," *HL*, Feb. 1938, 384–388; ʿAbd al-Rahman Sidqi, "Almaniya al-Naziyya Tuqimu Nahdataha ʿala al-ʿUnsuriyya," *HL*, June 1939, 741–744; ʿAli Adham, "al-Harb wa Nazʿat al-Fikr al-Almani," *HL*, Nov. 1939, 59–64.

121. Ibid., 59–60.

122. Ibid., 61.

123. ʿAbd al-Rahman Sidqi, "Ayy al-Ajnas Ibtadaʿa al-Hadara?" *HL*, Jan. 1937, 273–277.

124. ʿAbd al-Rahman Sidqi, "Almaniya al-Naziyya Tukimu Nahdataha ʿala al-ʿUnsuriyya," *HL*, June 1939, 741–744.

125. Ibid., 744.

126. Ibrahim al-Misri, "Madhhab al-Bashariyya: Bayna al-Dimuqratiyya wa al-Fashism," *HL*, July 1939, 900–905 (quotation from 904).

127. ʿAli Adham, "al-Shuʿubiyya fi al-ʿAsr al-Hadith," *HL*, Feb. 1938, 384–388.

128. Ibid., 387–388.

129. Ibid., 388.

130. Ibid., 384–388.

131. ʿAbd al-Rahman Sidqi, "Almaniya al-Naziyya Tukimu Nahdataha ʿala al-ʿUnsuriyya," *HL*, June 1939, 741–744 (quotation from 744).

132. Sami al-Jaridini, "Idtihad al-Yahud," *HL*, Dec. 1938, 148–149.

133. For example, see *HL*, Apr. 1938, 700–701; *HL*, Dec. 1938, 217–219; *HL*, Mar. 1939, 527; *HL*, July 1939, 929–931, *HL*, Aug. 1939, 1049–1063.

134. "Madha Rabiha al-Alman min Ibʿad al-Yahud?" *HL*, July 1939, 944.

135. "Laysa al-Yahud Jinsan," *HL*, Dec. 1938, 225–226.

136. Ibid.

137. Ibid.

138. "al-Yahud wa Filastin," *HL*, Feb. 1939, 479; see also *HL*, Mar. 1939, 558–600.

139. Editorial, "Bayna al-Islam wa al-Yahudiyya," *RS*, Dec. 12, 1938, 2037.

140. Editorial, "Shayluk al-Hadith," *TQ*, Mar. 21, 1939, 1–3.

141. "al-Qadiyya al-Filastiniyya ʿala Dawʿ al-Kitab al-Abyad," *TQ*, May 30, 1939, 1–4.

142. ʿAbd al-Rahman Shukri, "Mushkilat al-Yahud fi al-ʿAlam," *RS*, July 31, 1939, 1485–1487.

143. Ibid., 1486–1487.

Chapter 5

1. Salama Musa, "Musulini wa al-Habasha," *MJ*, Aug. 1935, 3–4; Musa, "al-Ghazat wa al-Harb," *MJ*, Dec. 1935, 33–38; editorial, "al-Fashiyya wa al-Naziyya," *MJ*, Nov. 1936, 83–84.

2. Editorial, "Sir al-Hawadith: Nahnu wa ʿUsbat al-Umam," *MJ*, Oct. 1935, 3. See also the editorials, "Sir al-Hawadith," *MJ*, Apr. 1935, 3; "Italiya wa al-Habasha," *MJ*, July 1935, 5; "Musulini wa al-Habasha," *MJ*, Aug. 1935, 3–4; "Sir al-Hawadith," "al-ʿUsba wa

Italiya," and "al-Hal fi al-Habasha," *MJ*, Sept. 1935, 3–5; "Sir al-Hawadith" and "Nahnu wa ʿUsbat al-Umam," *MJ*, Oct. 1935, 3.

3. Salama Musa, "al-Ghazat wa al-Harb," *MJ*, Dec. 1935, 33–38.

4. Editorial, "Tawahhush Italiya," *MJ*, Feb. 1936, 5–6.

5. Editorial, "Musulini wa al-Ummahat al-Habashiyyat," *MJ*, May 1937, 89–91.

6. Editorial, "Mustaʿmarat Italiya fi al-Bahr al-Mutawassit," *MJ*, Apr. 1937, 86–87; editorial, "Hujum Italiya ʿala Misr," *MJ*, Aug. 1937, 4–5.

7. ʿAbbas Mahmud al-ʿAqqad, "Musulini: min al-Salam ila al-Harb," *HL*, Dec. 1935, 130–133.

8. ʿAbbas Mahmud al-ʿAqqad, "al-Bahr al-Abyad al-Mutawassit: Mihwar li al-Siyasa al-Urubbiyya fi al-Waqt al-Hadir," *HL*, Feb. 1937, 373–376.

9. ʿAbbas Mahmud al-ʿAqqad, "Siyasat al-ʿAlam: Hal Aflahu fi Tawjih Siyasatiha?" *HL*, July 1937, 961–964.

10. Ibid.; ʿAbbas Mahmud al-ʿAqqad, "Mawatin al-Khatar fi Urubba: Min Ayna Taʾti al-Harb al-Muqbila?" *HL*, Jan. 1937, 241–246.

11. ʿAbbas Mahmud al-ʿAqqad, "Siyasat al-ʿAlam: Hal Aflahu fi Tawjih Siyasatiha?" *HL*, July 1937, 963–964. See also ʿAqqad, "Athr al-Ajanib fi Nahdat Misr," *HL*, June 1937, 841–844; ʿAqqad, "al-Nizam al-Maliki fi Misr," *HL*, Aug. 1937, 1086–1089.

12. Muhammad ʿAbdalla ʿInan, "al-Siraʿ bayna al-Habasha wa al-Istiʿmar al-Gharbi," *RS*, Dec. 24, 1934, 2088–2091.

13. Muhammad ʿAbdalla ʿInan, "Misr wa Maʾ al-Nil wa Hawadith al-Habasha," *RS*, Jan. 7, 1935, 6–9.

14. Ahmad Hasan al-Zayyat, "Asalib al-Istiʿmar: Qadiyyat al-Habasha—Qadiyyat al-Sharq wa Qadiyyat al-Hurriyya," *RS*, Aug. 5, 1935, 1241–1242.

15. Ibid.

16. Ahmad Hasan al-Zayyat, "Misr wa ʿUsbat Janif," *RS*, Sept. 9, 1935, 1441–1442.

17. Ahmad Hasan al-Zayyat, "Khaybat al-Madaniyya," *RS*, Oct. 28, 1935, 1721–1722.

18. Muhammad ʿAbdalla ʿInan, "Ahlam al-Salam wa Kayfa Inharat fi Khamsat ʿAshr ʿAman," *RS*, Oct. 21, 1935, 1687–1689; see also Diblumasi Kabir [ʿInan], "Usbat al-Umam wa Tatbiq al-ʿUqubat: Tahrim al-Harb min al-Wujha al-Dawliyya," *RS*, Oct. 21, 1935, 1728–1730.

19. Diblumasi Kabir [ʿInan], "al-Maʾsa al-Fashistiyya," *RS*, Nov. 11, 1935, 1809–1810; Diblumasi Kabir [ʿInan], "al-Siraʿ al-Hasim bayna al-Tughyan wa al-Dimuqratiyya," *RS*, July 13, 1936, 1129.

20. See Diblumasi Kabir [ʿInan], "al-Maʾsa al-Fashistiyya," *RS*, Nov. 11, 1935, 1810–1811; Muhammad ʿAbdalla ʿInan, "Asalib al-Kifah al-Dawli bayna al-Ams wa al-Yawm," *RS*, Feb. 17, 1936, 249–351; ʿInan, "al-Masʾala al-Habashiyya bayna Italiya wa Inkiltara," *RS*, May 11, 1936, 767–769; Diblumasi Kabir [ʿInan], "Baʿda Inhiyar al-Habasha: al-Khatar al-Fashisti wa al-Siraʿ bayna al-Fashistiyya wa al-Imbiraturiyya al-Biritaniyya," *RS*, June 1, 1936, 887–889; Diblumasi Kabir [ʿInan], "Khatar al-Fashistiyya ʿala Salam al-ʿAlam wa Mushkilat al-Bahar al-Abyad al-Mutawassit," *RS*, Nov. 23, 1936, 1910–1913.

21. Diblumasi Kabir ['Inan], "al-Ma'sa al-Fashistiyya," *RS*, Nov. 11, 1935, 1809–1811; Diblumasi Kabir ['Inan], "Ba'da Inhiyar al-Habasha: al-Khatar al-Fashisti wa al-Sira' bayna al-Fashistiyya wa al-Imbiraturiyya al-Biritaniyya," *RS*, June 1, 1936, 887–889.

22. Diblumasi Kabir ['Inan], "Khatar al-Fashistiyya 'ala Salam al-'Alam wa Mushkilat al-Bahr al-Abyad al-Mutawassit," *RS*, Nov. 23, 1936, 1910–1913; Muhammad 'Abdalla 'Inan, "Tatawwur Khatir fi al-Siyasa al-Dawliyya," *RS*, Dec. 7, 1936, 1985–1988; 'Inan, "Tawr Jadid fi Ta'rikh Urubba al-Siyasi," *RS*, Dec. 21, 1936, 2063–2065.

23. Diblumasi Kabir ['Inan], "Misr wa Italiya: 'Ibar al-Madi Dala'il al-Hadir," *RS*, Dec. 6, 1937, 1965–1967.

24. Muhammad 'Abdalla 'Inan, "Tawr Jadid fi Ta'rikh Urubba al-Siyasi," *RS*, Dec. 21, 1936, 2063–2065; for the same theme, see Diblumasi Kabir ['Inan], " 'Asifa fi al-Sharq al-Aqsa," *RS*, Jan. 4, 1937, 5–7.

25. Diblumasi Kabir ['Inan], "al-Sira' al-Hasim bayna al-Tughyan wa al-Dimuqratiyya," *RS*, July 13, 1936, 1127–1129; Diblumasi Kabir ['Inan], "al-Harb al-Ahliyya al-Isbaniyya: Sira' bayna al-Tughyan wa al-Hurriyya," *RS*, Nov. 9, 1936, 1833–1835; Diblumasi Kabir ['Inan], "Ma'arakat al-Mabadi' wa al-Nuzum," *RS*, Aug. 24, 1936, 1365–1367.

26. Diblumasi Kabir ['Inan], "Ilama Yasiru al-'Alam? Tariq al-Harb wa Tariq al-Salam," *RS*, Nov. 8, 1937, 1804–1806.

27. Diblumasi Kabir ['Inan], "al-Sira' al-Hasim bayna al-Tughyan wa al-Dimuqratiyya," *RS*, July 13, 1936, 1127–1129.

28. See Jaridini's commentaries in *HL*, Apr. 1938, 644–648, and *HL*, May 1938, 765–767.

29. Sami al-Jaridini, "Sijill al-Ayyam," *HL*, July 1938, 1010–1015.

30. Editorial, "Ittijahat al-Siyasa al-Hadira—al-Sira' Bayna Jabhatayn: al-Dimuqratiyya wa al-Fashiyya," *HL*, Aug. 1938, 1089–1092.

31. Ahmad Hasan al-Zayyat, " 'Usbu' Mahmum: bayna al-Dimuqratiyya wa al-Diktaturiyya," *RS*, Sept. 26, 1938, 1561–1562.

32. Ibid.

33. Ibrahim al-Misri, "al-Diktaturiyyat Tuhaddidu al-Duwal al-Dimuqratiyya," *HL*, Nov. 1938, 36–37.

34. "Sawt min Maqburat Tshikuslufakiya," *RS*, Aug. 7, 1939, 1565–1566.

35. Editorial, "al-Thaqafa fi Khidmat al-Siyasa," *RS*, Dec. 5, 1938, 1995.

36. Salama Musa, "al-Dawla al-Jami'a wa al-Dawla al-Dimuqratiyya," *MJ*, Dec. 1938, 65–66.

37. Niqula Yusuf, "Rajul al-Wataniyya Yad'u ila al-Wahda al-'Alamiyya," *MJ*, Nov. 1938, 35–43.

38. Editorial, "al-Sira' bayna al-Diktaturiyya wa al-Dimuqratiyya," *TQ*, Jan. 3, 1939, 8–12. For other uses of the terms in *al-Thaqafa*, see 'Abbas Mahmud al-'Aqqad, "al-'Ibra bi al-Khawatim," *TQ*, Feb. 7, 1939, 1–4; editorial, "al-Mawqif al-Dawli al-Hadir," *TQ*, May 9, 1939, 1–5.

39. Editorial, "al-Sira' bayna al-Diktaturiyya wa al-Dimuqratiyya," *TQ*, Jan. 3, 1939, 8.

40. Ibid., 8–12.

41. Ibid., 10–12.

42. Ibid., 11–12.

43. "Ba'da Intisar Franku," *MJ*, Feb. 1939, 3–5.

44. 'Abbas Mahmud al-'Aqqad, "Athar al-Azma al-Dawliyya fi al-'Alam al-'Arabi," *HL*, Jan. 1939, 257–260.

45. Ibrahim al-Misri, "Almaniya Tazhafu ila al-Sharq," *HL*, Feb. 1939, 399–403.

46. "Sijill al-Ayyam," *HL*, Mar. 1939, 524–528.

47. Niqula al-Haddad, "Tujjar al-Mawt Alladhina Yasuqun al-Shu'ub ila al-Harb," *HL*, Mar. 1939, 537–542.

48. Muhammad 'Awad Muhammad, "al-Ma'sa al-Isbaniyya," *TQ*, Mar. 7, 1939, 1–6.

49. "Mas'alat al-Bahr al-Abyad al-Mutawassit," *TQ*, Apr. 4, 1939, 1–5.

50. Editorial, "al-Ma'sa al-Tshikuslufakiyya," *TQ*, Mar. 28, 1939, 1–5.

51. "Almaniya al-Jadida," *MJ*, Apr. 1939, 3–5.

52. "Masra' Albaniya: Mihnat Umma Saghira Basila," *TQ*, Apr. 18, 1939, 1–5, 42.

53. Muhammad 'Awad Muhammad, "Misr Wasat 'Awasif al-Siyasa al-Dawliyya," *TQ*, Apr. 25, 1939, 1–5, 44.

54. Ahmad Hasan al-Zayyat, "Uqtulu al-Ju' Taqtulu al-Harb," *RS*, Apr. 24, 1939, 800.

55. Editorial, "La Sadaqa li al-Islam ma'a al-Isti'mar," *RS*, May 29, 1939, 1078. For variations on this theme in *al-Risala*, see *RS*, June 12,1939, 1172–1174; *RS*, July 24, 1939, 1468–1470; *RS*, Aug. 7, 1939, 1565–1567; *RS*, Aug. 28, 1939, 1710–1711.

56. Editorial, "al-Khilaf bayna Almaniya wa Buluniya wa Mas'alat Dantsij wa al-Mamir," *TQ*, May 16, 1939, 1–4.

57. Editorial, "Al-Mawqif al-Dawli al-Hadir wa Ihtimalat al-Harb wa al-Salam," *TQ*, May 9, 1939, 1–5.

58. Editorial, "Rusiya al-Sufyatiyya wa Jabhat Muqawamat al-I'tida'," *TQ*, June 13, 1939, 1–4.

59. Ibid.

60. Ibrahim al-Misri, "al-Mawqif al-Siyasi al-Urubbi," *HL*, June 1939, 745–752.

61. Ibid., 747–752.

62. Editorial, "Suhub fi Ufq Urubba: Tawali' al-Harb wa al-Salam," *TQ*, July 11, 1939, 1–4.

63. Editorial, "Bayna al-Ams wa al-Yawm: Kafya Yu'idu al-Ta'rikh Nafsahu," *TQ*, Aug. 15, 1939, 1–4.

64. Editorial, "Qunbulat Musku," *TQ*, Aug. 29, 1939, 1–4.

65. For example, see *MJ*, Mar. 1939, 3–5, 96–100; *MJ*, May 1939, 3–8, 77–79; *MJ*, June 1939, 8–21; *MJ*, Aug. 1939, 40–45.

66. "Mukafahat al-Ta'atul fi al-Wilayat al-Muttahida," *MJ*, May 1939, 3–5; "Mahiyat al-Dimuqratiyya al-Amrikiyya," *MJ*, July 1939, 4–6.

67. See *MJ*, Mar. 1939, 3–5; *MJ*, June 1939, 3–10; *MJ*, Aug. 1939, 3–5, 52–55.

68. Ahmad Hasan al-Zayyat, "Uqtulu al-Ju'," *RS*, Apr. 24, 1939, 800.

69. Editorial, "Mas'alat al-Bahr al-Abyad al-Mutawassit," *TQ*, Apr. 4, 1939, 1–6.

70. Ibid., 5–6; for similar statements, see *TQ*, 25 Apr. 1939, 1–5, 44; *TQ*, July 4, 1939, 3–4.

71. Editorial, "al-Mithaq al-Faransi al-Turki wa al-Tawazun fi Sharqi Bahr al-Abyad al-Mutawassit," *TQ*, July 4, 1939, 1–4.

72. For example, see *HL*, Mar. 1939, 589–591; *HL*, May 1939, 651–656 and 709–711; *HL*, June 1939, 772–776.

73. Muhammad ʿAwad Muhammad, "Misr Wasat ʿAwasif al-Siyasa al-Dawliyya," *TQ*, Apr. 25, 1939, 1–5, 44; editorial, "al-Mithaq al-Faransi al-Turki," *TQ*, July 4, 1939, 1–4.

74. See *HL*, June 1939, 772–776; *HL*, July 1939, 890–892.

75. Niqula al-Haddad, "al-Silm Arjahu: Bahth Yuthbitu Tafawwuq al-Duwal al-Dimuqratiyya," *HL*, May 1939, 637–642.

76. Editorial, "al-Mawqif al-Dawli al-Hadir wa Ihtimalat al-Harb wa al-Salam," *TQ*, May 4, 1939, 1–5.

77. See *HL*, June 1939, 772–776; *HL*, July 1939, 890–892.

78. Ibid., 892.

79. "Imtihan al-Nizam al-Dimuqrati," *MJ*, Mar. 1939, 97–98.

80. Editorial, "al-Harb," *MJ*, Oct. 1939, front page.

81. Niqula Yusuf, "Sira ʿIshrin Sana bayna Rusul al-Salam wa Zabaniyat al-Harb," *MJ*, Oct. 1939, 17–23.

82. Niqula al-Haddad, "Sind al-Dimuqratiyya," *HL*, July 1936, 1014–1020.

83. Ibrahim al-Misri, "al-Shabab wa Ruh al-Quwwa," *HL*, May 1936, 763–768.

84. Ahmad Hasan al-Zayyat, "Min Ahadith al-Shabab: Hawla al-Dimuqratiyya," *RS*, Apr. 26, 1937, 681–682; Ahmad Hasan al-Zayyat, "Ila al-Shabab: Hawla al-Dimuqratiyya Aydan," *RS*, May 3, 1937, 721–722.

85. Khalil Hindawi, "Risalat al-Shabab fi al-Hadir," *RS*, May 31, 1937, 907–908.

86. ʿAbd al-Majid Nafiʿ, "al-Islam wa al-Dimuqratiyya," pt. 1, *RS*, June 7, 1937, 937–940; Nafiʿ, pt. 2, *RS*, June 14, 1937, 982–985.

87. Salama Musa, "Masaʾil al-Shabab al-Misriyyin," *MJ*, Apr. 1938, 83–84.

88. ʿAbd al-Rahman Sidqi, "al-Jamahir ka al-Atfal," *HL*, May 1938, 780.

89. Ibid.

90. Ibrahim al-Misri, "Li man Yaktubu al-Katib fi Misr: al-Jumhur La Yaktarithu li al-Haraka al-Fikriyya," *HL*, July 1938, 988–991; see also Ibrahim al-Misri, "al-Tabaqa al-ʿAliya fi Misr wa Hal Tuʾaddi Wajibuha Nahwa al-Shaʿb?" *HL*, Mar. 1939, 507–510.

91. ʿAbd al-Rahman Sidqi, "al-Jamahir ka al-Atfal," *HL*, May 1938, 779–780; Ibrahim al-Misri, "Li man Yaktubu al-Katib fi Misr: al-Jumhur La Yaktarithu li al-Haraka al-Fikriyya," *HL*, July 1938, 988–991.

92. Taha Husayn, "al-Dimuqratiyya wa al-Taʿlim al-Awwali," *HL*, Jan. 1939, 244–248. The text is republished from Husayn's *Mustaqbal al-Thaqafa fi Misr* (Cairo, 1938), 94–102.

93. "Imtihan al-Nizam al-Dimuqrati," *MJ*, Mar. 1939, 97–98; see also "Shuʿun al-Taʿlim: al-Taʿlim wa al-Dimuqratiyya," *MJ*, Apr. 1939, 76–80.

94. ʿAbbas Mahmud al-ʿAqqad, "Masir al-Madhahib al-Ijtimaʿiyya al-Hadira idha Waqaʿat al-Harb," *HL*, June 1939, 721–725.

95. Niqula al-Haddad, "al-Diktaturiyya Humma ʿAridatun la Khatar minha ʿala al-Dimuqratiyya," *HL*, June 1939, 753–758.

96. 'Abd al-Razzaq al-Sanhuri, "al-Ta'bir 'an Ray' al-Umma," pt. 1, *HL*, Apr. 1938, 601–606; pt. 2, *HL*, May 1938, 734–739.

97. Editorial, "al-Dimuqratiyya wa al-Idha'a," *RS*, June 19, 1939, 1221.

98. Ibid.

99. 'Abbas Mahmud al-'Aqqad, "Islah al-Sihafa," *RS*, Nov. 28, 1938, 1921–1923.

100. Tawfiq al-Hakim, "Hal Fahama Udaba'una al-Mu'asirun Haqiqat Risalatihim?" *TQ*, Apr. 25, 1939, 9; for further discussion of Hakim, see Israel Gershoni, "Confronting Nazism in Egypt: Tawfiq al-Hakim's Anti-Totalitarianism, 1938–1945," *Tel Aviver Jahrbuch für deutsche Geschichte*, 26 (1997), 121–150.

101. Niqula Yusuf, "Rajul al-Wataniyya Yad'u ila al-Wahda al-'Alamiyya," *MJ*, Nov. 1938, 35–43.

102. 'Ali Adham, "al-Niza' al-'Alami," *HL*, Dec. 1938, 165–168.

103. Salama Musa, "Thaqafa Bashariyya am Thaqafat Wataniyya Muta'addida," *MJ*, Feb. 1939, 17–19.

104. Ibid., 18–19.

105. 'Abbas Mahmud al-'Aqqad, "Hukuma 'Alamiyya," *HL*, May 1939, 601–604.

106. Ibrahim al-Misri, "Madhab al-Bashariyya: Bayna al-Dimuqratiyya wa al-Fashism," *HL*, July 1939, 900–905.

Part III Prologue

1. See the Prologue to Part II, "Public Sphere and Public Discourse in Interwar Egypt," for a discussion of the terms *effendi/effendiyya*.

2. In addition to the works of Lucie Ryzova, cited earlier, see Gershoni and Jankowski, *Redefining the Egyptian Nation*, 1–31, and Deeb, *Party Politics in Egypt*, passim. For a study of the phenomenon in another Arab country, see Michael Eppel, "The Elite, the *Effendiyya*, and the Growth of Nationalism and Pan-Arabism in Hashemite Iraq, 1921–1958," *International Journal of Middle East Studies*, 30 (1998), 227–250.

3. Mitchell, *Society of the Muslim Brothers*, is the classic study of the movement's early history. It has recently been supplemented by Brynjar Lia's important study *Society of the Muslim Brothers in Egypt*.

4. See Jankowski, *Egypt's Young Rebels: 'Ali Shalabi, Misr al-Fatah wa Dawruha fi al-Siyasa al-Misriyya, 1933–1941* (Cairo, 1982).

5. See Ahmed Abdalla, *The Student Movement and National Politics in Egypt* (London, 1985), 39–43; Haggai Erlich, *Students and University in Twentieth Century Egyptian Politics* (London, 1989), 95–123.

6. Erlich, *Students*, 123–133; James P. Jankowski, "The Egyptian Blue Shirts and the Egyptian Wafd, 1935–1938," *Middle Eastern Studies*, 6 (1970), 77–95.

Chapter 6

1. In addition to Mitchell's *Society of the Muslim Brothers* and Lia's *Society of the Muslim Brothers in Egypt*, see James Heyworth-Dunne, *Religious and Political Trends in Modern Egypt* (Washington, 1950); I. M. Husaini, *The Moslem Brethren: The Greatest of Modern Islamic Movements* (Beirut, 1956); Christina P. Harris, *Nationalism and Revolution in*

Egypt: The Role of the Muslim Brotherhood (The Hague, 1964); Ramadan, *Tatawwur*, 1:279–330; Rifʿat al-Saʿid, *Hasan al-Banna: Mata . . . Kayfa . . . wa li Madha?* (Cairo, 1977); Charles Wendell, *Five Tracts of Hasan al-Banna' (1906–1949)* (Berkeley, CA, 1978); Zakariya Sulayman Bayumi, *al-Ikhwan al-Muslimun wa al-Jamaʿat al-Islamiyya fi al-Hayat al-Siyasiyya al-Misriyya, 1928–1948* (Cairo, 1979); ʿAbd al-ʿAzim Muhammad Ramadan, *Dirasat fi Taʾrikh Misr al- Muʿasir* (Cairo, 1981), 259–306. See also the memoirs of Hasan al-Banna, *Mudhakkirat al-Daʿwa wa al-Daʿiya* (Cairo, [1943?]), trans. by M. N. Shaikh as *Memoirs of Hasan al-Banna Shaheed* (Karachi, 1981).

2. For example, see Heyworth-Dunne, *Trends*, 23, 86 n. 20; Malcolm Halpern, *The Politics of Social Change in the Middle East and North Africa* (Princeton, NJ, 1963), 135–136; Ramadan, *Tatawwur*, 1:307–315; Tareq Y. Ismael and Jacqueline S. Ismael, *Government and Politics in Islam* (London, 1985) , 77; Shimon Shamir, "The Influence of German National Socialism on Radical Movements in Egypt," in *Germany and the Middle East, 1835–1939*, ed. J. L. Wallach, 200–204 (Tel Aviv, 1976); most recently Matthias Küntzel, *Jihad and Jew-Hatred: Islamism, Nazism and the Roots of 9/11* (New York, 2007), 6–31.

3. For these features, see Mitchell, *Society of the Muslim Brothers*, 163–294, and Lia, *Society of the Muslim Brothers in Egypt*, 161–197 (both of whom do not go so far as to characterize the movement as "fascist").

4. Hasan al-Banna, "Hal Nahnu Qawm ʿAmaliyun?" *JIM*, Jumada al-Ula 19, 1353, as quoted in Bayumi, *al-Ikhwan al-Muslimun*, 192–193.

5. See ibid., 192–195. Bayumi also went on to point out the criticism and rejection of fascist ideology found in brotherhood texts; see 194–197.

6. See Gershoni and Jankowski, *Redefining the Egyptian Nation*, 79–96; Israel Gershoni, "Rejecting the West: The Image of the West in the Teachings of the Muslim Brotherhood, 1928–1939," in Dann, *The Great Powers in the Middle East, 1919–1939*, 370–390.

7. Among other works, see ʿAwatif ʿAbd al-Rahman, *Misr wa Filastin* (Cairo, 1980); James Jankowski, "Egyptian Responses to the Palestine Problem in the Interwar Period," *International Journal of Middle East Studies*, 12 (1980), 1–38; Thomas Mayer, *Egypt and the Palestine Question, 1936–1945* (Berlin, 1983); Israel Gershoni, "The Muslim Brothers and the Arab Revolt in Palestine, 1936–1939," *Middle Eastern Studies*, 22 (1986), 367–397; Lia, *Society of the Muslim Brothers in Egypt*, 235–247; Abd Al-Fattah Muhammad El-Awaisi, *The Muslim Brothers and the Palestine Question, 1928–1947* (London, 1998) 34–101.

8. "Notes on Wilhelm Stellbogen," Oct. 23, 1939, FO, WO 208:502, as cited in Lia, *Society of the Muslim Brothers in Egypt*, 179–180.

9. "The Ikhwan al-Muslimin Reconsidered," Dec. 14, 1942, FO 141:838 as quoted in Lia, *Society of the Muslim Brothers in Egypt*, 176.

10. Hasan al-Banna, *Daʿwatuna* (Cairo, 1937), 11–14.

11. Ibid., 14–15.

12. Hasan al-Banna, *Ila Ayy Shay' Nadʿu al-Nas?* (Cairo, 1936), 20–30.

13. Banna, *Daʿwatuna*, 15.

14. Ibid., 17–18.

15. Ibid., 18–19.

16. Ibid., 19.

17. Hasan al-Banna, *Nahwa al-Nur* (Cairo, 1937), 11.

18. Ibid., 15.

19. Hasan al-Banna, "al-Ikhwan al-Muslimun fi ʿAshr Sanawat," *ND*, Dhu al-Hijja 17, 1357, 3–34; later published as a pamphlet entitled *Risalat al-Muʾtamar al-Khamis* (Cairo, 1940).

20. Banna, "al-Ikhwan al-Muslimun fi ʿAshr Sanawat," 26–27.

21. Ibid., 32–35.

22. Ibid., 33–34.

23. Hasan al-Banna, "Ila al-Shabab," *ND*, Dhu al-Hijja 5, 1358, 9–13; later published in pamphlet form under the title *Ila al-Shabab* (Cairo, 1941). Banna expounded further on these themes in an address delivered at the Cairo headquarters of the Brothers on Apr. 4, 1939, also published in *ND*; see Hasan al-Banna, "al-Khitab al-Jamiʿ alladhi Alqahu Fa-dilat al-Murshid al-ʿAmm," *ND*, Dhu al-Hijja 5, 1358 (Jan. 15, 1940), 1–7.

24. Banna, "Ila al-Shabab," 9–13.

25. Muhammad al-Ghazzali, "al-Ikhwan al-Muslimun—Haqiqat al-Wataniyya bayna Hadarat al-Gharb," *ND*, Rabiʿ al-Thani 3, 1358, 6–8.

26. Ibid.

27. Salih Mustafa ʿAshmawi, "al-Kufr Milla Wahida wa al-Istiʿmar Dhull Wahid," *ND*, Muharram 29, 1358, 3–5.

28. Ibid., 4–5.

29. Ibid., 5.

30. Jankowski, *Egypt's Young Rebels*, 39–40.

31. Ibid., 40, 74–76.

32. Banna, "al-Ikhwan al-Muslimun fi ʿAshr Sanawat," 31–32.

33. Salih Mustafa ʿAshmawi, "Ila Allazina Yuriduna min al-Ikhwan an Yattahidu maʿa Misr al-Fatah," *ND*, Jumada al-Ula 1, 1358, 5, 10.

34. ʿAbd al-Hafiz Muhammad ʿAbd al-Jawad, "al-Ikhwan al-Muslimun wa Misr al-Fatah," *ND*, Ramadan 8, 1357, 7–10. On this issue, see also Bayumi, 236–244; Ramadan, *Tatawwur*, 307–315.

35. *ND*, Ramadan 15, 1357, as cited in El-Awaisi, *Muslim Brothers and the Palestine Question*, 70.

36. See ibid., 70–71.

37. *ND*, Dhu al-Hijja 3, 1357, as cited in ibid., 71.

38. Ibid., 74–75.

39. Hasan al-Banna, *Majmuʿat Rasaʾil al-Imam al-Shahid Hasan al-Banna*, as quoted in El-Awaisi, *Muslim Brothers and the Palestine Question*, 6.

40. Banna, *Daʿwatuna*, 19.

41. Muhammad al-Ghazzali, "al-Ikhwan al-Muslimun—Haqiqat al-Wataniyya bayna Hadarat al-Gharb," *ND*, Rabiʿ al-Thani 3, 1358, 6–8.

42. El-Awaisi, *Muslim Brothers and the Palestine Question*, 7, 203.

43. See Bayumi, *al-Ikhwan al-Muslimun*, 33–96; Heyworth-Dunne, *Trends*, 11–35; Mitchell, *Society of the Muslim Brothers*, 5–11; Lia, *Society of the Muslim Brothers in Egypt*, 29–30, 55–60, 163–165, 215–216.

44. Muhibb al-Din al-Khatib, "Watan Wahid, Umma Wahida, Lugha Wahida," *FH*, Muharram 22, 1357, 3–4; Khatib, "al-Qawmiyya al-ʿArabiyya wa al-Qawmiyya al-Almaniyya," *FH*, Rajab 20, 1357, 3–4.

45. Khatib, "Watan Wahid, Umma Wahida, Lugha Wahida," 3–4.

46. Khatib, "al-Qawmiyya al-ʿArabiyya wa al-Qawmiyya al-Almaniyya," 4.

47. Ibid.

48. Khatib, "al-Qawmiyya al-ʿArabiyya wa al-Qawmiyya al-Almaniyya," 4. See also his editorials "Faragh fi Hayat al-Qawmiyya al-ʿArabiyya," *FH*, Jumada al-Ula 2, 1357, 3–4, and "Taʿawum al-Natiqin bi al-Dad fi ʿIshrin Sana," *FH*, Jumada al-Akhira 24, 1358, 3–4.

49. Khatib, "Watan Wahid, Umma Wahida, Lugha Wahida," 3–4.

50. Muhibb al-Din al-Khatib, "Mawqif al-Kutlatayn al-Dawliyyatayn min al-Qawmiyya al-ʿArabiyya," *FH*, Jumada al-Ula 2, 1358, 3–4. See also Khatib, "Taʿawum al-ʿArab li Inqadh Qawmiyyatihim," *FH*, Jumada al-Ula 25, 1358, 3–4.

51. Banna, "al-Ikhwan al-Muslimun fi ʿAshr Sanawat," 21–24.

52. Hasan al-Banna, "Kalimat al-Usbuʿ," *ND*, Shawwal 13, 1357, 5.

53. Ibid., 4–5.

54. Ibid., 3–6.

55. Ibid., 4.

56. Banna, "al-Ikhwan al-Muslimun fi ʿAshr Sanawat," 21.

57. Ibid., 22.

58. Ibid., 22–23; for similar statements, see also "Fi Muhit al-Ikhwan al-Muslimin," *ND*, Muharram 1, 1358, 25–26; Salih Mustafa ʿAshmawi, "Siyasatuna," *ND*, Rabiʿ al-Awwal 30, 1357, 6.

59. Banna, "al-Ikhwan al-Muslimun fi ʿAshr Sanawat," 19–21.

60. *ND*, Rabiʿ al-Awwal 30, 1357, 3–5.

61. Banna, "al-Ikhwan al-Muslimun fi ʿAshr Sanawat," 13–14.

62. Discussed in Lia, *Society of the Muslim Brothers in Egypt*, 248–251.

63. See Jankowski, *Egypt's Young Rebels*, 37–43.

64. See Mitchell, *Society of the Muslim Brothers*, 17–18, and Lia, *Society of the Muslim Brothers in Egypt*, 247–256.

65. "Special Comprehensive Report [*Taqrir Ijmali Khass*]," as quoted in Lia, *Society of the Muslim Brothers in Egypt*, 253–254.

66. Hasan al-Banna, "Wajibat al-Ikhwan fi al-ʿAdat wa al-Libas wa al-Manzar," as quoted in ibid., 255.

67. Mitchell, *Society of the Muslim Brothers*, 22–23; Lia, *Society of the Muslim Brothers in Egypt*, 261–266.

68. Heyworth-Dunne, *Trends*, 39–41; Mitchell, *Society of the Muslim Brothers*, 6–27; Lia, *Society of the Muslim Brothers in Egypt*, 268–269.

69. Killearn to Eden, June 16, 1943, FO 371:35536, J 2855:2:16.

70. Lia, *Society of the Muslim Brothers in Egypt*, 172–177.

71. On this body, see ibid., 177–181; El-Awaisi, *Muslim Brothers and the Palestine Question*, 110–119; Mitchell, *Society of the Muslim Brothers*, 30–32 (who dates its inception later in the war).

72. See Lia, *Society of the Muslim Brothers in Egypt*, 151–154.

73. Kellar to Loxley, July 19, 1943, FO 371:35536, J 3177:2:16.

74. Ibid.

Chapter 7

1. For studies of the movement, see Jankowski, *Egypt's Young Rebels*; Shalabi, *Misr al-Fatah*; Ramadan, *Tatawwur*, 1:175–277; Rifʿat al-Saʿid, *Ahmad Husayn: Kalimat wa Mawaqif* (Cairo, 1979). The most important accounts by the movement's leader Ahmad Husayn are his autobiographical *Imani* (Cairo, 1936), 2d ed. (Cairo, 1946) (Citations are to both editions); Husayn, *Murafaʿat al-Raʾis Ahmad Husayn fi ʿAhd Hukumat al-Wafd* (Cairo, 1938); Husayn, *Nisf Qarn Maʿa al-ʿUruba wa Qadiyyat Filastin* (Beirut, 1971).

2. For studies dealing totally or partially with youth movements and fascist influence in other eastern Arab lands in the 1930s, see Hanna Batatu, *The Old Social Classes and the Revolutionary Movements in Iraq* (Princeton, NJ, 1978); John P. Entelis, *Pluralism and Party Transformation in Lebanon: al-Kataʾib, 1936–1970* (Leiden, 1974); Eppel, "The Elite, the *Effendiyya*," 227–250; Philip S. Khoury, *Syria and the French Mandate: The Politics of Arab Nationalism, 1920–1945* (Princeton, NJ, 1987); Reeva S. Simon, *Iraq Between the Two World Wars: The Creation and Implementation of a Nationalist Ideology* (New York, 1986); Thompson, *Colonial Citizens*; Watenpaugh, *Being Modern in the Middle East*; Peter Wien, *Iraqi Arab Nationalism: Authoritarian, Totalitarian, and Pro-Fascist Inclinations, 1932–1941* (New York, 2006); Meir Zamir, *Lebanon's Quest: The Road to Statehood, 1926–1939* (New York, 1997); Labib Zuwiyya Yamak, *The Syrian Social Nationalist Party: An Ideological Analysis* (Cambridge, MA, 1966); Götz Nordbruch, *Nazism in Syria and Lebanon: The Ambivalence of the German Option, 1933–1945* (London, 2009).

3. *MSA*, Oct. 21, 1933, 7 (italics in the original).

4. Ibid.

5. *MSA*, Oct. 21, 1933, 5.

6. Ibid.

7. *MSA*, Jan. 14, 1935, 2. For a similar statement from a speech of 1936, see Husayn, *Imani* (1946 ed.), 274–275.

8. *MSA*, Mar. 31, 1934, 13.

9. The phrase is that of Hamada al-Nahil writing in *MTH*, Apr. 24, 1937, 8, discussed further below.

10. Stein Ugelvik Larsen, "Was There Fascism Outside Europe? Diffusion from Europe and Domestic Impulses," in *Fascism Outside Europe*, ed. Stein Ugelvik Larsen (New York, 2001), 727, 732.

11. U.S. National Archives, Microfilm Series T-120 (*Deutsches Auswärtiges Amt*), roll 4873, L310544–L310545.

12. Discussed in Williams, *Mussolini's Propaganda*, 121–122, 131.

13. *AH*, June 23, 1936, 2.

14. See *BL*, June 24, 1936, 1, for an account of the subsequent furor.

15. See *AH*, June 24, 1936, 9; ibid., June 25, 1936, 9; ibid., July 10, 1936, 10; ibid., Oct. 10, 1936, 10; Husayn, *Murafaʿat al-Raʾis*, 110–124; Husayn, *Imani* (1946 ed.), 281–284.

16. *JMF*, Apr. 12, 1939, 6.

17. Muhammad Subayh, *Min al-ʿAlamayn* (Cairo, 1963), 23. For the "Gentleman's Agreement" and its effect in reducing Italian anti-British propaganda in the Middle East in 1938–1939, see Williams, *Mussolini's Propaganda*, 53, 87–88.

18. A similar phenomenon has been observed for Iraq in the 1930s, where Peter Wien has noted that "Germany was only one reference for nationalists among others"; Wien, *Iraqi Arab Nationalism*, 2.

19. Fathi Radwan, *Taʾrikh Ghandi* (Cairo, 1932).

20. From a speech of 1935, as cited in Husayn, *Imani* (1946 ed.), 162–163.

21. Fathi Radwan, *Difalira* (Cairo, 1937), 6.

22. Muhammad Subayh, *al-Yaban: Bilad al-Shams al-Mushriqa* (Cairo, 1937), 3.

23. *JMF*, Apr. 14, 1938, 4.

24. *JMF*, July 18, 1938, 3.

25. From a speech of Mar. 1936, as quoted in Husayn, *Imani* (1936 ed.), 315.

26. *JMF*, Mar. 19, 1938, 5.

27. Ibid.

28. *MSA*, Dec. 30, 1933, 3.

29. *MSA*, Oct. 6, 1934, 5.

30. *MSA*, Aug. 25, 1934, 5.

31. Ibid. See also ibid., Sept. 1, 1934, 5; ibid., Sept. 8, 1934, 9.

32. *AH*, Sept. 27, 1934, 8; *MSA*, Sept. 28, 1934, 9.

33. Husayn, *Murafaʿat al-Raʾis*, 128–131; idem, *Imani* (1946 ed.), 155.

34. *BL*, Aug. 17, 1935, 4.

35. See the editorials in *Wadi al-Nil* (an Alexandria daily briefly associated with the movement in the mid-1930s), July 10, 1935, 1; ibid., July 24, 1935, 1; ibid., Aug. 8, 1935, 1; ibid., Aug. 29, 1935, 1.

36. Quoted in *AH*, Oct. 3, 1935, 1.

37. See *MSA*, Nov. 12, 1935, 4.

38. Fathi Radwan, *Musulini* (Cairo, 1937), 4–6.

39. Ibid., 157–160.

40. Radwan, *Difalira*, 3–4.

41. Muhammad Subayh, *Hitlar* (Cairo, 1937), 4–88.

42. Ibid., 54–57, 120–145.

43. Ibid., 145–150.

44. From an interview by an unnamed spokesman of the society with *MLM*, June 29, 1936, 7.

45. *MSA*, Oct. 21, 1933, 5.

46. For Young Egypt's opposition to the treaty in 1936, see *AH*, Sept. 6, 1936, 11; ibid., Sept. 23, 1936, 9; ibid., Oct. 26, 1936, 10; ibid., Nov. 1, 1936, 10; Ahmad Husayn, *Ra'y Jam'iyyat Misr al-Fatah fi Mu'ahadat Sanat 1936* (Cairo, 1936).

47. *MTH*, Apr. 24, 1937, 8. The essay carried a disclaimer to the effect that the views in it did not represent the position of the Young Egypt Party.

48. Ibid.

49. See Ramadan, *Tatawwur*, 1:220–227.

50. *JMF*, Mar. 31, 1938, 1.

51. *JMF*, Apr. 4, 1938, 2.

52. *JMF*, July 18, 1938, 5.

53. *JMF*, Jan. 24, 1938, 11.

54. Ibid.

55. *JMF*, Apr. 14, 1938, 4.

56. *JMF*, Jan. 24, 1938, 11.

57. *JMF*, Apr. 14, 1938, 5;

58. Ibid.

59. *JMF*, Feb. 21, 1938, 4.

60. *JMF*, Mar. 14, 1938, 3.

61. *JMF*, Aug. 23, 1938, 13–14.

62. Ibid.

63. In his interview with *Lavoro Fascista* as reported in *JMF*, Aug. 1, 1938, 2.

64. *JMF*, Aug. 23, 1938, 14–15.

65. Ibid., 15–16.

66. *JMF*, Mar. 7, 1938, 8.

67. For an account of Badawi's early career and his enthusiasm for fascism, see his autobiography *Sirat Hayati* (Beirut, 2000), 1:86–149.

68. *JMF*, Apr. 1, 1938, 3, 7; ibid., Apr. 11, 1938, 4, 10; ibid., May 2, 1938, 4, 11.

69. *JMF*, Aug. 1, 1938, 4.

70. *JMF*, Aug. 11, 1938, 4.

71. *JMF*, Aug. 15, 1938, 4, 9.

72. *JMF*, Sept. 1, 1938, 5.

73. *JMF*, Sept. 8, 1938, 6.

74. *JMF*, Aug. 29, 1938, 4.

75. See *JMF*, Oct. 29, 1938, 3; ibid., Oct. 31, 1938, 3; ibid., Nov. 3, 1938, 6–7.

76. *JMF*, July 15, 1939, 1.

77. *JMF*, July 29, 1939, 3, 5.

78. *JMF*, July 10, 1939, 9.

79. *JMF*, Aug. 7, 1939, 2.

80. See Jankowski, *Egypt's Young Rebels*, 39.

81. *JMF*, July 27, 1939, 1, 4.

82. *JMF*, Feb. 28, 1938, 1.

83. *JMF*, Apr. 1, 1938, 3, 7.

84. *JMF*, June 29, 1938, 3.

85. *JMF*, Dec. 8, 1938, 11.

86. See *JMF*, May 15, 1939, 7.

87. *JMF*, Mar. 14, 1938, 2.

88. Ibid., 3.

89. Ibid., 3.

90. *JMF*, Sept. 26, 1938, 4.

91. *JMF*, Sept. 29, 1938, 1.

92. *JMF*, Sept. 24, 1938, 2.

93. *JMF*, Nov. 5, 1938, 5.

94. *JMF*, Oct. 8, 1938, 6.

95. *JMF*, Oct. 10, 1938, 3.

96. For specifics, see *JMF*, Sept. 29, 1938, 7; ibid., Oct. 1, 1938, 4–5; ibid., Oct. 8, 1938, 7; ibid., Oct. 13, 1938, 1, 5, 9.

97. *JMF*, Nov. 3, 1938, 3; ibid., Nov. 10, 1938, 6; ibid., Nov. 19, 1938, 4; ibid., Nov. 28, 1938, 5.

98. *JMF*, Apr. 10, 1939, 1.

99. *JMF*, Apr. 12, 1939, 6.

100. *JMF*, Apr. 10, 1939, 1.

101. *JMF*, Apr. 12, 1939. 6.

102. Husayn's open letter to Hitler was published, in both Arabic and French, in *JMF*, July 6, 1939, 1–4. It was reprinted in pamphlet form, with texts in Arabic and English, after the war as Ahmed Hussein, *Message to Hitler!* (New York, 1947).

103. Ibid., 6.

104. Ibid., 8–9.

105. *JMF*, Aug. 31, 1, 4.

106. Ibid., 5.

107. *JMF*, Aug. 31, 1939, 3.

108. *JMF*, Sept. 2, 1939, 3.

109. *JMF*, Aug. 24, 1939, 12.

110. *JMF*, Aug. 28, 1939, 1.

111. *JMF*, Sept. 2, 1939, 4.

112. *JMF*, Sept. 13, 1939, 4.

113. See *JMF*, Jan. 15, 1940, 3; ibid., Jan. 25, 1940, 5; ibid., Jan. 2, 1941, 8.

114. The new program was first published in *JMF*, Mar. 18, 1940, 4–8.

115. See Lampson to Eden, Apr. 29, 1941, FO 407:225, 29–34; Cairo to Foreign Office, May 27, 1941, FO 371:27429, J 1646:18:16; Lampson to Eden, June 2, 1941, FO 371:27431, J 1737:18:16; Lampson to Eden, Feb. 12, 1942, FO 403:466, 16237, 5–10.

116. Details in Lampson to Eden, June 7, 1941, 371:27431, J 1805:18:16; Lampson to Eden, June 17, 1941, FO 371:27431, J 2157:18:16; Lampson to Eden, July 23, 1941, FO 371:27431, J 2418:18:16; Husayn, *Imani* (1946 ed.), 323; Ahmad Husayn, *Wara' al-Qudban* (Cairo, 1949), 5–10.

Conclusion

1. For example, see Majid Khadduri, *Independent Iraq: A Study in Iraqi Politics Since 1932* (London, 1951), 127–205; Elie Kedourie, "Pan-Arabism and British Policy," in his *The Chatham House Version and other Middle Eastern Studies* (London, 1970), 213–235; Kedourie, "The Kingdom of Iraq: a Retrospect," ibid., 236–285; Mohammad A. Tarbush, *The Role of the Military in Politics: A Case Study of Iraq to 1941* (London, 1982); Phebe Marr, *The Modern History of Iraq* (Boulder, 1985); Marr, "The Development of Nationalist Ideology in Iraq, 1921–1941," *The Muslim World*, 75, no. 2 (1985), 85–101; Simon, *Iraq Between the Two World Wars*; Walid Hamdi, *Rashid Ali al-Gailani and the Nationalist Movement in Iraq, 1939–1941* (London, 1987); Liora Lukitz, *Iraq: The Search for National Identity* (London, 1995).

2. For examples, see A. L. Tibawi, *A Modern History of Syria Including Lebanon and Palestine* (London, 1969), 363–378; Zuwiyya Yamak, *The Syrian Social Nationalist Party*; Itamar Rabinovich, "Germany and the Syrian Political Scene in the late 1930s," in *Germany and the Middle East, 1835–1939*, ed. J. L. Wallach, 191–198 (Tel Aviv, 1975); Khoury, *Syria and the French Mandate*, 395–580, 626–630; Miloš Mendel and Zdeněk Müller, "Fascist Tendencies in the Levant in the 1930s and 1940s," *Archív Orientálni* 55 (1987), 1–17; Zamir, *Lebanon's Quest*, 233–239; Shafiq Jaha, *al-Haraka al-'Arabiyya al-Sirriyya: Jama'at al-Kitab al-Ahmar, 1935–1945* (Beirut, 2004).

3. See 'Ali Muhafaza, *al-'Alaqat al-Almaniyya al-Filastiniyya, 1841–1945* (Beirut, 1981); Martin Kramer, the chapter entitled "Congresses of Collaboration: Islam and the Axis, 1938–1945," in his *Islam Assembled: The Advent of the Muslim Congresses* (New York, 1986), 157–165; Bernard Lewis, the chapter entitled "The Nazis and the Palestine Question" in his *Semites and Anti-Semites: An Inquiry into Conflict and Prejudice* (New York, 1986), 140–163; Philip Mattar, *The Mufti of Jerusalem: Hajj Amin al-Husayni and the Palestinian National Movement* (New York, 1988); Zvi Elpeleg, trans. by David Harvey, *The Grand Mufti: Haj Amin al-Hussaini, Founder of the Palestinian National Movement* (London, 1993); 'Abd al-Rahman 'Abd al-Ghayni, *Almaniya al-Naziyya wa-Filastin, 1933–1945* (Beirut, 1995), 187–405; Klaus-Michale Mallmann and Martin Cüppers, *Halbmond und Hakenkreuz: Das Dritte Reich, die Araber und Palästina* (Darmstadt, 2006); cf. Klaus Gensicke, *Der Mufti von Jerusalem und die Nationalsozialisten: Eine politische Biographie Amin el-Husseinis* (Darmstadt, 2007).

4. See E. Marston, "Fascist Tendencies in Pre-War Arab Politics: A Study of Three Arab Political Movements," *Middle East Forum*, 35 (1959), 19–35; Tillmann, *Deutschlands Araberpolitik im Zweiten Weltkrieg*; Robert L. Melka, "The Axis and the Arab Middle East, 1930–1945," Ph.D. diss., University of Minnesota, 1966; Hirszowicz, *The Third Reich and the Arab East*; Be'eri, *Army Officers in Arab Politics and Society*; Schröder, *Deutschland und der Mittlere Osten*; Elie Kedourie, *Politics in the Middle East* (New York, 1992).

5. See, for example, Sylvia Haim, *Arab Nationalism: An Anthology* (Berkeley, CA, 1962), 36–72; Lewis, *Semites and Anti-Semites*, 140–163; Yehoshua Porath, *In Search of Arab Unity, 1930–1945* (London, 1986).

6. The phrase is that of Francis Nicosia in his "Arab Nationalism and National Socialist Germany, 1933–1939: Ideological and Strategic Incompatibility," *International Journal of Middle East Studies*, 12 (1980), 351–372. See also Nicosia, *The Third Reich and the Palestine Question* (London, 1985); Wild, "National Socialism in the Arab Near East"; Francis R. Nicosia, "Fritz Grobba and the Middle East Policy of the Third Reich," in *National and International Politics in the Middle East: Essays in Honour of Elie Kedourie*, ed. Edward Ingram, 206–228 (London, 1986); Hillgruber, "The Third Reich and the Near and Middle East," 274–282.

7. For works in this vein, see Christoph Schumann, *Radikalnationalismus in Syrien und Libanon: Politische Sozialisation und Elitenbildung, 1930–1958* (Hamburg, 2001); Schumann, "The Generation of Broad Expectations: Nationalism, Education, and Autobiography in Syria and Lebanon, 1930–1958," *Die Welt des Islams*, 41 (2001), 174–205; Schumann, "The Experience of Organized Nationalism: Radical Discourse and Political Socialization in Syria and Lebanon, 1930–1958," in *From the Syrian Land to the States of Syria and Lebanon*, ed. Thomas Philipp and Christoph Schumann, 343–358 (Würzburg, 2004); Thompson, *Colonial Citizens*, 191–196; Keith David Watenpaugh, "Steel Shirts, White Badges and the Last Qabaday: Fascism, Urban Violence and Civic Identity in Aleppo Under French Rule," in *France, Syrie et Liban, 1918–1946—les ambiguïtés et les dynamiques de la relation mandataire*, ed. N. Méouchy, 325–347 (Damascus, 2003); Watenpaugh, *Being Modern in the Middle East*, 255–278.

8. Orit Bashkin, "Protecting Pluralism, 1931–1945," in *The Other Iraq: Pluralism and Culture in Hashemite Iraq* (Stanford, CA, 2008), 52–86.

9. Wien, *Iraqi Arab Nationalism*, 78, 113–115.

10. See Zamir, *Lebanon's Quest*, 84–233, 240–247; Eyal Zisser, "Writing a Constitution: Constitutional Debates in Syria in the Mandate Period," in *Liberal Thought in the Eastern Mediterranean: Late 19th Century Until the 1960s*, ed. Christoph Schumann, 195–215 (Leiden/Boston, 2008).

11. Manfred Sing, "Between Lights and Hurricanes: Sami al-Kayyali's Review *al-Hadith* as a Forum of Modern Arabic Literature and Liberal Islam," in *The Middle Eastern Press as a Forum for Literature*, ed. Horst Unbehaun, 119–141 (Frankfurt, 2004); Sing, "Illiberal Metamorphoses of a Liberal Discourse: The Case of Syrian Intellectual Sami al-Kayyali (1898–1972)," in Schumann, *Liberal Thought*, 293–322.

12. See Khoury, *Syria and the French Mandate*; Zamir, *Lebanon's Quest*; Thompson, *Colonial Citizens*; Kais M. Firro, *Inventing Lebanon: Nationalism and the State under the Mandate* (London, 2003).

13. Discussed in Nordbruch, *Nazism in Syria and Lebanon*, 37–38, 138.

14. René Wildangel, *Zwischen Achse und Mandatsmacht: Palästina und der Nationalsozialismus* (Berlin, 2007). See also Mustafa Kabha, " 'My Enemy's Enemy—A Friend': Attitudes of the Palestinian National Movement Toward Fascism and Nazism, 1925–1945," *Zmanim*, 17 (1999), 79–86 [Hebrew]; Mustafa Kabha, *Writing Up a Storm: The Palestinian Press as Shaper of Public Opinion, 1929–1939* (London, 2007), 141–154, 252–254. Additional contributions to the new narrative concerning the entire Arab Middle East

can be found in Gerhard Höpp, Peter Wien, and René Wildangel, eds., *Blind für die Geschichte? Arabische Begegnungen mit dem Nationalsozialismus* (Berlin, 2004).

15. See Nordbruch, *Nazism in Syria and Lebanon*, 34–42, 68–70, 112–114, 123–126, 138–140; Götz Nordbruch, "Bread, Freedom, Independence—Opposition to Nazi Germany in Lebanon and Syria and the Struggle for a Just Order," in "Intellectual History in Middle Eastern Studies," guest editors Amy Singer and Israel Gershoni, special issue, *Comparative Studies of South Asia, Africa and the Middle East*, 28, no. 3 (2008), 416–422.

16. Nordbruch, *Nazism in Syria and Lebanon*, 69–70, 79, 112–114, 123, 125–126, 139–140; Nordbruch, "Bread, Freedom, Independence," 420–422.

17. Ra'if Khuri, "Taqrir al-Lajna al-Tahdiriyya fi Mu'tamar Mukafahat al-Fashistiyya," *al-Tali'a*, May 1939, 358, as cited in Nordbruch, "Bread, Freedom, Independence," 421–422.

18. Nordbruch, "Bread, Freedom, Independence." See also Nordbruch, "Defending the French Revolution during World War II: Raif Khoury and the Intellectual Challenge of Nazism in the Levant," *Mediterranean Historical Review*, 21, no. 2 (Dec. 2006), 219–238.

19. Khalid Bakdash, *al-'Arab wa al-Harb al-Ahliyya fi Isbaniya* (Damascus, 1937), 33. We thank Götz Nordbruch for providing this source.

20. Stanley Payne, *A History of Fascism, 1914–1945* (Madison, WI, 1995), 352.

21. Ibid., 352–353.

22. Ibid., 352.

23. See the positive reaction to Küntzel's book in Jeffrey Goldberg, "Seeds of Hate," *New York Times*, Jan. 6, 2008; and Stephen Schwartz's enthusiastic review, *Weekly Standard*, 013, no. 31 (Apr. 28, 2008). Schwartz goes as far as to claim that "the Muslim Brotherhood *did* [emphasis in original] become an open ally of Hitler in seeking enhanced German influence in the Islamic world." In his foreword to the book, Jeffrey Herf endorses the book's conclusions about the Muslim Brothers, stating that "[i]n ideology and organization, it [the Egyptian Muslim Brothers] echoed themes of European fascism and Nazism" that "all created points of commonality with fascism and Nazism"; Matthias Küntzel, *Jihad and Jew-Hatred: Islamism, Nazism, and the Roots of 9/11* (New York, 2007), x.

24. Küntzel, *Jihad and Jew-Hatred*, xxiii.

25. Ibid., 3.

26. Ibid., 6–60

27. In reaching the conclusion that Nazi-inspired anti-Semitism was appropriated from Nazi Germany, the work ignores the findings of one of its main sources. As noted in Chapter 6, El-Awaisi's study of the pro-Palestinian and anti-Jewish activism of the Muslim Brothers in the later 1930s makes no mention of Nazi influence on the Muslim Brothers in the later 1930s and contains little that echoes the deep-seated and comprehensive anti-Semitism of the Nazis. Rooted in primary sources, El-Awaisi's conclusion is worth citing: "The hostility of the Society to the Jews had its origins in a particular reading of the Qur'an, the Prophetic Tradition, the Prophetic Biography, Islamic history, and modern

history. Nevertheless, the Society emphasised the possibility of co-existing peacefully with the Jews, were it not for the events in Palestine" (El-Awaisi, *The Muslim Brothers and the Palestine Question*, 203).

28. Küntzel, 31–46.

29. Ibid., 37.

30. Ibid., 25–37.

31. Banna, *Daʿwatuna*, 19, as translated and quoted in Wendell, *Five Tracts of Hasan Al-Banna'*, 54.

32. Küntzel, 27–28, citing Edmund Cao-Van-Hoa, *"Der Feind meines Feindes . . . ,"* *Darstellungen des nationalsozialistischen Deutschland in ägyptischen Schriften* (Frankfurt-am-Main, 1990), 98. The latter work, rather than demonstrating an ideological predisposition toward Nazism on the part of Egyptians, presents certain Egyptian attitudes toward Nazi Germany as based on the tactical and instrumental "the-enemy-of-my-enemy-is-my-friend" grounds characteristic of the old narrative.

33. Stanley Payne's admonition at the close of a chapter considering "Fascism Outside Europe?" is pertinent: "Thus it seems that the full characteristics of European fascism could not be reproduced on a significant scale outside Europe. . . . It is consequently doubtful that a typology derived from European fascism can be applied to non-European movements or regimes with full accuracy or specificity. . . . [F]ascism was a historical phenomenon primarily limited to Europe during the era of world wars." Payne, *History of Fascism*, 353–354.

34. Saul Friedländer, *Nazi Germany and the Jews: The Years of Persecution, 1933–1939* (London, 1997), 73–112.

35. Marc Bloch, *The Historian's Craft* (New York, 1953), 31. Marc Bloch was himself a victim of Nazism.

Bibliography

Archival Repositories and Collections

Bourne, Kenneth, D. Cameron Watt, and Michael Partridge, general eds. *British Documents on Foreign Affairs: Reports and Papers from the Foreign Office Confidential Print.* Pt. 2, ser. G, *Africa, 1914–1939: Egypt and the Sudan,* edited by Peter Woodward. 20 vols. Lanham, MD: University Publications of America, 1994–1995 [BDFA].

Great Britain. Public Record Office. Records of the Foreign Office [FO 371].

United States National Archives. Microfilm ser. T-120. *Deutsches Auswärtiges Amt.*

Egyptian Periodicals Consulted

al-Ahram
al-Balagh
al-Fath
al-Hilal
al-Ithnayn wa al-Dunya
Jaridat al-Ikhwan al-Muslimin
Jaridat Misr al-Fatah
al-Jihad
al-Majalla al-Jadida
Majallat al-Lata'if al-Musawwara
Majallat al-Sarkha
Majallat al-Thughr
al-Misri
al-Muqattam
al-Musawwar
al-Nadhir
al-Risala

Ruz al-Yusuf
al-Thaqafa

Arabic Books and Articles Cited

ʿAbd al-Ghayni, ʿAbd al-Rahman. *Almaniya al-Naziyya wa Filastin, 1933–1945.* Beirut, 1995.

ʿAbd al-Nasir, Jamal. *Falsafat al-Thawra.* Cairo, 1954. Translated as *The Philosophy of the Revolution.* Buffalo, 1959.

ʿAbd al-Rahman, ʿAwatif. *Misr wa Filastin.* Cairo, 1980.

ʿAtiq, Wajih. *Al-Jaysh al-Misri wa al-Alman fi Athnaʾ Harb al-ʿAlamiyya al-Thaniyya.* Cairo, 1993.

———. *Al-Malik Faruq wa Almaniya al-Naziyya: Khams Sanawat min al-ʿAlaqat al-Sirriyya.* Cairo, 1992.

Badawi, ʿAbd al-Rahman. *Sirat Hayati.* 2 vols. Beirut, 2000.

al-Banna, Hasan. *Daʿwatuna.* Cairo, 1937.

———. *Ila al-Shabab.* Cairo, 1941.

———. *Ila Ayy Shayʾ Nadʿu al-Nas?* Cairo, 1936.

———. *Mudhakkirat al-Daʿwa wa al-Daʿiya.* Cairo, [1943?]. Translated by M. N. Shaikh as *Memoirs of Hasan al-Banna Shaheed.* Karachi, 1981.

———. *Nahwa al-Nur.* Cairo, 1937.

Bayumi, Zakariya Sulayman. *al-Ikhwan al-Muslimun wa al-Jamaʿat al-Islamiyya fi al-Hayat al-Siyasiyya al-Misriyya, 1928–1948.* Cairo, 1979.

Fuʾad, Niʿmat Ahmad. *Qimam Adabiyya: Dirasat wa Tarajim li Aʿlam al-Adab al-Misri al-Hadith.* Cairo, 1966.

Haykal, Muhammad Husayn. *Mudhakkirat fi al-Siyasa al-Misriyya.* 2 vols. Cairo, 1951, 1953.

Husayn, Ahmad. *Imani.* Cairo, 1936. 2d ed., Cairo, 1946.

———. *Murafaʿat al-Raʾis Ahmad Husayn fi ʿAhd Hukumat al-Wafd.* Cairo, 1938.

———. *Nisf Qarn Maʿa al-ʿUruba wa Qadiyyat Filastin.* Beirut, 1971.

———. *Raʾy Jamʿiyyat Misr al-Fatah fi Muʿahadat Sanat 1936.* Cairo, 1936.

———. *Waraʾ al-Qudban.* Cairo, 1949.

Husayn, Taha. *Mustaqbal al-Thaqafa fi Misr.* Cairo, 1938.

Jaha, Shafiq. *al-Haraka al-ʿArabiyya al-Sirriyya: Jamaʿat al-Kitab al-Ahmar, 1935–1945.* Beirut, 2004.

al-Jundi, Anwar. a*l-Maʿarik al-Adabiyya fi al-Shiʿr wa al-Nathr wa al-Thaqafa wa al-Lugha wa al-Qawmiyya al-ʿArabiyya.* Cairo, 1961.

———. *al-Maʿarik al-Adabiyya fi Misr, 1914–1939.* Cairo, 1983.

Muhafaza, ʿAli. *al-ʿAlaqat al-Almaniyya al-Filastiniyya 1841–1945.* Beirut, 1981.

Muhammad, Muhammad Sayyid. *al-Zayyat wa al-Risala.* Riyadh, 1982.

Musa, Salama. *al-Dunya baʿda Thalathin Sana.* Cairo, 1936.

al-Nahhas, Mustafa. *Mudhakkirat Mustafa al-Nahhas: Rabʿ Qarn min al-Siyasa fi Misr, 1927–1952.* Edited by Ahmad ʿIzz al-Din. 2 vols. Cairo, 2000.

Radwan, Fathi. *Difalira*. Cairo, 1937.

———. *Musulini*. Cairo, 1937.

———. *Ta'rikh Ghandi*. Cairo, 1932.

al-Rafi'i, 'Abd al-Rahman. *Fi A'qab al-Thawra al-Misriyya*. 3 vols. Cairo, 1947–1951.

Ramadan, 'Abd al-'Azim Muhammad. *Dirasat fi Ta'rikh Misr al-Mu'asir*. Cairo, 1981.

———. *al-Sira' bayna al-Wafd wa al-'Arsh, 1936–1939*. Cairo, 1979.

———. *Tatawwur al-Haraka al-Wataniyya fi Misr, 1937–1948*. 2 vols. Cairo, 1972.

al-Sadat, Anwar. *Asrar al-Thawra al-Misriyya*. Cairo, 1957. Translated as *Revolt on the Nile*. New York, 1957.

———. *In Search of Identity: An Autobiography*. New York, 1977.

———. *Qissat al-Thawra Kamilatan*. Cairo, 1956.

al-Sa'id, Rif'at. *Ahmad Husayn: Kalimat wa Mawaqif*. Cairo, 1979.

———. *Hasan al-Banna: Mata . . . Kayfa . . . wa li Madha?* Cairo, 1977.

Shalabi, 'Ali. *Misr al-Fatah wa Dawruha fi al-Siyasa al-Misriyya, 1933–1941*. Cairo, 1982.

Subayh, Muhammad. *Hitlar*. Cairo, 1937.

———. *Min al-'Alamayn*. Cairo, 1963.

———. *al-Yaban: Bilad al-Shams al-Mushriqa*. Cairo, 1937.

Cited Books and Articles in Other Languages

Abdalla, Ahmed. *The Student Movement and National Politics in Egypt*. London, 1985.

American Christian Palestine Committee. *The Arab War Effort: A Documented Account*. New York, [1946?].

Arielli, Nir. "Fascist Italy in the Middle East, 1935–1940." Ph.D. dissertation, University of Leeds, March 2008.

Ayalon, Ami. "Egyptian Intellectuals Versus Fascism and Nazism in the 1930s." In *The Great Powers in the Middle East, 1919–1939*, edited by Uriel Dann, 391–404. New York, 1988.

———. *The Press in the Arab Middle East: A History*. New York, 1995.

Baker, Keith Michael. "Politics and Public Opinion under the Old Regime: Some Reflections." In *Press and Politics in Pre-Revolutionary France*, edited by Jack R. Censer and Jeremy D. Popkin, 204–246. Berkeley, CA, 1987.

Bashkin, Orit. *The Other Iraq: Pluralism and Culture in Hashemite Iraq*. Stanford, CA, 2008.

Batatu, Hanna. *The Old Social Classes and the Revolutionary Movements in Iraq*. Princeton, NJ, 1978.

Be'eri, Eliezer. *Army Officers in Arab Politics and Society*. New York, 1970.

Berque, Jacques. *Egypt: Imperialism and Revolution*. London, 1972.

Bloch, Marc. *The Historian's Craft*. New York, 1953.

Brugman, J. *An Introduction to the History of Modern Arabic Literature in Egypt*. Leiden, 1984.

Calhoun, Craig, ed. *Habermas and the Public Sphere*. Cambridge, MA, 1992.

Cao-Van-Hoa, Edmond. *"Der Feind meines Feindes . . ." Darstellungen des nationalsozialistischen Deutschland in ägyptischen Schriften*. Frankfurt-am-Main, 1990.

Ciano, Galeazzo. *Diary, 1937–1943*. New York, 2002.

Coury, Ralph. "Who 'Invented' Egyptian Arab Nationalism?" *International Journal of Middle East Studies*, 14 (1982), 249–281, 459–479.

Cowan, Brian. "Mr. Spectator and the Coffeehouse Public Sphere." *Eighteenth Century Studies*, 37, no. 3 (2004), 345–366.

Deeb, Marius. *Party Politics in Egypt: The Wafd and Its Rivals, 1919–1939*. London, 1979.

Edgar, Andrew. *The Philosophy of Habermas*. Montreal, 2005.

Egger, Vernon. *A Fabian in Egypt: Salamah Musa and the Rise of the Professional Classes in Egypt, 1909–1939*. Lanham, MD, 1986.

El-Awaisi, Abd Al-Fattah Muhammad. *The Muslim Brothers and the Palestine Question, 1928–1947*. London, 1998.

Elpeleg, Zvi. *The Grand Mufti: Haj Amin al-Hussaini, Founder of the Palestinian National Movement*. Translated by David Harvey. London, 1993.

Entelis, John P. *Pluralism and Party Transformation in Lebanon: al-Kata'ib, 1936–1970*. Leiden. 1974.

Eppel, Michael. "The Elite, the *Effendiyya*, and the Growth of Nationalism and Pan-Arabism in Hashemite Iraq, 1921–1958." *International Journal of Middle East Studies*, 30 (1998), 227–250.

Eppler, John W. *Rommel Ruft Kairo: Aus dem Tagesbuch eines Spions*. Gutersloh, 1959.

Erlich, Haggai. "Periphery and Youth: Fascist Italy and the Middle East." In *Fascism Outside Europe*, edited by Stein Ugelvik Larsen, 393–423. New York, 2001.

———. *Students and University in Twentieth Century Egyptian Politics*. London, 1989.

Firro, Kais M. *Inventing Lebanon: Nationalism and the State Under the Mandate*. London, 2003.

Fraser, Nancy. "Rethinking the Public Sphere: A Contribution to the Critique of Actually Existing Democracy." In *Habermas and the Public Sphere*, edited by Craig Calhoun, 109–142. Cambridge, MA, 1992.

Friedländer, Saul. *Nazi Germany and the Jews: The Years of Persecution, 1933–1939*. London, 1997.

Gensicke, Klaus. *Der Mufti von Jerusalem und die Nationalsozialisten: Eine politische Biographie Amin el-Husseinis*. Darmstadt, 2007.

Gershoni, Israel. "Confronting Fascism in Egypt: Tawfiq al-Hakim's Anti-Totalitarianism, 1938–1945." *Tel Aviver Jahrbuch für deutsche Geschichte*, 26 (1997), 121–150.

———. "Egyptian Liberalism in an Age of 'Crisis of Orientation': *al-Risala's* Reaction to Fascism and Nazism, 1933–1939." *International Journal of Middle East Studies*, 31 (1999), 551–576.

———. *Light in the Shade: Egypt and Fascism, 1922–1937*. Tel Aviv, 1999 [in Hebrew].

———. "The Muslim Brothers and the Arab Revolt in Palestine, 1936–1939." *Middle Eastern Studies*, 22 (1986), 367–397.

———. "Rejecting the West: The Image of the West in the Teachings of the Muslim Brotherhood, 1928–1939." In *The Great Powers in the Middle East, 1919–1939*, edited by Uriel Dann, 270–290. New York, 1988.

Gershoni, Israel, and James Jankowski. *Redefining the Egyptian Nation, 1930–1945.* Cambridge, UK, 1995.

Göçek, Fatma Müge, ed. *Political Cartoons in the Middle East.* Princeton, NJ, 1998.

Gross, Alan G. "Habermas, Systematically Distorted Communication, and the Public Sphere." *Rhetoric Society Quarterly,* 36, no. 3 (2006), 309–330.

Habermas, Jürgen. "The Public Sphere." *New German Critique,* 3 (1974), 49–55.

———. *The Structural Transformation of the Public Sphere: An Inquiry into a Category of Bourgeois Society.* Translated by Thomas Burger. Cambridge, MA, 1989. First published in German, 1962.

Haim, Sylvia G. *Arab Nationalism: An Anthology.* Berkeley, CA, 1962.

Halpern, Malcolm. *The Politics of Social Change in the Middle East and North Africa.* Princeton, NJ, 1963.

Hamdi, Walid. *Rashid Ali al-Gailani and the Nationalist Movement in Iraq, 1939–1941.* London, 1987.

Harris, Christina P. *Nationalism and Revolution in Egypt: The Role of the Muslim Brotherhood.* The Hague, 1964.

Heyworth-Dunne, James. *Religious and Political Trends in Modern Egypt.* Washington, DC, 1950.

Hillgruber, Andreas. "The Third Reich and the Near and Middle East, 1933–1939." In *The Great Powers in the Middle East, 1919–1939,* edited by Uriel Dann, 274–282. New York, 1988.

Hirszowicz, Lukasz. *The Third Reich and the Arab East.* London, 1966.

Hoexter, Miriam, Shmuel N. Eisenstadt, and Nehemia Levtzion, eds. *The Public Sphere in Muslim Societies.* Albany, NY, 2002.

Holub, Robert C. *Jurgen Habermas: Critic in the Public Sphere.* London, 1991.

Höpp, Gerhard, Peter Wien, and René Wildangel, eds. *Blind für die Geschichte? Arabische Begegnungen mit dem Nationalsozialismus.* Berlin, 2004.

Hourani, Albert. *Arabic Thought in the Liberal Age, 1798–1939.* Oxford, 1962.

Husaini, I. M. *The Moslem Brethren: The Greatest of Modern Islamic Movements.* Beirut, 1956.

Hussein, Ahmed [Ahmad Husayn]. *Message to Hitler!* New York, 1947.

Ismael, Tareq Y. and Jacqueline S. *Government and Politics in Islam.* London, 1985.

Jankowski, James. "The Egyptian Blue Shirts and the Egyptian Wafd, 1935–1938." *Middle Eastern Studies,* 6 (1970), 77–95.

———. "Egyptian Regional Policy in the Wake of the Anglo-Egyptian Treaty of 1936: Arab Alliance or Islamic Caliphate?" In *Britain and the Middle East in the 1930s: Security Problems, 1935–39,* edited by Michael J. Cohen and Martin Kolinsky, 81–97. London, 1992.

———. Egyptian Responses to the Palestine Problem in the Interwar Period." *International Journal of Middle East Studies,* 12 (1980), 1–38.

———. *Egypt's Young Rebels: "Young Egypt," 1933–1952.* Stanford, CA, 1975.

———. "The Government of Egypt and the Palestine Question, 1936–1939." *Middle Eastern Studies,* 17 (1981), 427–453.

Kabha, Mustafa. "'My Enemy's Enemy—A Friend': Attitudes of the Palestinian National Movement towards Fascism and Nazism, 1925–1945." *Zmanim*, 17 (1999) 79–86 [in Hebrew].

———. *Writing Up a Storm: The Palestinian Press as a Shaper of Public Opinion, 1929–1939*. London, 2007.

Kedourie, Elie. "Egypt and the Caliphate, 1915–52." In *The Chatham House Version and Other Middle-Eastern Studies*, 177–212. London, 1970.

———. "The Kingdom of Iraq: A Retrospect." In *The Chatham House Version and Other Middle-Eastern Studies*, 236–285. London, 1970.

———. "Pan-Arabism and British Policy." In *The Chatham House Version and Other Middle-Eastern Studies*, 213–235. London, 1970.

———. *Politics in the Middle East*. New York, 1992.

Khadduri, Majid. *Independent Iraq: A Study in Iraqi Politics Since 1932*. London, 1951.

Khoury, Philip S. *Syria and the French Mandate: The Politics of Arab Nationalism, 1920–1945*. Princeton, NJ, 1987.

Kirk, George. *Survey of International Affairs, 1939–1946*. Vol. 2, *The Middle East in the War*. London, 1952.

Kramer, Martin. *Islam Assembled: The Advent of the Muslim Congresses*. New York, 1986.

Küntzel, Matthias. *Jihad and Jew-Hatred: Islamism, Nazism, and the Roots of 9/11*. New York, 2007.

Lacouture, Jean. *Nasser: A Biography*. New York, 1973.

Lacouture, Jean and Simonne. *Egypt in Transition*. 1956. Reprint, New York, 1958.

Larsen, Stein Ugelvik. "Was There Fascism Outside Europe? Diffusion from Europe and Domestic Impulses." In *Fascism Outside Europe*, edited by Stein Ugelvik Larsen, 705–818. New York, 2001.

Lewis, Bernard. *Semites and Anti-Semites: An Inquiry Into Conflict and Prejudice*. New York, 1986.

Lia, Brynjar. *The Society of the Muslim Brothers in Egypt: The Rise of an Islamic Mass Movement, 1928–1942*. Reading, UK, 1998.

Lukitz, Liora. *Iraq: The Search for National Identity*. London, 1995.

MacDonald, Callum A. "Radio Bari: Italian Wireless Propaganda in the Middle East and British Countermeasures." *Middle Eastern Studies*, 13 (1977), 195–207.

Maghraoui, Abdeslam M. *Liberalism Without Democracy: Nationhood and Citizenship in Egypt, 1922–1936*. Durham, NC, 2006.

Mallmann, Klaus-Michale, and Martin Cüppers. *Halbmond und Hakenkreuz: Das Dritte Reich, die Araber und Palästina*. Darmstadt, 2006.

Mansfield, Peter. *Nasser's Egypt*. Baltimore, 1965.

Marr, Phebe. "The Development of Nationalist Ideology in Iraq, 1921–1941," *The Muslim World*, 75, no. 2 (1985), 85–101.

———. *The Modern History of Iraq*. Boulder, CO, 1985.

Marsot, Afaf Lutfi al-Sayyid. "The Cartoon in Egypt." *Comparative Studies in Society and History*, 13 (Jan. 1971), 2–15.

———. *Egypt's Liberal Experiment, 1922–1936*. Berkeley, CA, 1977.

Marston, E. "Fascist Tendencies in Pre-War Arab Politics: A Study of Three Arab Political Movements." *Middle East Forum*, 35 (1959), 19–35.

Mattar, Philip. *The Mufti of Jerusalem: Hajj Amin al-Husayni and the Palestinian National Movement*. New York, 1988.

Matthews, Weldon C. *Confronting an Empire, Constructing a Nation: Arab Nationalism and Popular Politics in Mandate Palestine*. London, 2006.

Mayer, Thomas. *Egypt and the Palestine Question, 1936–1945*. Berlin, 1983.

McKeon, Michael. "Parsing Habermas' 'Bourgeois Public Sphere.'" *Criticism*, 46, no. 2 (2004), 273–277.

Melka, Robert L. "The Axis and the Arab Middle East, 1930–1945." Ph.D. dissertation, University of Minnesota, 1966.

Mendel, Miloš, and Zdeněk Müller. "Fascist Tendencies in the Levant in the 1930s and 1940s." *Archív Orientální*, 55 (1987), 1–17.

Mitchell, Richard. *The Society of the Muslim Brothers*. London, 1969.

Musa, Salama. *The Education of Salama Musa*. Translated by L. O. Schuman. Leiden, 1961.

Nation Associates, The. *The Record of Collaboration of King Farouk of Egypt with the Nazis and Their Ally, the Mufti*. New York, 1948.

Nicosia, Francis. "Arab Nationalism and National Socialist Germany, 1933–1939: Ideological and Strategic Incompatibility." *International Journal of Middle East Studies*, 12 (1980), 351–372.

———. "Fritz Grobba and the Middle East Policy of the Third Reich." In *National and International Politics in the Middle East: Essays in Honour of Elie Kedourie*, edited by Edward Ingram, 206–228. London, 1986.

———. *The Third Reich and the Palestine Question*. London, 1985.

Norbrook, David. "Women, the Republic of Letters, and the Public Sphere in the Mid-Seventeenth Century." *Criticism*, 46, no. 2 (2004), 223–240.

Nordbruch, Götz. "Bread, Freedom, Independence: Opposition to Nazi Germany in Lebanon and Syria and the Struggle for a Just Order." In "Intellectual History in Middle Eastern Studies," guest editors Amy Singer and Israel Gershoni, special issue, *Comparative Studies of South Asia, Africa and the Middle East*, 28, no. 3 (2008), 416–422.

———. "Defending the French Revolution During World War II: Raif Khoury and the Intellectual Challenge of Nazism in the Levant." *Mediterranean Historical Review*, 21, no. 2 (2006), 219–238.

———. *Nazism in Syria and Lebanon: The Ambivalence of the German Option, 1933–1945*. London, 2009.

"Note sur la presse égyptienne et la presse palestinienne à la fin de 1944." *Cahiers de l'Orient contemporaine*, 1 (1944–1945), 124–127.

Nutting, Anthony. *Nasser*. New York, 1972.

Pask, Kevin. "The Bourgeois Public Sphere and the Concept of Literature." *Criticism*, 46, no. 2 (2004), 241–256.

Payne, Stanley. *A History of Fascism, 1914–1945*. Madison, WI, 1995.

Philipp, Thomas. *Gurgi Zaydan: His Life and Thought*. Beirut, 1979.

Porath, Yehoshoa. *In Search of Arab Unity, 1930–1945*. London, 1986.

Rabinovich, Itamar. "Germany and the Syrian Political Scene in the late 1930s." In *Germany and the Middle East, 1835–1939*, edited by J. L. Wallach, 191–198. Tel Aviv, 1975.

Ryzova, Lucie. *L'effendiyya ou la modernité contestée*. Cairo, 2004.

———. "Egyptianizing Modernity through the 'New Effendiya': Social and Cultural Constructions of the Middle Class in Egypt Under the Monarchy." In *Re-Envisioning Egypt, 1919–1952*, edited by Arthur Goldschmidt, Amy J. Johnson, and Barak A. Salmoni, 124–163. Cairo, 2005.

Sachar, Howard Morley. *Europe Leaves the Middle East, 1936–1954*. New York, 1972.

Safran, Nadav. *Egypt in Search of Political Community*. Cambridge, MA, 1961.

Sansom, Alfred William. *I Spied Spies*. London, 1965.

Schröder, Bernd Philipp. *Deutschland und der Mittlere Osten im Zweiten Weltkrieg*. Göttingen, 1975.

Schumann, Christoph. "The Generation of Broad Expectations: Nationalism, Education, and Autobiography in Syria and Lebanon, 1930–1958." In *From the Syrian Land to the States of Syria and Lebanon*, edited by Thomas Philipp and Christoph Schumann, 342–358. Würzburg, 2004.

———, ed. *Liberal Thought in the Eastern Mediterranean: Late 19th Century Until the 1960s*. Leiden/Boston, 2008.

———. *Radikalnationalismus in Syrien und Libanon: Politische Sozialisation und Elitenbildung, 1930–1958*. Hamburg, 2001.

Segré, Claudio G. "Liberal and Fascist Italy in the Middle East, 1919–1939: The Elusive White Stallion." In *The Great Powers in the Middle East, 1919–1939*, edited by Uriel Dann, 199–212. New York, 1988.

Shamir, Shimon. "The Influence of German National Socialism on Radical Movements in Egypt." In *Germany and the Middle East, 1835–1939*, edited by J. L. Wallach, 200–209. Tel Aviv, 1976.

Simon, Reeva S. *Iraq Between the Two World Wars: The Creation and Implementation of a Nationalist Ideology*. New York, 1986.

Sing, Manfred. "Between Lights and Hurricanes: Sami al-Kayyali's Review *al-Hadith* as a Forum of Modern Arabic Literature and Liberal Islam." In *The Middle Eastern Press as a Forum for Literature*, edited by Horst Unbehaun, 119–141. Frankfurt, 2004.

———. "Illiberal Metamorphoses of a Liberal Discourse: The Case of Syrian Intellectual Sami al-Kayyali (1898–1972)." In *Liberal Thought in the Eastern Mediterranean: Late 19th Century Until the 1960s*, edited by Christoph Schumann, 293–322. Leiden/Boston, 2008.

Smith, Charles D. "The 'Crisis of Orientation': The Shift of Egyptian Intellectuals to Islamic Subjects in the 1930s." *International Journal of Middle East Studies*, 4 (1973), 382–410.

———. *Islam and the Search for Social Order in Modern Egypt: A Biography of Muhammad Husayn Haykal*. Albany, NY, 1983.

Somers, Margaret R. "What's Political or Cultural about Political Culture and the Public Sphere? Toward an Historical Sociology of Concept Formation." *Sociological Theory*, 13, no. 2 (1995), 113–144.

Steffens, Hans von. *Salaam: Geheimcommando zum Nil, 1942*. Neckargemund, Germany, 1960.

Stephens, Robert. *Nasser: A Political Biography*. New York, 1972.

St. John, Robert. *The Boss: The Story of Gamal Abdel Nasser*. New York, 1960.

Tarbush, Mohammad A. *The Role of the Military in Politics: A Case Study of Iraq to 1941*. London, 1982.

Thompson, Elizabeth. *Colonial Citizens: Republican Rights, Paternal Privilege, and Gender in French Syria and Lebanon*. New York, 2000.

Tibawi, A. L. *A Modern History of Syria Including Lebanon and Palestine*. London, 1969.

Tillmann, Heinz. *Deutschlands Araberpolitik im Zweiten Weltkrieg*. Berlin, 1965.

Tripp, Charles. "Ali Mahir and the Politics of the Egyptian Army, 1936–1942." In *Contemporary Egypt: Through Egyptian Eyes. Essays in Honour of P. J. Vatikiotis*, edited by Charles Tripp, 45–71. London, 1993.

Vatikiotis, P. J. *The Modern History of Egypt*. New York, 1969.

———. *Nasser and His Generation*. New York, 1978.

Vaucher, Georges. *Gamal Abdel Nasser et son Equipe*. 2 vols. Paris, 1959.

Watenpaugh, Keith David. *Being Modern in the Middle East: Revolution, Nationalism Colonialism, and the Arab Middle Class*. Princeton, NJ, 2006.

———. "Steel Shirts, White Badges, and the Last Qabaday: Fascism, Urban Violence and Civic Identity in Aleppo Under French Rule." In *France, Syrie, et Liban, 1918–1946: Les ambiguïtés et les dynamiques de la relation mandataire*, edited by N. Méouchy, 325–347. Damascus, 2003.

Wendell, Charles. *Five Tracts of Hasan al-Banna' (1906–1949)*. Berkeley, CA, 1978.

Wheelock, Keith. *Nasser's New Egypt*. New York, 1960.

Wien, Peter. *Iraqi Arab Nationalism: Authoritarian, Totalitarian, and Pro-Fascist Inclinations, 1932–1941*. New York, 2006.

Wild, Stefan. "National Socialism in the Arab East Between 1933 and 1939." *Die Welt des Islams*, 25 (1985), 126–173.

Wildangel, René. *Zwischen Achse und Mandatsmacht: Palästina und der Nationalsozialismus*. Berlin, 2007.

Williams, Manuela A. *Mussolini's Propaganda Abroad: Subversion in the Mediterranean and the Middle East, 1935–1939*. London, 2006.

Wynn, Wilton. *Nasser of Egypt: The Search for Dignity*. Cambridge, MA, 1960.

Yamak, Labib Zuwiyya. *The Syrian Social Nationalist Party: An Ideological Analysis*. Cambridge, MA, 1966.

Zamir, Meir. *Lebanon's Quest: The Road to Statehood, 1926–1939*. New York, 1997.

Zisser, Eyal. "Writing a Constitution: Constitutional Debates in Syria in the Mandate Period." In *Liberal Thought in the Eastern Mediterranean; Late 19th Century Until the 1960s*, edited by Christoph Schumann, 195–215. Leiden/Boston, 2008.

Index